Android™ Development with Flash®

Your visual blueprint™ for developing mobile apps

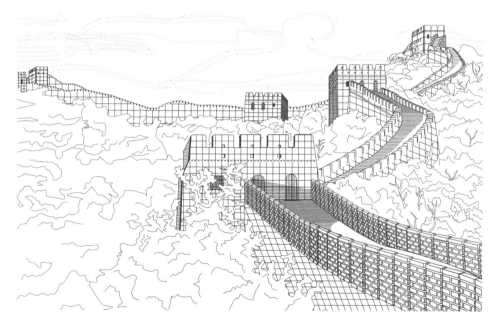

By Julian Dolce

WILEY

Wiley Publishing, Inc.

Android™ Development with Flash®: Your visual blueprint™ for developing mobile apps

Published by
Wiley Publishing, Inc.
10475 Crosspoint Boulevard
Indianapolis, IN 46256

www.wiley.com

Published simultaneously in Canada

Library of Congress Control Number: 2010934750

ISBN: 978-0-470-90432-9

Manufactured in the United States of America

10 9 8 7 6 5 4 3 2 1

Trademark Acknowledgments

Contact Us

For general information on our other products and services, please contact our Customer Care Department within the U.S. at 877-762-2974, outside the U.S. at 317-572-3993 or fax 317-572-4002.

For technical support, please visit www.wiley.com/techsupport.

The Great Wall of China

The Great Wall of China is the world's longest structure built by human hands, stretching more than 4,000 miles. Begun during the 5th century B.C., construction on the Great Wall of China continued into the 16th century. Building materials were often determined by the surrounding topography and include packed earth, stones, bricks, tiles, and quarried limestone. Like a dragon, the Wall winds through mountains, grasslands, deserts, and plateaus — and through the heart of Chinese history and culture.

Learn more about the Great Wall and other marvels of China in *Frommer's China,* 4th Edition (ISBN 978-0-470-52658-3), available wherever books are sold or at www. Frommers.com.

WILEY

Sales

Contact Wiley
at (877) 762-2974
or (317) 572-4002.

Credits

Acquisitions Editor
Aaron Black

Project Editor
Dana Rhodes Lesh

Technical Editor
Paul Geyer

Copy Editor
Dana Rhodes Lesh

Editorial Director
Robyn Siesky

Editorial Manager
Rosemarie Graham

Business Manager
Amy Knies

Senior Marketing Manager
Sandy Smith

Vice President and Executive Group
Publisher
Richard Swadley

Vice President and Executive Publisher
Barry Pruett

Project Coordinator
Sheree Montgomery

Graphics and Production Specialists
Carrie A. Cesavice
Andrea Hornberger
Jennifer Mayberry

Quality Control Technicians
Rebecca Denoncour
Lindsay Littrell

Proofreader
Mildred Rosenzweig

Indexer
Valerie Haynes Perry

Media Development Project Manager
Laura Moss

Media Development Assistant
Project Manager
Jenny Swisher

Media Development
Associate Producers
Josh Frank
Marilyn Hummel
Doug Kuhn
Shawn Patrick

Screen Artists
Ana Carillo
Cheryl Grubbs
Jill A. Proll
Ronald Terry

Cover Art Illustrator
Cheryl Grubbs

About the Author

Julian Dolce is the senior Flash developer at QNX Software Systems, specializing in mobile AIR applications. Julian has spoken at numerous conferences around the world, where he has taught workshops on moving from Flash development to iPhone development, as well as a number of AIR for Android development workshops. He also maintains a personal development blog, www.deleteaso.com, in which he writes about his life as a Flash developer.

Author's Acknowledgments

This book would not have been possible without the support of my close friends, Thomas, Elissa, Miles, Marco, Lori, Neil, and Sherisse. You guys put up with me for six months and made sure that I did not go insane. You are the best friends anyone could ask for.

Erin, your love, support and encouragement throughout my entire career has been a source of strength and inspiration. Your courage and determination has taught me that any dream, no matter how big, is never out of reach. You never stopped believing in me, and I cannot thank you enough for it.

Finally, to my parents and the rest of my family. You have supported me throughout my entire life, and I could not have gotten to where I am today without you.

How to Use This Visual Blueprint Book

Who This Book Is For

This book is for intermediate-to-advanced Flash developers who want to use their knowledge of Flash and ActionScript to develop AIR Android applications. This book specifically focuses on the Android platform, but many of the topics and examples can be used to develop for any AIR mobile platform.

The Conventions in This Book

① Steps

This book uses a step-by-step format to guide you easily through each task. Numbered steps are actions you must do; bulleted steps clarify a point, step, or optional feature; and indented steps give you the result.

② Notes

Notes give additional information — special conditions that may occur during an operation, a situation that you want to avoid, or a cross-reference to a related area of the book.

③ Extra or Apply It

An Extra section provides additional information about the preceding task — insider information and tips for ease and efficiency. An Apply It section takes the code from the preceding task one step further and allows you to take full advantage of it.

④ Bold

Bold type shows text or numbers you must type.

⑤ Courier Font

`Courier font` indicates the use of scripting language code such as statements, operators, or functions, and code such as objects, methods, or properties.

● Italics

Italic type introduces and defines a new term.

Web Site

You can find the code samples throughout the book on the Wiley Web site, www.wiley.com. Search the site for this book's page; then you can find the code samples on the Downloads tab.

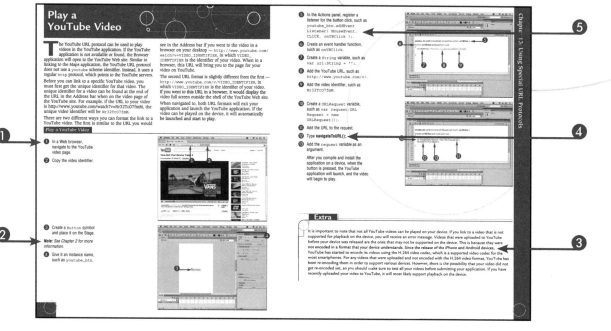

TABLE OF CONTENTS

TABLE OF CONTENTS

TABLE OF CONTENTS

Introducing Android Devices

I t is an exciting time to be a Flash developer. Adobe has taken big steps in making the Flash platform available on as many devices as possible. The Open Screen Project is an Adobe-led initiative whose goal is to "enable consumers to engage with rich Internet experiences seamlessly across any device, anywhere," as it says on its Web site, at www.openscreenproject.org.

Flash Player 10.1 will be available for multiple mobile platforms, such as Google Android, RIM's BlackBerry, Palm Pre, and Nokia, as well as numerous other devices such as TVs, set top boxes, tablets, and netbooks. Adobe is working with these and over 50 other partners to optimize Flash Player 10.1 in order to work better with the different devices.

Flash Player 10.1

There are two very different parts to the Flash platform on mobile devices. Flash Player 10.1 has been optimized for use in mobile browsers. The intent is to have all the content that you would normally see on a desktop browser work just as you would expect on a mobile device. Flash Player 10.1 also takes advantage of some of the new mobile device APIs, such as multitouch and geolocation. If you currently have Flash content on the Web, it is a good idea to test it on an Android device with Flash Player 10.1 installed. Consider updating the content to better support mobile devices if possible. As mobile devices become more popular, users will demand that content work seamlessly across all platforms. The Flash Player 10.1 plug-in is available now for supported Android 2.2 devices in the Android Market.

AIR for Mobile Devices

The other piece of the Flash platform mobile story is AIR for mobile devices. AIR (Adobe Integrated Runtime) was originally designed and developed for the desktop, and some features do not translate well to mobile platforms. To help with this, Adobe has created the mobile profile for AIR, which is a subset set of AIR. To find out which APIs are available, see the sections "Introducing the Available APIs" and "Check What APIs Are Not Available" later in this chapter.

Currently, the AIR mobile profile is available for iPhone OS and Android devices. However, because of the new terms of use by Apple, you can no longer use Flash CS5 to create and submit applications to the Apple iTunes App Store. The AIR Runtime is available on Android devices and needs to be installed on the device in order to run any AIR applications. Similarly to the desktop runtime, the mobile runtime will be installed if the user tries to install an AIR for Android application without the runtime.

The AIR Runtime is currently supported on Android devices with Android 2.2, also known as *Froyo,* installed or higher. It also is currently supported only on Android devices with an ARMv7 processor. Most new devices should support the AIR Runtime; however, you will want to double check before you purchase a device.

Because the Android platform is open source, many device manufacturers ship their devices with custom Android skins. As Google releases new versions of Android, each manufacturer must convert its skins to the new version before the device can be updated. Because of this, it is a good idea to stay away from devices that have highly customized skins, such as the Sony Ericsson Xperia X10, which is capable of running AIR except that it currently ships with Android 1.6.

The following are a few of the devices that are currently available that support the AIR Runtime and Android AIR applications. You may still need to update them to Android 2.2, but after they are updated, they should run all applications.

Google Nexus One

The Nexus One is manufactured by HTC for Google and can be purchased from Google unlocked. Being able to purchase an unlocked device is attractive for developers, as they are not restricted to a specific network provider. This also means that you can purchase one if you plan to use it only as a development device and not as an everyday mobile phone. There are two versions available that support the different cell network providers and can be purchased for the United States, Canada, and Europe.

The Nexus One ships with Android 2.1, a 1GHz Snapdragon processor, and 512MB of memory. It also has 512MB of Flash memory storage and a 4GB microSD card. The SD card can be upgraded to a 32GB card. The Nexus One has a screen resolution of 480 x 800 pixels and has a 5.0 megapixel camera, which can shoot 720 x 480 video at 20fps or higher.

Motorola Droid

Outside of the United States, the Motorola Droid is referred to as the Motorola *Milestone.* Both devices currently support Android 2.1. There are two big differences between the Droid and the Nexus One: The Droid has a slide-out keyboard and a screen resolution of 480 x 854 pixels.

HTC Desire

The HTC Desire is one of the more popular Android phones on the market today, and it is very similar to the Nexus One. The biggest difference between the two devices is the Desire's HTC Sense Android user interface. The Desire also has tactile buttons across the bottom as opposed to the Nexus One's touch-sensitive buttons.

Android Tablets

There are a number of Android tablet devices that are set to release in the last half of 2010, and there are too many to discuss here. However, the most important thing to understand is the difference in screen resolution. 1024 x 768, 1366 x 768, 800 x 600, and 1024 x 600 are just some of the different screen resolutions for tablets that will support AIR Android applications. Testing how your application will look and respond on these different screen resolutions will ensure that users have a good user experience across devices.

As you can see, there are many differences between all the different models, and the tablets are a game changer. There are lots of tips and things to think about in this book when developing your applications to support multiple platforms. It is a good exercise to try and take all of these into consideration early on in development. Some things to ask yourself are, "What does my application look like in multiple resolutions?" and "How does a user interact with my application on a non–touch-enabled device?." Even if

you ever plan to support only one device today, allowing for multiple platforms in the future will prove to be worthwhile. The iPad is a great example of developers never planning for a different resolution or platform. When the iPhone SDK first came out, developers were fortunate and had to design for only one screen size and resolution. Now with the release of the iPad and the fourth generation iPhone, developers have to redesign and even rewrite their applications in order to support these new platforms.

Introducing the Development Tools

If you have developed Flash applications before, you will already be familiar with some of the tools that will be explored throughout this book. However, some of them may be new to you. The following are all the different tools that are discussed throughout the book.

Flash CS5 Professional

Flash CS5 is the main integrated development environment (IDE) for developing Flash applications for the Web, desktop, and Flash Lite–enabled mobile devices. In this 11th version of Flash, Flash CS5 introduced us to the ability to publish Flash applications to native iPhone applications, which ships with the product. In the fall of 2010, Adobe released an update for Flash CS5 and AIR, which enables you to develop and publish applications for Android devices. The update can be downloaded through the Adobe CS5 Updater application or from the Adobe Web site. If you are not sure if you have the latest version, select Updates from the Help menu in Flash CS5.

Flash Builder

Flash Builder, formerly know as *Flex Builder*, is an Eclipse-based IDE for creating Flex and AS3 projects. Flash Builder is Adobe's main ActionScript coding application. Flash CS5 does have the capability to write separate ActionScript code and classes; however, Flash Builder provides a much more feature-rich development environment. With the newest version of Flash Builder, Adobe has also integrated a better workflow between it and Flash CS5. You are now able to publish .fla files directly from Flash Builder without having to switch between applications. One of the benefits of Flash Builder is that it is built on top of Eclipse, a popular open source IDE. This enables you to take advantage of the many plug-ins built for Eclipse, which provide additional functionality that you do not get in Flash CS5. There are many plug-ins for managing source control, build integration, and support for other programming languages.

FDT

FDT (Flash Development Tool) is an Eclipse-based IDE similar to Flash Builder. FDT provides many features that speed up development, such as code templates, quick fixes, quick assist, and organized imports — just to name a few. FDT 4 is currently in beta and is quickly becoming one of the most popular ActionScript editors among many of the best Flash developers in the community. FDT 4 gives developers the ability to create their own plug-ins for FDT. This allows community members and developers to create a workflow that is best suited for them. It is only a matter of time before a FDT Android plug-in is released to help with publishing and installing Android applications.

Android SDK

The Android SDK is developed and released by Google, and it enables developers to create native Android applications. There are several tools that come with the Android SDK that are extremely helpful in developing Android applications. Before you begin to develop your application, make sure to download this SDK from the Google Web site. For more details, see the section "Get the Android SDK" later in this chapter.

Android Emulator

The Android emulator comes included in the Android SDK and can be used to test your AIR Android applications on your development computer. The emulator can be configured in a number of different ways, which is extremely useful for testing your application on multiple types of devices. You can also simulate a number of device-specific actions that would normally be available only on a device, such as a voice call, SMS message, and geolocation events.

AIR Runtime for Android

In order for your AIR Android applications to run on an Android device, you must first have the AIR Runtime installed. If an AIR Android application attempts to install without the runtime, it will prompt the user to download the runtime first. This process is very similar to the process of installing an AIR application on the desktop. Having the runtime installed is true for both Android devices and any Android emulators you have created. The AIR Runtime is installed the same way as any other Android application.

Android adb Tool

The Android Debug Bridge (adb) is a tool that comes with the Android SDK. It enables you to manage the state of an Android emulator instance or a connected device. It can be found in the tools folder of the Android SDK and is used by the Flash IDE to install applications onto your connected devices. If you are comfortable with using the command line, you can use adb to drop into a remote shell on an emulator or device instance, and you can issue shell commands on these instances. You can also use the adb tool to push or pull files from your device. This can be extremely useful if you want to better examine a file that your application has created on the device. For more details and other adb commands, check out the adb page on the Android Developers site, http://developer.android.com/guide/developing/tools/adb.html.

Adobe ADT Tool

The AIR Developer Tool (ADT) is used to compile your Android applications from your Flash and AIR applications. The ADT tool can be found in the bin directory of the AIR SDK, as well as the AIK2.5/bin folder in the Adobe Flash CS5 directory. ADT can be used by the command line to package your applications. For more details on compiling Android applications with the command line, see Chapter 3, "Developing Your First Application." You can also create a self-signed certificate, which can be used to digitally sign your AIR Android applications. It is important to note that applications uploaded to the Android Market must be signed with a certificate that have a validity period ending after October 22, 2033.

Android Market

The Android Market is a place where you can download and install applications to your Android device. It is similar to the iTunes App Store for the iPhone, except it does not have a desktop version and is available only on your device. If you want to submit your application to the Android Market, you need to register with Google for an Android developer account, which costs $25 US. After registration, you will be able to submit applications through the Android Market Web site. For more details on preparing and submitting your applications, see Chapter 17, "Deploying Your Application." Both the Flash Player 10.1 plug-in for browsers and the AIR Runtime can be downloaded from the Android Market, and you should install them on your device if they are not already.

Introducing the
Available APIs

With the ability to publish Android applications from Flash CS5 comes a set of new APIs that enable you to take advantage of some of the features the Android platform has to offer. However, Adobe's strategy is not to support only the Android platform but as many platforms as possible. This is the reason you may not see as many Android-specific features as you may like or think. Adobe is being very pragmatic about what new features it introduces and how its APIs will look on future platforms, mobile or otherwise. Adobe's goal is to provide one consistent API for all platforms. For example, the ActionScript code should be the same for accessing a camera whether you are developing applications for the Web, desktop, Android, iPhone, or any other future supported platform.

Accelerometer

The new `Accelerometer` class, which can be found in the `flash.sensors` package, gives you the ability to interact with the accelerometer that is built into the device. The Android accelerometer is a three-axis accelerometer capable of measuring both acceleration and gravity. The accelerometer is used to detect the device's rotation as well as any movements such as shakes.

Geolocation

The `flash.sensors.Geolocation` class enables you to interact with the device's location sensor. With this class, you can retrieve the location of your device anywhere in the world. Coordinates are reported to you in the form of latitude and longitude. There are differences in the ways each device figures out your location. It is important to understand that every device that has the Android OS installed does not necessarily have the same location sensor and that accuracy will differ greatly between the devices.

Camera Roll

The `flash.media.CameraRoll` class enables you to save a `BitmapData` instance to the device's camera roll. You can also use the `CameraRoll` class to enable the user to select an image from the Gallery application on the device.

Stage Orientation

There are a few new classes and methods to help handle stage orientation changes and updates. The `flash.display.StageOrientation` class defines a set of valid orientations in which the Stage can be set. The `flash.display.Stage.setOrienation` method, which is new in AIR 2.0, enables you to set the orientation of the Stage based on one of the static properties in the `StageOrientation` class. And finally, there is a `flash.events.StageOrienationEvent` class, which allows you to listen for when the Stage orientation is changing and has changed.

Touch Event

The `flash.events.TouchEvent` class is used to detect when a user touches the screen with his or her finger. The `TouchEvent` class is very much the alternative to the `MouseEvent` class but for touches. As well as being available on Android devices, the `TouchEvent` class is also available on AIR applications in Windows 7 with a touch-enabled screen and Flash CS5 iPhone applications.

Gesture Transform Event

The `flash.events.GestureTransformEvent` class is used to detect specific user interactions with multiple fingers. Touch-enabled interfaces are still very much in their infancy; however, there is already a standard set of gestures that a user understands and expects when interacting with your applications. The `GestureTransformEvent` class can detect four different types of gestures: swipe, rotate, pinch and zoom, and pan. Swipe detects a single finger swiping across the screen in the left, right, up, or down direction. The rotate gesture allows you to place two fingers on an object and rotate one finger around the other to rotate the object. The pinch and zoom gesture enables you to zoom in and out of objects by moving your fingers closer or farther apart from each other. Finally, the pan gesture lets you pan an object in any direction with two fingers. Some of these gestures are supported in Windows 7, Mac OS X 10.5.3, and Windows Mobile 6.5, as well as on iPhone and Android devices. If you plan on supporting more than one platform, you should double check which gestures are fully supported on each before starting development.

NetConnection

Adobe has added `NetConnection` support for Android applications. The `NetConnection` class gives you the ability to connect to a Flash Media Server to create peer-to-peer applications, as well as view streaming video on your device. It will also allow you to communicate with Flash Remoting and the AMF protocol.

FLV

FLV is Adobe's Flash Video format. There are two methods of playing an FLV video on a Android device. The first is to import the video onto the Timeline in an FLA file. This will create a `MovieClip` with your video in it, and you will be able to control it just as you would a normal `MovieClip`. The second method is to bundle the file with the application and load it at runtime. Both of these methods are covered in Chapter 8, "Working with Video," later in the book.

Shared Objects

`SharedObjects` are Flash's version of a browser cookie. They allow your Flash application to save user data on the device. This allows your application to load the save data when you come back to the application.

SQLite Database

The SQLite database is the most widely deployed SQL database in the world. When Adobe released AIR 1.0, it included the ability to communicate with SQLite databases from your applications. This gives you the ability to save large and complex data locally on the device. The Android platform also has SQLite libraries to develop with. A lot of the data on your device is stored in SQLite databases, such as your Contacts and Call History. Adobe has given us the ability to create, save, and load data from a SQLite database.

Check What APIs Are Not Available

Some of the AIR features that you are familiar with on the desktop are not currently available in the mobile profile of AIR. The omission of some of the features makes perfectly good sense, such as the concept of windows, as an Android application can have only one window, but some may not be so obvious. It is still the early days for the AIR mobile profile, so Adobe has decided to release the AIR Runtime without some of the features instead of having us wait longer for more features. Also, the AIR mobile profile started out with creating native iPhone applications. Apple placed certain restrictions on applications, which prevented Adobe from developing these features from the start. Adobe is committed to making the AIR Android Runtime a success and is constantly working to include new features and updates for developers to take advantage of.

HTML Loader

The `HTMLLoader` class provides AIR with the capability to render Web pages inside the application. Adobe has bundled a version of WebKit inside the AIR Runtime for the desktop, which provides a number of advanced features that are most likely not needed for mobile devices. In order to provide support for `HTMLLoader`, Adobe would have to bundle WebKit with the Android AIR Runtime, which would increase both its file size and the memory footprint. You can use the `StageWebView` class in order to load and display HTML text and Web pages within your application. However, the `StageWebView` class does not provide developers with the same level of communication between ActionScript and the JavaScript as `HTMLLoader` provides.

New AIR 2.0 Networking Classes

With the most recent release of AIR 2.0, Adobe has introduced some new networking classes. The `ServerSocket` class enables you to create your own socket server and have other AIR clients connect to it via the `Socket` class. This feature allows you to pass data to and from applications. The `ServerSocket` class is currently not available, but you can create a `Socket` in your Android application and connect to one running on your computer.

The `DatagramSocket` class enables you to send and receive UDP data. This can be used to create peer-to-peer applications or gaming. It is more unreliable than a TCP socket because you cannot guarantee the order of the data you will receive and lost packets are not retransmitted or even detected.

Adobe has also introduced a set of classes that can be used in conjunction with the new socket and server classes. For example, the `NetworkInfo` class provides you with a list of all available network interfaces available on the current machine. From those, you are able to find out what type of interface they are as well as the IP for the address. This comes in handy when you are creating peer-to-peer applications in which you may not know the IP address of the other peer.

There is technically no reason why these classes are not part of the Flash to Android offering, and they have been a highly requested feature. Adobe does plan on implementing these sometime in the future — when, however, is very hard to say.

Pixel Bender

Currently, Pixel Bender kernels and the `Shader` class are not supported in the Android AIR Runtime. These were originally not supported because the Apple App Store terms of use state that an application cannot execute any interpreted code. This may be something that Adobe visits with Android, but it is most likely lower on the priority list for Adobe and developers.

AS1 and AS2

This may come as a surprise to some developers, but there are still many developers who have not adopted AS3 and are still using AS2 or AS1. If you are one of these developers or have some older projects that you are looking to convert, you will need to start learning AS3 and start converting your projects. Currently, the AIR packager works only with AS3, and there will not be support for any earlier version of ActionScript. All the tasks and code in this book are in ActionScript 3, so if you are not familiar with it, I suggest you read up on ActionScript in order to get up to speed first; I recommend the book *ActionScript: Your visual blueprint for creating interactive projects in Flash CS4 Professional,* available from Wiley Publishing.

Alchemy

Adobe Alchemy is an Adobe Labs project, which enables developers to compile C and C++ code that would run in the ActionScript Virtual Machine (AVM). The exciting thing about this project is that it allows you to add functionality to the Flash Player that currently does not exist. Some community examples include being able to play external .wav audio files and open and preview .psd Photoshop files. Currently, this is not officially supported, but if there is some Alchemy library that you want to use, test it on your device to see if it does work.

Notifications

Android devices have a notifications area in the status bar, which can be used by applications to notify the user of an event. This is commonly used for new email notifications as well as application updates. Currently, only native Android applications can post notifications to the notification area, not AIR Android applications.

Widgets

You can develop many types of applications for the Android platform. As well as a regular application that a user would launch from the home screen or Android menu, the Android SDK allows you to develop widget applications and services. *Widget applications* are no more than a miniature application view that can be placed on the home screen. Widget applications provide users with small amounts of data or statuses, such as the weather or news. Currently, you cannot build widget applications with the Android AIR Runtime.

Become an Android Developer

I f you want to submit your AIR Android applications to the Android Market, you must first create an Android developer account. The registration fee for the Android Market is $25.00 US and can be paid using Google Checkout during the registration process. This is a one-time fee and does not require a renewal every year like other mobile development platforms.

In order to sign up for an Android Market account, you must first log in to your existing Google account. If you do not have an account, you can click a link on the sign-up page to create one. After you are signed in with your Google account, you will be presented with the Getting Started page. This page has a form on it that will be used to create your Android Market account. The information will also determine how you appear to customers in the Market.

The developer name that you choose will appear underneath your application listing in the Android Market. Feel free to enter your name if you are an individual developer or your company name if you plan on selling your applications. Your developer name will also be a link that sends users to the URL provided in the Website URL field.

After you have filled out all the information correctly and submitted it, you will be brought through the payment process of your application. Google uses its Google Checkout service to process your payment. After your payment has been accepted, your application will be approved, and you will be brought to your developer home screen. From here, you can upload your applications to the Android Market. For more details on submitting your applications, see Chapter 17.

Become an Android Developer

Start the Registering Process

1 In a browser, go to http://market.android.com/publish.

2 Sign in with your Google account.

OR

2 Click Create an Account Now.

Note: *If you already have a Google account, skip to step **10**.*

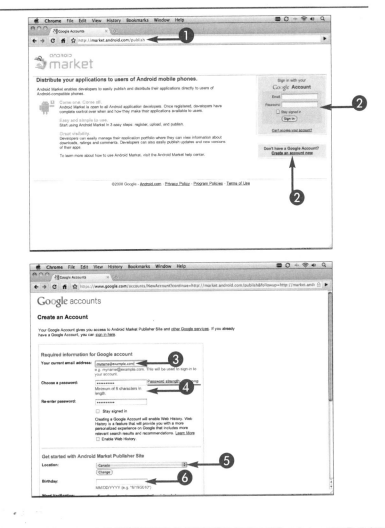

Create a Google Account

3 Type your current email address.

4 Type and confirm a password.

5 Click here and choose a location.

6 Type your birthday.

7 Scroll down and type the word shown in the image.

8 Click I Accept. Create My Account.

The Account Create Confirmation screen appears.

9 Click Click Here to Continue.

Create an Android Market Account

The Getting Started page appears.

⑩ Type a developer name.

⑪ Double check that your prefilled-in email address is correct.

⑫ Type the URL of your Web site.

⑬ Type your phone number.

⑭ Click Continue.

The Registration Fee page appears.

⑮ Click Continue.

The Google Checkout page appears.

⑯ Fill in all the necessary information and pay the $25.00 registration fee.

Your Android Market developer page appears.

● You can click Setup Merchant Account and follow the site's instructions if you plan on selling your applications.

Extra

If you plan on selling your applications, you will need to set up a merchant account with Google Checkout. To set up your account, you will need to enter additional banking information as well as tax ID numbers. Make sure to have these ready before you start. If you plan on uploading only free applications, you can skip this step. To set up your merchant account, click the Setup Merchant Account link at the bottom of your developer home page. You will be presented with a form that you will need to completely fill out in order to create your account. The processing fee for the Android Market purchases is different from a regular Google Checkout purchase. When an application is sold in the Android Market, Google will keep 30% of the application price. For example, if your application is sold for $10.00, you will receive a payment of $7.00, and Google will keep $3.00 as a transaction fee. If you do not have all your business, banking, and tax information ready during the sign-up process, you can enter it any time to set up your merchant account. However, you will not be able to charge customers for your applications until you do.

Get the Android SDK

The Android SDK is not required to develop AIR Android applications; however, it is required to interact with your device in order to install your application. The Flash CS5 IDE uses the SDK to install the compiled Android application on your device when you publish. The SDK also includes an emulator that allows you to test your applications locally before testing on a device. It is highly recommend that you download the SDK before you begin developing your application.

The SDK can be downloaded from the Android Developers site. There is a separate download for Windows, Mac OS X, and Linux; simply choose the version for the operating system on which you will be developing. After the .zip file has finished downloading, extract it and place the extracted contents in a location where you can access it conveniently.

In the root of the SDK, there is a tools folder. This folder contains several of the tools or executables that you will use to interact with your device and the emulator. The android executable provides a user interface for managing the SDK. Running this application will bring up the Android SDK and AVD Manager window. From here, you can download all the up-to-date components of the SDK. Be sure to download all of the Android 2.2 API 8 packages. There is no need to download the documentation or the samples, but as long as you download the SDK platform, you should have everything you need in order to develop AIR Android applications.

Get the Android SDK

1️⃣ In a Web browser, go to http://developer.android.com/sdk/index.html.

2️⃣ Click the SDK package for your operating system.

The License Agreement page appears.

3️⃣ Click I Agree to the Terms of the Android SDK License Agreement.

4️⃣ Click Download.

The SDK is downloaded.

5️⃣ Extract the SDK .zip package.

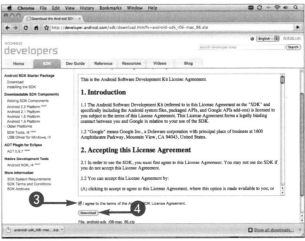

6 On Mac OS X, in a Terminal window, run the android tool in the tools folder of the SDK.

OR

6 In Windows, execute the SDK Setup.exe at the root of the SDK folder.

The Android SDK and AVD Manager interface appears.

7 Click Available Packages.

8 Click the packages to download and install.

9 Click Install Selected.

The packages are downloaded and installed.

Extra

To make life easier when using the tools in the SDK through the command line, add the tools folder of the SDK to your System Path variable. This can be done on Mac OS X by creating a .bash_profile file in the root of your user directory and placing the following text in it, making sure to replace <PATH TO SDK> with the full path to the root folder of your SDK:

```
export PATH=${PATH}:<PATH TO SDK>/tools
```

This process for Windows is different for each version, and much more complicated. A Google search for "Adding folders to Path variable for Windows" will give you many results on how to do this.

Get the Android Eclipse Plug-in

The Android Eclipse Plug-in is primarily used for developing native Android applications with Java. However, it provides many valuable features that you can use to help debug your applications. This is especially useful if you are already using an Eclipse-based IDE, such as Flash Builder or FDT, as your primary ActionScript editor. Even if you are not currently using Eclipse, the Android plug-in can be useful if you are not comfortable with using the command line in order to interact with the SDK.

You can install the plug-in using the Install New Software option in Eclipse or your Eclipse-based IDE, such as FDT or Flash Builder. Have the URL https://dl-ssl.google.com/android/eclipse/ handy because you need to enter it in the Install dialog box. Eclipse searches this URL for any available Eclipse software and plug-ins. If the URL is entered correctly, the Development Tools item will appear in the dialog box. You can select this to begin the download and installation process.

After the plug-in is downloaded and installed, you will be asked to restart Eclipse. When you restart, you will be prompted to enter the path to your Android SDK location. If you have not downloaded the Android SDK, see the preceding section, "Get the Android SDK," for more details.

From Eclipse, you can access the Android SDK and AVD Manager window by selecting Window → Android SDK and AVD Manager from the main menu. In that window, you can set up new emulator instances.

The Eclipse plug-in also installs the DDMS (Dalvik Debug Monitor Service) perspective, which provides a number of different ways to interact with your device and emulator instances.

Get the Android Eclipse Plug-in

Get and Install the Plug-in

1 In Eclipse, click Help.

2 Click Install New Software.

The Install dialog box appears.

3 Type **https://dl-ssl.google.com/android/eclipse/**.

4 Click to check Developer Tools.

5 Click Next.

The Install Details page of the dialog box appears.

6 Click Finish.

The plug-in begins to download and install.

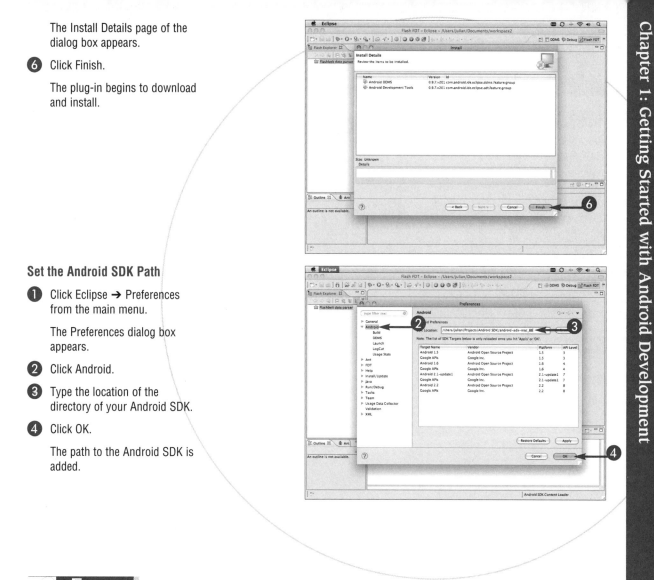

Set the Android SDK Path

1 Click Eclipse → Preferences from the main menu.

The Preferences dialog box appears.

2 Click Android.

3 Type the location of the directory of your Android SDK.

4 Click OK.

The path to the Android SDK is added.

The most useful feature of the DDMS perspective is the File Explorer panel. With a device selected, this panel will show the file system of that device. This can help you ensure that files are being created in the correct location. It also allows you to push and pull files to and from the device. By default, you will not have access to some of the folders on the device, such as the data directory. This is because that folder is owned by the root user of the device. In order to gain access to that folder, you must root your phone, which will void your warranty but also give you more access. Unless there is a very good reason for doing so, it is not recommended that you root your device. There are many tutorials online on how to do this if you are interested. Make sure to follow the instructions for your device, or it may result in a bricked device.

There are also many useful utilities in the DDMS perspective that can be used to debug your applications. For more details, see Chapter 16, "Debugging Your Application."

Enable
USB Debugging

I n order to install applications on your device, you must first have it set up to enable debugging. Depending on which operating system you are currently developing on, the number of steps may vary.

If you are developing on a Windows computer, you will need to download and install the USB driver package using the Android SDK and AVD Manager. This process is the same as installing the additional Android SDK components. For more details, see the section "Get the Android SDK" earlier in this chapter. If you already completed the steps in that section and selected all the available packages, there is a good chance that you have already installed this. You can check to see if it has been downloaded by looking for the usb_driver directory in the root of your SDK. The process for installing the drivers is

different for each version of Windows, and I suggest that you follow the instructions on the Android Developers site, http://developer.android.com/sdk/win-usb.html, in order to install them correctly.

If you are using a Mac OS X computer for development, you can skip having to install the USB drivers. The steps below should just work.

You can now connect your device to your computer with the USB cable included with your device. If it has connected correctly, you should see the USB symbol in the notifications area of the status bar. The next step is to turn on USB debugging when the device is connected. To do so, on your device, you go to the list of options that can be used during development and choose to debug applications on the device.

Enable USB Debugging

 Connect your device with a USB cable.

 Tap Settings.

The Settings application is launched.

③ Tap Applications.

The Application Settings are displayed.

④ Tap Development.

The Development settings are displayed.

⑤ Tap USB Debugging.

A confirmation dialog box appears.

⑥ Tap OK.

Your device is now ready for USB debugging.

Extra

There are two additional options in the Development list that are also very useful when developing and debugging applications. The Stay Awake option prevents the screen from going to sleep while it is connected to a USB cable or while charging. This can be useful when developing if you are testing and continuously reinstalling your application on the device. More times than not, the screen will go to sleep when you are compiling and installing your application. If you turn this on, make sure to turn it off when you are testing to see if your system idle code works correctly. For more details on setting the system Idle mode, see Chapter 12, "Using the Location and WiFi Features."

The third option is Allow Mock Locations. If this option is checked, you can simulate the device being at a specific geolocation coordinate. This is extremely useful when testing geolocation features of your application without physically being at a specific location. For more details on simulating geolocation coordinates on your device, see the section "Debug with the Android Eclipse Plug-in" in Chapter 16.

Create an
Android Virtual Device

Android Virtual Devices (AVDs) are configured emulator instances, which enable you to set up an emulator to mimic the behavior of an actual device. Creating an Android Virtual Device gives you full control over the entire specifications of the emulator. This allows you to set up an emulator just like a device that you may want to test your application on.

Each Android Virtual Device is made of up several parts. The first is which version of the SDK you want to use on the device. In order to make sure that the device has Android 2.2 or higher installed, choose a target with an API level greater or equal to 8. Next, you can specify a specific skin and screen resolution for your device. Several of the popular device screen resolutions come preinstalled with the SDK; however, you can enter a

custom resolution if you prefer. You can also specify the size of the SD card that you want your device to have, and you can select an image of an SD Card in order to have it be populated with files when created. You can also adjust the hardware profile of the device. There are a number of items that you can add to your device, such as support for a directional pad, touch-screen capability, a GPS, a camera, a trackball, and keyboard support.

Google has done a great job in allowing you to model your Android Virtual Device after an actual device as closely as possible. This keeps you from having to have a physical device for all the different Android devices in order to test your application. However, this does not replace testing on an actual device, which should always be done.

Create an Android Virtual Device

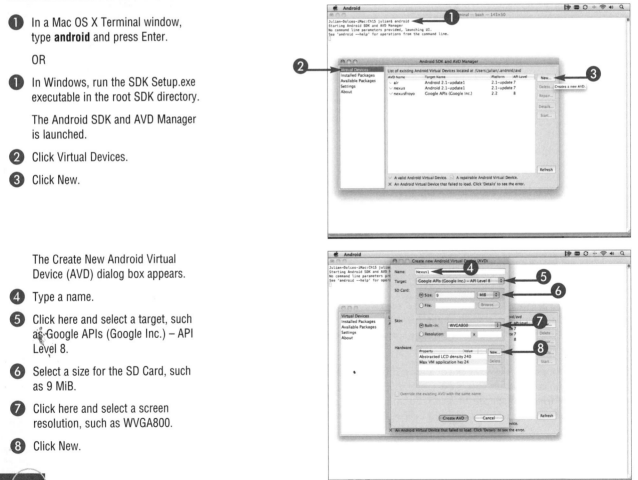

① In a Mac OS X Terminal window, type **android** and press Enter.

OR

① In Windows, run the SDK Setup.exe executable in the root SDK directory.

The Android SDK and AVD Manager is launched.

② Click Virtual Devices.

③ Click New.

The Create New Android Virtual Device (AVD) dialog box appears.

④ Type a name.

⑤ Click here and select a target, such as Google APIs (Google Inc.) – API Level 8.

⑥ Select a size for the SD Card, such as 9 MiB.

⑦ Click here and select a screen resolution, such as WVGA800.

⑧ Click New.

The hardware features dialog box appears.

9 Click here and select a hardware feature, such as Touch-Screen Support.

10 Click OK.

11 Repeat steps **8** to **10** for each hardware feature that you want to add.

You are returned to the Create New Android Virtual Device (AVD) dialog box.

12 Click Create AVD.

A result dialog box appears.

13 Click OK.

The AVD is created.

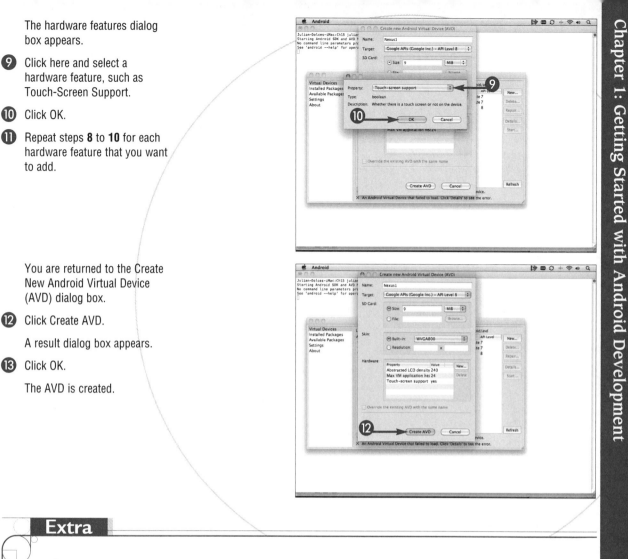

Extra

In order to see a complete list of all the available Android Virtual Devices, you can enter the following command in a Terminal or command prompt window:

```
android list avds
```

This will print out a list of the AVDs as well as their configurations. The name, path to the .avd file, the target framework and API, and the skin are displayed for each AVD.

After some time, chances are that you will create a number of different AVDs in order to simulate the different devices on the market. As this list grows, you may want to remove any unwanted AVDs. The android tool has the ability to delete a specific AVD. The syntax for deleting a AVD is as follows:

```
android delete avd -n <name>
```

The name argument can be found when you use the list command. For example, if I had an AVD named nexusone, I would use the following command in order to delete it:

```
android delete avd -n nexusone
```

Start the Emulator

After you have created your Android Virtual Device, you can start it. Starting an Android Virtual Device causes the emulator application to be launched with the configuration of the device that you have set. If you have not created an Android Virtual Device, see the preceding section, "Create an Android Virtual Device."

There are two main ways to start an Android Virtual Device, from the command line and from the Android SDK and AVD Manager window. From the command line, you use the emulator executable in the tools folder of the Android SDK. The emulator executable has many options you can use when starting up an Android Virtual Device. The main option you will want to use is the -avd switch. This switch enables you to specify the name of the

Android Virtual Device that you want to start. If you are unsure of what the name of the Android Virtual Device is, you can get a list of all available devices using the command mentioned earlier, android list avds.

If you are using the Eclipse plug-in or are not comfortable with the command line, you can use the Android SDK and AVD Manager in order to start the Android Virtual Device that you want. The Virtual Devices selection displays a list of all the available devices. This is similar to the android list avds command.

It may take a while for your device to fully boot up to the home screen of the device. Also, before you can install your applications onto the device, you will need to install the AIR Runtime for the emulator.

Start the Emulator

Start the Emulator with the Command Line

1 In a Terminal or a command prompt window, type **emulator –avd**.

2 Type the name of the AVD that you want to start, such as Nexus1.

3 Press Enter.

The emulator launches the AVD.

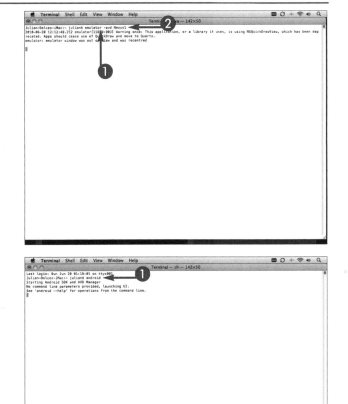

Start the Emulator with the Android SDK and AVD Manager

1 In a Mac OS X Terminal window, type **android**.

OR

1 In Windows, run the SDK Setup.exe executable in the root SDK directory.

2 Press Enter.

The Android SDK and AVD
Manager appears.

3 Click Virtual Devices.

4 Click a device.

5 Click Start.

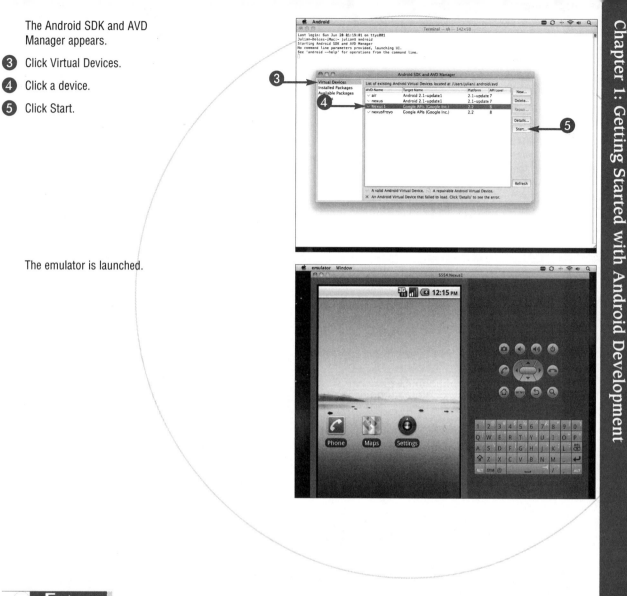

The emulator is launched.

Extra

After your emulator is launched, you can telnet into it to perform more commands on it. When the emulator is fully booted to the home screen, you will notice that there is a number before the name in the title bar of the emulator window. In the example in this section, that number is 5554. This number is the port that the emulator is connected to. You can telnet into the emulator by typing the following command into a Terminal window:

```
telnet localhost 5554
```

This will start a telnet session with the emulator, which will allow you to interact with the emulator a number of ways. After you are connected, type **help** into the Terminal window to see a list of available commands.

Using the Actions Panel

The Flash Actions panel is where all your scripting or ActionScript coding is done within an FLA (Flash animation) file. The Actions panel consists of three main sections: the Actions toolbox, at the top left of the panel, which groups similar ActionScript elements together; the Script navigator, at the bottom left, which enables you to jump to your different scripts easily; and the Script pane, on the right, which is where you write your ActionScript code.

The Actions toolbox is a listing of all the internal ActionScript classes and methods provided by Adobe, which allow you to program your Flash application. If there are times when you cannot remember what a class's method name is, you can find it in the list and double-click it to have it added to the Script pane.

You can write scripts on a frame in the Timeline or on an object on the Stage. It is best practice to write only frame scripts because they are easier to find and keep all your code grouped together. There will be times when you will write code on multiple frames and sometimes on different Timelines. The Script navigator gives you the ability to quickly jump between all the scripts in your file. This can be a big timesaver because it allows you to keep the Actions panel open while writing code.

The Script pane is where you will write all your ActionScript code. It is a basic text editor with some code editor features that will help you be a more efficient programmer. Many of these features can be accessed from the toolbar above the editor window. You can format your code, check its syntax, add and remove comments, and collapse blocks of code.

Using the Actions Panel

Using the Actions Panel to Code

1. Click the frame on the Timeline for which you want to write ActionScript.

2. Click Window.

3. Click Actions.

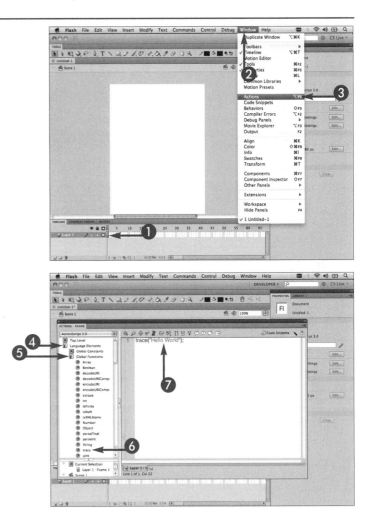

The Actions panel appears.

4. Click an Actions main category, such as Language Elements.

5. Click a subcategory, such as Global Functions.

6. Click an action, such as `trace`.

   The action appears in the Script pane.

7. Type text in the action, such as **"Hello World"** for a `trace` action.

Commenting Code

- Click here to apply block comments to selected code.

- Click here to apply single-line comments to a selected line.

- Click here to remove comments.

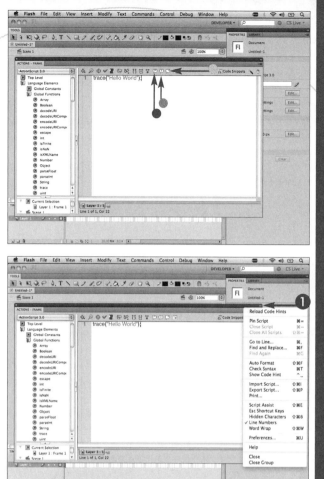

Using Actions Panel Commands

1 Click the additional options button.

The many commands that you can use while using the Actions panel appear.

Note: *Learning the keyboard shortcuts for these commands will help speed up development.*

Extra

A new feature introduced in Flash CS5 is the ability to introspect your custom code and provide code hinting. This can drastically speed up development time, as this will save you from typing more than you need to. If you bring up code hinting on an object, it will bring up all its public methods and properties, which acts like an outline for its help file. This saves you from having to remember all of a class's public attributes and gives you the ability to quickly look them up. To bring up the code hint window as you type, press Ctrl+spacebar. Depending on where your cursor is, different options will appear. If you do not have anything selected, a list of all the available ActionScript classes and objects will appear. If you are on an instance of a class, a list of public methods and properties will appear. When the code hint window appears, you can continue to type what you are looking for, and it will narrow the search for you. You will also notice that when you are using code completion, any `import` statements for that class will be added. As you go through the examples in the book, try to use this feature as much as possible, as it is a good habit to pick up.

Create a Skeleton Custom Class

As your scripts become more complex, you will want to create custom classes for them in order to better organize your code. To do this, you will need to create a separate .as file, which you can do in the IDE (integrated development environment). However, if you are working on a project with many custom classes, you may want to look at a more full-featured programming environment, such as Flash Builder, to write your ActionScript code.

A custom class consists of a few key parts: The first is a package, which is a way to group similar classes together. If you do not give your class a package name, it resides in the default package of your application. The second part is a constructor, which is the main entry point to

your class. The *constructor* is simply a function method with the exact same name as the file or class. When you create a new instance of your class, the code in the constructor will be fired. This is where you will place any initialization that needs to occur for your class to work correctly. It is a good practice to limit the amount of code in your constructors. Having a constructor call a separate `init()` method that does all the initialization is a good way to achieve this. The reason for limiting the code in your constructor is that this code is not optimized when you compile your application.

After you have the base of a class created, you can add properties and methods to give your class the functionality that you need.

Create a Skeleton Custom Class

1️⃣ Click File.

2️⃣ Click New.

The New Document dialog box appears.

3️⃣ Click ActionScript 3.0 Class.

4️⃣ Click OK.

The Create ActionScript 3.0 Class dialog box appears.

⑤ Give your class a name, such as `MyClass`.

⑥ Click OK.

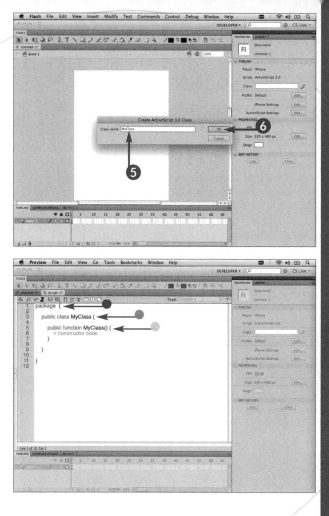

A skeleton class is generated for you.

● You place the package declaration here.

● You place the class declaration here.

● You place the class constructor method here.

Extra

When naming your packages, it is a good practice to use the reverse-domain naming convention. This makes sure that your classes will not conflict with any other classes created by another developer that have the same name. For example, the URL of my blog is www.deleteaso.com, so my packages would look like this: `com.deleteaso`. If you give your packages a name, you will also have to place your class file in a set of folders that mimics your package name. In my case, my classes would go in a folder named com/deleteaso. After you have your main package defined, you can create more packages within it to better group similar classes. For example, all of my custom event classes may go in a package named `com.deleteaso.events`. Try to follow a similar naming convention to group classes to the one that Adobe has adopted for the internal ActionScript classes. This will give other developers an idea of which package to look in for certain functionality.

Set the Source Path

As your projects get more complex and have more custom classes and more .fla files, you are going to want to organize them in a way that makes sense for you. A common way to do this is to have all your classes in a Classes folder and all your .fla files in an src folder. Doing this early in your development will save you lots of time as your project grows.

After you place your .fla files no longer in the same directory as your .as files, you need to tell Flash where to find them so that they can be compiled with your application. To do this, you need to set the source path to the folder where your classes are located.

You can set this individually in each of your .fla files. This is done from the Advanced ActionScript 3.0 Settings

dialog box. When the dialog box first appears, the Source Path tab will be selected, and a list of folder locations is shown underneath it. The default location is always set to . ,which refers to the same folder in which the .fla file is in. You add your new location to the list. If you prefer, you can select the folder icon to select the folder in a File Browser window.

You can also set the source path globally for every .fla file that you create. This is done from the ActionScript 3.0 Advanced Settings dialog box accessed from the Preferences dialog box. The process is the same for adding paths globally as it is for an individual .fla file.

Set the Source Path

Set the Source Path for a File

1 Click File.

2 Click ActionScript Settings.

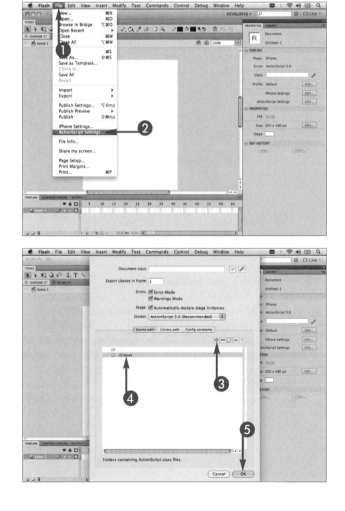

The Advanced ActionScript 3.0 Settings dialog box appears.

3 Click the + button to add a new path.

4 Enter the path to your classes, such as ./Classes.

5 Click OK.

The source path is set for the file.

Set the Source Path Globally

1 Press ⌘+U (Ctrl+U).

The Preferences dialog box appears.

2 Click ActionScript.

The ActionScript settings appear.

3 Click ActionScript 3.0 Settings.

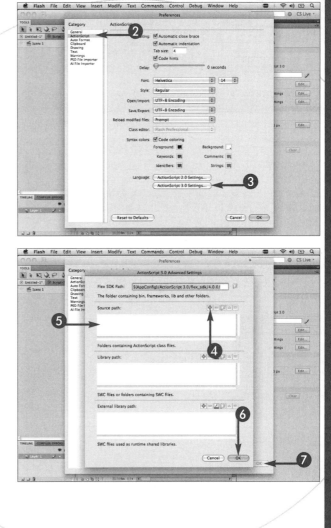

The ActionScript 3.0 Advanced Settings dialog box appears.

4 Click the + button.

5 Enter the new source path.

6 Click OK.

You are returned to the Preferences dialog box.

7 Click OK.

The source path is set globally.

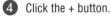

Extra

When setting your source path, it is a good practice to use relative paths instead of absolute paths. This is really important if multiple people are working on the same project on different computers. If you use absolute paths, your class paths will likely not be the same. Using relative paths is easy if you understand a few concepts. If you want to reference a directory that is a level up from the current one, you can use `../`. If you want to reference two levels up, you simply double that, `../../`. So if you wanted to create a relative path for the example shown in this section, you would have used `../Classes`. This tells Flash to go up a level from inside the src folder and select the Classes folder.

Along with a folder for your .fla files and your .as files, it is a good idea to create a folder in which Flash will create all of the .swf files for your project. This folder is usually called bin, or something similar. This will make it easy if you ever have to deploy your .swf files to a server. Make sure to also use relative paths when setting the output location for your .swf.

Create
MovieClips

hen you want to interact with assets in your Flash project, you will need to create or convert current assets into symbols. Symbols come in a few different forms, the main one being a MovieClip. A MovieClip symbol consists of a Timeline, which can contain other types of symbols. You can also control the playback of the Timeline independently of other Timelines. MovieClips can also be scripted with ActionScript. These are by far the most powerful symbols in Flash, so the majority of the symbols you create will be MovieClips.

You can convert any asset that is already on the Stage to a MovieClip using the Convert to Symbol dialog box, in which you can name the MovieClip, select its type, select

the folder in the Library to create it in, and set the registration point of the symbol.

The *registration point* is the location in which your MovieClip's contents will be placed. By default, the registration point is set to the top left, or 0,0. Most of the time this will work; however, there are times when you will want to change this. There are examples later in the book that use the center of the object as its registration point. This is commonly used when you want objects to rotate or scale from the center and not from the top left of the object.

You can also create an empty MovieClip by clicking Insert → New Symbol or by pressing ⌘+F8. After the symbol has been created, Flash will open it in Edit mode so that you can add assets to it.

Create MovieClips

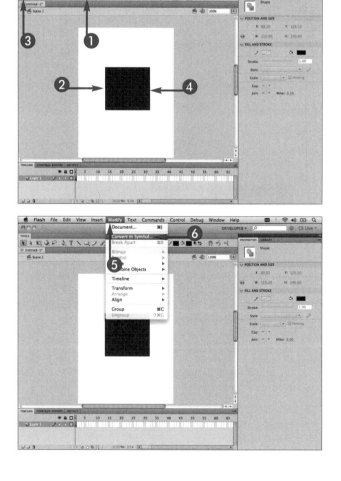

1 Select a shape tool, such as the Rectangle tool.

2 Draw the shape on the Stage.

3 Click the Selection tool.

4 Select the shape on the Stage.

5 Click Modify.

6 Click Convert to Symbol.

Note: *You can also use the keyboard shortcut F8.*

The Convert to Symbol dialog box appears.

⑦ Give your symbol a name, such as square_mc.

⑧ Click here and select Movie Clip as the type.

⑨ Click here and set the registration point of the symbol.

⑩ Click OK.

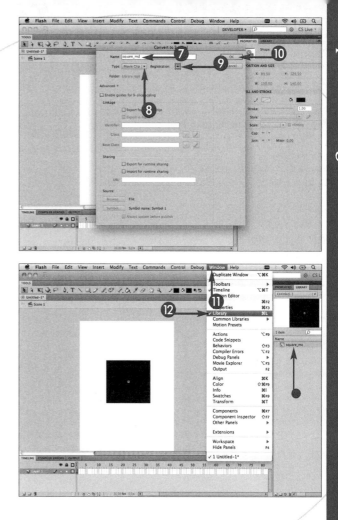

⑪ Click Window.

⑫ Click Library to display the Library panel if it is not already checked.

● The symbol you just created appears in the Library.

Note: *You can use the ⌘+L (Ctrl+L) keyboard shortcut to toggle the visibility of the Library panel.*

Extra

You can also create a MovieClip with ActionScript. There are many reasons why you would want to create it with code instead of with the Flash authoring environment, which will become apparent as you work through the other samples in the book. Here is the syntax for creating a MovieClip with code:

```
var mymc:MovieClip = new MovieClip();
```

Another symbol that is similar to a MovieClip is a Sprite. A Sprite is a MovieClip without a Timeline. Oftentimes, if you do not need to do any Timeline animation, you will create a Sprite object instead. These cannot be created in the IDE and must be created with code. Here is the syntax to create a Sprite instance:

```
var mysprite:Sprite = new Sprite();
```

Create Buttons

Whereas MovieClips are great for working with animations and displaying content, buttons are used to allow your users to interact with your application. Button symbols respond to various interactive events, such as rollovers, mouse clicks, and touches when developing touch-enabled applications.

Buttons are simple four-frame interactive MovieClips. The first three frames represent different visual states for the button, and the fourth represents the overall hit area of the button. The play head or Timeline never plays but goes to the appropriate frame when it reacts to the mouse or a touch.

The first frame is the *up state*. This is the frame that is shown when nothing is interacting with it. The second

frame is the *over state*. This is the frame that is shown when a user places the mouse cursor over the button. The third frame is the *down state*. This is the frame that is shown when the user presses the mouse button down while over the button. This frame is also shown when a user touches down on the button of a touch-enabled device, such as the Android. The fourth and last frame is the overall hit area of the button. This sets the bounding box of the button in which the user can interact with it. This frame is invisible when the file is published.

After your button is created, you can receive events from it when the user interacts with it. This will give you the ability to respond to a user's interaction and update the screen as needed. For more details on handling events, see the section "Work with Events" later in this chapter.

Create Buttons

Create a Button

① Click Insert.

② Click New Symbol.

Note: *You can also use the ⌘+F8 (Ctrl+F8) keyboard shortcut to create a new symbol.*

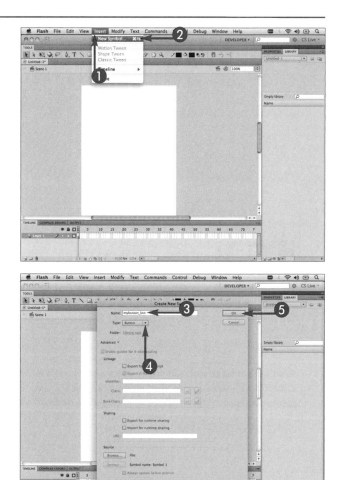

The Create New Symbol dialog box appears.

③ Name your symbol, such as mybutton_btn.

④ Click here and select Button as the type.

⑤ Click OK.

The button is created.

Create the Visual State of the Button

⑥ Select a shape tool, such as the Rectangle tool.

⑦ Select the Up frame in the Timeline.

⑧ Draw a shape.

⑨ Click Scene 1 to exit the button Timeline.

Place an Instance of Your Button

⑩ Click your button in the Library and drag it to the Stage.

An instance of the button is created.

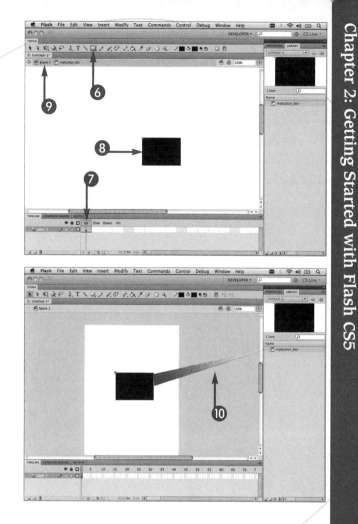

Extra

Button symbols provide you with a very quick and easy way to add interactivity to your projects. However, there will come a time when you will want to use animation or create some more complex button states, instead of the static four frames of a basic button. In order to do this, you may look at creating buttons from MovieClip symbols. MovieClip and button symbols respond to the same interactions from a mouse or touch. By listening for these events, you can play or show different animations for each state. This is shown in more detail in Chapter 5, "Handling Interaction." If you want to have the mouse cursor turn to the hand when you roll over a MovieClip button, simply set the buttonMode property to true:

```
mymc.buttonMode = true;
```

Edit Properties in Flash

After you have created some symbols, you can add them to the Stage. When they are on the Stage, you can set many of their properties in the Properties panel.

Setting the instance name of the symbol allows you to reference it through code. Many of the examples later in the book require you to set the instance name for an object. It is always a good idea to name your instances when they are added to the Stage.

You can also adjust the size and position of your object. The x property will set your object's position along the x-axis, left to right, and the y property will set the its position along the y-axis, top to bottom. Adjusting the width and height properties will change the size of your object.

There are also many Color Effects settings that you can apply to your object, such as Brightness, Tint, Advanced, and Alpha. One that you will probably use the most is the Alpha setting. This will set the initial alpha property of the object, or transparency. It is important to note that you can set only one color effect to your object in the Properties panel. However, you can also set them with code, which will allow you to apply multiple effects at once.

You can also apply filters to your object. Flash comes with a bundle of filters, similar to those in Photoshop: Drop Shadow, Blur, Glow, Gradient Glow, Gradient Bevel, and Adjust Color. Unlike the color effects, you are able to apply multiple filters to your objects. You can also save filter presets, which allow you to apply the same set of filters to multiple objects in your file.

Edit Properties in Flash

1 Select a shape tool, such as the Rectangle tool.

2 Draw a shape on the Stage.

3 Click the Selection tool.

4 Select the shape on the Stage.

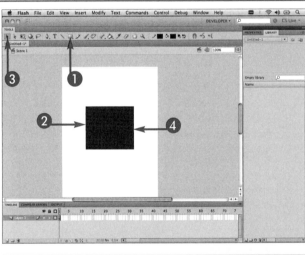

5 Press F8.

The Convert to Symbol dialog box appears.

6 Give your symbol a name, such as square_mc.

7 Click here and select Movie Clip as the type.

8 Set the registration point of the symbol.

9 Click OK.

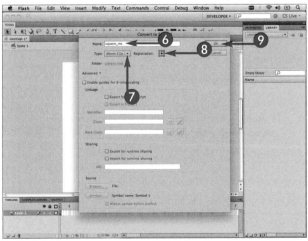

⑩ Click Window.

⑪ Click Properties if the Properties panel is not already visible.

Note: *You can also use the ⌘+F3 (Ctrl+F3) keyboard shortcut to toggle the visibility of the Properties panel.*

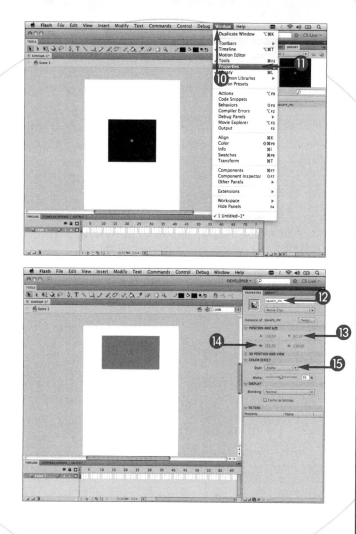

⑫ Give your symbol an instance name, such as `square_mc`.

⑬ Change the y position.

⑭ Change the width property.

⑮ Click here and select a Color Effect style, such as Alpha.

You can set other properties in the panel as well.

Apply It

As mentioned earlier, the Properties panel is just one way to set your object's properties. You will often want to change these properties at runtime and will need to do so through code. First, make sure that you have given any objects you want to affect an instance name. Here is what setting some of the properties you can set in the IDE would look like in ActionScript:

```
myinstance.x = 100;
myinstance.y = 250;
myinstance.width = 50;
myinstance.height = 64;
myinstance.alpha = 0.5;
```

Add Objects to the Stage with Code

Adding items to the Stage is simply a matter of dragging them from the Library onto it. However, there will be times in your project when you want to add objects to the Stage with code. The Stage in this case is called the display list. The *display list* is a hierarchal tree of every visual item that is displayed at any given time. The order of the list is important because the lower an item is on the list, the lower the depth at which it will appear visually.

To add an object to the display list, you need to create one with ActionScript. You could simply instantiate a new `MovieClip` instance with the following syntax:

`var mc:MovieClip = new MovieClip();`

Alternatively, you can create a new instance of an item that resides in your Library. To do so, you must set the item to Export for ActionScript in the item's Properties panel. When you give it a class name, choose something that well represents it so that the name is easy to remember. If you do not already have an .as file for that class, Flash will automatically generate one for you when you compile your project. This will not create an actual file but simply create the class so that it gets compiled with your .swf. To instantiate your Library asset, use the same syntax that you use for a `MovieClip`, except replace `MovieClip` with the class name you gave your Library item.

After you have created an object, you can add it to the display list. You can do this by calling the `addChild()` method on any `DisplayObjectContainer` class. This is the base class for any objects that can serve as display list containers. The two most common are `MovieClip` and `Sprite`.

Add Objects to the Stage with Code

 Create a `MovieClip` symbol and select it in the Library.

Note: For more details on how to create `MovieClip` symbols, see the section "Create MovieClips" earlier in this chapter.

 Right-click the item.

❸ Click Properties.

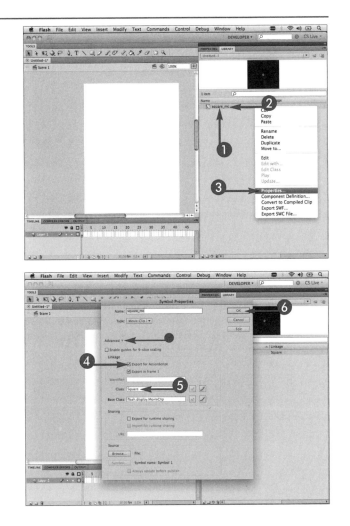

The Symbol Properties dialog box appears.

● You may have to click here to expand the Advanced properties.

❹ Click Export for ActionScript.

 Give your symbol a class name, such as `Square`.

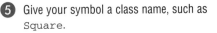 Click OK.

Note: If a dialog box appears saying, "A definition for this class could not be found in the classpath, so one will be automatically generated in the SWF file upon export," click OK.

7 Select a frame in the main Timeline.

8 Open the Actions panel.

Note: *See the section "Using the Actions Panel" for more information.*

9 Create a new `Square` variable, such as `var mc:Square = new Square();`.

10 Add your object to the Stage, such as `addChild( mc );`.

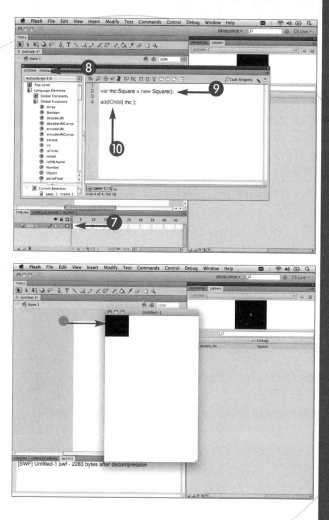

11 Press ⌘+Enter (Ctrl+Enter) to test your movie.

● Your object is now added to the Stage.

Chapter 2: Getting Started with Flash CS5

Extra

When you add an object to the display list using the `addChild()` method, it gets added to the top of the list. This means that the object will be shown on the topmost layer and will overlap any items at lower depths at the same location. There are times when you want to add items at a certain index in the display list. To do this, you can use the `addChildAt()` method. This method is very similar to `addChild()`, with the addition of an extra index parameter. The index parameter specifies which index in the display list you would like to add the object at:

```
var mc:MovieClip = new MovieClip();
addChildAt( mc, 5 );
```

Be careful to make sure that you are adding your object to an index that is in range of the current display list. This means that you cannot add an item to an index that is higher than the total number of children currently on the list. For example, if there are currently four items in the list, you cannot add your item at index 6.

Remove Objects from the Stage with Code

Just as you can add objects to the display list with `addChild()` and `addChildAt()`, you can remove objects with `removeChild()` and `removeChildAt()`. `removeChild()` takes a reference to the object that you want to remove as its only parameter. `removeChildAt()` takes the index of the child in the display list that you want to remove. If you try to remove a child at an index that does not exist, an error will be thrown.

It is important to note that removing an object from the display does not remove it from memory. You can add it back onto the display list later if you like. If you want to make sure that it gets cleared from memory, set the instance of your object to null, after it has been removed. You will also want to remove any other references to your object, such as event listeners. For more details on how to

remove event listeners, see the section "Work with Events" later in this chapter.

Being able to re-add your objects back onto the display list is convenient; however, the trade-off is that you will have to be diligent in making sure that it can be cleared from memory. Memory management is not an exact science, and there are many things to take into account. The topic alone could be a whole book in and of itself. There are many great resources and examples online on how to make sure that your objects get cleared from memory or garbage collected. I strongly recommend reading as much information as you can on the subject and finding out what works best for your specific situations.

Remove Objects from the Stage with Code

① Create a `MovieClip` symbol and place it on the Stage.

Note: *See the section "Create MovieClips" earlier in this chapter for more information.*

② Click the Selection tool.

③ Select the symbol.

④ Give it an instance name, such as `square_mc`.

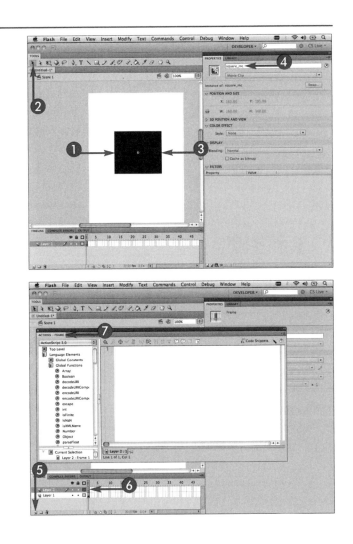

⑤ Click the New Layer button in the Timeline panel.

A new layer is created.

⑥ Select a frame in the new layer.

⑦ Open the Actions panel.

Note: *See the section "Using the Actions Panel" for more information.*

8 Remove the instance from the Stage, such as removeChild(square_mc);.

9 Press ⌘+Enter (Ctrl+Enter) to test your movie.

● Your object is now removed from the Stage.

Apply It

The removeChild() and removeChildAt() methods are great at removing one object from the display list at a time. But what happens if you have hundreds of items that you want to remove at once? You would expect there to be a removeAll() method, but this does not exist. If you ever need to write your own, similar method, you can use the following code:

```
while( numChildren ){
    removeChildAt( 0 );
}
```

This removes all the objects from the display list at once.

Work with Events

In ActionScript, an object dispatches an event when an action takes place. Events can be fired when the user interacts with your application, such as clicks a button, or the Flash Player can dispatch them when it is executing specific tasks, such as adding an object to the display list. Events are one of the main mechanics in which one or more objects talk to each other.

You can listen for when events occur by adding an event listener to an object, which dispatches the event. To add an event listener, use the addEventListener() method. The first two parameters, which are required, are the type of event that you want to listen for and a reference to an event handler function.

An *event handler* is simply a function that will be called when the event is dispatched. Every event handler takes one parameter, which is the type of event that it is listening for. The Event object will have all the necessary information that you need in order to respond correctly to an event being dispatched.

Like all things in ActionScript, if you can add events, you can remove them as well. When you no longer need to listen for a particular event, make sure to remove the listener by calling the removeEventListener() method. It is important to remove all unwanted event listeners when you no longer need your objects. This will help make sure that they are cleared from memory by the garbage collector.

Work with Events

① Select a frame in the Timeline in which you want to add your ActionScript code.

② Open the Actions panel.

Note: *See the section "Using the Actions Panel" for more information.*

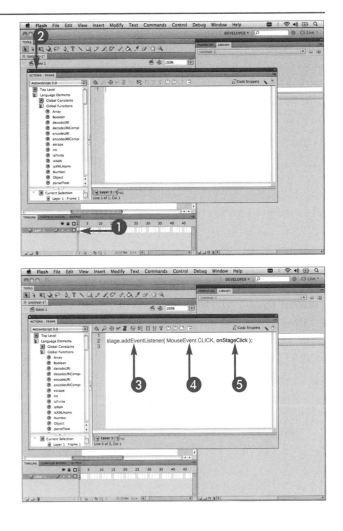

③ Add an event listener to the Stage object, such as stage.addEventListener();.

④ Specify the type of event, such as MouseEvent.CLICK.

⑤ Specify an event handler, such as onStageClick.

6 Create an event handler method, such as `function onStageClick()`.

7 Add an event object as its parameter, such as `event:MouseEvent`.

8 Add a `trace` statement when clicked, such as `trace( "stage click" );`.

9 Remove the event listener, such as `stage.removeEventListener( MouseEvent.CLICK, onStageClick );`.

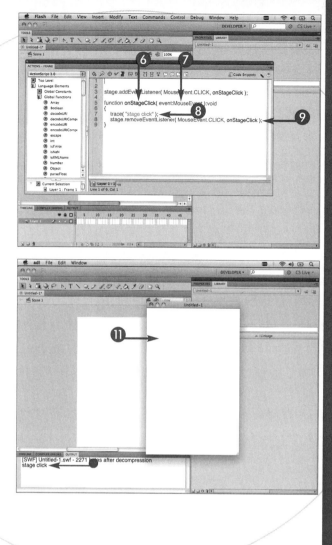

10 Press ⌘+Enter (Ctrl+Enter) to test your movie.

11 Click the Stage of the movie.

● Your `trace` statement appears in the Output panel.

Note: *Clicking the stage a second time will not show the* `trace` *statement because you removed the listener.*

Extra

Now that you know how to add, remove, and listen for events, you can start to dispatch your own events. The `EventDispatcher` class, and any object that is added to the display list, can dispatch events. The `dispatchEvent()` method is what you will use to dispatch your event. It takes an `Event` object as its only argument. This is the same object that will be passed to your event handler that is listening for your event. Here is an example of an event being dispatched when an animation has completed:

```
dispatchEvent( new Event( "animationComplete" ) );
```

As you get more comfortable with events, you can create your own classes that subclass `Event`, which then can be passed into the `dispatchEvent()` method.

Using the Drawing API

The drawing API (application programming interface) enables you to draw vector shapes with ActionScript. This is the code equivalent of drawing shapes, such as rectangles and circles, in the Flash authoring environment. You can draw in two different types of objects, Shapes and Sprites. Both of these objects have a graphics property, which is where all the drawing occurs.

The Shape class is a lightweight DisplayObject whose sole purpose is to draw shapes in. The Sprite class can also be used if you need to add items to its display list, whereas the Shape class cannot. However, with this added functionality, the Sprite class will consume more memory.

The Graphics class contains all the methods that you can use to draw vector shapes. There are three steps to drawing a shape: First, you want to set the fill color and

alpha of the shape with the beginFill() method. Next, you can use any of the draw shape methods to draw the actual shape. The drawRect() and drawCircle() methods are two of the simpler and more popular shape methods. After you have drawn your shape, close the fill by calling the endFill() method.

The Graphics class also gives you the ability to draw lines with code. First, set the line style that you want to draw with the lineStyle() method. This method allows you to set the thickness, color, and alpha of the line, as well as some other more advanced properties. To draw the line, call the drawLine() method. This draws a line from the current position to the one passed into the method. If you want to move to a new position without drawing a line, you can use the moveTo() method.

When you want to clear your drawing, call the clear() method.

Using the Drawing API

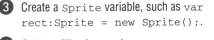

① Select a frame in the Timeline in which you want to add your ActionScript code.

② Open the Actions panel.

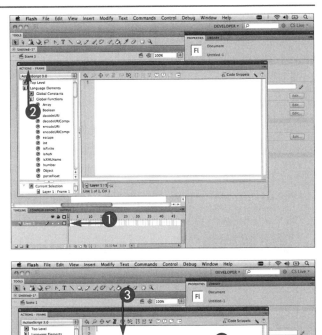

③ Create a Sprite variable, such as var rect:Sprite = new Sprite();.

④ Select a fill color, such as rect. graphics.beginFill(0x000000);.

⑤ Draw a shape, such as rect.graphics. drawRect(0,0,100,100);.

⑥ End the fill, such as rect.graphics. endFill();.

⑦ Add the shape to the Stage, such as addChild(rect);.

8 Create a `Sprite` variable, such as `var line:Sprite = new Sprite();`.

9 Set the line style, such as `line.graphics.lineStyle( 5, 0x000000 );`.

10 Set the start position, such as `line.graphics.moveTo( 0, 200 );`.

11 Draw a line, such as `line.graphics.lineTo( 100, 200 );`.

12 Add the line to the Stage, such as `addChild( line );`.

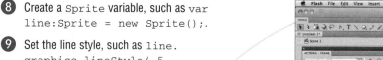

13 Press ⌘+Enter (Ctrl+Enter) to test your movie and see your drawings.

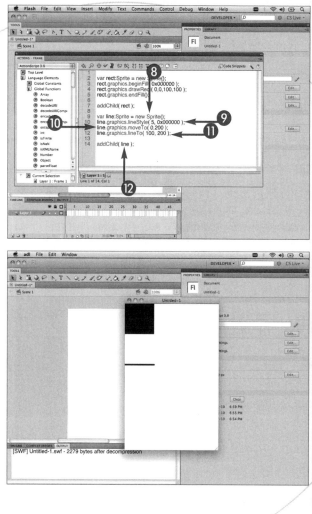

Using Flash CS5 Help

With the release of CS5, Adobe has created a new AIR application called Adobe Help, which can be launched by pressing F1. The Help application aggregates all the help files for the CS5 products in one central location. With the Help application, you are able to store all your help files locally so that you can access them when you are offline. It also provides an easy way to receive help updates from Adobe when they become available.

There are three sections of the Help application: the Search pane, the Feedback & Rating pane, and the browser pane. The browser pane is a simple Web browser that displays HTML content. There are back and forward buttons that enable you to navigate to previously viewed pages, just as you would in a real Web browser. The URL for the page is also in the top right of the pane, and clicking it will open the page in your default browser.

The Search pane allows you to search your local help content, Adobe's Web site (www.adobe.com), and many of the community sites. By selecting Community Help in the Search Location drop-down list, you will get results of some of the more popular forum and tutorial sites on the Web. It is like having Google integrated into the Help application.

Some of the help documents allow you to leave feedback and give ratings. You can use this as a place to report bugs in the documentation or ask for more clarification if you still do not understand the concepts on the page.

Using Flash CS5 Help

1 Click Help.

2 Click Flash Help.

Note: *You can use the F1 keyboard shortcut to launch the Help application.*

The Help application launches.

3 Click ActionScript 3.0 Language and Components Reference.

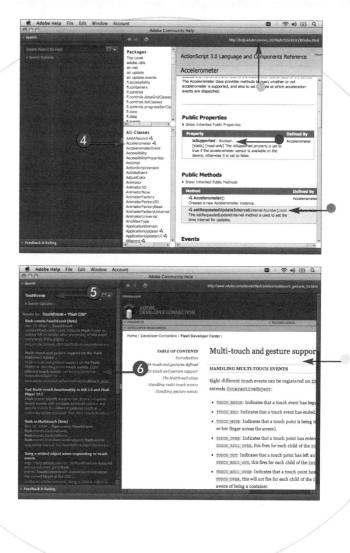

④ Select a class in the class list, such as `Accelerometer`.

● You can click a property in the summary to go to its help.

● You can click a method in the summary to go to its help.

● You can click the page URL to open it in a Web browser.

⑤ Enter a search term, such as **TouchEvents**.

⑥ Click a search result.

● The page will be loaded in the application.

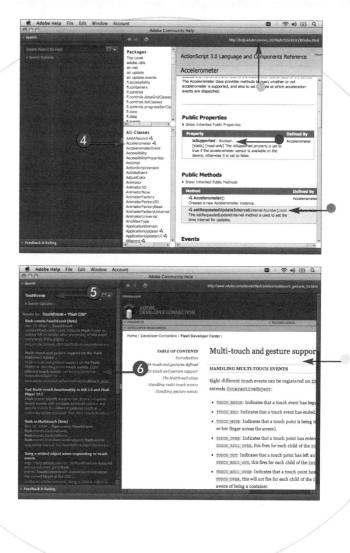

Extra

It is really important that you set any of the important Help packages to be available for offline viewing. The last thing that you will want is to find yourself without Internet access and struggling to remember how to do something. You can manage your local content from the Preferences dialog box in the application. It will also show you if there are any updates to the documents that you have on your computer. Keeping your Help files up to date is critical, as they may contain bugs just like your code can. They can also contain new features and APIs for newer versions of the Flash Player and AIR. Before the Adobe Help application, it was difficult to keep everything up to date, and you never knew if you had the most up-to-date files. Adobe recognized these issues and is committed to making the Help application as easy as it possibly can be.

Create a New Project

Adobe has developed a new project template for creating Android applications. When you select the AIR for Android template in the New Document dialog box, an .fla will be created with the Stage dimensions of 800 x 480, which is the full-screen resolution of most Android phones in Portrait mode. Your file will also be set up to publish with ActionScript 3.0 and with the default Android settings.

If you are creating an application that will be in only Landscape mode, you can change the Stage dimensions to 480 x 800 in the Document Settings dialog box.

In the Document Settings dialog box, you can also set the background color and frame rate of your application. The default frame rate for a new .fla file is 24 frames per

second. This is the standard frame rate for animations; however, you may want to change this if you are creating a game. 30 frames per second is a commonly used frame rate for Flash games and Web sites, but feel free to experiment with this to find what works best for you. The faster your frame rate, the faster your animations will happen. The downfall to this is that you may be redrawing your graphics more often, which may cause the performance of your application to decrease.

There is also a Make Default button in the Document Settings dialog box. Clicking this button will set the current document's settings to the new default for any new file that you create. This will affect every type of .fla and not just your AIR for Android projects.

---

① Click File.

② Click New.

Note: *You can also use the ⌘+N (Ctrl+N) keyboard shortcut to open the New Document dialog box.*

The New Document dialog box appears.

③ Click the Templates tab.

The New from Template options appear.

④ Click the AIR for Android category.

⑤ Click 480x800Android.

⑥ Click OK.

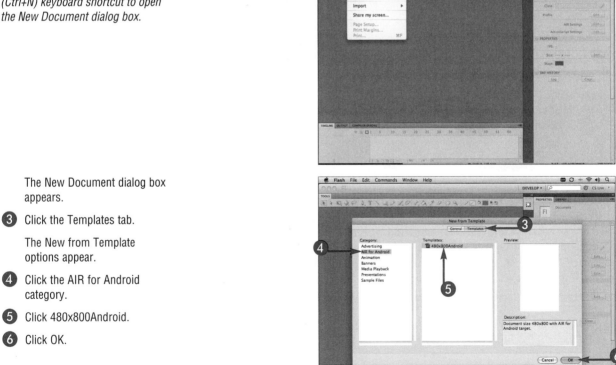

A new, blank AIR for Android project is created.

7 Click Modify.

8 Click Document.

Note: *You can also use the ⌘+J (Ctrl+J) keyboard shortcut to open Document Settings dialog box.*

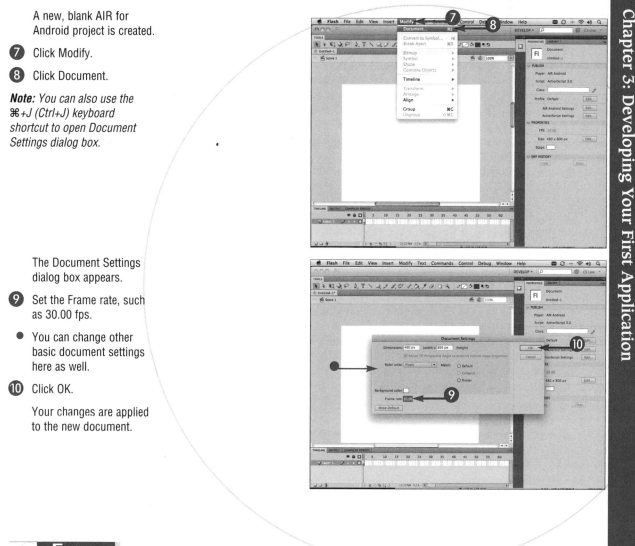

The Document Settings dialog box appears.

9 Set the Frame rate, such as 30.00 fps.

● You can change other basic document settings here as well.

10 Click OK.

Your changes are applied to the new document.

Extra

Flash CS5 has introduced a new file format for your Flash projects, .xfl. This file format is an uncompressed version of the .fla format. To save your file in this format, select Flash CS5 Uncompressed Document (*.xfl) from the Format drop-down list in the Save dialog box. This will create a folder with the same name as the filename you specified. Inside that folder is a folder structure that contains all the information about your file, as well as the assets in your Library. If you used CS5 to import any images or audio files to the Library, they can be found in the LIBRARY folder. This enables you to update assets without having to open the file or re-import them. The DOMDocument.xml file is an XML representation of your file. It contains all the ActionScript on any frames and any shapes or assets on the Stage.

The .xfl format makes adding Flash files to a source control system, such as Subversion, a lot easier. Because the file format is text, as opposed to the binary .fla file format, you will have the ability to merge changes between two versions of your files. This will make working with large teams a lot more efficient.

Configure Publish Settings

electing the AIR for Android template from the New from Template dialog box sets up some of the major publish settings for you. However, there are many other settings that can affect your final output. You can set these in the Publish Settings dialog box. By default, there are three tabs across the top: Formats, Flash, and HTML. The Formats tab enables you to select multiple types of files to output your file to. Because you are only concerned about creating Android applications, you can deselect the HTML check box, which removes the HTML tab from the top.

The text input area beside the Flash check box is the location where Flash will output the compiled .swf for your application. This enables you to set the location to

another folder other than the same one as the .fla. It is a good practice to use relative paths to your file just in case you copy the project folder to a new location or you are working with a team of developers and designers.

The Flash tab has all the settings that will affect the output of your .swf file. Changing the compression settings for images and sounds will greatly affect the file size and the quality of your application. You can also publish the file from the Publish Settings dialog box by clicking the Publish button at the bottom. Publishing your file will export your file to the .swf file specified on the Formats tab and create the Android application in the same directory.

Configure Publish Settings

1 Click File.

2 Click Publish Settings.

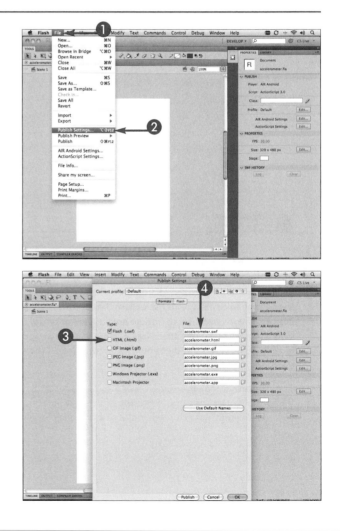

The Publish Settings dialog box appears.

3 Click here to uncheck the HTML check box.

4 Set the path to your .swf file.

Note: *The default .swf file location and name is the same folder as your .fla file with the same name.*

5 Click the Flash tab.

6 Set the default JPEG quality settings, such as to 100.

7 Click OK.

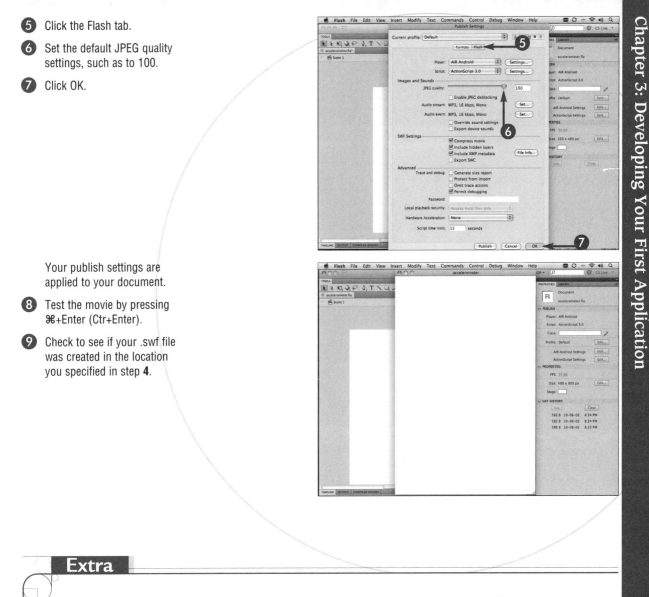

Your publish settings are applied to your document.

8 Test the movie by pressing ⌘+Enter (Ctrl+Enter).

9 Check to see if your .swf file was created in the location you specified in step **4**.

Extra

If you often find yourself adjusting the Publish settings the same way, you can save that profile to be used later. At the very top of the Flash tab in the Publish Settings dialog box, there is a drop-down list with the currently selected profile and a set of buttons to the right of it. The first button exports and imports the publish profiles. These are exported as .xml files and can be imported from another file to change the settings. The next two buttons are Create New Profile and Duplicate Profile, which essentially do the same thing. These add a new profile to the .fla file. This comes in very handy if you are targeting multiple platforms. For example, you could create a profile that targets the Android, one that targets the iPhone, and one that targets the Web. This enables you to publish to multiple platforms quickly during development when you make changes to your application. It also gives you control over being able to optimize your assets for the different platforms. On the desktop, you will want your assets at their best quality, whereas on the Web you will probably compromise quality for file size. The fourth button enables you to rename the currently selected profile. Finally, the fifth button deletes the currently selected profile.

Set Your Application Output

There are other settings besides those in the Publish Settings dialog box that will affect your final output. You can find these settings in the AIR Android Settings dialog box, which can be accessed from the Flash tab of the Publish Settings dialog box or as shown below. The General tab contains the main settings for your application.

The output file is the location and name of the .apk file that will be created when you publish the file. This is the file that you will install onto your device. You can name your file anything you like, but it is a good idea to keep it consistent with other output files that you create, such as your .swf file.

The app name is the name that you want to give your application. This is the text that will appear underneath the icon on the home screen of your Android device. There is limited space underneath the icon, so be sure to pick a good name.

The Version input area of the AIR Android Settings dialog box is where you set the version number of your application. When you install your application to your device, the version number is used to determine if your application needs to be updated. This means that if you make changes to your application and do not update the version number, the device will not recognize that the application has been updated, so your application will not be updated on the device. This does not affect the development process when installing the application from Flash CS5. For more details about version numbers, see the section "Update Your Version Number" later in this chapter.

Set Your Application Output

① Click File.

② Click AIR Android Settings.

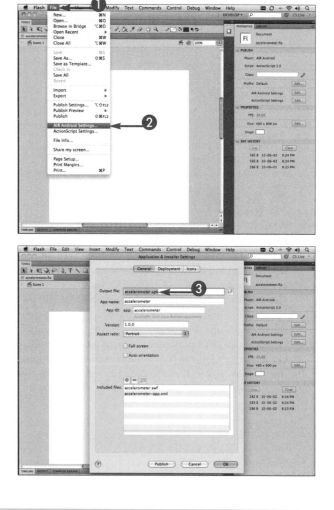

The Application & Installer Settings dialog box appears.

③ Change the name and location of your .apk file.

④ Select a name for your application.

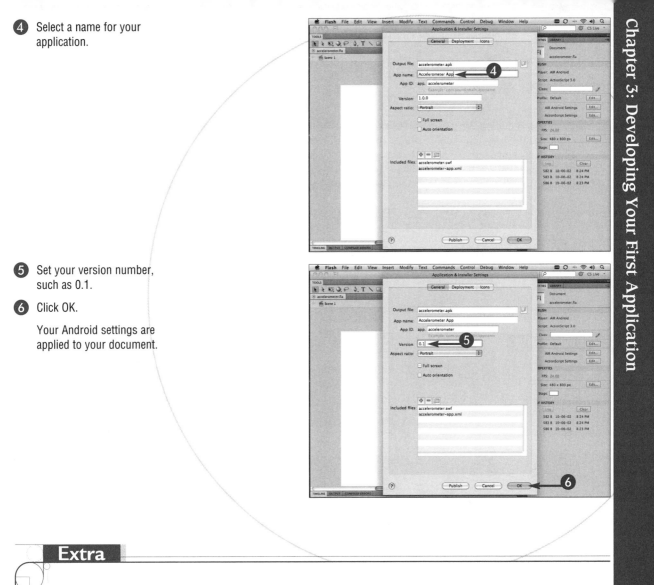

⑤ Set your version number, such as 0.1.

⑥ Click OK.

Your Android settings are applied to your document.

Extra

When you publish your application, Flash creates a file with the .apk extension. An .apk file is an Android application file. However, an .apk file is no more than a fancy zip file. To examine the file in greater detail, you can rename the file to have a .zip extension and extract it. This will extract a folder with the same name as the file. Opening the folder will show you the entire contents and folder structure of your application. This folder structure mimics that of a native Android SDK application.

The AndroidManifest.xml file describes the properties and configuration of the application. The assets folder is where the main .swf file for your application resides. You will also find any other files that you have bundled with your application in this directory.

In the assets/META-INF/AIR folder is an application.xml file. This is a copy of your application descriptor file for your application. You can retrieve the contents of this file using the following syntax:

```
var appDescriptor:XML = NativeApplication.nativeApplication.applicationDescriptor;
```

Create a P12 Certificate

An Android device requires that all applications be digitally signed with a certificate whose private key is held by the application developer. The device uses this certificate to identify the developer of an application and to establish a trust relationship between applications. If you have done any iPhone development, you may familiar with this process, as every iPhone application also needs to be digitally signed. Unlike the iPhone platform, the Android platform does not require that a certificate authority sign the certificate. It is perfectly fine, and often standard practice, to use a self-signed certificate in order to digitally sign your Android application.

Flash Professional CS5 gives you all the tools that you need to create a suitable certificate file to digitally sign your application. This can be done from the Deployment tab of the AIR Android Settings dialog box. Clicking the Create button presents you with a form, in which you can enter all your information in order to link you with your certificate.

The first three input fields are personal information about the developer. The Country drop-down field enables you to select which country you live in. The two password fields enable you to set a password for the certificate. Make sure to use something that you will remember, as you will need to enter this when you compile your application. The default type of certificate is 1024-RSA, but Google recommends using a 2048-RSA certificate. All certificates require a validity period, and the Android Market requires it to be valid until the year 2033.

After you have created your certificate, you can add it to the Certificate field on the Deployment tab in order to digitally sign your application with it.

Create a P12 Certificate

① Click File ➔ AIR Android Settings.

The Application & Installer Settings dialog box appears.

② Click the Deployment tab.

③ Click Create.

The certificate-creation form appears.

④ Enter a publisher name.

⑤ Enter an organization unit.

⑥ Enter an organization name.

⑦ Click here and select a country.

⑧ Enter a password and confirm it.

⑨ Click here and select a type, such as 2048-RSA.

⑩ Enter a validity period, such as 25.

⑪ Click the folder icon.

The Open dialog box appears.

⑫ Click here and select a folder to save your certificate to.

⑬ Click Open.

You are returned to the creation form.

⑭ Click OK.

A certificate creation pop-up box appears.

⑮ Click OK.

You are returned to the Deployment tab.

● Your certificate is inserted in the Certificate field.

⑯ Enter your certificate password.

⑰ Click here to check Remember Password for This Session.

⑱ Click OK.

Your application will now be digitally signed when it is compiled.

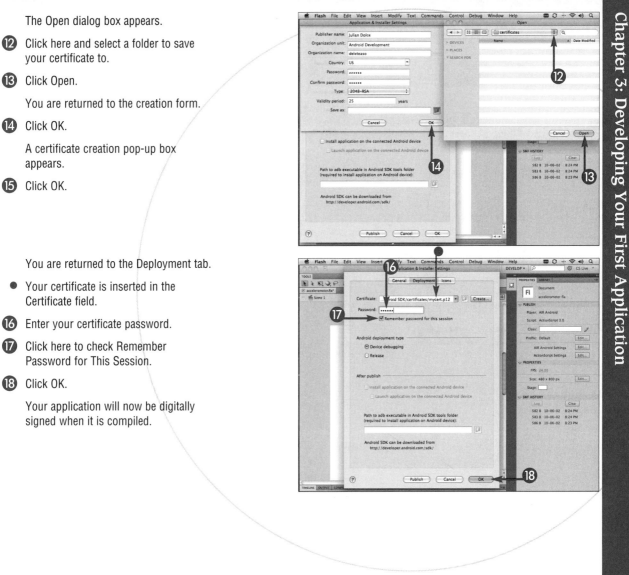

Extra

There are several other ways to create your digital certificate not using the Flash Professional CS5 tools. You can also use the adt executable, which comes with the AIR SDK, to create your certificate from the command line. The adt executable can be found in the bin folder of the AIR SDK. Make sure that you are using the most recent version of the SDK that supports AIR Android development. In a Terminal window, the following syntax can be used in order to create a certificate. Simply replace the values with your own information:

```
adt -certificate -cn "Neil Coelho" -c "CA" -validityPeriod 25 2048-RSA clcert.p12 mypassword
```

Compile from Flash Professional CS5

After you have created an AIR for Android file in Flash Professional CS5 and properly set all the publish settings, you are ready to compile the file to an Android application. Adobe has made the process for compiling and installing the application on your device as seamless as possible. If you add the path to the Android SDK to your publish settings, Flash will automatically install the application to the device when it has finished publishing it. You can also have the application automatically launch after it has been installed. If you have not downloaded the Android SDK, see Chapter 1, "Getting Started with Android Development," for more details.

To set the path to the Android SDK, you use the AIR Android Settings dialog box's Deployment tab. The After Publish section offers you options for what Flash should

do after it has finished compiling the application. Here you can set the path to the `adb` executable in the tools folder of the Android SDK.

You can test your application on your computer; however, some of the features may not work, if your application uses ones that are available only on your device, such as the accelerometer and geolocation features. The entire process to compile and install your application on your device can take up valuable development time. If you can test your application, even in parts, on your computer before installing it to your device, this will save you a lot of time. After you are satisfied that your application works on your computer, install and test it on a device because it will run differently than on your computer.

Compile from Flash Professional CS5

① Click File.

② Click AIR Android Settings.

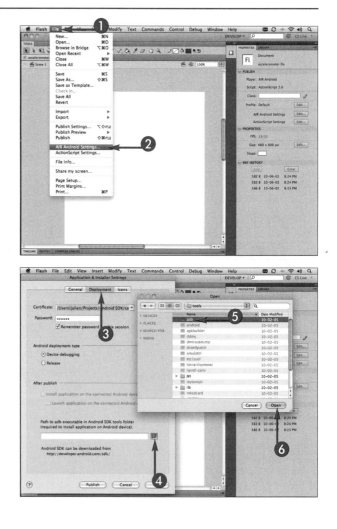

The Application & Installer Settings dialog appears.

③ Click the Deployment tab.

④ Click the folder icon.

The Open dialog box appears.

⑤ Select the `adb` executable.

⑥ Click Open.

You are returned to the Deployment tab.

7 Click here to check Install Application on the Connected Android Device.

8 Click here to check Launch Application on the Connected Android Device.

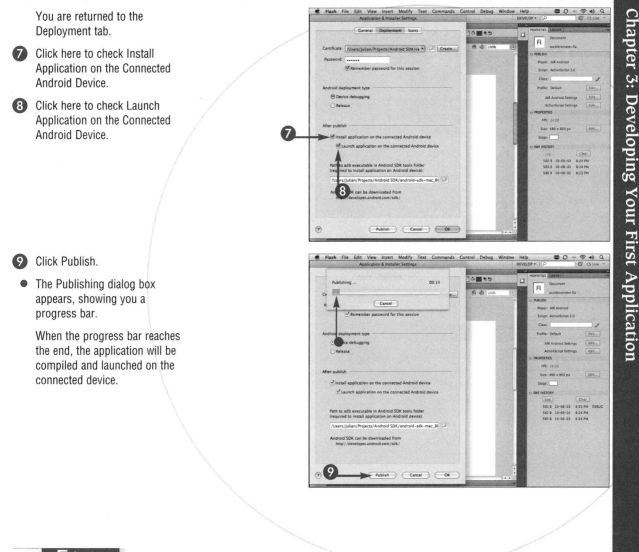

9 Click Publish.

● The Publishing dialog box appears, showing you a progress bar.

When the progress bar reaches the end, the application will be compiled and launched on the connected device.

Extra

When you are testing your application, be sure to check the Compiler Errors panel. If there is a problem with any of the ActionScript you have written, the Flash compiler will stop and throw an error, which is displayed in the panel. Each error will give you the location and line number of the error, as well as a description of what the error is. Clicking the error in the panel will bring you to the line number and position of the error in your code.

The Compiler Errors panel shows warnings as well as errors. These warnings are not severe enough to cause Flash to not compile your file; however, it is probably a good idea to investigate each one and try and resolve them because they may cause unexpected behavior in your application. Some examples of the errors that you may encounter are duplicate variable names, duplicate frame labels, and AS3 migration issues.

In Flash CS5, you can now toggle the visibility of the errors and warnings by clicking the representative icons at the bottom of the Compiler Errors panel.

Compile from the Command Line

The `adt` executable is a tool that can be used to compile an AIR Android application from an .swf file. This is the application that Flash Professional CS5 uses when compiling your project to an Android application. You can also use this application to compile your application from the command line. The `adt` executable can be found in the AIK2.5/bin folder in the Adobe Flash CS5 installation folder.

Before you start, you will need to get the full paths to the `adt` executable file and your certificate .p12 file. After you have the paths to those files, open a command shell or a Terminal window and navigate to the location of your .swf file.

The `adt` packager has a number of switches that are used to configure how your application is compiled. The `-target`

switch enables you to select which type of application you want to compile. You have the same options that are available on the Deployment tab of the AIR Android Settings dialog box in the Flash IDE. The `-storetype` switch specifies the type of certificate you are using, which in this case is pkcs12. The `-keystore` switch specifies the file path to your .p12 certificate file. The `-storepass` switch is the password for your certificate file.

The parameters are as follows: the path to the .apk file that you want to compile, your application descriptor file, and the .swf file of your application. These are all the required parameters and switches to compile your AIR Android application. If you have included any paths to icons or default images in your application descriptor file, you can add these after the required fields.

Compile from the Command Line

1 Open a Terminal or command-line window.

2 Navigate to the folder with your .swf file, such as cd ~/Desktop/Accelerometer, and press Enter.

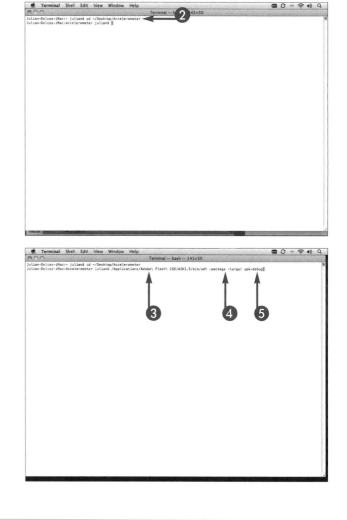

3 Enter the path to the `adt` executable, such as /Applications/Adobe\ Flash\ CS5/AIK2.5/bin/adt.

4 Type **–package –target**.

5 Enter a valid `-target` option, such as `apk-debug`.

⑥ Type **-storetype pkcs12 –keystore**.

⑦ Type the full path to your .p12 file, such as /Users/julian/Desktop/ Accelerometer/mycert.p12.

⑧ Type **–storepass**.

⑨ Type your certificate password.

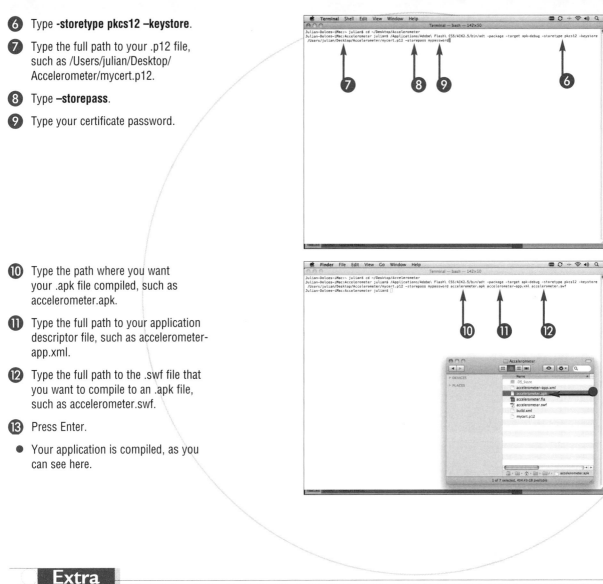

⑩ Type the path where you want your .apk file compiled, such as accelerometer.apk.

⑪ Type the full path to your application descriptor file, such as accelerometer-app.xml.

⑫ Type the full path to the .swf file that you want to compile to an .apk file, such as accelerometer.swf.

⑬ Press Enter.

● Your application is compiled, as you can see here.

Extra

There are currently two valid values for the -target switch, which specifies the Android deployment type. The example in this section uses the apk-debug option in order to specify that the application can be debugged. This enables you to receive trace statements and debug the application on the device.

When you are ready to submit the application to the Android Market, you will need to use the apk value for the -target switch. The following example is the same as the one shown here, except that it uses the apk value:

```
/Applications/Adobe\ Flash\ CS5/AIK2.5/bin/adt -package -target apk -storetype pkcs12 -keystore
    mycert.p12 -storepass mypassword accelerometer.apk accelerometer-app.xml accelerometer.swf
```

Install Your Application on Your Device

The section "Compile from Flash Professional CS5" earlier in this chapter shows an application being installed on the device immediately after it was compiled. This method works great if you are using Flash CS5 to develop all your applications. However, it is quite possible that you develop all your applications without the use of Flash and use only an ActionScript editor, such as Flash Builder or FDT. If this is the case, you will need to compile your applications from the command line; for more details, see the preceding section, "Compile from the Command Line."

After your application has been compiled, you will then need to install the application on your device from the command line. From the command line, you can install the application to a device connected with USB or to an emulator that is running. For more details on running the emulator, see Chapter 1.

The adb executable in the tools folder of the Android SDK enables you to install applications from the command line. Telling adb where to install an application can be done with either the -e switch or the -d switch. Specifying the -e switch will tell adb to install the application on the emulator, whereas the -d switch will install it on your device. If you have more then one type of device connected, you can use the -s switch and specify the serial number of the device to install it on that device.

After you have specified which device to target, you can use the install command followed by the path to the .apk file in order to install your application on the device.

Install Your Application on Your Device

Install Your Application on Your Device

1 Type **adb**.

2 Specify a target device, such as −d for a connected device.

3 Type **install**.

4 Type the full path to your .apk file, such as ~/Desktop/Accelerometer/ accelerometer.apk.

5 Press Enter.

● The application is successfully installed on the device.

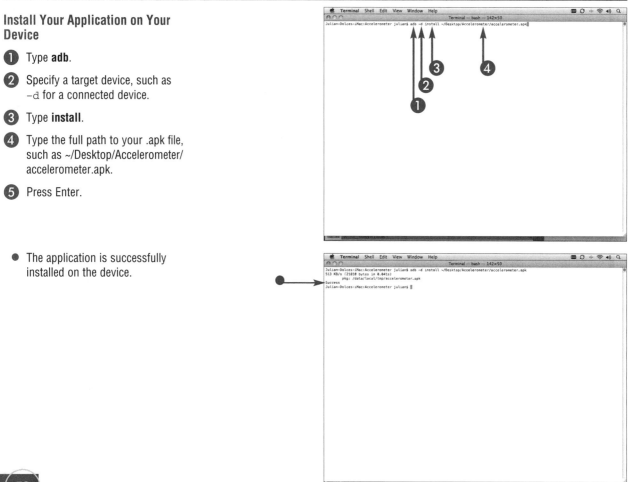

Reinstall Your Application on Your Device

1 Type **adb**.

2 Specify a target device, such as −d for a connected device.

3 Type **install**.

4 Type **−r**.

5 Type the full path to your .apk file, such as ~/Desktop/Accelerometer/accelerometer.apk.

6 Press Enter.

● Your application is reinstalled on your device.

Uninstall Your Application on Your Device

1 Type **adb**.

2 Specify a target device, such as −d for a connected device.

3 Type **uninstall**.

4 Type **app.**.

5 Type the App ID for your application.

6 Press Enter.

● Your application is uninstalled.

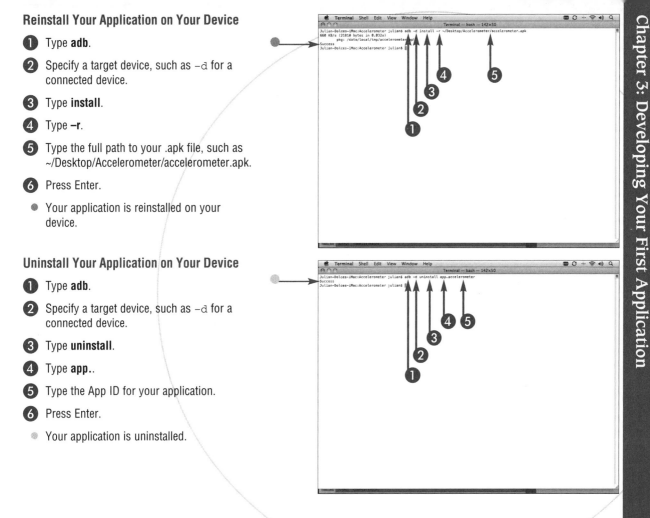

Apply It

If you are developing your application with an Eclipsed-based ActionScript editor, such as Flash Builder or FDT, you can use ANT to run your command-line commands. This will save you from having to switch between your editor and a command line in order to install the application. A powerful feature of FDT is being able to set an ANT script to be run after your application has been compiled. Copy the following into a build.xml file to use it with ANT:

```xml
<?xml version="1.0" encoding="UTF-8"?>
<project name="Android Install" basedir="." default="install">
                <target name="install">
                    <exec executable="adb">
                        <arg line="-d install accelerometer.apk" />
                    </exec>
                </target>
</project>
```

Update Your Version Number

Setting the version number helps you distinguish between different versions of your application. A common number scheme is *major.minor.build*. The major number is incremented when you release a version to the Market, the minor number is incremented when you release a new build to testers or a small set of features after its major release has been completed, and the build number gets incremented every time you publish the file during development. When you increment a number, also set the number to the right of it to 0.

You can set the version number in two places. The first, and easiest, is on the General tab of the AIR Android Settings dialog box. The version number input area is under where you added the name for your application.

The second place is in the app descriptor file that is created when you publish your application. This .xml file is created in the same directory as your .swf file and is named <swfname>-app.xml. To edit the version, open the file in Flash CS5 or any other text editor and find the `<version>` node. Simply replace the current version with the new one and save the file.

Being able to update the version from this file allows you to write a batch script to automatically update the version for you. There are several ways to create this script, depending on the workflow you have set up in order to compile your applications. One way is to write a JSFL (JavaScript Flash) script that could do this. If you are unfamiliar with JSFL, you can check the Flash Help for more details.

Remember, you can find the code samples throughout the book, such as accelerometer.fla and accelerometer-app.xml below, on the Wiley Web page for the book on the Downloads tab, at www.wiley.com/WileyCDA/WileyTitle/productCd-0470904321.html.

Update Your Version Number

Update the Version Number in Flash

1. Click File.

2. Click AIR Android Settings.

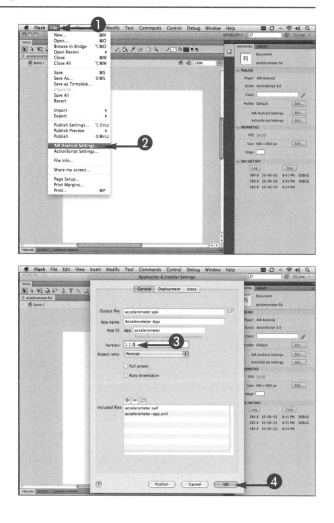

The Application & Installer Settings dialog box appears.

3. Increment the version number, such as 1.1.0.

4. Click OK.

The version number is updated.

Update the Version Number in the App Descriptor File

1 Click File → Open.

The Open dialog box appears.

2 Click your application descriptor file.

3 Click Open.

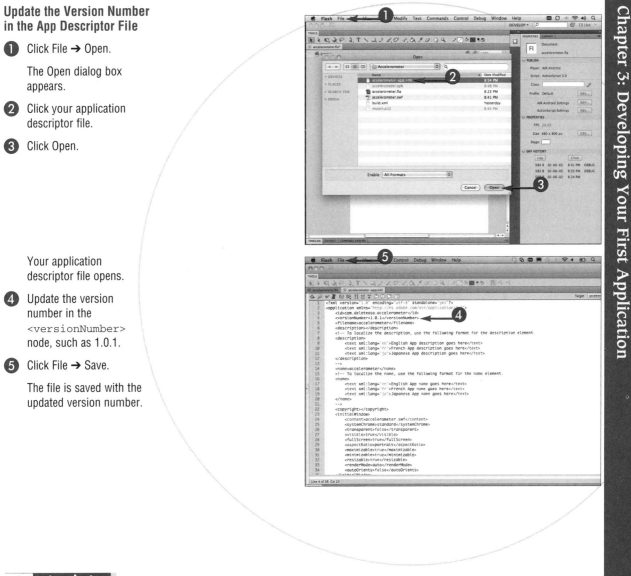

Your application descriptor file opens.

4 Update the version number in the `<versionNumber>` node, such as 1.0.1.

5 Click File → Save.

The file is saved with the updated version number.

Apply It

When you are sending builds to your testers, it is a good idea to display the version number somewhere in the interface. This will allow them to log bugs to a specific version and will prevent any confusion on which build they actually have on their phones. Here is the syntax to retrieve the version number with ActionScript:

```
var appDescriptor:XML = NativeApplication.nativeApplication.applicationDescriptor;
var ns:Namespace = appDescriptor.namespace();
var appVersion:String = appDescriptor.ns::versionNumber;
```

Set Application Permissions

I n order for an Android application to interact with certain parts of the device, the application must be granted certain permissions. When an application is installed on a device, the permissions that are required by the application are displayed to the user. These permissions are granted to the application at the time of installation, and no checks with the user are performed when an application is running. This gives the user a good understanding of what device services the application is using.

For an application to request the proper permissions, one or more <uses-permission> nodes should be added to the application descriptor file. When your Flash application is compiled to an Android application, the permission nodes are added to the AndroidManifest.xml file bundled with your application.

There are a number of permissions that an Android application can set to gain access to certain features of the device. However, only a small subsection of these are required for AIR applications, as not all the device features are exposed to the AIR Runtime.

There are currently eight permissions that you can set for your applications. Some features required of the AIR Runtime will require multiple permissions to be set. Writing to an SD card, accessing the Internet, disabling sleep mode, accessing GPS locations, muting any audio for incoming phone calls, and accessing the camera and microphone all require one or more permissions to be set. As these features are introduced throughout the book, you will examine which permissions need to be set for that feature. The following is a complete list and explanation for each permission.

Set Application Permissions

Create the Android Node

1 Open your application descriptor file.

2 Add the <android> </android> node.

3 Add the <manifestAdditions> </manifestAdditions> node.

4 Add the <manifest> </manifest> node.

5 Add the <data></data> node.

6 Add the <![CDATA[ ]]> tag.

Your file is ready to have permissions set for it.

Set Application Permissions

1 To write to the external memory card of the device, add <uses-permission android:name="android.permission. WRITE_EXTERNAL_STORAGE"/>.

2 To access the Internet, add <uses-permission android:name="android. permission.INTERNET"/>.

3 To access GPS data, add <uses-permission android:name="android.permission. ACCESS_FINE_LOCATION"/>.

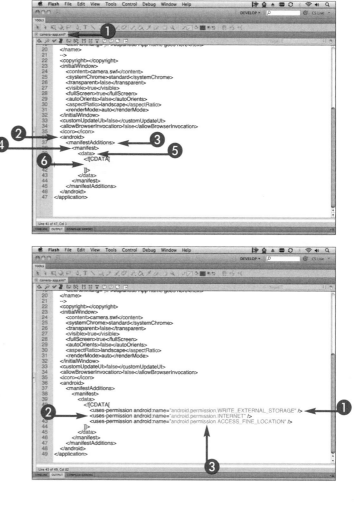

④ To access the camera, add `<uses-permission android:name="android.permission.CAMERA"/>`.

⑤ To access the microphone, add `<uses-permission android:name="android.permission.RECORD_AUDIO"/>`.

⑥ To mute audio during an incoming call, add `<uses-permission android:name="android.permission.READ_PHONE_STATE"/>`.

⑦ To prevent the device screen from sleeping, add `<uses-permission android:name="android.permission.WAKE_LOCK"/>`.

⑧ Also, add `<uses-permission android:name="android.permission.DISABLE_KEYGUARD"/>`.

The application permissions are now set.

Extra

It is very easy to forget to add these permissions during development. If a feature does not work as you would expect it to, there is a good chance that you have forgotten to grant permission for that feature. There are some things that you can watch for while debugging your application in order to catch a missing permission. Watching the output of a connected device with the `logcat` tool can give you insight on how your application is interacting with the Android OS. The `logcat` tool can be started from a command prompt or Terminal window by executing the following command:

```
adb logcat
```

The following output is an example of what you would see if you forgot to add the permission for accessing the camera:

```
W/ServiceManager(   59): Permission failure: android.permission.CAMERA from uid=10060 pid=10090
E/CameraService(   59): Permission Denial: can't use the camera pid=10090, uid=10060
```

Some features may also throw errors in ActionScript. Debugging each feature will be different, but the `logcat` tool is a good place to start.

Set a Custom Application URI

O ne of the powerful features of the Android platform is being able to launch applications from other applications or from a Web browser. When an application is launched, you can also pass arguments to the application so that it can be launched in a certain configuration. If an application is already running, it can still receive the arguments in order to change its state. In order for your application to be launched by other applications, you specify a custom URI, which specifies that your application recognizes this type of URL. For example, if you are creating a Twitter client, you may consider setting your application URI to `twitter://`. When the Android OS recognizes a URL with `twitter://` at the beginning, your application would be launched. Setting a custom URI for your application can be done in the application descriptor file for your application.

When your application is launched, the `NativeApplication` class dispatches an `InvokeEvent`. `INVOKE` event. The `InvokeEvent` instance that is passed to your event handler method contains an `arguments` property. If the URL that was used to launch the application contains arguments, the first element of this `arguments` array will contain the full URL used to launch your application, including the URI. It is your responsibility to do the necessary parsing of the URL in order to act on the event.

You should always add the listener for the `InvokeEvent`. `INVOKE` event at the very start of your application. If one or more events occur before the listener is added, the events are queued and dispatched after the listener has been added. However, there is no guarantee that the events will be fired in the same order that they were received.

Set a Custom Application URI

Add a Custom URI

1. Open the application descriptor file.

2. Add the `<android></android>` node.

3. Add the `<manifestAdditions></manifestAdditions>` node.

4. Add the `<launcherActivity></launcherActivity>` node.

5. Add the `<data> </data>` node.

6. Add the `<![CDATA[ ]]>` node.

7. Add the `<intent-filter></intent-filter>` node.

8. Add `<action android: name="android.intent.action.VIEW"/>`.

9 Add `<category android:name="android.intent.category.BROWSABLE"/>`.

10 Add `<category android:name="android.intent.category.DEFAULT"/>`.

11 Add the `data` node, such as `<data android:scheme=/>`.

12 Set your custom URI, such as `"myapp"`.

The custom URI is set.

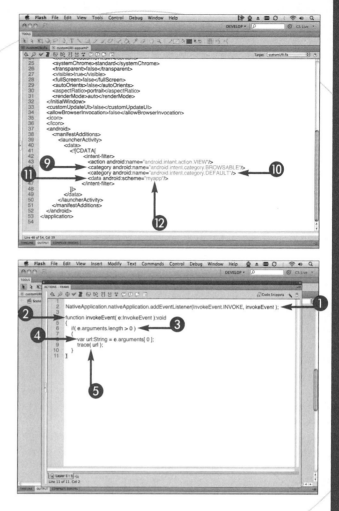

Listen for InvokeEvent

1 Add a listener for the `INVOKE` event, such as `NativeApplication.nativeApplication.addEventListener(InvokeEvent.INVOKE, invokeEvent );`.

2 Create an event handler, such as `invokeEvent`.

3 Check to see if there are arguments.

4 Get a reference to the full URL, such as `var url:String = e.arguments[ 0 ];`.

5 Output the full URL, such as `trace( url );`.

The application will detect when it has been launched with arguments.

Extra

There are three different methods of launching an application with an HTML link. A user can click a link on a Web page in the native browser application, a link in a `StageWebView` instance, or a link in `htmlText` of a `TextField` instance. The following is an example of a link in a `TextField`:

```
myTextField.htmlText = "<u><a href=\"myapp://arg1=value1&arg2=value2\">Launch App</a></u>";
```

If there is more than one application with the custom URI, a menu will be presented to the user, enabling him or her to select which application is launched. On Android devices, this occurs when a YouTube or Google Maps link is launched, offering the user the option to launch the URL in the browser or in its native application.

Mobile User Interface Guidelines

I f you have spent a lot of time on a specific mobile platform, such as Android or iPhone, you have probably realized that many of the applications have a similar look and feel. This allows users to become familiar and comfortable with applications quickly. In order to help developers with this, Google has created a set of useful controls and components that are beautifully designed. If you have used enough apps, you can start to pick out which elements are part of the Android SDK. Currently, there is not a way to incorporate the native controls with your Flash CS5 or AIR application; however, there are many Photoshop templates online that will enable you to make your own controls look like Google's. If you decide to use buttons and graphics that look like the ones provided in the SDK, make sure that they behave the same way that Google had intended. If you implement a button or graphic that does not do what Google designed it to do, there is a good chance that it will confuse users and give them a bad experience.

One Screen

One of the biggest differences between designing for the desktop and mobile platforms is the amount of windows that your application can have. On a desktop, an application can theoretically have as many windows as it needs. On a mobile device, however, you are able to show only one screen at a time. There are exceptions to this rule, such as the different alert and modal windows, but plan for your application to have only the one window. Your application can have multiple screens, but only one can be shown at a time. If your application requires the use of multiple windows, you will need to try and design it into a sequence of screens or rethink the user flow of your application.

One Application at a Time

With any mobile device, memory is going to be limited, and Android devices are no different. Developers need to make sure that their applications use the least amount of memory as possible. To stop applications from using memory when it is no longer being used, you can listen for the `Event.DEACTIVATE` event, which is fired by the Android operating system. This allows you to free up as much memory as possible and stop any CPU-intensive tasks in order to conserve battery life.

If the device is in need of more memory, it will try to free up more by exiting applications that have been placed in the background. If this occurs to your application, the user will expect that his data is not lost when he returns. To help combat data loss, it is important to save the state of your application when it makes sense. You may also want to save the last screen or state in which the user left the application. When the user returns to the application, you can load the necessary data and take him to the last part of the application that he was interacting with.

For more details on the several different ways to save data and states in your application, see Chapter 10, "Saving State."

Think Top Down

When designing your application, you will need to take into consideration how you display information to the user. Because a user will be using her fingers or thumbs in order to interact with your application, portions of the screen will be blocked from view by her hand. This is an important user experience problem that designers and developers need to solve as touch-enabled devices and screens become more ubiquitous. It is a good practice to place any important information higher up on the screen than you normally would. Any changes in your interface as the user interacts with it should always be above where she is touching the screen. This will make sure that the user's hand does not block any important information.

Minimize Input

One big difference between the different smartphones on the market is whether they have a physical keyboard or not. Some devices, such as the Nexus One, have decided to not include a physical keyboard in order to keep a small form factor. Instead, there is a touch-screen keyboard that appears when user input is required. Typing on this keyboard is suitable for typing short amounts of text in small bursts, but this is less than ideal when trying to type a long email. Having users enter lots of information with the keyboard can cause them to become frustrated and leave your application. Limiting the amount of information that users must input before having something meaningful occur is a good way to keep them happy. It is also a good idea to make users enter that information only once. Saving it to the device in a text file or `SharedObject` is an option for doing this.

Focus

Users' typical interaction with their mobile device comes in short bursts when they are not at their computers. Because of this, their attention span will be extremely short; they will want the information that they are looking for quickly. Keeping the focus of your application to a simple task will give you a better opportunity to effectively communicate with your users. Too much information or too many features can complicate the user experience of an application quickly. For example, using an application to check up-to-date sports scores probably loses focus if the user can purchase tickets for the game as well. These two features would probably serve your users better if they were separate applications.

Keeping your application focused on a single task will reduce the amount of help you need to provide to your users. When you present the users with a screen, they should not have to ask themselves what they are supposed to do. Because screen real estate is at a premium, you should avoid having large pieces of text explaining what to do. If you find yourself having to explain your app's functionality to the user, chances are that it is too complicated. It is good to discover this as early in development as possible. Creating storyboards and mock-ups will allow you to plan effectively. Have an unbiased party look these over and see if he or she understands the goal of your application. The more planning and focus group testing that you can do upfront, the more time you will save in development.

Understanding
Screen Resolutions

When designing your application to run on the Android platform, it is extremely important to factor in its compact screen size. Creating a device that is portable and fits in your pocket can create many design challenges. Designing for the 3.7-inch diagonal screen size of most Android phones is much different than designing for a 19-inch desktop monitor.

When designing an application to run on an Android mobile phone, you will have to take into account the different screen resolutions for the different devices. This is not a lot different than designing for multiple resolutions on the Web.

The Nexus One and HTC Incredible phones have a screen resolution of 800 x 480 when in Portrait mode and 480 x 800 when in Landscape mode, whereas the Motorola DROID phone has a screen resolution of 854 x 480 when in Portrait mode and 480 x 854 when in Landscape

mode. If you design your application to have the status bar visible, you will need to account for it during design. The default height of the status bar is 38 pixels, and this should be taken into consideration when designing your application. If the status bar is not a required element of your application, you can create a full-screen application that will hide it from the user. See the following section, "Create Full-Screen Applications," for more details.

Considering screen real estate when designing your application will force you to make sure that you include only necessary elements for interacting with your application. Crowding the interface with unnecessary design elements can confuse your users and provide a bad user experience. Every element on the screen should have a purpose, whether it is displaying information to the user or allowing him or her to interact with it.

Examples of Applications in Portrait Mode

The following application is 762 x 480.

Ⓐ The content height is 762 pixels.

Ⓑ The content width is 480 pixels.

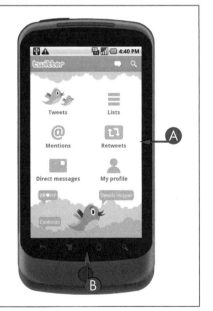

Examples of Applications in Portrait Mode *(continued)*

The following application is 800 x 480.

Ⓐ The content height is 800 pixels.

Ⓑ The content width is 480 pixels.

Android Tablet Screen Resolution

In 2010, we are going to see a number of new style devices called *tablets*. The most popular one to date is by far the iPad. However, there are a number of Android and other tablets that will launch later in the year, for which you can develop Flash and AIR applications. With so many new devices set to release, all with different screen sizes and resolutions, it will be important to plan for your application to function correctly on any sized resolution. There are two common screen resolutions for tablets, 1024 x 600 and 1024 x 768.

If you plan on supporting multiple devices, or multiple platforms, consider how your application would readjust its layout based on a new screen resolution at runtime. You can easily test how your application will respond to screen size changes by resizing the window when testing on your computer.

Of course, this goes beyond tablets. Thinking about how your application would look on any sized platform early on is never a bad idea. Even if you plan on never supporting other platforms today, you never know what the future holds. iPhone developers never thought they would be converting their apps to the iPad a year ago.

Examples of Applications in Landscape Mode

The following application is 480 x 800.

Ⓐ The content height is 480 pixels.

Ⓑ The content width is 800 pixels.

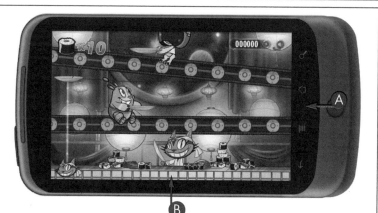

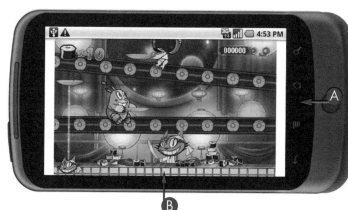

The following application is 480 x 800. Notice how the content is scaled to fit when the status bar is shown.

Ⓐ The content height is 480 pixels.

Ⓑ The content width is 800 pixels.

Create Full-Screen Applications

The status bar is the top bar on your device. It contains some important information, such as battery life, the time, cell signal, cell carrier, the currently connected network interface, and any notifications. This can be important information for some applications but unnecessary for others. The default height for the status bar on Android phones is 38 pixels high, and the status bar accounts for the total screen resolution of the device.

If you are creating an application that needs the extra screen real estate and does not need the status bar, you can hide it by creating a full-screen application. Most games hide the status bar because they want to fully immerse the user in the experience of playing the game.

To hide the status bar to create full-screen applications, you use the AIR Android Settings dialog box. When you open it, the General tab should be selected by default; however, if it is not, select it to find the Full Screen check box. Leaving this option unchecked will create your application with the status bar visible, and checking it will cause your application to take over the entire screen.

You can also create full-screen applications by editing the application descriptor file for your application. You can use this method if you are not using Flash CS5 to develop your applications. In the <initialWindow> node of the application descriptor file, there is a <fullScreen> node. This value can be set to either true or false. Setting it to true causes your application to be created in full screen. This value is set to false by default.

Set Your Application to Full Screen

1. Click File.

2. Click AIR Android Settings.

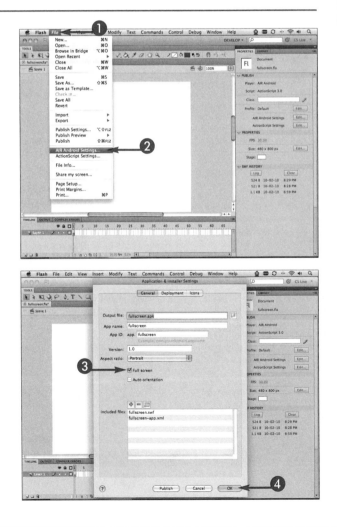

The Application & Installer Settings dialog box appears.

3. Click here to check the Full Screen check box.

4. Click OK.

Your application is set to run full screen.

Check Your App Descriptor File's <fullScreen> node

1 Click File → Open.

The Open dialog box appears.

2 Click your app descriptor file.

3 Click Open.

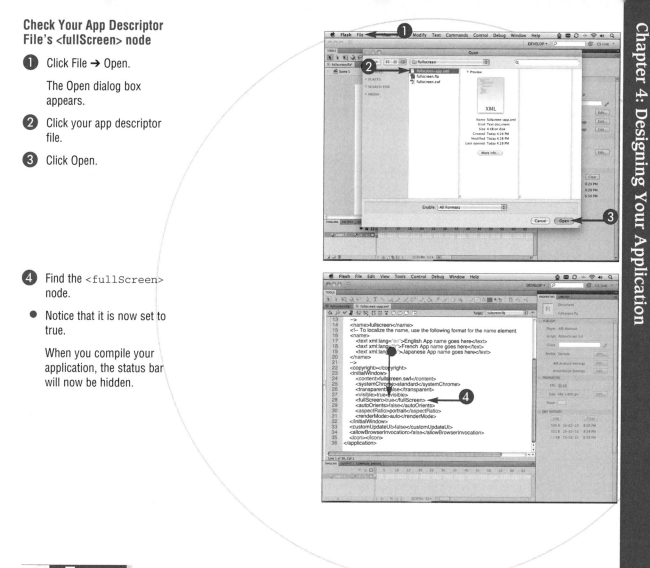

4 Find the `<fullScreen>` node.

● Notice that it is now set to true.

When you compile your application, the status bar will now be hidden.

Extra

Currently, you are not able to show and then hide the status bar with a Flash CS5 or AIR Android application. You may have noticed some applications on your device that do this while your application is running. For example, the Goggles application will hide the status bar when you are taking a photo and show it after the application has analyzed the image. This allows the user to see the camera view port full screen and only shows the status bar when it is necessary.

With this in mind, make sure that the user will never need the status bar when creating full-screen applications. If you choose to hide it, the user will have to leave your application and return to the home screen of the device to check for any of the information that the status bar holds. It is probably a good idea to display the status bar if your application does a lot of communicating with a network because your user will want to see if his or her data is being sent over WiFi or 3G.

Understanding Screen Orientation

ndroid phones, such as the Nexus One, come equipped with three-axis accelerometers. The Android OS uses the accelerometer to determine in which orientation you are holding the device. As the user rotates the device in his or her hands, the Android OS will let your application know which orientation the device is currently in, enabling you to adjust your content.

You can have your application start in one of two different orientation modes, Portrait or Landscape. You can specify this using the AIR Android Settings dialog box's General tab's Aspect Ratio drop-down list.

You can also have your content auto rotate to the correct orientation. When the device rotates your content, you may need to adjust it. To listen for orientation changes, you can add an event listener on the Stage for a

StageOrientationEvent.ORIENTATION_CHANGE event. This event will tell you the new orientation as well as the previous one.

If you choose not to have your content rotate automatically, you can manually set the orientation. The Stage.setOrientation() method allows you to specify one of four valid orientations. These valid orientations can be found in the StageOrientation class: StageOrientation.DEFAULT, StageOrientation.ROTATED_LEFT, StageOrientation.ROTATED_RIGHT, and StageOrientation.UPSIDE_DOWN.

If you plan on supporting multiple devices, you can also check to see if your device currently supports Stage orientations, before trying to call the Stage.set Orientation() method. Stage.supportsOrientation Change is a static property that returns true if your device is able to change its orientation.

Set Auto Orientation

1 Click File.

2 Click AIR Android Settings.

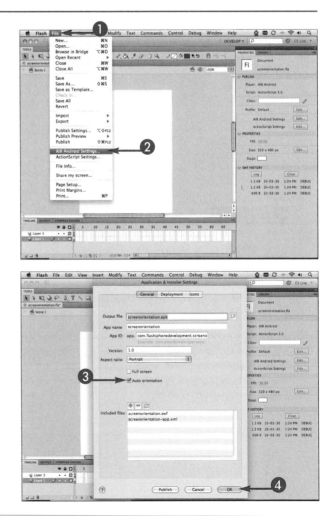

The Application & Installer Settings dialog box appears.

3 Click here to check the Auto Orientation check box.

4 Click OK.

Your application is set to rotate automatically with the device.

Create a Text Field to Display the Orientation

1. Click the Text tool.

2. Create and select a text field on the Stage.

3. Click here and select Classic Text.

4. Click here and select Dynamic Text.

5. Give the text field an instance name, such as `orientation_txt`.

6. Click here and select a font family, such as Helvetica.

Display the Orientation in the Text Field

7. Open the Actions panel.

8. Listen for the Stage to change orientations, such as `stage.add EventListener(StageOrient ationEvent.ORIENTATION_ CHANGE, onChange);`.

9. Create an event handler function.

10. Set the text of your `TextField` to the orientation of the Stage.

11. Vertically center the `TextField`, such as `orientation_txt. y = Math.round((stage. stageHeight/2) - (orientation_txt. height/2));`.

12. Compile and install the application on your device.

13. Rotate your device to see the orientation change.

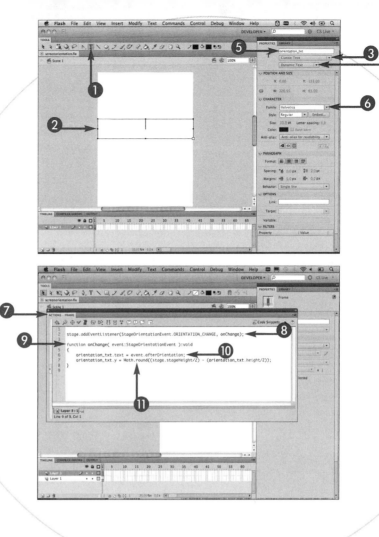

Extra

If you plan on supporting both aspect ratios, it is recommended that you always start your application in Portrait mode. If your application supports Landscape mode, make sure that it supports both modes. If you set your application to start in Landscape mode, it will start with an orientation of `StageOrientation.ROTATED_RIGHT`. This means that the bottom of the device, the one with the connector input, will be in your right hand. When a user is holding the device in Landscape mode, his or her hands may be covering the speakers. This may make the audio very hard to hear, so in this case, you should not rely on sounds as a way of communicating to your user.

To create your application in Landscape mode, change the Stage dimensions of your Flash project to a screen resolution for landscape, such as 480 x 800. This enables you to properly lay out your content in the correct orientation when designing your application. With the Stage selected, you can change this in the Document Settings dialog box by clicking the Edit button next to the screen dimensions in the Properties panel. You can also bring up this dialog box by pressing Ctrl+J (⌘+ J).

Create Usable Hit States

sing a mouse as a means of interacting with an application gives you pinpoint accuracy when trying to click or interact with elements on the screen. An item that is 1 x 1 pixel in size can be clicked on, although this may be difficult. When designing touch-enabled applications, on the other hand — when the user is using his or her finger as an input device — you must take into account the size of your interactive controls.

Designing items too small or placing them too close together will cause a user to spend extra time and attention trying to tap the correct element. Additionally, there will be times when users will be using only one hand when interacting with your application. In this case, there is a good chance that their thumb is doing all the tapping, which will cause the taps to be less accurate.

It is important to give your users a big enough target to account for their being less accurate with their touches. A good rule is to make sure that the target area for a touch is no smaller than 44 x 44 pixels. Depending on your application, every situation is going to be different, and it will be up to you to make sure that your elements are at an appropriate size.

It is also a good idea to provide visual feedback to the users when they tap the screen. Creating a highlighted state for your elements is a great way to do this. This will let the users know that their touch registered. Without any visual feedback, the users may think that their touch did not register if the interface does not immediately reflect their touch. For more details on how to create proper visual states for your buttons, see Chapter 5, "Handling Interaction."

Create Usable Hit States

Create a Symbol

1. Click a shape tool, such as the Rectangle tool.

2. Draw the shape on the Stage.

3. Click the Selection tool.

4. Select the shape.

5. Click Modify.

6. Click Convert to Symbol.

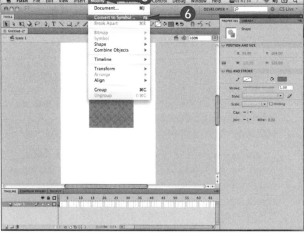

The Convert to Symbol dialog box appears.

7 Give your shape a name, such as `mybutton_btn`.

8 Click here and select Button as the type.

9 Click OK.

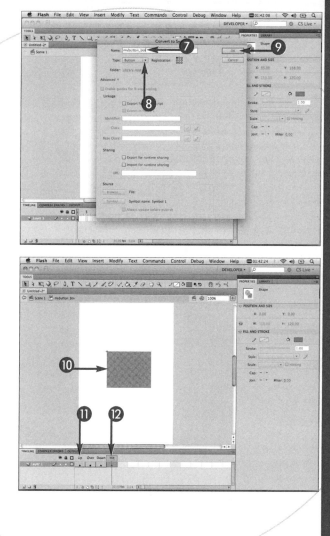

Set the Symbol's Hit States

10 Double-click the shape on the Stage to enter Edit mode.

11 Select the Up frame and press F6 three times to insert new keyframes.

12 Make sure that the Hit frame has a shape big enough to detect touches.

Note: *The contents of the Hit frame do not appear when publishing your file. They are only used to determine the hit area of your button.*

Extra

To try and compensate for the accuracy of your finger, your device takes into account a certain offset from where your finger actually is. This also happens because when your finger taps an item, it will most likely cover it up. So to account for this, the device will offset the hit target a little lower than you may be expecting. If your application supports being only right side up, in any orientation, then you will not have to worry about this.

However, there are certain situations in which this can come into play. Imagine that you are creating a board game such as chess or another two-player game. You could have your device on a table with each player on either side of the device where their game pieces are located. The user who is trying to tap elements on the screen when the device is upside down for her will notice that she has to touch a lot higher on the item than usual. The way to get around this is to change the orientation of device when it is the other user's turn to interact.

Understanding Layout

There is no specific guideline on how you should lay out your designs; however, the following are some suggestions to take into consideration. To begin with, elements should not be placed against the edge of the screen and should have a 20-pixel padding from any edge. However, any background images are exempt from this rule. Further, elements should be no less than 10 pixels apart from each other. Placing items too close to each other can cause users to tap on incorrect elements. These are just some guidelines to take into consideration, and these can be broken if necessary.

It is a good practice to keep touch elements away from the edge of the screen for a couple of reasons. The first reason is they can be hard to touch depending on their size and the device that your application is running on.

The second is that the user may inadvertently touch them while holding the device in certain orientations.

Supporting multiple screen sizes will most likely mean that you will need to reposition items when the screen resolution changes. You can listen for the Event.RESIZE event on the Stage to determine whether the screen resolution has changed. In your event handler, you can determine what the new dimensions are and adjust the position of your items to their new locations. Making sure that the Stage is aligned to the top left will make calculating your content's new positions a lot easier. To set the Stage alignment to the top left, you can use the following code:

```
stage.align = StageAlign.TOP_LEFT;
```

In the example shown here, you will create an application that auto rotates and keeps a symbol centered on the screen.

Understanding Layout

Set Auto Orientation

1 Click File → AIR Android Settings.

The Application & Installer Settings dialog box appears.

2 Click here to select the Auto Orientation check box.

3 Click OK.

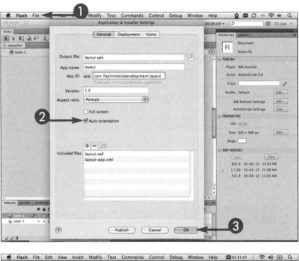

Create a Symbol

4 Create a MovieClip and select it on the Stage.

5 Give it an instance name, such as square_mc.

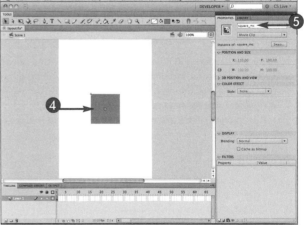

Set the Stage Properties

6 Open the Actions panel.

7 Set the Stage alignment, such as `stage.align = StageAlign.TOP_LEFT;`.

8 Set the Stage scale mode, such as `stage.scaleMode = StageScaleMode.NO_SCALE;`.

9 Add a listener for Stage resize events, such as `stage.addEventListener ( Event.RESIZE, onStageResize );`.

10 Create an event handler function for your listener, such as `onStageResize`.

Keep the Symbol Centered

11 Center your `MovieClip` on the x-axis based on the new Stage width, such as `square_mc.x = (stage.stageWidth/2) - (square_mc.width/2);`.

12 Center your `MovieClip` on the y-axis based on the new Stage height, such as `square_mc.y = (stage.stageHeight/2) - (square_mc.height/2);`.

Note: *These equations assume the registration point of your symbol is at 0,0.*

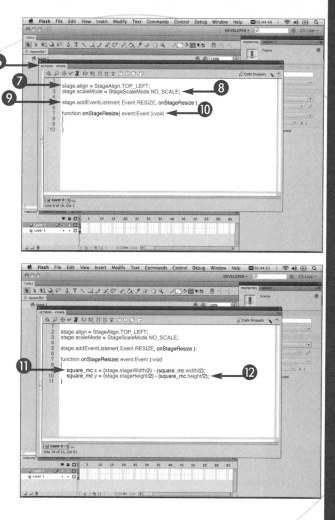

Extra

There are a number of different ways that you can align the Stage, instead of to the top left. The `StageAlign` class provides seven other options for Stage alignment. `StageAlign.TOP` centers the content horizontally and vertically and aligns it to the top of the screen. `StageAlign.BOTTOM` centers the content horizontally and vertically and aligns it to the bottom of the screen. `StageAlign.LEFT` horizontally aligns the content to the left and vertically centers it. `StageAlign.RIGHT` horizontally aligns the content to the right and vertically centers it. `StageAlign.TOP_RIGHT` aligns your content to the top and right sides of the screen. `StageAlign.BOTTOM_LEFT` aligns your content to the bottom and left sides of the screen. `StageAlign.BOTTOM_RIGHT` aligns your content to the bottom and right sides of the screen. I encourage you to experiment with all the different Stage alignments to see how your content is repositioned when the screen is resized. To initiate a resize event, you can simply drag the bottom corner of the window when testing locally on your computer.

Create Button States

O ne of the big differences between developing applications for a mobile device compared to a desktop computer is handling interaction. On a desktop, your application would make use of the mouse as a primary interaction input, whereas on a device, your fingers do most of the work.

The first thing you will probably realize is that you will not receive any MouseEvent.ROLL_OVER events because you cannot actually roll over any objects. Because of this, any buttons that may have rollover states for the desktop computer will not be shown. It is important, and good practice, to make sure that all your buttons have highlighted states, or mouse down states. This will give the users visual feedback that they actually touched on

the button that they intended to touch. Creating buttons without proper states may lead the users to think that your application is broken or that the device is frozen.

There are two ways to make sure that your buttons have the proper states. The easiest way is to create a Button symbol in the Flash IDE and create a new state for your button in the appropriate frame on the Timeline. The second way is to listen for the MouseEvent.MOUSE_DOWN event on a MovieClip through code. This allows you to change the appearance of your MovieClip through code when a finger is touched down on the hit area of your button. If you use this method, you need to ensure that you change the state back when the user lifts his or her finger off the button as well.

Create Button States

1. Create a Button symbol.

2. Create a MovieClip.

Note: See Chapter 2, "Getting Started with Flash CS5," for more details on these steps.

3. Select the MovieClip on the Stage.

4. Give the button an instance name, such as mc_btn.

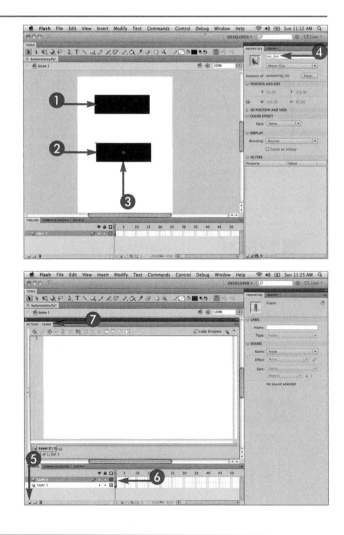

5. In the Timeline panel, click the New Layer button.

    A new layer is created.

6. Select the new layer.

7. Open the Actions panel.

8 Add a mouse down listener to your MovieClip, such as `mc_btn. addEventListener( MouseEvent. MOUSE_DOWN, mouseDown );`.

9 Add a mouse up listener to your MovieClip, such as `mc_btn. addEventListener( MouseEvent. MOUSE_UP, mouseUp );`.

10 Create a `mouseDown` event handler.

11 Create a `mouseUp` event handler.

Note: *For more details on creating event handlers, see Chapter 2.*

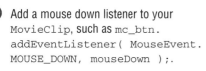

12 In your `mouseDown` function, create a new `ColorTransform` instance, such as `var trans:ColorTransform = new ColorTransform();`.

13 Set the `color` property, such as `trans. color = 0x000099;`.

14 Apply the `ColorTransform`, such as `mc_btn.transform. colorTransform = trans;`.

15 Repeat steps **12** to **14** in your `mouseUp` method and change the color, such as `trans.color = 0x00000;`.

16 Publish the file and click the buttons to see their states change.

Extra

Another thing to keep in mind when creating buttons is size. On a desktop computer, you could have a 1 x 1 pixel button and still be able to click it with the mouse. On a touch screen, your finger is less precise, which makes it really hard to click small buttons. So it is important to make your buttons big enough in size that the users can register a proper touch. It is also a good idea to keep your buttons far enough apart so that the users do not select a button that they did not intend to. When designing buttons in your application, try to give them the same look and feel as the ones that the Android OS uses in its applications. Creating similar buttons will make your users familiar with your application right away. In this section, the example shows creating simple color changes for the different states; however, you can also create a state that shows a circular highlight representing where the finger pressed on the screen.

Respond to Touch Events

or developing for platforms that can handle detecting a user's touch, Adobe has introduced the flash.events.TouchEvent class. This class is new and available on Flash Player 10.1, AIR 2.0, and the Android. Touch events can be thought of as mouse events for touch-enabled devices, in that they allow you to respond to basic touch interactions.

When a user interacts with the screen with a single or multiple fingers, multiple types of TouchEvents will be fired that allow you to respond correctly to the user. You can listen for TouchEvents on any InteractiveObject. Here is a typical sequence of events that will be fired during a single touch interaction: First, a TouchEvent. TOUCH_BEGIN event is fired when the user first presses his finger on the screen of the device. Second, a TouchEvent.TOUCH_MOVE is fired if the user drags his

finger on the screen while the object is still pressed. Lastly, a TouchEvent.TOUCH_END event is fired when the user lifts his finger off the screen.

In order to respond to these events, you need to add a listener to an InteractiveObject. This can be a Button, a MovieClip, or even the root Stage of your application. In the example below, I add a few listeners to the main Timeline of a blank .fla to create a very simple paint program to help illustrate what I have talked about.

If you are going to develop your application to support platforms other than the Android, you can detect to see if TouchEvents are supported on the device. flash. ui.Multitouch.supportsTouchEvents returns true if the device does support TouchEvents and false if it does not. Planning ahead of time to support multiple platforms is never a bad thing; it will save you development time down the road.

Respond to Touch Events

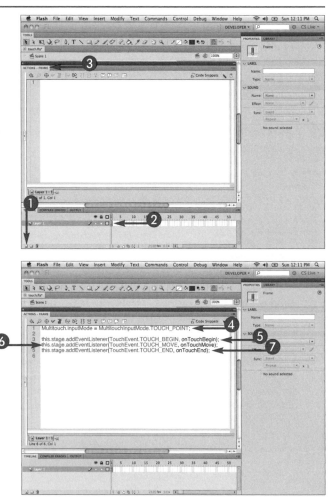

1. In the Timeline panel, click the New Layer button.

   A new layer is created.

2. Select the new layer.

3. Open the Actions panel.

4. Set the multitouch input mode to touch, such as
   Multitouch.inputMode =
   MultitouchInputMode.TOUCH_POINT;.

5. Add a TOUCH_BEGIN listener to the Stage,
   such as this.stage.addEventListener(
   TouchEvent.TOUCH_BEGIN, onTouchBegin
   );.

6. Add a TOUCH_MOVE listener to the Stage, such as
   this.stage.addEventListener(Touch
   Event.TOUCH_MOVE, onTouchMove);.

7. Add a TOUCH_END listener to the Stage, such
   as this.stage.addEventListener(
   TouchEvent.TOUCH_END, onTouchEnd);.

⑧ Create an `onTouchBegin` event handler for your listener.

⑨ Create an `onTouchMove` event handler for your listener.

⑩ Create an `onTouchEnd` event handler for your listener.

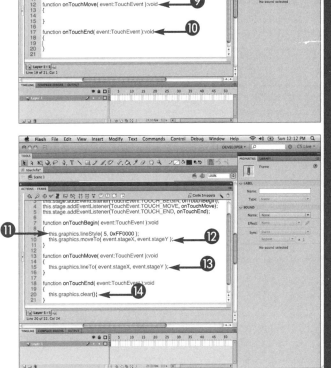

⑪ In the `onTouchBegin` method, set the line style, such as `this.graphics. lineStyle( 5, 0xFF0000 );`.

⑫ Move the drawing position to the touch location, such as `this.graphics. moveTo( event.stageX, event. stageY );`.

⑬ In the `onTouchMove` method, draw a line to the new touch location, such as `this. graphics.lineTo( event.stageX, event.stageY );`.

⑭ In the `onTouchEnd` method, clear the drawing, such as `this.graphics. clear();`.

⑮ Publish the file and install the application on your device.

Extra

It is really important to plan ahead when creating your applications. Even if at the time of development, you do not plan on supporting any other platforms, you never know when Adobe will support a new platform that you did not expect during development. The less amount of time it takes to get your application working on a new platform, the better. If you do not plan to support multiple touches or gestures in your application, you may want to consider using `MouseEvents` instead of `TouchEvents`. This will allow your application to be compatible with more platforms than touch-enabled ones.

The sequence of events is similar to those used in the example in this section. `MouseEvent.MOUSE_DOWN` is fired when the user presses down on the mouse button, `MouseEvent.MOUSE_MOVE` is fired when the user moves the mouse with the mouse button still pressed, and `MouseEvent.MOUSE_UP` is fired when the user releases the mouse button. If you have previous experience developing Flash applications, this concept is not new to you, and you can apply that knowledge the same way you would when developing applications for the Web or desktop.

Track Multiple Touches

Tracking multiple touches is not much harder than tracking a single touch. The TouchEvent. touchPointID property is a unique ID for each unique touch that occurs. This ID is assigned when the TouchEvent.TOUCH_BEGIN event is fired and can be used to track unique touches on the screen.

For each new touch that is detected, the touchPointID is incremented. For example, if you were to place two fingers on the screen and drag them around, you would receive touch event objects with touchPointID values of 1 and 2. If you lifted those fingers and placed them back on the screen, you would get touchPointID values 3 and 4. This makes it a little harder to track specific fingers because touchPointID 2 does not necessarily mean finger 2. In order to track specific fingers, you will

need to store which touchPointIDs are currently being used in an Array or Dictionary object, as you will see in the example below. You place the ID in this object during the TouchEvent.TOUCH_BEGIN event and remove it in the TouchEvent.TOUCH_END event.

Each touch screen device has a different number of touches that it can detect at once. Each Android device may support a different maximum touch. Currently, the Google Nexus One phone supports only 2. If you are planning on releasing your application on multiple platforms that support touch screens, you will want to plan for this number to change and be able to accommodate fewer or more touches. To do this, you can use the Multitouch.maxTouchPoints property to determine how many touches can be detected at the same time.

Track Multiple Touches

1. Set the input mode, such as Multitouch. inputMode = MultitouchInputMode. TOUCH_POINT;.

2. Create an array to hold a color for each finger, such as var colors:Array = [0x731931, 0x401323, 0x262226, 0x54594C, 0x888C65];.

3. Create a Dictionary instance to hold sprite references, such as var sprites:Dictionary = new Dictionary();.

4. Create a touch counter, such as var touchCount:int = 0;.

5. Add listeners and event handlers for the TOUCH_ BEGIN, TOUCH_MOVE, and TOUCH_END events.

6. Create a new Sprite instance and add it to the Stage, such as var mc:Sprite = new Sprite(); addChild(mc);.

7. Set the sprite's lineStyle, such as mc.graphics.lineStyle(5, colors[touchCount]);.

8. Set the initial drawing location to the touch position, such as mc.graphics.moveTo(event.stageX, event.stageY);.

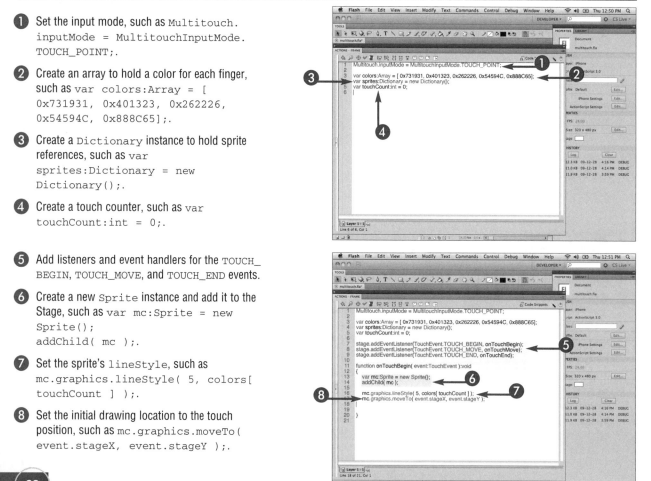

9 Increment the touch count, such as `touchCount++;`.

10 Store a reference to the sprite, such as `sprites[ event.touchPointID ] = mc;`.

11 Get the reference to the sprite, such as `var mc:Sprite = sprites[ event.touchPointID ] as Sprite;`.

12 Draw a line to the new touch position, such as `mc.graphics.lineTo( event.stageX, event.stageY );`.

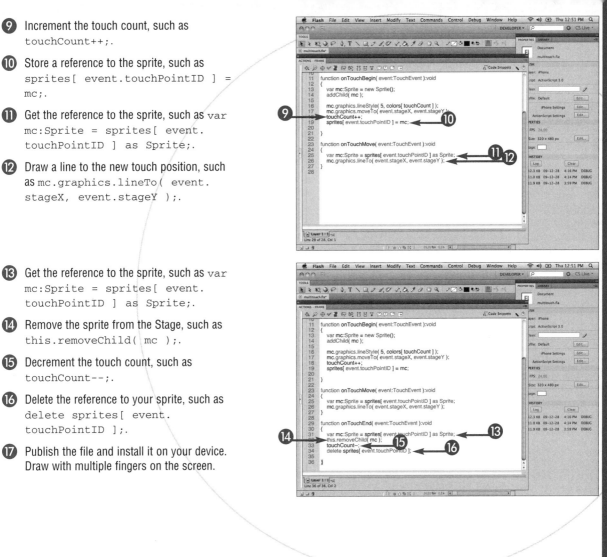

13 Get the reference to the sprite, such as `var mc:Sprite = sprites[ event.touchPointID ] as Sprite;`.

14 Remove the sprite from the Stage, such as `this.removeChild( mc );`.

15 Decrement the touch count, such as `touchCount--;`.

16 Delete the reference to your sprite, such as `delete sprites[ event.touchPointID ];`.

17 Publish the file and install it on your device. Draw with multiple fingers on the screen.

Extra

If you would like to play around with a different color scheme, you can easily find new ones in the Kuler panel. You can access this panel by clicking Window → Extensions> → Kuler in Flash Professional CS5. On this panel, you can browse different color schemes that other users have created. When you have found a scheme that you like, you can add the colors to the Swatches panel. If you do not find one that suits you, you can always edit an existing one or create a new one.

Respond to Zoom Events

O ne of the main user interactions for multitouch devices is the pinch and zoom gesture. It is most commonly used to scale objects up and down. You have probably used this gesture yourself a number of times to zoom in and out of Web sites in the browser or email on your device. If you are new to the platform, the zoom gesture, sometimes referred to just as *pinch,* is achieved by placing two fingers on the screen and moving them apart to zoom in and moving them closer to zoom out. It would be possible to achieve this effect by tracking multiple touch points, but that is harder than it sounds. Luckily, Adobe has provided the `TransformGestureEvent.GESTURE_ZOOM` event, which will take care of all the hard work.

In order to respond to this gesture, you simply add an event listener to any `InteractiveObject`, just as you have done in previous examples. When the event is fired, the event handler method will be called with a `TransformGestureEvent` object as a single argument.

This event contains all the information you need in order to scale the object in relation to a gesture. In particular, the two properties of interest are `scaleX` and `scaleY`. Your first thought may be to simply set the scale values that are returned from the event to your object, but that will give you an undesired result. The reason for this is that the scale properties that are returned are values based on the previous gesture event — not its current scale value. In order to calculate your object's new scale properties, you simply multiply the object's current scale by the event's scale values.

Respond to Zoom Events

① Create a `MovieClip`.

Note: *See Chapter 2 for more details on this step.*

② Give it an instance name, such as `square_mc`.

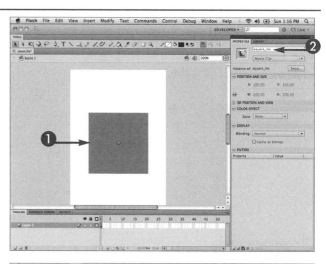

③ In the Timeline panel, click the New Layer button.

A new layer is created.

④ Select the new layer.

⑤ Open the Actions panel.

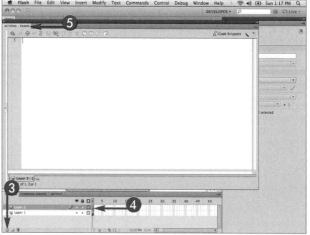

6 Set the input mode, such as
`Multitouch.inputMode = MultitouchInputMode.GESTURE;`.

7 Add a listener for the zoom event, such as
`square_mc.addEventListener( TransformGestureEvent.GESTURE_ZOOM, onZoom );`.

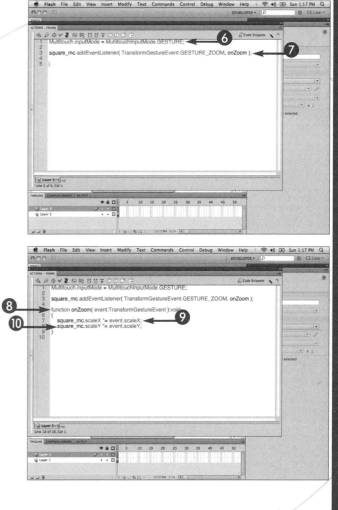

8 Create an event handler for your zoom listener.

Note: See Chapter 2 for more details on creating event handlers.

9 Set the `scaleX` of the square based on the gesture, such as `square_mc.scaleX *= event.scaleX;`.

10 Set the `scaleY` of the square based on the gesture, such as `square_mc.scaleY *= event.scaleY;`.

11 Publish the file and install it on your device.

12 Place two fingers close together on the square and move them apart.

Extra

A tip for creating smooth-looking zoom gestures is to make sure that your registration point is at the center of your object instead of the default top left, or 0,0. This will ensure that your object is scaled from its center and will be consistent with all other objects that react to this gesture in other applications on your device. There are a couple of different ways that you can set the registration point. The easiest is way is to set it in the Convert to Symbol dialog box by selecting the center dot as the registration point. The other way is through code and will require you to have your object in a parent `DisplayObjectContainer`:

```
child.x = -child.width;
child.y = -child.height;
```

This will center the child object to its parent's registration point, assuming that it is at 0,0.

Respond to Rotate Events

A nother commonly used multitouch interaction, aside from the pinch and zoom gesture, is the two-finger rotate gesture. To rotate an object, place one finger on it and rotate a second finger around the first. It is important to note that only one finger needs to be on the object that you are rotating. The second finger can be outside of the hit area of the object, but it must remain on the screen at all times.

In order to detect for this gesture, you can listen for the `TransformGestureEvent.GESTURE_ROTATE` event on any `InteractiveObject` on the Stage. If a rotate gesture is detected, this event will be fired, and your event handler will be called with a `TransformGestureEvent` object as its argument. This object contains all the

information that you need in order to rotate your object. The `TransfromGestureEvent.rotation` property contains the rotation of the object since the previous rotation event. In order to have this affect your object, you add the event's rotation value to the current rotation value of your object.

It is a good idea for all the objects that respond to a rotation gesture to have their registration be at their center. This will ensure that your fingers are always on the object as you rotate it. If you had your object's registration point at the default top left, or 0, 0, you could rotate the object off the screen, which could produce some undesirable results.

Respond to Rotate Events

① Create a `MovieClip`.

Note: See Chapter 2 for more details on this step.

② Give it an instance name, such as `square_mc`.

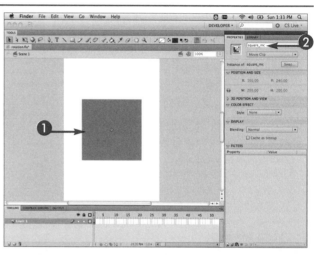

③ In the Timeline panel, click the New Layer button.

A new layer is created.

④ Select the new layer.

⑤ Open the Actions panel.

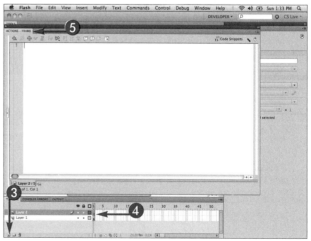

6 Set the input mode, such as `Multitouch. inputMode = MultitouchInputMode.GESTURE;`.

7 Add a listener for the rotate gesture, such as `square_mc.addEventListener( TransformGestureEvent.GESTURE_ ROTATE, onRotate );`.

8 Create an event handler for your rotate listener.

Note: See Chapter 2 for more details on this step.

9 Set the new rotation, such as `square_ mc.rotation += event.rotation;`.

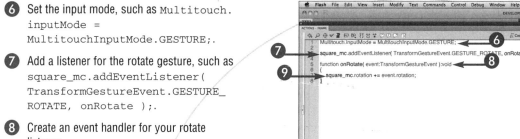

10 Publish and install the application on your device.

11 Place two fingers on the square and rotate one around the other.

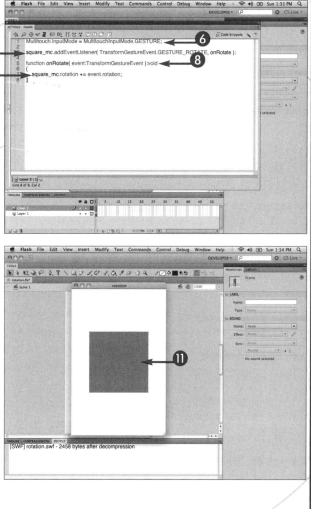

Apply It

If you are feeling adventurous and want to try and program this gesture yourself, you can do so by tracking two fingers. One way to determine the new rotation of your object is to find the angle between two lines. To do this, you will need to store the previous location of the two touches. Those two points will form line 1, and the current touch points will form line 2. Here is a method that calculates the angle in degrees from two lines:

```
function angleBetweenLines( line1Start:Point,  line1End:Point,  line2Start:Point,
  line2End:Point):Number{
var a:Number = line1End.x - line1Start.x;
var b:Number = line1End.y - line1Start.y;
var c:Number = line2End.x - line2Start.x;
var d:Number = line2End.y - line2Start.y;
var degs:Number = Math.cos(((a*c) + (b*d)) / ((Math.sqrt(a*a + b*b)) * (Math.sqrt(c*c +
  d*d))));
return degs * ( 180 / Math.PI );
}
```

Respond to Pan Events

Because of the limited screen real estate, there will be times when your content will be bigger than the viewing area. When this happens, you will want to give the users the ability to scroll or pan the content so that they can see any hidden content. This can also happen when you zoom in on objects, and objects scale up past the bounds of the screen. For example, consider a photo gallery application. When you initially display the image, you would show it at a size that fills the screen. But you may allow the user to zoom into specific areas of the image using the `TransformGestureEvent.GESTURE_ZOOM` event. The user scales the image up twice its original size, and now the part of the image that she is interested in is off the screen. You will want to let her pan the image around in order to see any areas that were off-screen.

To detect for a pan gesture, you can listen for the `TransformGestureEvent.GESTURE_PAN` event on any `InteractiveObject`. This event is fired when it is detected that the user has placed two fingers on the object and is dragging them around the screen. Only one finger must be on the targeted object, and the other controls the direction in which to pan the object. The `TransformGestureEvent` object that gets passed to the event handler contains two properties that you will use to move your object. `TransformGestureEvent.offsetX` and `TransformGestureEvent.offsetY` give the difference in position since the last pan event. To move the targeted object, add the current x and y values of your object to these values.

Respond to Pan Events

Set Panning on an Image

1 Import an image onto the Stage.

Note: *See Chapter 6, "Working with Images," for more details.*

2 Convert the image to a `MovieClip`.

Note: *See Chapter 2 for more details on this topic.*

3 Give the `MovieClip` an instance name, such as `image_mc`.

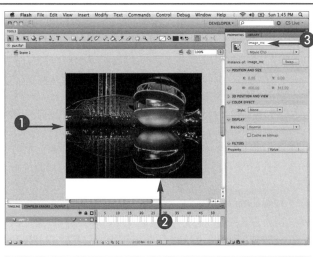

4 In the Timeline panel, click the New Layer button.

A new layer is created.

5 Select the new layer.

6 Open the Actions panel.

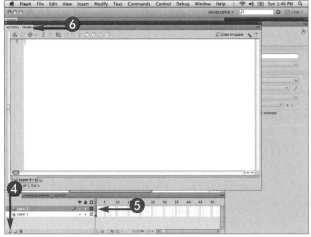

7 Set the input mode, such as `Multitouch. inputMode = MultitouchInputMode. GESTURE;`.

8 Add a listener for the pan gesture, such as `image_mc.addEventListener( TransformGestureEvent.GESTURE_ PAN, onPan );`.

9 Create an event handler for your pan listener.

10 Set the new x position based on the gesture, such as `image_mc.x += event. offsetX;`.

11 Set the new y position based on the gesture, such as `image_mc.y += event. offsetY;`.

Test the Application

12 Publish and install the application on your device.

13 Place two fingers on the image and move them around the screen to pan the image.

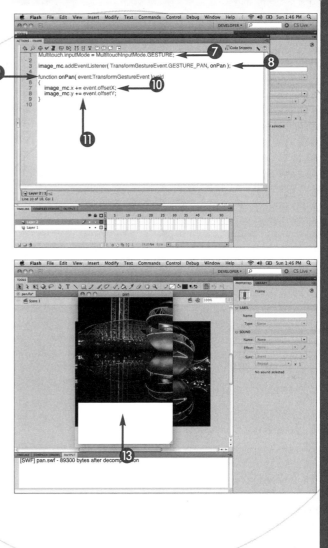

There are other ways to pan objects than using the `TransformGestureEvent.GESTURE_PAN` event. For example, you could use `TouchEvent.TOUCH_MOVE` to drag the object around if you wanted to, as in the following:

```
Multitouch.inputMode = MultitouchInputMode.TOUCH_POINT;
this.stage.addEventListener(TouchEvent.TOUCH_MOVE, onTouchMove);
function onTouchMove( event:TouchEvent ):void{
image_mc.x = event.stageX;
image_mc.y = event.stageY;
}
```

However, you cannot detect for gestures and touches at the same time in your application. So if want to detect for any other gestures and want the ability to pan and drag, you will need to use the `TransformGestureEvent. GESTURE_PAN` event.

Respond to Swipe Events

The swipe is a relatively simple gesture. It can be initiated by swiping your finger either vertically or horizontally in a straight line with a single finger. This gesture is most commonly used to navigate through a set of content. A good example of this is the Gallery application, which uses swipe gestures to navigate through the photos on your device.

You can listen for a swipe gesture on any `InteractiveObject` by adding listening for its `TransformGestureEvent.GESTURE_SWIPE` event. When a swipe gesture is detected, a `TransformGestureEvent` object is passed as an argument to your event handler. The `offsetX` property will return either 1 for a swipe right or -1 for a swipe left. The `offsetY` property will return either 1 for a swipe down or -1 for a swipe up.

As soon as you know which way the swipe occurred, you can adjust your content accordingly.

The example below shows importing two images to the Stage and moving them left or right depending on the direction of the swipe. When you first load the application, you are going to place the first image on the Stage and have it take up the entire screen area. Because it is the first image, you are going to only allow for left swipes. If you swiped the content right, there would not be an image to move into its place. When you swipe left, you are going to animate the current image off-screen to the left and animate the second image on-screen from the right. When the second image is shown, you are going to check for right swipes. When a right swipe is detected, you are going to animate the second image off-screen to the right and animate the first image in from the left.

Respond to Swipe Events

Set Swiping for Two Images

1 Import an image onto the Stage.

Note: See Chapter 6 for more details.

2 Convert the image to a `MovieClip`.

Note: See Chapter 2 for more details.

3 Place the image at 0,0.

4 Give it an instance name, such as `image1_mc`.

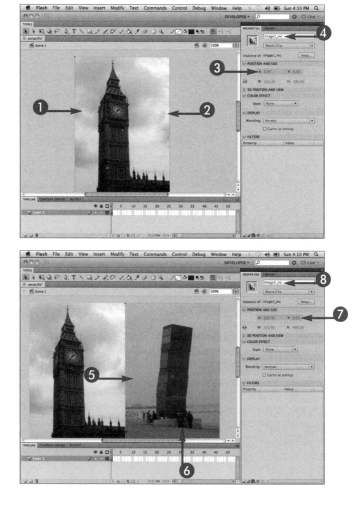

5 Import a second image onto the Stage.

Note: See Chapter 6 for more details.

6 Convert the image to a `MovieClip`.

Note: See Chapter 2 for more details.

7 Place the image at 320,0.

8 Give it an instance name, such as `image2_mc`.

⑨ Open the Actions panel.

⑩ Set the input mode, such as `Multitouch.inputMode = MultitouchInputMode.GESTURE;`.

⑪ Add a swipe gesture listener to both images.

⑫ Create an event handler, such as `onSwipe`.

⑬ Check to see which image detected the swipe gesture.

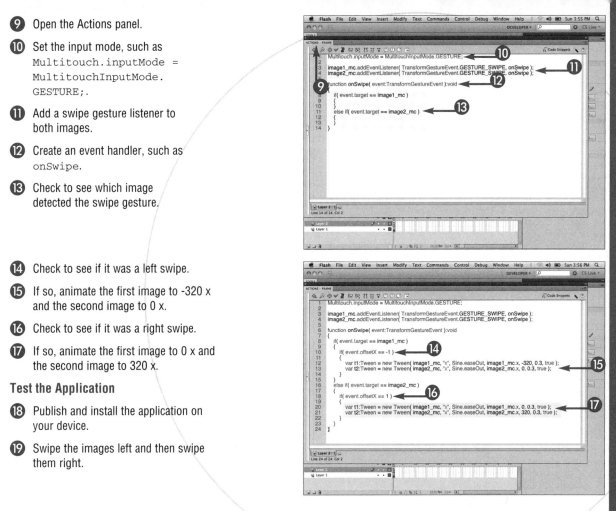

⑭ Check to see if it was a left swipe.

⑮ If so, animate the first image to -320 x and the second image to 0 x.

⑯ Check to see if it was a right swipe.

⑰ If so, animate the first image to 0 x and the second image to 320 x.

Test the Application

⑱ Publish and install the application on your device.

⑲ Swipe the images left and then swipe them right.

Apply It

The way shown in this section is the easiest way to detect for swipes, but you can also detect touches independently and determine which direction a swipe is going. By doing this, you have more control over how fast and how far the swipe has to go before it is classified as a swipe:

```
image1_mc.addEventListener( TouchEvent.TOUCH_BEGIN, onBegin );
image1_mc.addEventListener( TouchEvent.TOUCH_MOVE, onMove );
var startX:Number;
var startY:Number;
function onBegin( event:TouchEvent ):void{
    startX = event.stageX;
    startY = event.stageY;
}
function onMove( event:TouchEvent ):void{
if( startX > event.stageX ){
            // left swipe detected
        }else{
            //right swipe detected
        }
}
```

Listen for Accelerometer Events

A popular interaction with mobile devices, especially among games, is the use of the accelerometer. Driving games use the accelerometer, allowing the users to rotate their devices back and forth in order to steer their vehicle. Also, shaking the device has become a popular way to incorporate Easter eggs into your game or application.

The new `Accelerometer` class lets you receive acceleration data from the on-board accelerometer chip of the device. As the device moves, you will receive linear acceleration data along the x, y, and z axes. To receive this data, listen for the `AccelerometerEvent.UPDATE` event on the `Accelerometer` object. An `AccelerometerEvent` object will be passed to your event handler, which contains `accelerationX`,

`accelerationY`, and `accelerationZ` properties, a value for each axis.

The `accelerationX` property represents the acceleration measured in Gs along the x-axis. This axis runs from the left to the right of the device when it is in its upright position. The `accelerationY` property represents the acceleration measured in Gs along the y-axis. This axis runs from the bottom of the phone to the top. In the case of an Android, this axis runs from the earpiece to the bottom of the device. The `accelerationZ` property represents the acceleration measured in Gs along the z-axis. The axis runs perpendicular to the face of the phone, and the value will be positive as it moves closer to you.

The example below shows moving a ball around the screen as the device is tilted and moved around.

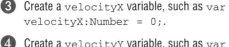

Create a Ball That Moves with the Device

1. Create a circle `MovieClip`.

2. Give it an instance name, such as `circle_mc`.

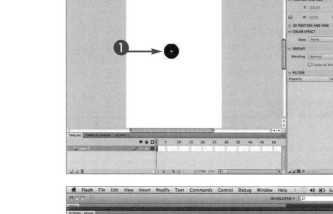

3. Create a `velocityX` variable, such as `var velocityX:Number = 0;`.

4. Create a `velocityY` variable, such as `var velocityY:Number = 0;`.

5. Create an `Accelerometer` variable, such as `var am:Accelerometer = new Accelerometer();`.

6. Set the update interval of the accelerometer.

7. Add an update listener to the accelerometer.

8. Create an event handler, such as `onUpdate`.

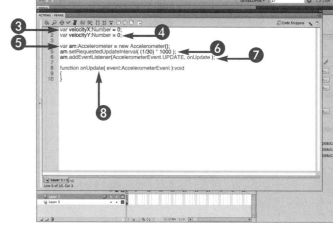

9. Create a Number variable, such as
`var velocityMultiplier: Number = 0.5;`.

10. Apply the `accelerationX` value to calculate the velocity of `x`.

11. Apply the `accelerationY` value to calculate the velocity of `y`.

12. Set the `x` property of the circle instance, such as `circle_mc.x += velocityX`.

13. Set the `y` property of the circle instance, such as `circle_mc.y -= velocityY`.

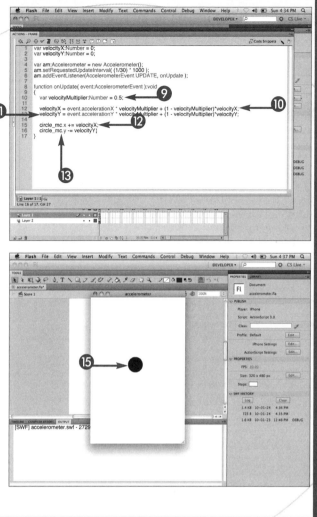

Test the Application

14. Publish and install the application on your device.

15. Move the device around to move the circle on the screen.

Apply It

One thing to keep in mind when trying to animate an object with values from the accelerometer is that you are not guaranteed to get values at a regular interval. So if you are trying to create nice, smooth, time-based animations based on that data, you will need to store the time between each accelerometer update and factor that into your equation.

Another option is to animate the object on a `Timer` or `EnterFrame` event and only update the velocities in the accelerometer update handler. To do so, remove the following code from the `onUpdate` method:

```
circle_mc.x += velocityX;
circle_mc.y -= velocityY;
```

And add the following code to the example:

```
stage.addEventListener( Event.ENTER_FRAME, onFrame );
function onFrame( event:Event ):void{
    circle_mc.x += velocityX;
    circle_mc.y -= velocityY;
}
```

91

Determine If the Accelerometer Is Available

When developing an application that takes advantage of the accelerometer, you are going to need to place the application on your device in order to test it. This can slow down development if every time you make changes to your application, you need to test it on the device. This is extremely inefficient, especially if you are not testing the portion of your application that uses the accelerometer. To get around this issue, a good practice is to detect to see if the accelerometer is available and give yourself another way of interacting with your application if it is not.

For example, if you need to detect for a shake motion, you could place a button on the screen that when pressed would simulate a shake. Doing this allows you to test on your computer, and when you are satisfied that

everything is working, you can put your application on the device to test your accelerometer code.

The `Accelerometer` class has a static property on it named `isSupported` to detect if it is available. It is a read-only property that is set to true if it is available; otherwise, it is false.

The example below shows comparing the current acceleration data to the previous to see if there has been a big enough shake. If a shake has occurred, you are going to play a sound. To detect for the shake, compare the previous acceleration data of all three axes to the current data. If there was enough of a difference in acceleration in any direction, you can determine that the user has shaken the device.

Determine If the Accelerometer Is Available

Respond to a Shake with a Sound

① Import a sound effect audio file.

② Give the sound a class name, such as `Shake`.

Note: *For more details on importing sounds, check out Chapter 7, "Working with Sound."*

③ Open the Actions panel.

④ Create a `Sound` variable for the shake sound, such as `var sound:Sound = new Shake();`.

⑤ Check to see if the accelerometer is available.

⑥ Create `Number` variables for the previous x, y, and z positions, such as `lastX`, `lastY`, and `lastZ`.

⑦ Create a new `Accelerometer` variable, such as `var am:Accelerometer = new Accelerometer();`.

⑧ Add an update listener to the `Accelerometer`.

9 Create a `Sprite` and draw a rectangle in it.

Note: *See Chapter 2.*

10 Add the sprite to the Stage.

11 Add a listener for the mouse click.

12 Create an event handler, such as `onClick`, and call the `shake` method inside it.

13 Create a `shake` function.

14 Play the sound, such as `sound.play();`.

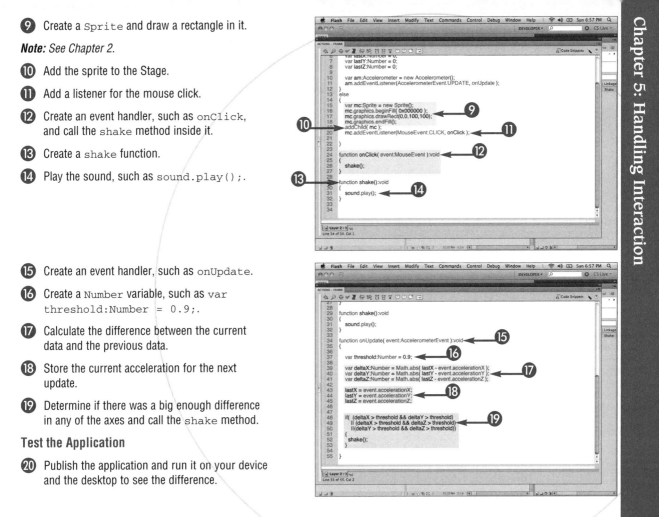

15 Create an event handler, such as `onUpdate`.

16 Create a `Number` variable, such as `var threshold:Number = 0.9;`.

17 Calculate the difference between the current data and the previous data.

18 Store the current acceleration for the next update.

19 Determine if there was a big enough difference in any of the axes and call the `shake` method.

Test the Application

20 Publish the application and run it on your device and the desktop to see the difference.

Apply It

There is also an `Accelerometer.muted` property that you can use to detect if the accelerometer is available. This is used to determine if the user has denied access to the accelerometer. Currently, Android devices do not have an option that allows the user to disable the accelerometer, but one may exist on other platforms. So if you are targeting multiple platforms, you may want to check this property as well for determining if the accelerometer is available. If you are just building Android applications, you do not have to worry about it. Here is how to use this property:

```
if( Accelerometer.isSupported || !Accelerometer.muted )
{
//Accelerometer is available.
}
```

Determine Device Orientation

Determining the orientation of the device can be easily achieved by reading the acceleration data from the accelerometer. You can detect to see if the device is positioned on any one of its six sides. This can be used in order to rotate content so that it matches the rotation of the device. It can also be used to detect user input. For example, say that you wanted the users to flip an object in a game. You could have the users actually flip their devices in order to flip the object in the game. Keep in mind, though, that the more extreme the gesture, the bigger the chance the users can have their devices flying out of their hands. And nobody will be doing that gesture more than you during development.

After you are familiar with reading the acceleration data from the accelerometer, determining the orientation is

pretty simple. The following example references the Nexus One and most other Android phones. If `accelerationX` is greater than 0.5, then the device is laying on its right side, the side opposite the volume controls. If `accelerationX` is less than -0.5, the device is laying on its left side, the side with the volume controls. If `accelerationY` is greater than 0.5, the device is laying on its top side, the side with the headphone jack and lock button. If `accelerationY` is less than -0.5, the device is standing up, with the side with the connector jack pointing to the floor. If `accelerationZ` is greater than 0.5, the device is lying with its screen down. If `accelerationZ` is less than -0.5, the device is lying with its back down.

Determine Device Orientation

Create a TextField That Displays the Device Orientation

1 Click the Text tool.

2 Create a `TextField` on the Stage.

3 Click here and select Dynamic Text as the `TextField`'s type.

4 Give the text field an instance name, such as `debug_txt`.

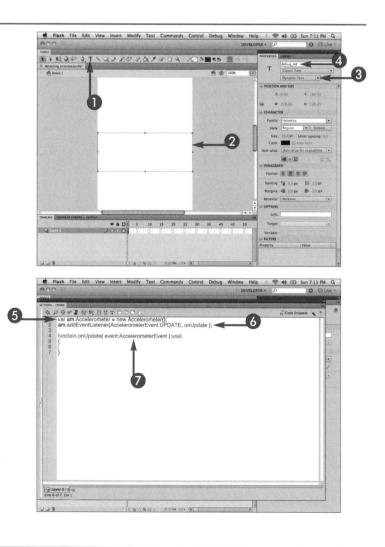

5 Create a new `Accelerometer` variable, such as `var am:Accelerometer = new Accelerometer();`.

6 Add an update event listener to the accelerometer variable.

7 Create an event handler, such as `onUpdate`.

8 Check to see if `accelerationX` is greater than 0.5.

9 Set the text field, such as `debug_txt.text = "Right Side";`.

10 Check to see if `accelerationX` is less than -0.5.

11 Set the text field, such as `debug_txt.text = "Left Side";`.

12 Check to see if `accelerationY` is greater than 0.5.

13 Set the text field, such as `debug_txt.text = "Upside Down";`.

14 Check to see if `accelerationY` is less than -0.5.

15 Set the text field, such as `debug_txt.text = "Standing Up";`.

16 Check to see if `accelerationZ` is greater than 0.5.

17 Set the text field, such as `debug_txt.text = "Face Down";`.

18 Check to see if `accelerationZ` is less than -0.5.

19 Set the text field, such as `debug_txt.text = "Face Up";`.

Test the Application

20 Publish and install the application on your device. Change the orientation.

Extra

After you have determined the orientation of the device, you will want to rotate your content for your user. If the device is lying on its left side, you will want to rotate content 90 degrees. If the device is lying on its right side, rotate your content -90 or 270 degrees. If the device is upside down or lying on its top, rotate your content 180 degrees. For the other three sides, the content's rotation should be set to 0 degrees. One thing to keep in mind when rotating content this way is that you will have to reposition it as well. You could also have separate views for each rotation and swap them as the device rotates. The advantage to this is that you can potentially show different sized graphics when the device is rotated to either its left or right side to maximize the change in screen real estate. There is no right way to do it, and you will have to decide which way works best for you on a case-by-case basis.

Detect Which Way Is Up

When you are developing applications that allow the user to rotate the device, it will be important for you to make sure that your content is rotated and displayed properly. You could implement something similar to the example in the section "Determine Device Orientation," or you could detect which side is pointing up. Detecting which side is pointing up allows you to rotate your content to a more precise angle, instead of just every 45 degrees.

First, set up the `Accelerometer` so that you can receive the update events. If you are unsure of how to do this, have a look at the example in the section "Listen for Accelerometer Events." After you have an event handler created and receiving acceleration data, you can use the `Math.atan2` method to calculate the angle in radians.

The `Math.atan2` method takes two arguments, `y` and `x`. It is important to note that the `y` property is always the first argument, which is usually different in any other method that accepts `x` and `y` properties as arguments. To calculate the angle, you pass in the `accelerationY` value and the negative value of `accelerationX`. Because a `DisplayObjects.rotation` property is expecting an angle in degrees, you will need to convert the radians to degrees in order to set the rotation of your content. The following equation shows you how to do the conversion:

```
var degrees:Number = radians * ( 180 / Math.PI
);
```

After you have the angle in degrees, you can set it to the rotation property of your object. Below is a very simple example that rotates an image of an arrow to which way points up.

Detect Which Way Is Up

Create an Arrow to Point Up

1️⃣ Import an arrow graphic and convert it to a MovieClip.

Note: See Chapter 2 for more details on this topic.

2️⃣ Give it an instance name, such as arrow_mc.

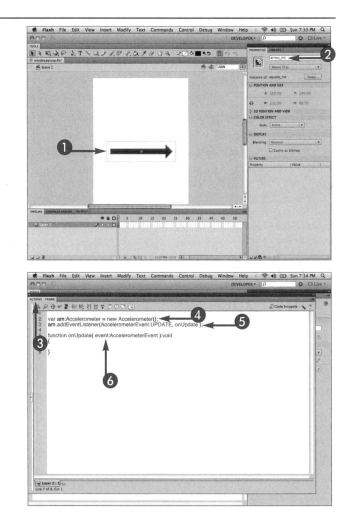

3️⃣ Open the Actions panel.

4️⃣ Create a new `Accelerometer` variable, such as `var am:Accelerometer = new Accelerometer();`.

5️⃣ Add an update event listener to the accelerometer variable.

6️⃣ Create an event handler, such as `onUpdate`.

7 Calculate the radians based on the acceleration values.

8 Convert the radians to degrees.

9 Set the rotation, such as `arrow_mc.rotation = degrees;`.

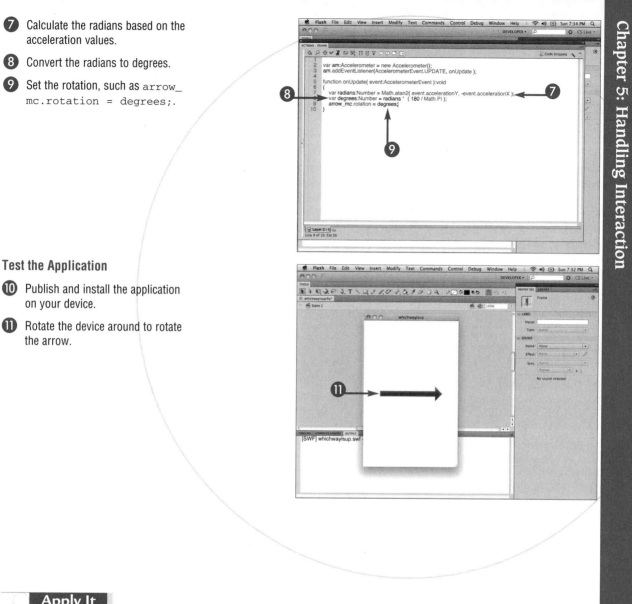

Test the Application

10 Publish and install the application on your device.

11 Rotate the device around to rotate the arrow.

Apply It

Changing the example so that the arrow is pointing to the side that is down is relatively easy. You simply need to change the values that you pass in to the Math.atan2 function to be negative accelerationY and positive accelerationX. This can be used to make sure that objects always fall the direction that gravity is pulling them. Here is what the function looks like with these changes:

```
var radians:Number = Math.atan2( -event.accelerationY, event.accelerationX );
```

Filter Accelerometer Data

I f you have been going through the other accelerometer examples or experimenting on your own, you have probably noticed that the data can sometimes contain some noise. Depending on how you are visualizing the data, this noise may cause your graphics to jump around quite a bit. To reduce the noise, you will want to smooth out the values from the `Accelerometer` by filtering out unwanted values. Smoothing data sets is used to capture patterns in the data while removing any noise. This technique is often used in analyzing images and sound waves.

The `accelerationZ` property in the `AccelerometerEvent` object represents gravity. To better understand this, place your device on a flat surface, like a table. You should see that the `accelerationX` and `accelerationY` properties are approximately 0, and the `accelerationZ` property should be approximately -1.

To remove the effects of gravity, you can use a *high-pass filter,* which reduces the amplitude of the cutoff frequency. This filter reduces some of the noise and gives you smoother results between updates.

The `dt` variable in the example below represents a time interval, and the `RC` variable represents a time constant. These two variables are used to calculate the `filterConstant` variable. A large `filterConstant` variable suggests that the data will decay very slowly over time and will also be strongly influenced by small changes in the accelerometer. A small `filterContstant` variable suggests that the data will decay quickly and will require large changes in the accelerometer in order to change the output. Changing the `rate` and `freq` variables in this example gives you more control over how you would like your acceleration data to be filtered.

Filter Accelerometer Data

Using a High-Pass Filter

1 Create a `Number` variable, such as `var rate:Number = 60;`.

2 Create a second `Number` variable, such as `var freq:Number = 5;`.

3 Create a third `Number` variable, such as `var dt:Number = 1.0/rate;`.

4 Create a fourth `Number` variable, such as `var RC:Number = 1.0/freq;`.

5 Create `Number` variables to store the acceleration data.

6 Create `Number` variables to store the filtered acceleration values.

7. Create a `filter` function.

8. Create a `Number` variable, such as `var filterConstant :Number= RC / (dt + RC);`.

9. Filter the data for all three axes.

10. Store the current acceleration values for the next update.

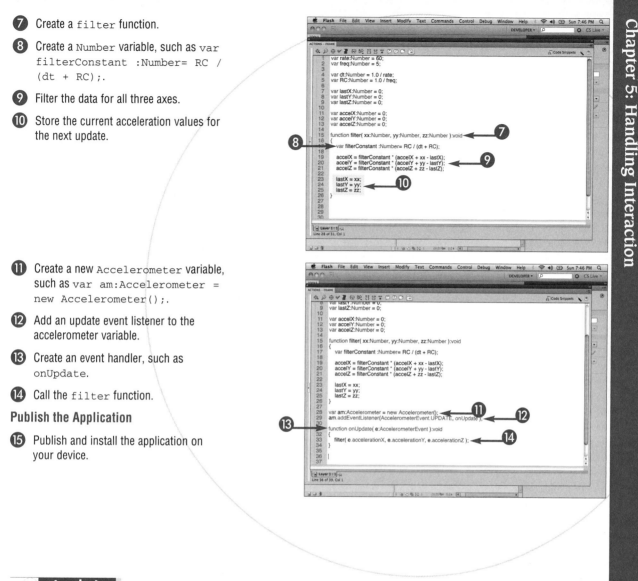

11. Create a new `Accelerometer` variable, such as `var am:Accelerometer = new Accelerometer();`.

12. Add an update event listener to the accelerometer variable.

13. Create an event handler, such as `onUpdate`.

14. Call the `filter` function.

Publish the Application

15. Publish and install the application on your device.

Apply It

You can also experiment with using a low-pass filter instead of a high-pass one. A *low-pass filter* reduces the amplitude of frequencies higher than the frequency cutoff and isolates the effects of gravity. To use this type of filter, you can simply replace the code in the `filter` method in the example shown here with the following:

```
var filterConstant:Number = dt / (dt + RC);
accelX = xx * filterConstant + accelX * (1.0 - filterConstant);
accelY = yy * filterConstant + accelY * (1.0 - filterConstant);
accelZ = zz * filterConstant + accelZ * (1.0 - filterConstant);
```

I encourage you to experiment with both filters and see which one works best for your specific implementation.

Prepare Your Images

Preparing your images before they are used in Flash can go a long way in the performance of your application. There are certain things that you will want to avoid and take into consideration when creating your images.

If you do most of your Flash development targeting the Web, you are used to trying to make your images as optimized as possible to reduce the file size. This usually means creating JPEG images and adjusting their compression settings. However, on the Android platform, PNG is the recommended image format to use. If you are converting an existing Flash application to a mobile platform, keep the existing image format the same and change them if you need to get some extra performance.

The maximum width and height of an image or a BitmapData instance is 2880 pixels. If your image is larger than this, it will not render on the screen. Slicing your image into several images will solve this issue. However, chances are in a mobile application that your image should never be this large.

It is also important to create your images at the size that they are intended to be shown. Never create them larger than needed and scale them down to size in Flash. Scaling your images is a very performance-intensive operation and should be avoided whenever possible. Also, make sure that there is not any unnecessary alpha in your images. If your images require a transparent background, crop them so that there is the least amount of alpha in the image as possible.

Following these simple guidelines will help you get the best performance out of your images in your applications.

Prepare Your Images

1. Open Photoshop, or some other image-editing software.

2. Click File → Open and open the image to prepare.

3. Click the Crop tool.

4. Crop the image to reduce unwanted alpha.

5. Click File.

6. Click Save As.

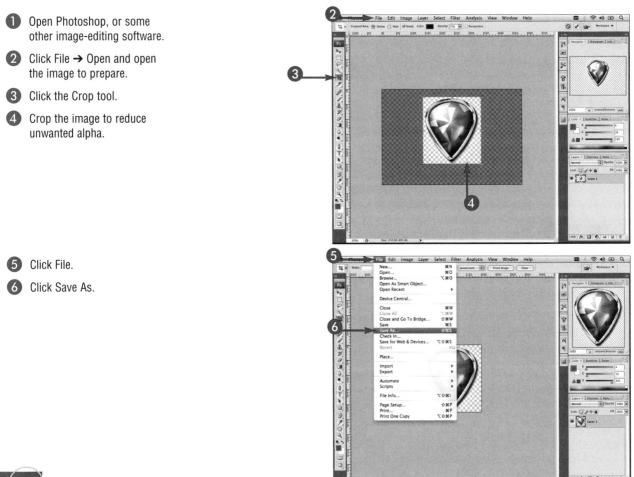

The Save As dialog box appears.

7 Click here and select PNG.

8 Name your file, such as gem.png.

9 Click Save.

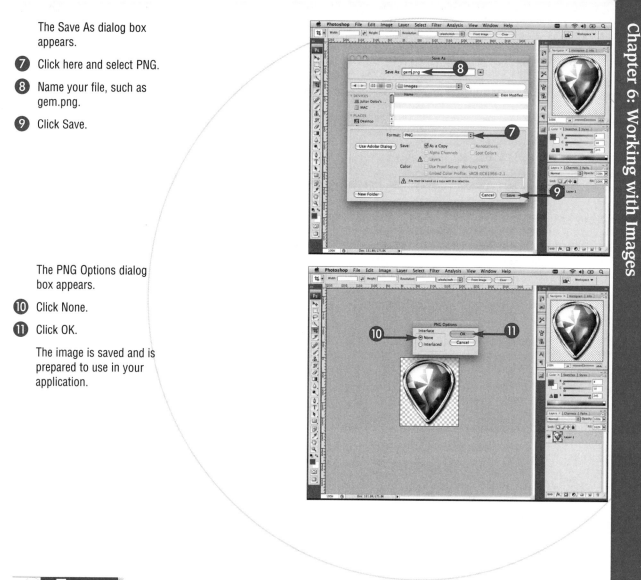

The PNG Options dialog box appears.

10 Click None.

11 Click OK.

The image is saved and is prepared to use in your application.

Extra

The PNG file format contains an alpha channel, which allows you to have transparency in your images. Oftentimes, you may have PNG images that are completely opaque and do not have any visible transparency. However, your image will still contain the alpha channel even if there is no transparency. There is a command-line program called pngcrush that enables you to remove the alpha channel of your PNG images in order to reduce the file size. You can download pngcrush from SourceForge.net, at http://pmt.sourceforge.net/pngcrush/. To remove the alpha channel for an image, run the following command in a Terminal or command prompt window:

```
pngcrush -cc imagewithalpha.png newimage.png
```

Import
Images

O ne way to include images in your application is to import them to the Library inside your Flash file. There are several advantages to this, the biggest one being that you are able to lay out your images accurately inside your file on the Stage.

When you import images to the Library, Flash compiles them into your .swf file. When you publish your Android application, your entire .swf file is compiled into the binary of your application. The more images in your Library, the bigger file size your application binary will have. When your application launches, your entire application is loaded into memory on your device. Therefore, the bigger your application binary, the longer the application will take to launch, and the more memory it will take up, even if you are not using the assets.

The advantage of this is that your images will be somewhat cached and you will not have to load them into memory every time, but this also means that you cannot remove them from memory. This is okay for images that you will use often, such as character animations in a game.

There are two options for importing images. You can import images to the Stage, or you can import them directly to the Library.

If you have an image sequence that you want to import, and if it is named properly, Flash will automatically detect that it is a sequence and import each image onto a separate frame on the Timeline. Images simply need to be named sequentially with a number suffix for Flash to recognize this. You just need to select the first image in the sequence when importing them.

Import Images

Import an Image to the Library

1 Click File.

2 Click Import.

3 Click Import to Library.

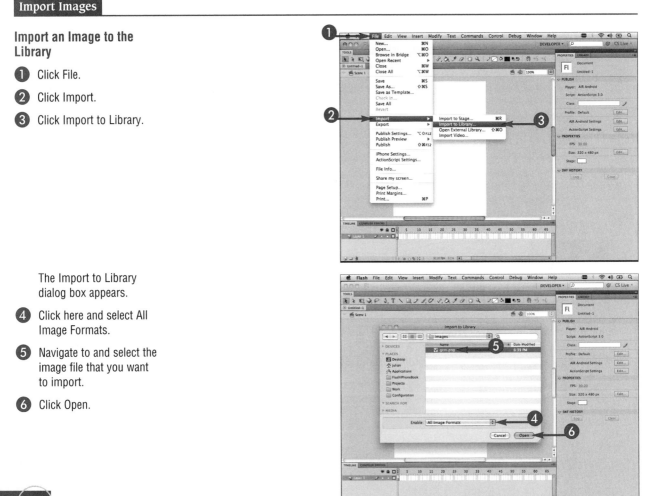

The Import to Library dialog box appears.

4 Click here and select All Image Formats.

5 Navigate to and select the image file that you want to import.

6 Click Open.

The image is imported to the Library.

7 Click Window → Library to open the Library panel.

● You can see your imported image here.

Note: For each image that you import, a graphic symbol is created in the Library. You can delete this symbol if you like and just use the bitmap.

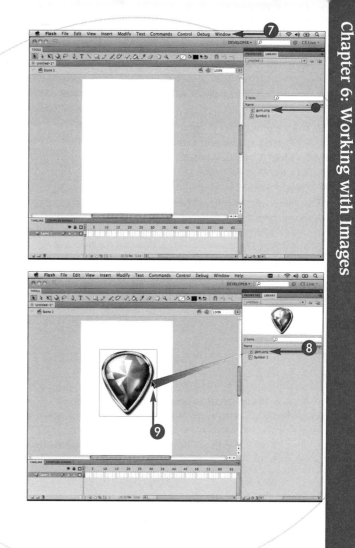

Place the Image on the Stage

8 Select your image in the Library.

9 Drag it onto the Stage.

Your image appears on the Stage.

Extra

After you have imported your images to the Library, you can edit them in an image-editing program, such as Photoshop. This allows you to make edits to your image and have them automatically updated in Flash. To edit an image, right-click it in the Library and select Edit with Adobe Photoshop CS5. If you do not have Photoshop CS5 installed on your machine, you can select the Edit With option instead, and it will prompt you to select your image-editing application. After your image-editing program has launched, your image will be opened so that you can begin editing it. After your edits are complete, save the image. When you go back to Flash, you will see your image updated in the Library. It will also be updated anywhere on the Stage where the image is placed.

Alternatively, you can simply overwrite the file on your hard drive with a new version and select Update from the right-click menu of the image. This allows you to update an image in the event that you are not the one editing the images.

Display Images

After you have added images to your Flash file, you will want to display them. The easiest way is to simply drag them from the Library onto the Timeline. Adding images to the Timeline allows you, or a designer, to visually lay out your design. In addition, it enables you to use motion tweens on the Timeline to animate properties of your images. This is usually the preferred method for images that do not need to be added or removed from the Stage at runtime.

If you have images that need to be added or removed from the display list at runtime, you can use ActionScript to display your images. In order to have your images be available to be accessed by ActionScript, you need to have them exported for ActionScript. There is a check box in

the Properties dialog box of the Library image that you can select to set this.

After your image has been exported for ActionScript, you will access it just as you would any other nonvisual ActionScript class. To do so, you will need to give your image a class name. When you select the Export for ActionScript check box, a class name is set to the same name as the Library item by default. Chances are you will want to change that in order to maintain some sort of consistency with the other ActionScript class naming conventions that you have adopted.

Your image gets exported to ActionScript as a `BitmapData` class. By instantiating your class, you can add it to a `Bitmap` instance, which then can be added to the display list.

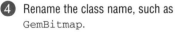

Display Images

 Right-click the image in the Library.

Note: For details on how to import images to the Library, see the previous section, "Import Images."

② Click Properties.

The Bitmap Properties dialog box appears.

③ Click Export for ActionScript.

④ Rename the class name, such as `GemBitmap`.

⑤ Click here and select Lossless (PNG/GIF).

⑥ Click OK.

Your image is ready to be accessed in ActionScript as a class.

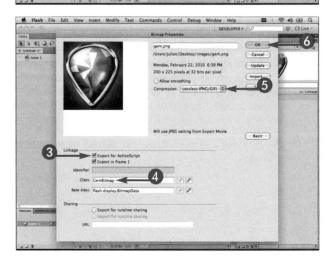

7 Open the Actions panel.

8 Instantiate your image from the Library, such as `var bd:GemBitmap = new GemBitmap();`.

9 Add it to a `Bitmap` instance, such as `var gem:Bitmap = new Bitmap( bd );`.

10 Add the `Bitmap` instance to the Stage, such as `addChild( gem );`.

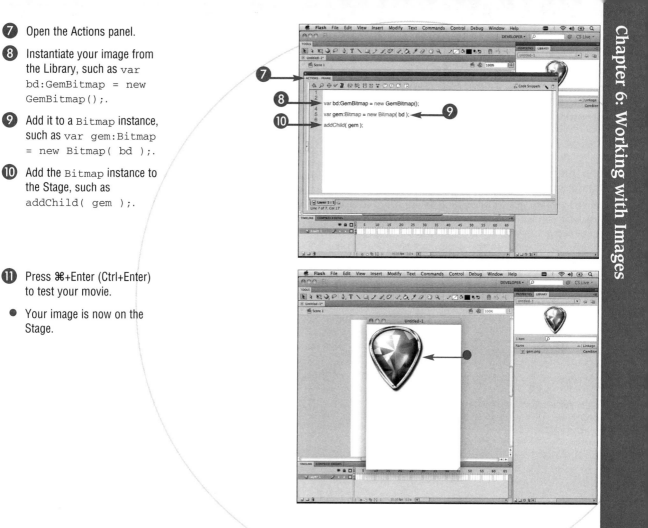

11 Press ⌘+Enter (Ctrl+Enter) to test your movie.

● Your image is now on the Stage.

Extra

Giving your image a better class name is entirely up to you. The important thing is to pick a convention and be consistent throughout your code. Adobe and the Flash community have adopted a set of naming conventions, which are consistent with those of ECMAScript. Choosing good names is very important because it makes your code clear and easy to understand. Even if you are the sole developer, chances are at some point another developer will look at your code and need to understand it.

Package names always start with a lowercase letter and continue with intercaps for subsequent words, such as `core` and `scrollClasses`. Namespaces start with a lowercase letter and use an underscore to separate words, such as `mx_internal`. Interface names start with a capital *I* and use intercaps for subsequent words, such as `IBitmapDrawable`.

Class names always start with a capital letter and use intercaps for any remaining words, such as `Accelerometer` and `CameraRoll`. `Event` and `Error` subclasses should following Adobe's naming convention and place the word at the end of the name, such as `AccelerometerEvent` and `IOError`.

Bundle Images with Your Application

Importing your images to the Library, which bundles them inside your application binary, is one way to bundle images with your application. For more details on this topic, see the section "Import Images" earlier in this chapter. The other method is to bundle the images externally from your application binary, which can be loaded and displayed at runtime with ActionScript.

This method has many benefits. First, by not including the images in the binary of the application, you reduce its size, which speeds up application load times. Secondly, the images get loaded into memory only after they have been loaded from the file system of the device. The images will also not be cached and can be freed from memory when they are no longer needed. This gives you more control over the memory consumption of your application.

This method is good for images that are not used frequently and at times when performance is not critical. Splash screens and help screens are good examples of these uses.

You can bundle files with your application from the Air Android Settings dialog box. At the bottom of the dialog box, there is a list of files that will be included with your application. By default, there are two in the list, your .swf file and your application descriptor file. You can add additional files or folders to this list.

It is a good idea to get in the habit of using relative path names for your files and folders. This will give you the ability to move your project folder to another location or computer if you are working with a team of designers and developers.

Bundle Images with Your Application

1 Click File.

2 Click AIR Android Settings.

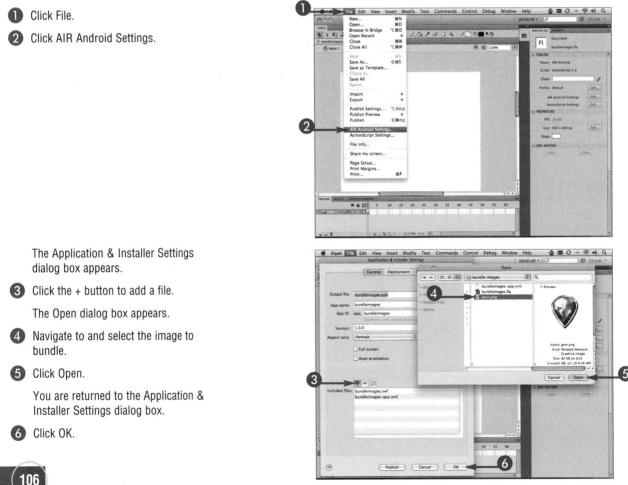

The Application & Installer Settings dialog box appears.

3 Click the + button to add a file.

The Open dialog box appears.

4 Navigate to and select the image to bundle.

5 Click Open.

You are returned to the Application & Installer Settings dialog box.

6 Click OK.

⑦ In a Finder window or Explorer, navigate to the folder with your compiled application.

⑧ Change the file extension of your compiled application from .apk to .zip.

⑨ Extract the ZIP file.

Your application is extracted to a folder with the same name.

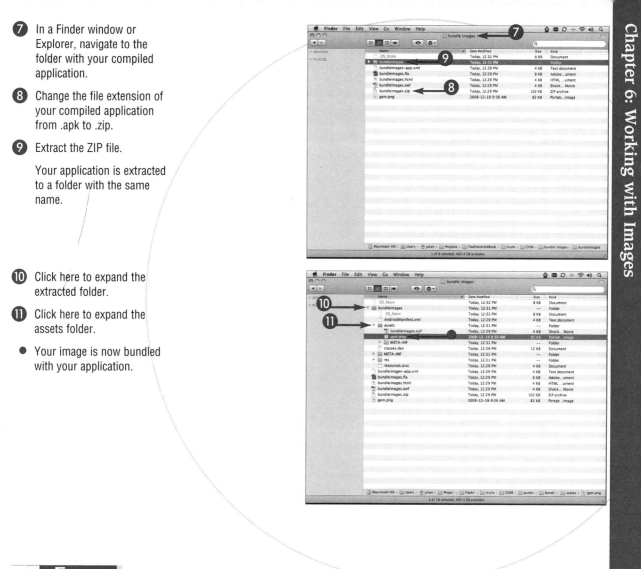

⑩ Click here to expand the extracted folder.

⑪ Click here to expand the assets folder.

● Your image is now bundled with your application.

Extra

There is no guideline to follow in deciding which images you should import into the Library to be compiled with your file and which images you should bundle with your application. Every instance and every application are going to be different, and it will be up to you to experiment, test, and decide which method works best. The question to ask yourself is if it is acceptable for the images to take a few seconds to load and appear on the screen. The more images you load at a given time, the longer it will take for all of the images to appear on the screen. This is due to the performance requirements for loading an image into memory and displaying it on the Stage. For elements such as user interface elements and backgrounds, this is probably acceptable. However, for any kind of image sequences or game elements, this may not be acceptable. Also, any items that have to be in sync with any other element, such as sound, may be better if they are imported into the Library.

Load Images at Runtime

Loading images at runtime can be accomplished by bundling them externally from your application. For more details on how to bundle your images, see the preceding section, "Bundle Images with Your Application." Images bundled with your application will be stored in the same directory as your application.

The Loader class is used to load external assets, such as images and SWF files. The Loader class extends the DisplayObjectContainer class and can be used as the parent container for the images that it loads. This allows you to add the instance of your Loader class to the display list before the asset has been completely loaded.

However, the Loader class can have only one child object, and you will not be able to add or remove any of its children as you would a normal DisplayObjectContainer

instance. The Loader class exposes the loaded asset by accessing the content property. It is accessible only after the file has completely finished loading.

To make sure that the image is available, you can listen for the Event.COMPLETE event on your Loader instance. This will ensure that the file has been completely loaded and is ready to be added to a different display list.

Even though you are loading the file locally from the device's file system, loading will not happen instantaneously. Depending on your assets, loading them can be a performance-intensive process, especially if you are trying to load multiple images at the same time. This may cause your images to flicker as they are loaded. Every situation will be unique, and you will have to test and make adjustments that create the best possible solution for your needs.

Load Images at Runtime

① Create a Loader instance, such as var loader:Loader = new Loader();.

② Create a URLRequest instance for the image that you bundled with your application, such as var request:URLRequest = new URLRequest("gem.png");.

Note: See the preceding section, "Bundle Images with Your Application," for more details.

③ Listen for when the image has finished loading, such as loader. contentLoaderInfo. addEventListener(Event. COMPLETE, onComplete);.

④ Create an event handler for the complete event, such as onComplete.

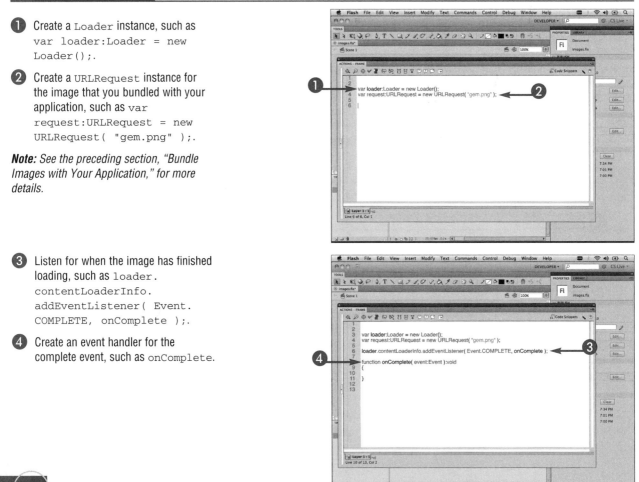

5 Get a reference to the loaded `Bitmap`, such as `var bitmap:Bitmap = loader.content as Bitmap;`.

6 Add the loaded `Bitmap` to the stage, such as `addChild( bitmap );`.

7 Load the image, such as `loader.load( request );`.

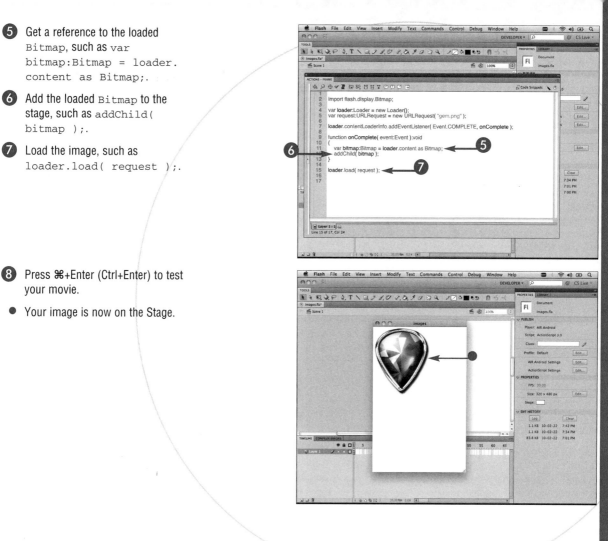

8 Press ⌘+Enter (Ctrl+Enter) to test your movie.

● Your image is now on the Stage.

Apply It

You can also load images from the Internet just as easily as you did from the local file system of the device. The only difference will be the URL that you pass to the `Loader` instance. One thing that you will have to keep in mind, however, is the load times over a network. You will want to indicate to your user that something is loading and potentially provide them with progress updates. To do so, you can listen for the `ProgressEvent.PROGRESS` event on your `Loader` instance, as follows:

```
var loader:Loader = new Loader();
loader.contentLoaderInfo.addEventListener( ProgressEvent.PROGRESS, onProgress );
function onProgress( event:ProgressEvent ):void{
var percent:Number = event.bytesLoaded/event.bytesTotal;
}
```

Create Images Dynamically

Earlier topics in this chapter explore developing with images that you created for your application in an image-editing application, such as Photoshop. But did you know that you can also create images dynamically at runtime with ActionScript? To create an image, you can use the BitmapData class in order to take a snapshot of a particular object or region of the screen. This is almost like taking a screenshot of your application, but it gives you more control over size and location. This technique is used often in user-generated applications to save the user's creations so that they can be preserved and viewed at a later time.

The BitmapData class is the pixel representation of a Bitmap object. The BitmapData class enables you to manipulate those pixels in various ways, as well as create new ones. The draw() method allows you to take a snapshot of a source object, which can later be saved as a Bitmap. Valid source objects are any DisplayObject, such as MovieClip, Sprite, Bitmap, Video, and TextField; also, you can specify another BitmapData object as the source.

You can also alter or apply effects to the drawn representation of your source object. The draw() method takes a number of optional parameters that provide you with this functionality, such as applying a colorTransfrom and blendMode, as well as using a Matrix instance to scale, rotate, or translate the bitmap.

After your object is drawn to a BitmapData instance, you can add it to a Bitmap instance to display it on the screen, or you can encode the data to an image format such as PNG and save it to the file system.

Create Images Dynamically

1. Create a BitmapData instance, such as var bd:BitmapData = new BitmapData();.

2. Give it a width, such as 320.

3. Give it a height, such as 480.

4. To make it not transparent, enter false as the third argument.

5. Enter an ARGB value as the background color, such as 0xFFFF0000;.

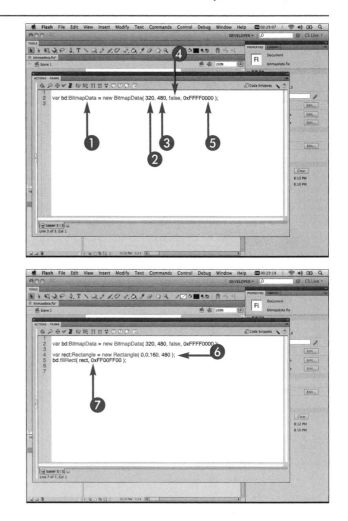

6. Create a Rectangle instance, such as var rect:Rectangle = new Rectangle(0,0,160, 480);.

7. Fill the rectangle with a color, such as bd.fillRect(rect, 0xFF00FF00);.

⑧ Create a `Bitmap` instance, such as `var bitmap:Bitmap = new Bitmap();`.

⑨ Add your `BitmapData` instance to the `Bitmap` instance.

⑩ Add the `Bitmap` instance to the Stage, such as `addChild ( bitmap );`.

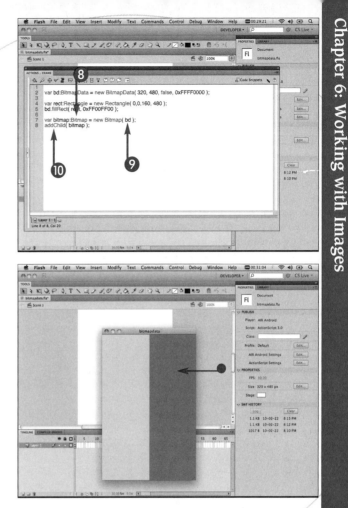

⑪ Press ⌘+Enter (Ctrl+Enter) to test your movie.

● Your dynamically created image is added to the Stage.

Apply It

Currently, the Flash Player does not have a method for encoding PNG images. However, there are several open source ActionScript 3.0 classes that do just that. `as3corelib`, which was created by Adobe and is available at http://code.google.com/p/as3corelib/, has a `PNGEncoder` class that allows you to pass it a `BitmapData` instance. The `PNGEncoder.encode` method returns a `ByteArray` encoded in the PNG image format. This allows you to save the `ByteArray` to the file system of your device, as follows:

```
var bd:BitmapData = new BitmapData( 200, 200, false, 0xFFFF0000 );
var png:ByteArray = PNGEncoder.encode( bd );
```

Save Images to the Camera Roll

Adobe has introduced the ability to save images to the camera roll, through a new class called `CameraRoll`. This allows your application to store images in a central location on the device. It also enables your users to share their images easily through different applications, such as email, Facebook, and Twitter.

The `CameraRoll` class is a very simple class that has only one static method and one static property. The `supportsAddImage` static property can be used to check whether the platform your application is running on supports adding images to the media library. In the case of an Android device, this should always return `true`; however, if your application is running on multiple platforms, it is a good idea to make this check.

The `addImage` static method enables you to save a `BitmapData` instance to the camera roll. There are a number of ways to create a `BitmapData` object, as shown earlier in this chapter. For example, if you are creating a painting program, in which users can paint on the screen with their fingers, you may want them to have the option to save their paintings. You could save them to the Documents directory of your application; however, this makes it a little more difficult for the users to get the images off their device. Saving the images to the camera roll gives them more options, the easiest being to just email the paintings to themselves from the Gallery application.

After the image has been successfully saved to the camera roll, the user can select it from the roll. See the following section, "Select Images from the Camera Roll," for more details.

Save Images to the Camera Roll

① Import an image to the Library.

Note: *See the section "Import Images" for more information.*

② Click and drag it onto the Stage.

③ Create a new `BitmapData` instance, such as `var bd:BitmapData = new BitmapData();`.

④ Give it a width the same as your image, such as `320`.

⑤ Give it a height the same as your image, such as `480`.

⑥ Type **false** to make it nontransparent.

⑦ Draw the Stage into your `BitmapData` instance, such as `bd.draw( stage );`.

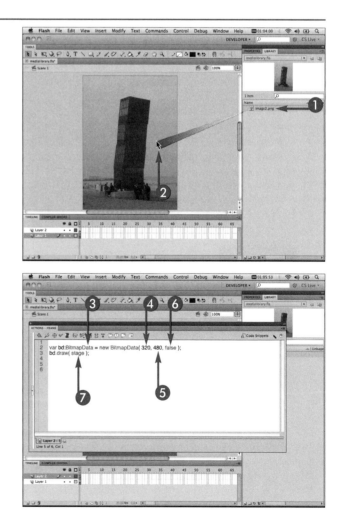

8. Check to see if the camera roll is supported.

9. Create a new `CameraRoll` instance, such as `var cr:CameraRoll = new CameraRoll();`.

10. Add the `BitmapData` to the `CameraRoll`, such as `cr.addBitmapData( bd );`.

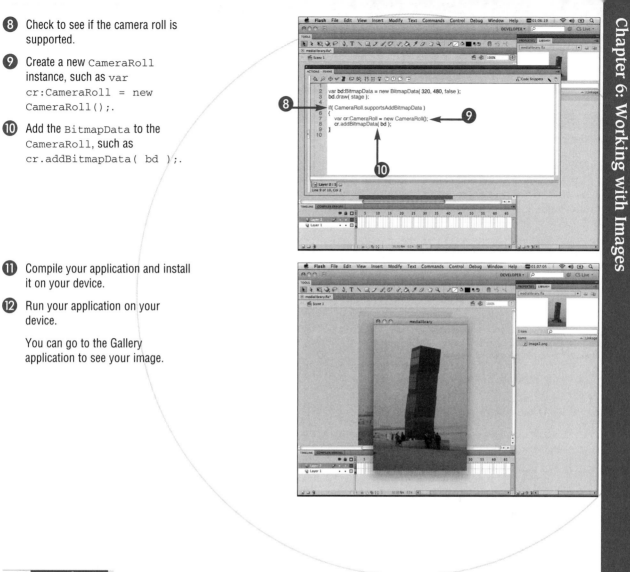

11. Compile your application and install it on your device.

12. Run your application on your device.

You can go to the Gallery application to see your image.

The `CameraRoll.addImage` static method also has a second parameter, which is a function that will be fired after the image has been successfully saved. This parameter is optional, but it is a good idea to implement it. You may want to show a progress indicator animation while it is saving. Implementing the second parameter will allow you to remove your animation and re-enable the user interface of your application.

```
var cr:CameraRoll = new CameraRoll();
cr.addImage( mybitmapdata, onComplete );
function onComplete():void {
trace( "image successfully saved" );
}
```

Select Images from the Camera Roll

After an image has been successfully saved to the camera roll, you can give the user the ability to select it. When your application prompts the user to select an image, the Gallery application is launched. From here, the user can select any image that is currently in the Gallery. In addition, the user can launch the Camera app from the Gallery application, take a picture, and return to the Gallery application in order to select it.

The static property supportsBrowseForImage of the CameraRoll class returns true if the device or platform supports browsing for images. Check this property if your application is developed for multiple platforms.

Calling the browseForImage method of a CameraRoll instance will launch and present the user with the Gallery application. A MediaEvent.SELECT event is fired when the user selects an image.

The MediaEvent object that is returned to your event handler contains all the information you need in order to load the selected image. The most important property of the MediaEvent object is data. The data property is a MediaPromise object, which can be loaded directly from the Loader class, using the loadFilePromise method. A MediaPromise object also has a file property, which is a File object that represents the image selected. This allows you to retrieve the filename, the full path to the file, and the URL of the image.

If your application needs to use the image in a subsequent session, it is a good idea to save the image to a location where the application can load it without having the user select it again. Also, do not store the location of the image in the camera roll; it may change, or the user may delete the image.

Select Images from the Camera Roll

① Check to see if selecting images is supported, such as if(CameraRoll. supportsBrowseForImage){}.

② Create a CameraRoll variable, such as var cr:CameraRoll = new CameraRoll();.

③ Listen for the SELECT event, such as cr.addEventListener(MediaEvent. SELECT, imageSelected);.

④ Browse for images, such as cr.browseForImage();.

⑤ Create an event handler, such as imageSelected.

⑥ Create a Loader variable, such as var loader:Loader = new Loader();.

⑦ Listen for the COMPLETE event, such as loader.contentLoaderInfo. addEventListener(Event.COMPLETE, imageLoaded);.

⑧ Load the selected image, such as loader. loadFilePromise(e.data);.

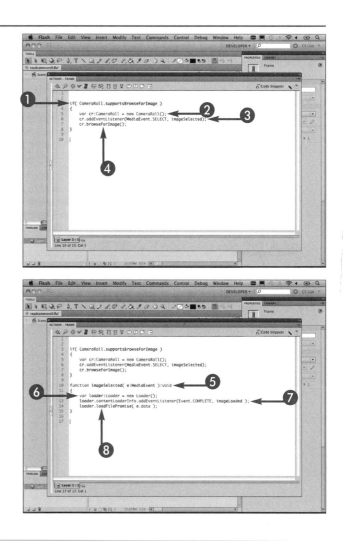

9 Create an event handler, such as `imageLoaded`.

10 Get a reference to the `LoaderInfo` object, such as `var info:LoaderInfo = e.target as LoaderInfo;`.

11 Remove the `COMPLETE` listener, such as `info.removeEventListener( Event.COMPLETE, imageLoaded );`.

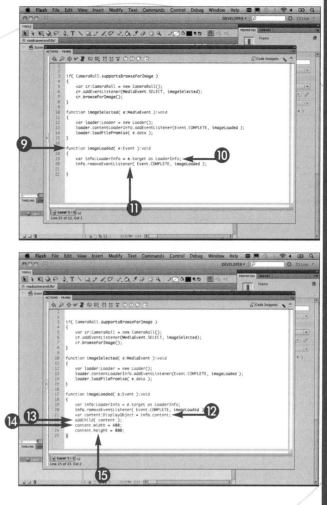

12 Get a reference to the loaded image, such as `var content:DisplayObject = info.content;`.

13 Add the content to the Stage, such as `addChild( content );`.

14 Set the width of the image, such as `content.width = 480;`.

15 Set the height of the image, such as `content.height = 800;`.

The selected image is added to the Stage.

Apply It

As well as listen for when the user selects an image, you can also listen for when the user does not select an image. The `Event.CANCEL` event will be fired if the user dismisses the Gallery application after it has been presented. Most of the time, this is caused by the user pressing the back button on the device. You can use the following syntax to listen for the cancel event:

```
var cr:CameraRoll = new CameraRoll();
cr.addEventListener( Event.CANCEL, imageSelectCancel );
function imageSelectCancel( e:Event ):void{
trace( "image select cancelled" );
}
```

Display the Camera

Throughout this chapter, the sections have discussed how to select, save, and take pictures using the `CameraRoll` class. These methods are useful if you are interested only in still images. However, there may be times when you would like to use the camera of the device as you would a Web camera on a desktop computer. This would allow you to create augmented reality and video streaming applications.

Conveniently, Adobe has implemented the `Camera` class in AIR for Android, which can be used the same way as on a desktop. There are, however, a few things to watch for. Currently, the live preview of the camera appears only in landscape, and it will show only upright video when your application is in Landscape mode.

Currently, only one camera on the device is supported. This is not an issue for Android devices, as there are no

devices with multiple cameras, but this could change in the future.

If you want to use the camera, you must first set the proper permissions in your application descriptor file, in order to give your application access to the camera. The permission name for the camera is `android.permission.CAMERA`. For more details on setting application permissions, see Chapter 3, "Developing Your First Application."

Calling the `Camera.getCamera()` method will return a reference to the camera. A `Camera` class instance can be attached to a `Video` class instance, which is used to display the camera on the Stage. The `Video` class is a `DisplayObject` and can be manipulated and modified just like any other `DisplayObject`. However, this may cause a decrease in performance.

Display the Camera

Set Camera Permissions

1. Open your application descriptor file.

2. Add the `<android> </android>` node.

3. Add the `<manifestAdditions> </manifestAdditions>` node.

4. Add the `<manifest> </manifest>` node.

5. Add the `<data></data>` node.

6. Add the `<![CDATA[ ]]>` tag.

7. Set the camera permissions, such as `<uses-permission android:name="android.permission.CAMERA"/>`.

Your application now has permission to use the camera.

Display the Camera

1. Click File → AIR Android Settings.

The Application & Installer Settings dialog box appears.

2. Click here and select Landscape.

3. Click here to check Full Screen.

4. Click OK.

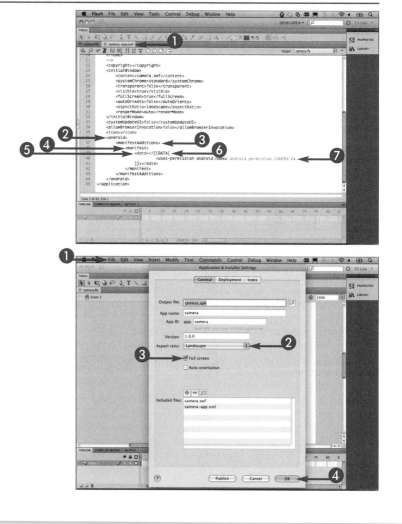

5. Open the Actions panel.

6. Set the scale mode of the Stage, such as `stage.scaleMode = StageScaleMode.NO_SCALE;`.

7. Set the align mode of the Stage, such as `stage.align = StageAlign.TOP_LEFT;`.

8. Create a `Camera` variable, such as `var camera:Camera = Camera.getCamera();`.

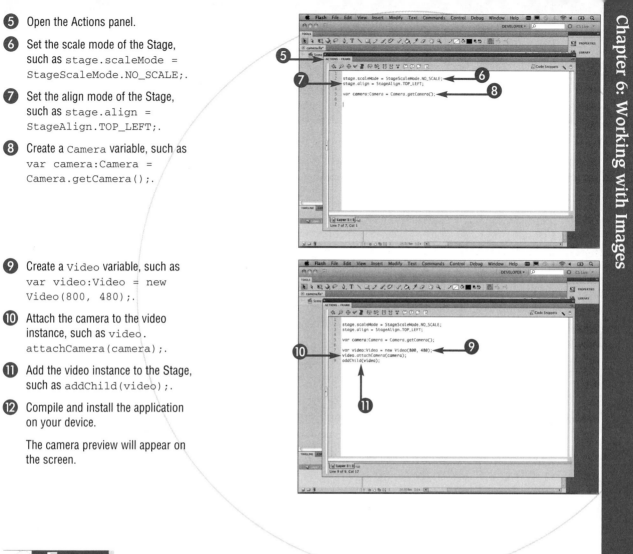

9. Create a `Video` variable, such as `var video:Video = new Video(800, 480);`.

10. Attach the camera to the video instance, such as `video.attachCamera(camera);`.

11. Add the video instance to the Stage, such as `addChild(video);`.

12. Compile and install the application on your device.

The camera preview will appear on the screen.

Extra

If you are looking to create augmenting reality applications, there are several open-source ActionScript libraries and resources available to help provide this functionality. The FLARToolKit, available at the Spark Project Web site (www.libspark.org/wiki/saqoosha/FLARToolKit/en), is the most popular library and is an ActionScript 3 port of the popular C++ library ARToolKit.

The FLARToolKit enables you to detect for predetermined glyphs or markers and track their movements within the screen. In most instances, when a marker or glyph is detected, a 3D model is shown. As the marker is rotated or moved closer or farther away from the camera, the model is scaled and rotated.

The loading of 3D models can be done with a number of open-source real-time 3D ActionScript libraries. Two of the more popular libraries are Away3D, at http://away3d.com/, and Papervision3D, at http://code.google.com/p/papervision3d/. Both libraries support loading COLLADA files, which can be exported from 3D software applications, such as Maya and 3D Studio Max.

117

Import Audio into Your Project

Using sounds in your application can either make or break it. Great sound design will enhance your application and provide an exceptional user experience. It can add a level of polish that can make a good application great. Bad sound design, on the other hand, can just as equally cripple an application. Repetitive sounds and unpleasant sounds can become annoying and cause users not to use your application.

There are a couple different ways to integrate sound into your applications, which are explored throughout this chapter. The first method is to import your sounds into the Library, just as you did with images in Chapter 6, "Working with Images." Importing sounds to the Library bundles them inside your application binary. This can cause the application binary to grow in file size quickly,

as sound files can be big. This is especially true for sounds such as background and music tracks.

When your application first loads, the entire binary for your application is loaded into memory. The bigger in file size the binary is, the longer it will take for your application to launch, and the more memory it will take to run your application. This is an important concept to understand and should be considered when importing audio files into your application. The method shown in this section is suitable for sound that you will play often, such as sound effects in a game.

When selecting your audio files for import, in the Import to Library dialog box, you choose All Sound Formats to let you know the supported types of audio files that can be imported into the Library.

Import Audio into Your Project

1 Click File.

2 Click Import.

3 Click Import to Library.

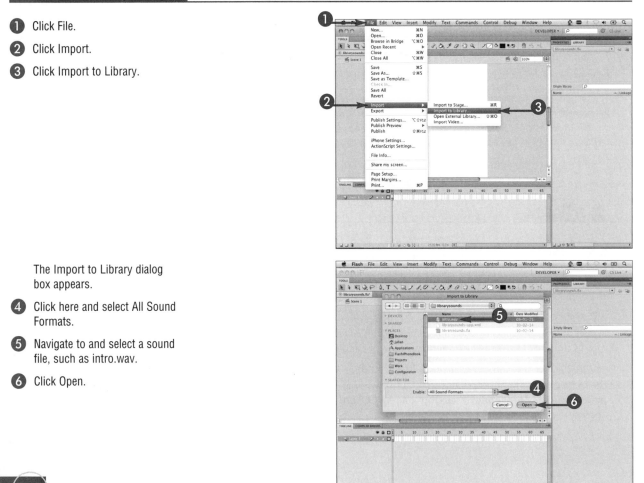

The Import to Library dialog box appears.

4 Click here and select All Sound Formats.

5 Navigate to and select a sound file, such as intro.wav.

6 Click Open.

The sound file is imported into the Library.

7 Click Window.

8 Click Library.

Note: *You can also use the ⌘+L (Ctrl+L) keyboard shortcut to show and hide the Library panel.*

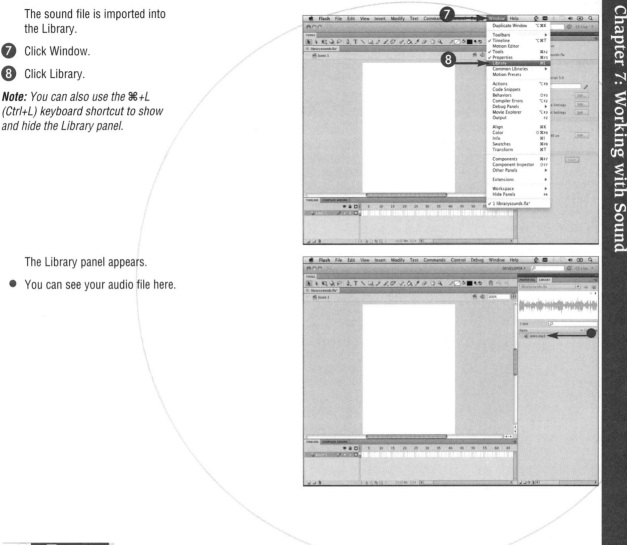

The Library panel appears.

● You can see your audio file here.

After you have imported your sound files to the Library, you can edit them in an audio-editing program, such as Adobe Soundbooth. This allows you to make edits to your sound file, such as change the volume or add filters, and have them automatically updated in Flash. To edit a sound file, right-click it in the Library and select Edit with Soundbooth. If you do not have Soundbooth installed on your machine, you can select the Edit With option instead, and it will prompt you to select your audio-editing application. Audacity is an excellent free audio-editing program that is available for both Windows and Mac OS X.

After your audio-editing program has launched, your sound file will be opened so that you can begin editing it. After your edits are complete, save the file, and your sound will be updated in Flash.

Alternatively, you can simply overwrite the file on your hard drive with a new version and select Update from the right-click menu of the sound in the Library. This allows you to update a sound file in the event that you are not the one editing the sound.

Choose an Audio Codec

hoosing the right audio codec for your sounds is extremely important. There are two different types of audio codecs: uncompressed, such as linear PCM and IMA4 (IMA ADPCM), and compressed, such as MP3 and AAC.

If you plan on looping your sound, most likely used for a background track, it is best to choose an uncompressed codec. When an audio file is encoded to an MP3, small silent gaps are added at the beginning and at the end of the audio file. When the sound is looped, you may hear a noticeable amount of silence between the end of the sound and the beginning of the loop. The best way to get around this is to use an uncompressed audio codec, which does not insert the silent gaps.

To use uncompressed sounds with your applications, you will need to import them into the Library of your file because Flash does not support the playback of any external uncompressed sounds. Changing the audio codec can be done from the Properties dialog box for a specific sound in the Library. There are three compressions you can choose from: ADPCM and RAW for uncompressed sounds and MP3 for compressed sounds.

If you plan on having your audio files loaded externally from your application, you will need to use the MP3 codec. Currently, this is the only codec that Flash supports when loading or streaming audio files. You can load files over the Internet as well as from your application bundle. For more details on bundling sounds with your application, see the following section, "Bundle Sounds with Your Application."

Choose an Audio Codec

Set an Audio Codec for a Library Sound

1 Right-click the sound file in the Library.

2 Click Properties.

The Sound Properties dialog box appears.

3 Click here and select the codec that you want, such as ADPCM.

4 Click here to choose to convert your stereo audio to mono.

5 Click here and select a sample rate, such as 44kHz.

6 Click here and select the number of bits, such as 4 bit.

7 Click OK.

The codec that you selected is applied to the sound file.

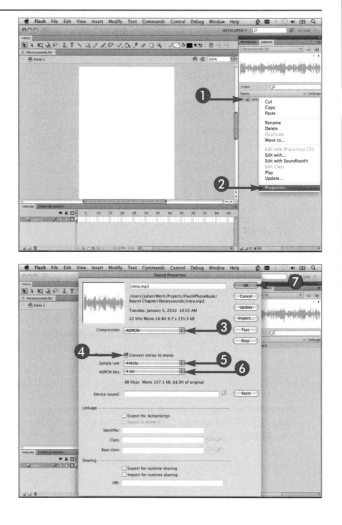

Set a Global Audio Codec

1. Click File.

2. Click Publish Settings.

   The Publish Settings dialog box appears.

3. Click the Flash tab.

4. Click the Set button for audio streams.

   The Sound Settings dialog box appears.

5. Click here and select the codec that you want.

6. Click here and select a sample rate, such as 44kHz.

7. Click here and select the number of bits, such as 5 bit.

8. Click OK.

   You are returned to the Publish Settings dialog box.

- You can click the Set button for audio events to set the audio compression settings.

9. Click OK.

   The codec that you selected is applied to all sound files.

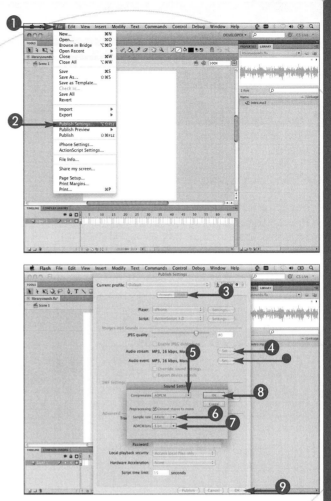

Extra

To get the most out of the audio in your application, you may want to experiment with several different audio codecs. If you have a lot of sounds in your Library, it is a pain and time-consuming to change them all individually. What you may have not known is that you can select multiple sounds in the Library and change the compression of them all at once. The process for changing multiple sounds at once is the same as changing it for an individual item. This puts a big emphasis on keeping your Library organized and similar files grouped together. For example, you may want to keep all your images in one folder and all your audio files in another. This will allow you to not only find your items quickly, but also select multiple items more easily. You may also want to group items that are related to specific sections of your application, such as all your assets for the Home section in one folder, and all the assets for your games in another.

Bundle Sounds with Your Application

A s well as import sounds to the Library and embed them into your application, you can bundle files externally with your application. These files will not be placed into memory when your application is launched, and you will have more control over their being released from memory when they are no longer needed.

Consider this method if you have large or long sound files. Having these not included in your application binary will help reduce the initial load time of your application. The downfall to using this method is that currently, Flash does not support playback for externally loaded uncompressed audio codecs. If you have smaller or shorter sound files, your best bet is to place them in the Library of your Flash file. Importing files is best used for sound effects and

other similar sound files. For more details on importing sounds to the Library, see the section "Import Audio into Your Project," earlier in this chapter.

You can bundle files with your application on the General tab of the AIR Android Settings dialog box. When you choose the files that you want to include, it is a good practice to use relative path names. This will allow you to develop your project on a different computer or allow you to work with multiple designers and developers as part of a team.

When your application is compiled, your files will be placed in the same location as your application binary. This makes it very easy to access them with ActionScript because the base path is the exact same as your application.

Bundle Sounds with Your Application

① Click File.

② Click AIR Android Settings.

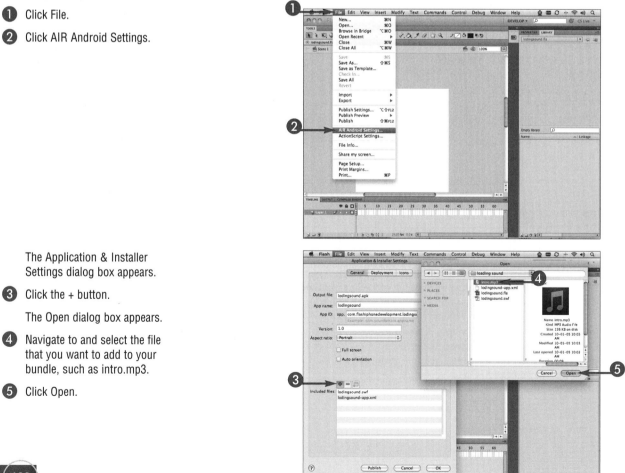

The Application & Installer Settings dialog box appears.

③ Click the + button.

The Open dialog box appears.

④ Navigate to and select the file that you want to add to your bundle, such as intro.mp3.

⑤ Click Open.

- Your file is now added to the list of files to bundle with your application.

6 Click OK.

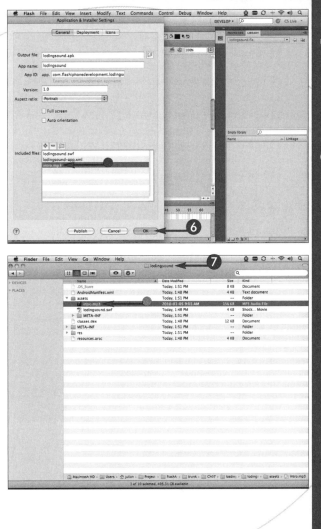

7 In a Finder window or Explorer, navigate to the folder with your compiled application.

- You can see that the audio file is bundled next to your application binary.

ffffffBundling your sounds with your application has many benefits, such as being able to control when they are added and removed from memory. This gives you greater control over the memory footprint of your application. The disadvantage of this method is that loading sounds can be a process-intensive task, especially if you are loading multiple sounds at the same time. Even though you are going to load the sounds locally from the file system of your device, there will be a slight delay from the time you load it to the time you are able to play it. This can cause sync issues as well as some performance issues. It is recommended that you preload your sounds before they are required to be played. If you have any experience building Flash applications for the Web, you should be familiar with this approach.

As well as preloading a sound before it is needed, it is also a good idea to play it once at zero volume. This will ensure that your sound plays back smoothly when played.

Load Sounds at Runtime

Loading sounds at runtime can be accomplished by bundling them externally from your application. For more details on how to bundle your sounds, see the preceding section, "Bundle Sounds with Your Application." Sounds bundled with your application will be stored in the same directory as your application. Currently, MP3 files are the only audio format that is supported for playing back external sounds with ActionScript.

You can also load an external MP3 file from a valid URL over the network. If you plan to load audio files over the network, you should make sure that it is really apparent to the users that they are going to be doing so. Downloading audio files over 3G has the potential to be very expensive for your users, and they should have the option to opt out

of that download or make sure that they are connected to a WiFi hotspot.

The `Sound` class enables you to load an external MP3, using the `load()` method. The `load()` method takes a `URLRequest` instance, which specifies the file that you want to load. After you have called the `load()` method and your file has begun loading, you can listen for `ProgressEvents`. This will allow you to monitor the progress of your file as it loads and enable you to display that to your user. Listening for `ProgressEvents` is really necessary only when loading sounds from the Internet, as loading sounds from the file system of the device should happen fairly quickly.

You can also listen for the `Event.COMPLETE` event on your sound object. This event will be fired when the sound file has been completely loaded.

Load Sounds at Runtime

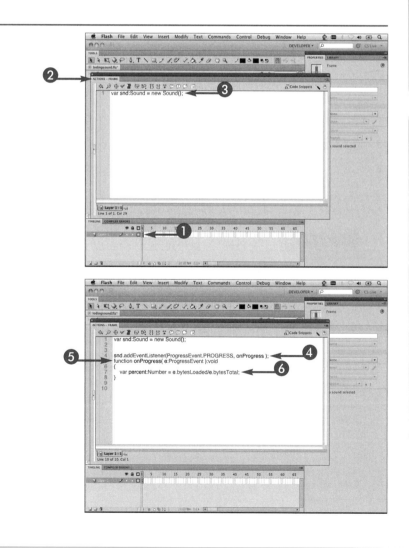

① Select a frame on the Timeline in which to place your ActionScript code.

② Open the Actions panel.

③ Create a `Sound` instance variable, such as `var snd:Sound = new Sound();`.

Note: *This example loads a sound file from your application bundle. For more details on how to bundle sound files with your application, see the preceding section, "Bundle Sounds with Your Application."*

④ Listen for the `ProgressEvent. PROGRESS` event on the `Sound` instance.

⑤ Create an event handler function, such as `onProgress`.

⑥ Calculate the percentage of the file downloaded, such as `var percent:Number = e.bytesLoaded/e. bytesTotal;`.

7. Listen for the `Event.COMPLETE` event on the `Sound` instance.

8. Create an event handler function, such as `onSoundLoaded`.

9. Create a `trace` statement to signal that the file has loaded.

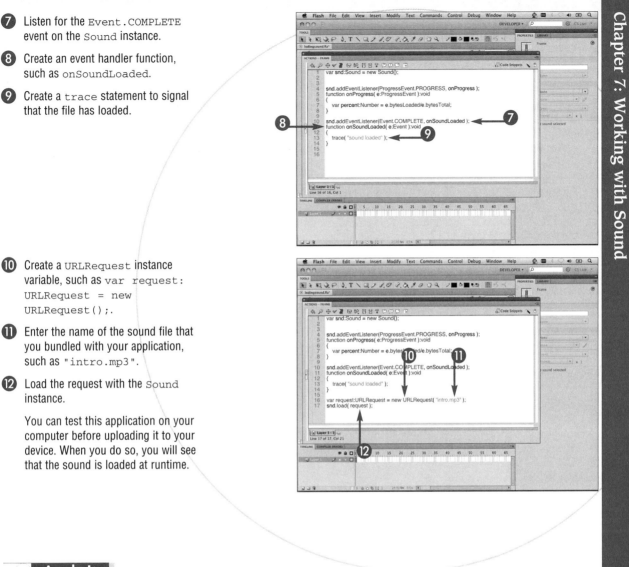

10. Create a `URLRequest` instance variable, such as `var request: URLRequest = new URLRequest();`.

11. Enter the name of the sound file that you bundled with your application, such as `"intro.mp3"`.

12. Load the request with the `Sound` instance.

You can test this application on your computer before uploading it to your device. When you do so, you will see that the sound is loaded at runtime.

Apply It

MP3 sound files can include ID3 tags, which are metadata that is embedded in the file. *Metadata* describes the file. You can access these tags with ActionScript by listening for the `Event.ID3` event on your sound object. This will fire an event when the ID3 data is available to be read when loading a sound:

```
var snd:Sound = new Sound();
snd.addEventListener( Event.ID3, onID3 );
function onID3( event:Event ):void{
var id3:ID3Info = Sound( event.target ).id3;
for (var propName:String in id3) {
trace(propName + " = " + id3[propName] );
}
```

Play Sounds

Playing sounds can be achieved through a `Sound` object instance. You can create a `Sound` object instance to load an external sound or create one from an audio file in your Library.

To make your sound files in your Library available to ActionScript, in order for you to instantiate them, you must export them to ActionScript and give them a class name. You do so using the Sound Properties dialog box. When you set the file to be exported in the dialog box, you will see the Class text input box become active, with a default class name the same as its name in the Library. Most likely, it will be the same as the actual filename you imported and does not fit with your class naming conventions. Make sure to change that to something

that reflects an ActionScript class so that you can remain consistent.

After you have created your `Sound` object instance, you can play it with the `play()` method. This method has three parameters: the start position of the sound, the number of times to loop the sound, and a `SoundTransform` object for your sound. All three of these parameters are optional and can be omitted if you want to play a sound quickly and only once.

The `play()` method also returns a `SoundChannel` instance, which allows you to control the sound. Each sound in your application is assigned to a `SoundChannel`, and each `SoundChannel` can be mixed independently from each other.

Play Sounds

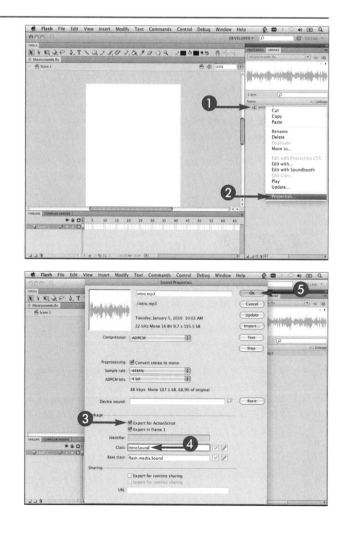

① Right-click the sound item that you want to play in the Library.

② Click Properties.

The Sound Properties dialog box appears.

③ Click Export for ActionScript.

④ Give your sound a class name, such as `IntroSound`.

⑤ Click OK.

Note: *For details on choosing compression settings, see the section "Choose an Audio Codec" earlier in this chapter.*

The sound is exported for ActionScript with a class name.

6 Click Window.

7 Click Common Libraries.

8 Click Buttons.

The Buttons Library panel appears.

9 Click a sample Play button.

10 Drag the button onto the Stage.

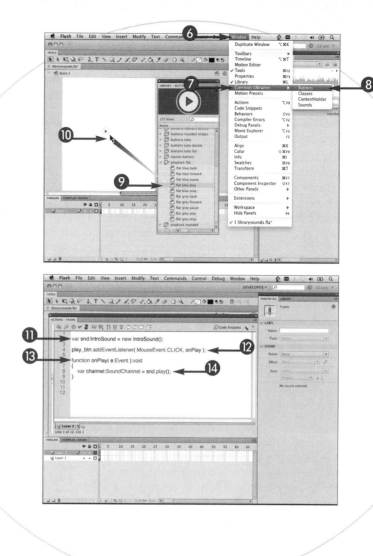

11 Create an instance of your sound from the Library, such as `var snd:IntroSound = new IntroSound();`.

12 Listen for a click event on the Play button on the Stage.

13 Create a click event handler function, such as `onPlay`.

14 Play the sound, such as `var channel:SoundChannel = snd.play();`.

The sound is played.

Apply It

When playing a sound, there are going to be times when you want to know when that sound has finished playing. One example for this would be to play another sound after the first one has finished. For example, you could create a bunch of small loops instead of one longer background track for the sound track of your application. This will give you lots of flexibility to have dynamic sound tracks, and they will not get repetitive and annoy the user.

You can add an event listener to the SoundChannel of your sound to determine when it has completed playing, such as the following:

```
var snd:Sound = new MyLibrarySound();
var channel:SoundChannel = snd.play();
channel.addEventListener( Event.SOUND_COMPLETE, onSoundComplete );
function onSoundComplete( event:Event ):void{
//sound has finished playing.
}
```

Stop Sounds

After you have started a sound using the `Sound.play()` method, you will want to stop it at some point. The first thing I am sure that you will be looking for is a `stop` method on the `Sound` class; however, this does not exist. The preceding section, "Play Sounds," discusses how the `play()` method returns a `SoundChannel` object instance. The `SoundChannel` class is what is used to control all aspects of your sound. You can think of it as a channel on a sound mixing board, with each of your sounds assigned to an input.

`SoundChannel` implements only one method, the `stop()` method. Calling the `stop()` method of a `SoundChannel` will stop the sound at the current position of the play head. It is a little confusing at first that the `play` and `stop`

methods are not from the same class, but after a while, you will get used to it, and it will seem like second nature.

This method is great for stopping individual sounds, but what if you want to stop all the sounds in your application? You could put references to all your active sound channels in an `Array` and loop through them to stop them individually. As mentioned earlier, a `SoundChannel` class is like a channel on a mixing board, and the `SoundMixer` class makes that analogy a good one. The `SoundMixer` class contains static methods and properties to control sounds globally in your application. The `stopAll()` method will stop all currently playing sounds. Just like the `SoundChannel.stop()` method, this method stops the sound at the current location of the play head.

Stop Sounds

① Click Window.

② Click Common Libraries.

③ Click Buttons.

The Buttons Library panel appears.

④ Click a sample Stop button.

⑤ Drag the button onto the Stage.

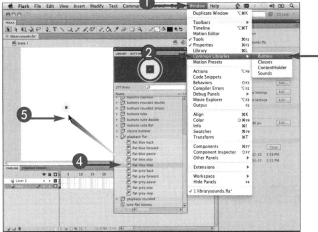

⑥ Select the Stop button on the Stage.

⑦ Click Window → Properties to open the Properties panel.

⑧ Give the button an instance name, such as `stop_btn`.

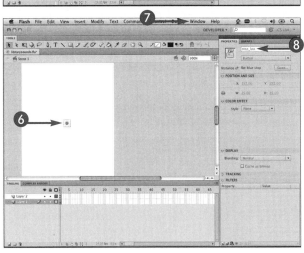

⑨ Select a frame on the Timeline in which to place your ActionScript code.

⑩ Open the Actions panel.

⑪ Create an instance variable for your sound in the Library, such as `var snd:IntroSound = new IntroSound();`.

⑫ Play the sound, such as `var channel:SoundChannel = snd.play();`.

Note: For more details on how to play sounds, see the preceding section.

⑬ Listen for a click event on the Stop button on the Stage.

⑭ Create a click event handler function, such as `onStop`.

⑮ Stop the sound, such as `channel. stop();`.

The sound is stopped.

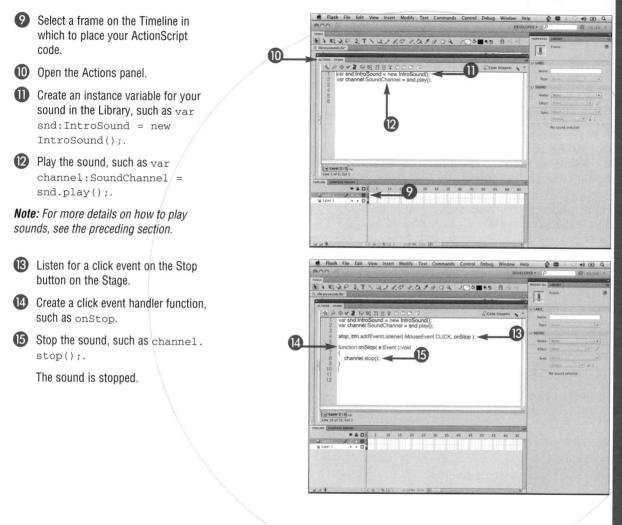

Apply It

After your sound is stopped, chances are at some point you will want to resume it from its current location. Unfortunately, there is not a `resume` method in the `SoundChannel` class for you to use, so you need to create your own. The first argument of the `Sound.play` method is the initial position in milliseconds where the sound should start to play. The `SoundChannel` class has a read-only `position` property that returns the position of the play head in milliseconds. With this, you can resume your sound from its current position, as follows:

```
var snd:Sound = new MySound();
var channel:SoundChannel = snd.play();
channel.stop();
snd.play( channel.position );
```

Set the Volume of a Sound

etting the volume of your sound is easily done with the SoundTransform class. The SoundTransform class has a volume property, which determines the volume of your sound. This value can be a number between 0 and 1. Setting the volume property to 0 will mute the sound, and setting the property to 1 will play the sound at its loudest volume.

Setting the volume of your sounds gives you control over the entire audio mix of your application. Making sure that all your sounds are set to the proper volume is an important part of sound design. If one sound is much louder than the others, it will stand out and cause a poor user experience. You can also increment or decrement the volume over time to fade sounds in and out.

After a SoundTransform instance has been created and its volume set, you can apply it to a SoundChannel instance through its soundTransform property. It is important to note that you cannot set the volume property of a SoundTransform instance that is already set on an object. For example, the following will not work:

```
mychannel.soundTransform.volume = 0.5;
```

Each time you would like to change the volume, you will need to reset the soundTransform property for the change in volume to take effect.

You can also apply a SoundTransform instance to other objects that have a soundTransform property. For example, you can set a SoundTransform instance to the soundTransfrom property of a MovieClip in order to control the volume of a sound that has been placed on its Timeline.

Set the Volume of a Sound

① Create a Sound instance from a sound in the Library.

② Create a Number instance variable, such as var volume:Number = 0;.

③ Create a SoundTransform instance variable, such as var sndtransform:SoundTransform = new SoundTransform();.

④ Set the volume of your SoundTransform instance variable.

Note: For details on how to export a sound for ActionScript, see the section "Play Sounds."

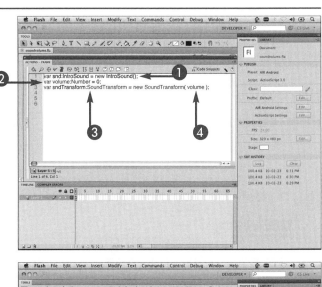

⑤ Play the sound, such as var channel:SoundChannel = snd.play();.

⑥ Set the start offset of the sound, such as 0.

⑦ Set the number of times to loop the sound, such as 100.

⑧ Set the initial SoundTransform of the sound.

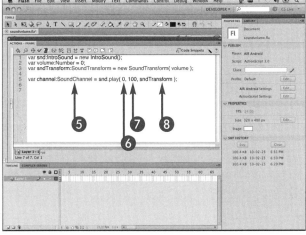

9 Add a listener to the Event.ENTER_ FRAME event of the stage.

10 Create an event handler function, such as fadeVolume.

11 Increment the volume instance every frame.

12 Check to see if the volume is greater than 1.

13 Remove the Event.ENTER_FRAME event listener.

14 Constrain the volume to 1.

15 Create a SoundTransform instance variable, such as var sndtransform: SoundTransform = new SoundTransform();.

16 Set the volume of your SoundTransform instance variable.

17 Apply the SoundTransform instance to the SoundChannel variable returned from the snd.play() method.

The volume of the sound is set.

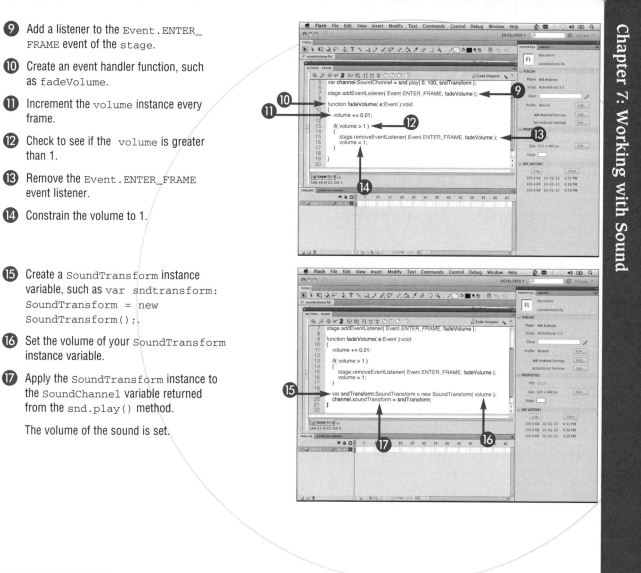

Apply It

In the section "Stop Sounds," the SoundMixer class was introduced. The SoundMixer class provides you with static methods and properties to control sounds globally in your application. Just like the SoundChannel class, SoundMixer has a soundTransform property that you can use to set the volume of all the sounds in your application, as in the following:

```
var sndTransform:SoundTransform = new SoundTransform();
sndTransform.volume = 0.5;
soundMixer.soundTransform = sndTransform;
```

Visualize the Sound Spectrum

The SoundMixer class has a method called computeSpectrum, which takes a snapshot of the current sound wave and places it into a ByteArray instance. This allows you to create some very cool audio visualizations of the sounds in your application. It is important to note that this takes into account every sound that is currently playing in your application. This means that you cannot visualize a specific sound if other sounds are playing at the same time.

The ByteArray that is produced from the computeSpectrum method has a fixed size of 512 floating-point values, in which the first 256 values

represent the left channel and the second 256 channels represent the right channel. Each floating-point value in the ByteArray will range from -1.0 to 1.0.

To visualize the sound as it is playing, you will have to call the computeSpectrum method at a steady interval. For this, you can use the Event.ENTER_FRAME event, which gets fired every time the Flash Player enters a new frame. It is a good practice to listen for the sound complete event on your sound so that you can remove the event listener. If you do not, you will be doing a lot of unnecessary calculations, which can cause the performance of your application to decrease.

Visualize the Sound Spectrum

① Create a Sound instance from a sound in the Library.

② Play the sound.

③ Listen for when the sound has completed playback.

④ Create a listener for the Event.ENTER_FRAME event.

⑤ Create an event handler function for the sound complete event.

⑥ Remove the Event.ENTER_FRAME event listener.

⑦ Create an event handler for the enter frame event.

⑧ Create a ByteArray variable.

⑨ Create an int constant, such as const PLOT_HEIGHT:int=200;.

⑩ Create another int constant, such as const CHANNEL_LENGTH:int = 256;.

⑪ Create a Number variable, such as var n:Number = 0;.

⑫ Compute the sound spectrum, such as SoundMixer.computeSpectrum (bytes, false, 0);.

13 Create a `Graphics` variable, such as `var g:Graphics = this.graphics;`.

14 Clear the current graphics context.

15 Set the line style.

16 Move the drawing cursor to its start location.

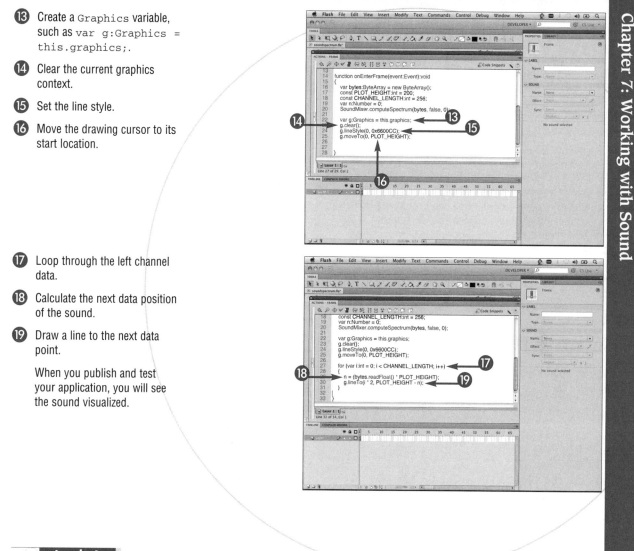

17 Loop through the left channel data.

18 Calculate the next data position of the sound.

19 Draw a line to the next data point.

When you publish and test your application, you will see the sound visualized.

Apply It

Earlier, it was mentioned that the `ByteArray` created by the `computeSpectrum` method returned 512 values, the first 256 representing the left channel and the second 256 representing the right. In the example in this section, you drew the representation of the left channel only. You can add the following code to the end of the `onEnterFrame` method to draw the right channel:

```
g.lineStyle(0, 0x00FF00);
g.moveTo(CHANNEL_LENGTH * 2, PLOT_HEIGHT);
for (i = CHANNEL_LENGTH; i > 0; i--) {
n = (bytes.readFloat() * PLOT_HEIGHT);
g.lineTo(i * 2, PLOT_HEIGHT - n);
}
g.lineTo(0, PLOT_HEIGHT);
```

Access the Microphone

The Microphone class enables you to interact with the microphone on the device. This is the same class and APIs that you would use in order to interact with the microphone on a desktop computer. The one restriction in AIR for Android is that you can connect to only one microphone. This should not be an issue, as almost all mobile devices have only one microphone.

If you want to use the microphone, you must first set the proper permissions in your application descriptor file, in order to give your application access to the microphone. The permission name for the microphone is android. permission.RECORD_AUDIO. For more details on setting application permissions, see Chapter 3, "Developing Your First Application."

The Microphone.getMicrophone() method will return a reference to the microphone on the device. The

Microphone class has a number of properties that give you control over the audio from the microphone.

The gain property can set to a number between 0 and 100 and will boost the signal of the microphone. The default value for this property is 50. The rate property defines the rate at which the microphone captures sound, measured in kHz. Valid values for the rate property are 5 (5,512Hz), 8 (8,000Hz), 11 (11,025Hz), 22 (22,050Hz), and 44 (44,100Hz).

activityLevel is a read-only property that returns the amount of sound detected by the microphone. If activityLevel returns 0, no sound has been detected. If activityLevel returns 100, a loud sound has been detected. This property can be used to determine a suitable value to supply to the setSilenceLevel() method, which sets the minimum input level to determine if there has been microphone activity.

Access the Microphone

Set Microphone Permissions

1. Open your application descriptor file.

2. Add the <android> </android> node.

3. Add the <manifestAdditions> </manifestAdditions> node.

4. Add the <manifest> </manifest> node.

5. Add the <data></data> node.

6. Add the <![CDATA[ ]]> tag.

7. Set the microphone permissions, such as <uses-permission android:name="android. permission. RECORD_AUDIO"/>.

   Your application now has permission to access the microphone.

Access the Microphone

1. Create a Microphone variable, such as var mic:Microphone;.

2. Get a reference to the microphone, such as = Microphone.getMicrophone().

3. Play audio captured from the microphone out the device speakers, such as mic. setLoopBack(true);.

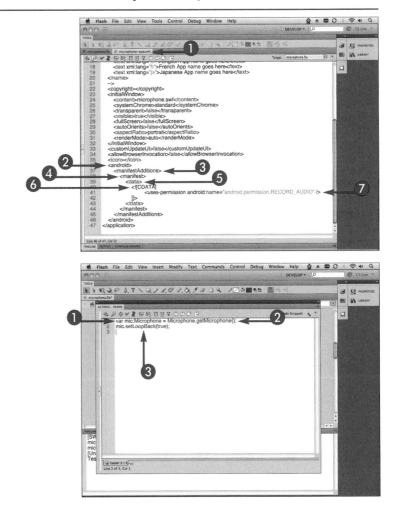

④ Check to see if the reference to the microphone is not null, such as if (mic != null) {}.

⑤ Add an activity event listener, such as mic. addEventListener(ActivityEvent. ACTIVITY, micActivity);.

⑥ Add a status event listener, such as mic. addEventListener(StatusEvent. STATUS, micStatus);.

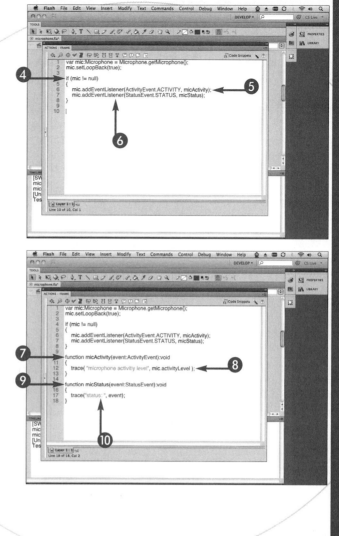

⑦ Create an event handler, such as micActivity.

⑧ Output the microphone activity level, such as trace("microphone activity level", mic.activityLevel);.

⑨ Create an event handler, such as micStatus.

⑩ Output the status event, such as trace("status: ", event);.

⑪ Compile and install your application.

Audio captured from the microphone will be played through the device speakers.

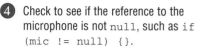

Apply It

If you plan on developing your application to run on multiple platforms, you should be prepared to handle a situation in which the device or platform does not have access to or does not support a microphone. Depending on the level of interaction your application requires from the microphone, you may choose not to support such a device. However, simply displaying a dialog box stating that the application could not access the microphone will allow the user to take the necessary actions to get your application to run properly. The following example can be used to determine if the Microphone class is supported on the current platform:

```
if( Microphone.isSupported ){
//initialize microphone
}
else{
trace( "microphone not supported" );
}
```

Explore Available Video Formats and Encode a Video File

Over the last few releases of the Flash Player, there have been many advancements in Flash Video. Currently, it supports three different codecs: Sorenson Spark, On2 VP6, and H.264. In May of 2010, Adobe announced that it would also support Google's open source VP8 video codec. Each codec has its advantages and disadvantages; however, H.264 has become a standard for video on the Web.

Currently, AIR for Android applications support the Sorensen Spark, On2 VP6, and H.264 video formats. These video formats can be integrated with your application a number of different ways. You can bundle them with your application as a separate file and play them with a `NetStream` object. You can progressively download a video over the network from one of your Web servers. You can use a Flash Media Server to stream the video to your device. Finally, you can embed the video on a Timeline inside your Flash file.

All of these methods produce different results, and it depends on your desired goals in order to pick what method works best for you. The following sections of this chapter discuss more about each method.

Currently, H.264 videos with the AAC audio codec are not supported on Android 2.1, code name *Eclair,* but will work on Android 2.2, code name *FroYo.* This may factor in to which codec you will use for your content. If your video does not have audio embedded in it, you should have no issues with H.264. However, targeting only Android 2.2 and higher will limit the amount of users who can install your application.

Explore Available Video Formats and Encode a Video File

Encode a Video File

 Open Adobe Media Encoder CS5.

Note: You can find the encoder in the folder /Applications/Adobe Media Encoder CS5/ on Mac OS X and in the Adobe Media Encoder CS5 folder in your Program Files directory in Windows.

2 Click Add.

The Open dialog box appears.

3 Navigate to and select the video file to encode.

4 Click Open.

5 Click here and select a video format, such as FLV | F4V.

Note: FLV is a Flash Video file, and F4V is a Flash renamed MP4 file. With this option, you are given the choice of several presets with different associated codecs.

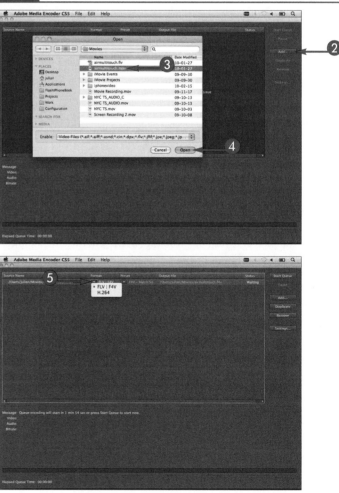

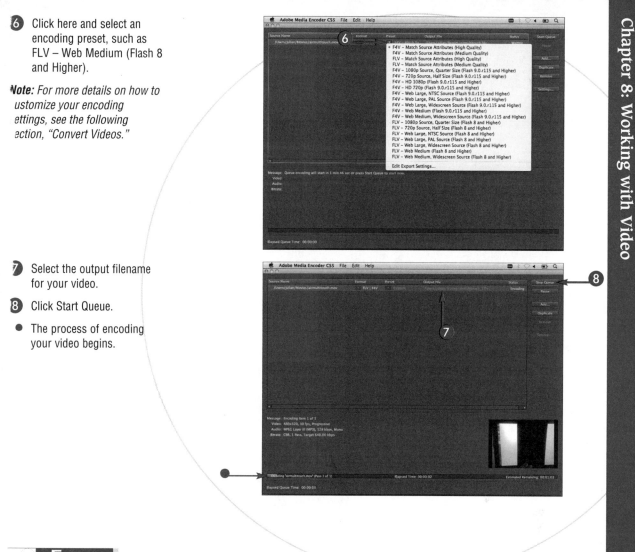

6 Click here and select an encoding preset, such as FLV – Web Medium (Flash 8 and Higher).

Note: For more details on how to customize your encoding settings, see the following section, "Convert Videos."

7 Select the output filename for your video.

8 Click Start Queue.

● The process of encoding your video begins.

Extra

Playing video can be an expensive process on the hardware of your device. When playing video, try to have as little else going on in your application as possible. This allows the CPU to use as much processing power as it can to ensure the fastest decoding and smoothest playback possible.

Also, try to minimize the amount of ActionScript that you have executing while the video is playing. Running timers and enter frame loops as well as the Timelines will have an impact on how well your video plays back.

Try to also minimize the amount of other visual elements that are redrawn on the screen at the same time the video is playing back. This is especially true for elements that intersect or overlap the video in any way. Even if these elements are underneath the video and hidden from view, they will still be redrawn and take up precision processing power.

If you need to add controls for your video, try not to place them on top of it. Instead, place them below the video or at any location where they will not overlap. If you need to update the visual state of the controls, do so as infrequently as possible. For example, instead of updating the progress every frame, do so every second.

Convert
Videos

There is a real science to converting your videos into a Flash video format. Every single video is going to compress differently at the same compression settings. Getting the best results for your videos will take some time and lots of experimenting.

The most important thing to do when converting your video is to make sure that the final video is the same dimensions as it will be when it is played back. If your application has to scale the video in order to make it fit, you will be causing unnecessary performance increases when playing it back.

There are a number of applications that enable you to convert your video. When you installed Flash CS5, you had the option to install Adobe Media Encoder C5 as well. This application does everything you will need in order to encode your videos in any Flash video format.

After you have selected a video to encode, you can adjust the settings to best suit your needs. To encode your video in the On2 VP6 video format, be sure to select FLV on the Format tab of the Export Settings window.

On the Video tab, set the size of your video to the final dimensions that you want. If you have to resize your video, make sure to resize it in the same aspect ratio as your original. In the Frame Rate drop-down list, select the frames per second that you want, setting this to the same as your source so that the converted video will use the same FPS as your source video. The Bitrate level drop-down list has several preset values that you can use, and the Custom option will give you more control.

The Audio tab enables you to set the compression settings for the audio in your video.

Convert Videos

① In Adobe Media Encoder CS5, click Add and choose the video to convert.

The video is added to the queue.

② Select your video in the list.

③ Click Settings.

Note: *For more details on how to add a video to the queue, see the preceding section, "Explore Available Video Formats and Encode a Video File."*

The Export Settings window appears.

④ Click here to check Export Video.

⑤ Click here to check Export Audio.

⑥ Click the Format tab.

⑦ Click here to select FLV.

8 Click the Video tab.

9 Click Resize Video.

10 Set the width of the video, such as 480.

11 Set the height of the video, such as 320.

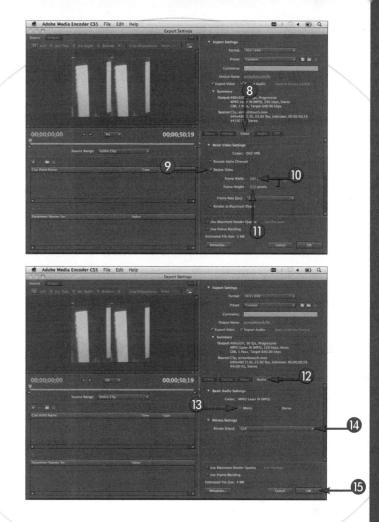

12 Click the Audio tab.

13 Set your audio to be Mono or Stereo.

14 Click here and select the bitrate of your audio, such as 128.

15 Click OK.

You are returned to the main screen.

16 Click Start Queue.

The process of converting your video begins.

Extra

There are a number of features in the Adobe Media Encoder application that go beyond just encoding your video. On the left side of the application, there are a number of tools that allow you to select only portions of your video to encode. You can trim the video from the start or the end to encode a subsection of your video.

You can also select the Crop tool, which is located on the Source tab, to crop unwanted parts of your video out. You can also make sure to crop your video to a specific aspect ratio, which helps you keep dimensions constrained.

You can also add cue points at specific times throughout your video. There are two types of cue points. *Navigation cue points* are placed on a key frame in your video. These are used for items such as bookmarks or as entry points into your video. *Event cue points* are placed at a specific time and are usually used to trigger other events in your application. To capture the cue points in ActionScript, set the `client` property on the `NetStream` object of your video.

Embed a Video

Y, ou can embed your video into your Flash file and place it on the Timeline. This enables you to control the video just as you would the Timeline of a MovieClip. When you import your video inside your Flash file, it will be compiled inside the binary of your application. When your application loads, it loads the entire binary into memory. This can create unnecessary memory overhead for your application, which may not be desirable. If you plan on playing your video often throughout your application, then having it always in memory may be a good idea, as loading it into memory can cause a decrease in performance.

Importing a video into your file is the same process as importing other media types, such as images and audio. However, after you select the video file that you want to

import, you will be presented with several options on how you would like it imported.

The first page of the Import Video dialog box will ask you the location of your video file, and the file that you selected will be preselected. The second page of the dialog box will give you options on how you would like to embed the video in your application. There are three different symbol types to choose from: embedded video, movie clip, and graphic. Selecting Embedded Video will import your video to the Library. Selecting Movie Clip will import your video to the Library as well as create a MovieClip symbol with the video placed on its Timeline. Selecting Graphic will import your video to the Library and create a Graphic symbol with your video on its Timeline.

You also have the option to place the instance on the Stage and expand its Timeline if needed.

Embed a Video

1. In Flash, click File.

2. Click Import.

3. Click Import Video.

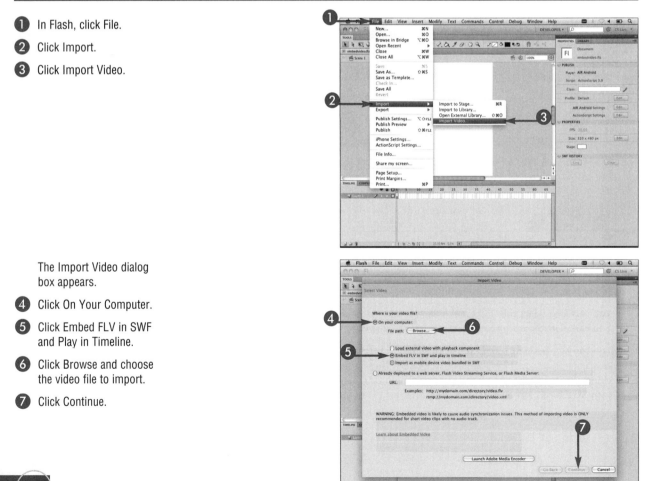

The Import Video dialog box appears.

4. Click On Your Computer.

5. Click Embed FLV in SWF and Play in Timeline.

6. Click Browse and choose the video file to import.

7. Click Continue.

The Embedding page of the dialog box appears.

8 Click here and select a symbol type, such as Embedded Video.

9 Click Place Instance on Stage.

10 Click Expand Timeline If Needed.

11 Click Include Audio, if your video has audio.

12 Click Continue.

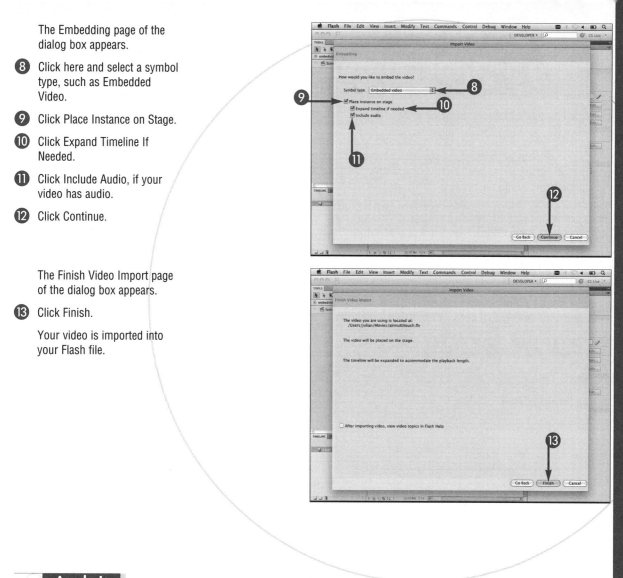

The Finish Video Import page of the dialog box appears.

13 Click Finish.

Your video is imported into your Flash file.

Apply It

You can also import a video into a separate Flash file and compile it as a separate .swf file. You can then load this video into your application at runtime. Embedding your video onto a Timeline enables you to control the video like a `MovieClip` symbol as opposed to a `NetStream` object. This can be advantageous in certain situations as it allows your application to control visual assets with a common interface.

Loading your SWF file is similar to loading other assets:

```
var loader:Loader = new Loader();
var request:URLRequest = new URLRequest( "video.swf" );
loader.load( request );
```

Bundle a Video with Your Application

As well as import videos to the Library of your Flash file, you can bundle them with your application when it is compiled. This includes the file inside your application package at the same level as your application binary.

When a user loads your application on his or her device, it takes a few seconds for the application to load and start up. The time that it takes to load an application varies from application to application. When an application is loaded, your entire application binary is loaded into memory. The bigger the file size of your application binary, the longer it will take to load, and the more memory it will use for the duration of the session.

Bundling your video with your application externally from your application binary will keep the file size of your application lower. It will also give you more control over the memory consumption of your application.

Determining which method to use when delivering and using video in your application will require some experimentation. Many games and other applications play a short video as an introduction, which is never played again. This type of video is a great example of when to bundle the video with your application.

You can add your video files to be bundled with your application on the General tab of the AIR Android Settings dialog box. There are three icons above the list on this screen that allow you to add files and folders, as well as remove items from the list. Adding a folder to the list will cause its contents to be bundled with it.

Bundle a Video with Your Application

1 Click File.

2 Click AIR Android Settings.

The Application & Installer Settings dialog box appears.

3 Click the + button.

The Open dialog box appears.

④ Navigate to and select the video file to bundle with your application, such as airmultitouch.flv.

⑤ Click Open.

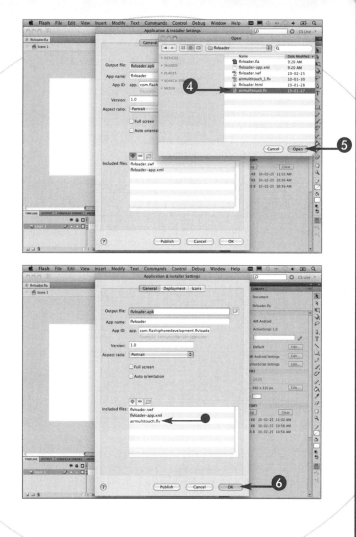

You are returned to the Application & Installer Settings dialog box.

● Your file appears in the Included Files list.

⑥ Click OK.

When your application is compiled, your image file will now be bundled with it.

Extra

Android AIR applications have the ability to play video streams from a Flash Media Server. Streaming video files is done over RTMP (real time messaging protocol). You can download and purchase Adobe Flash Media Streaming Server 3.5 from the Adobe Web site, www.adobe.com. This allows you to set up and run the server yourself. Additionally, you can install it on your development machine to use for testing for free.

If you are unable to set up and install a server on your own, there are many hosted solutions that you can use. Influxis, at www.influxis.com, is one of the premiere Flash Media Server hosting companies available. Its staff are experts in the field and can walk you through every step in order to get your videos online.

Streaming video to the phone can use up a lot of data over the network. You will want to make sure that your users are aware that the video is streaming so that they can make sure they are connected to a WiFi hotspot. Your customers will be angry if your application uses up their data plan without their knowing it.

Load
a Video

L oading a video file can be done from the file system of the device or over the Internet. This method of loading a video is sometimes referred to as a *progressive download*. This is similar to how YouTube loads and plays a video.

To load a video, you will need to create an instance of a NetConnection object and an instance of a NetStream object. The NetConnection class is often used to connect to a Flash Remoting or Flash Media Server. However, in this instance, it will not be connecting to a server, but you still need to call the connect method. The NetStream object is a channel within the NetConnection object, which will receive the stream data of your video.

The Video class is a DisplayObject, which is used to display the video stream data of the NetStream object.

It can be added to the display list just like all the other DisplayObjects that you are familiar with, such as MovieClip. There is a method on the Video class called attachNetStream(), which allows it to display any video data that it receives from the NetStream.

To start playing your video, you use the play() method on the NetStream object. You will pass the filename of your video in as an argument into the play() method. Once called, your video will begin to load and start to play.

When your video starts to play, you can monitor the bytesLoaded and bytesTotal properties on the NetStream object. This will enable you to monitor the loading of your video and display it to the user. This is necessary only if you are loading a video from the Internet, as a video from the file system should load quickly.

Load a Video

① Create a NetConnection variable, such as var nc:NetConnection = new NetConnection();.

② Connect the NetConnection variable, such as nc.connect(null);.

③ Create a NetStream variable, such as var ns:NetStream = new NetStream(nc);.

④ Play a stream, such as ns.play("airmultitouch.flv");.

Note: This will play a video that is bundled with your application.

⑤ Create a Video variable, such as var vid:Video = new Video();.

⑥ Set the width of the video, such as vid.width = 480;.

⑦ Set the height of the video, such as vid.height = 320;.

⑧ Add the video to the display list, such as addChild(vid);.

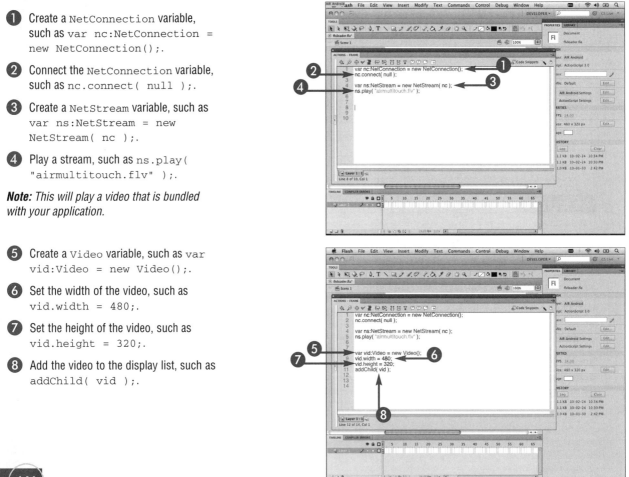

9 Set the x position of the video, such as `vid.x = 0;`.

10 Set the y position of the video, such as `vid.y = 0;`.

11 Attach the stream to the video, such as `vid.attachNetStream( ns );`.

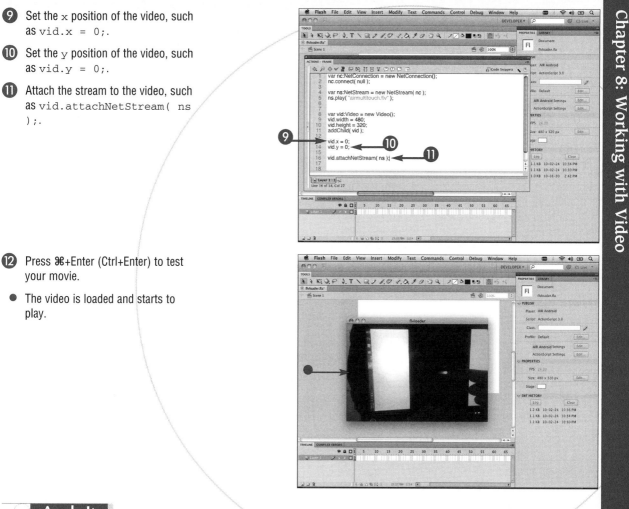

12 Press ⌘+Enter (Ctrl+Enter) to test your movie.

● The video is loaded and starts to play.

Apply It

The metadata of a video contains important information about the video. Each video encoder will embed different information into its metadata; however, most set at the very least the width, height, and duration of the video. You can retrieve the metadata of your video by creating an `onMetaData` method on the object that is set to the `client` property of the `NetStream` instance:

```
var nc:NetConnection = new NetConnection();
nc.connect( null );
var ns:NetStream = new NetStream( nc );
ns.client = this;
function onMetaData( info:Object ):void{
trace( info.width, info.height, info.duration );
}
```

If your video has metadata embedded inside of it and you do not implement this, you will receive an error similar to the following:

```
flash.net.NetStream was unable to invoke callback onMetaData.
```

Buffer a Video

When using progressive download to load a video over the Internet, you will want to implement some buffering techniques that will give your user the best playback possible. When you play a video, it does not wait for it to be loaded before it plays. The NetStream object fills up its buffer and then plays all the data in the buffer. As data in the buffer is played and emptied, the NetStream object tries to download more of the video and place it in the buffer, keeping it full. This helps deal with bandwidth fluctuation and gets your video playing as quickly as possible.

A good buffering technique to implement is called *dual threshold buffering.* This allows you to set a very low buffer time, in order to get the video playing as quickly as possible. Then when the initial buffer is full, switch to a larger buffer size to allow for a more continuous playback. This technique enables you to deal with fluctuation bandwidth and keep your video playing as smoothly as possible.

You can listen for when the buffer is full and empty by listening to the NetStatusEvent.NET_STATUS event. This event is fired when there has been a change in status or error in the NetStream instance. There is an info property, which is an object, on the event that contains all the information about the new status. The info.level property specifies if the event is a status change or an error. The info.code property tells what specific event occurred. An event with an info.code value of NetStream.Buffer. Empty means that the buffer is empty, and NetStream. Buffer.Full means that the buffer is full.

Buffer a Video

① Create a Video variable, such as
```
var vid:Video = new
Video();.
```

② Set the width of the video, such as
```
vid.width = 480;.
```

③ Set the height of the video, such as
```
vid.height = 320;.
```

④ Add the video to the display list, such as `addChild( vid );`.

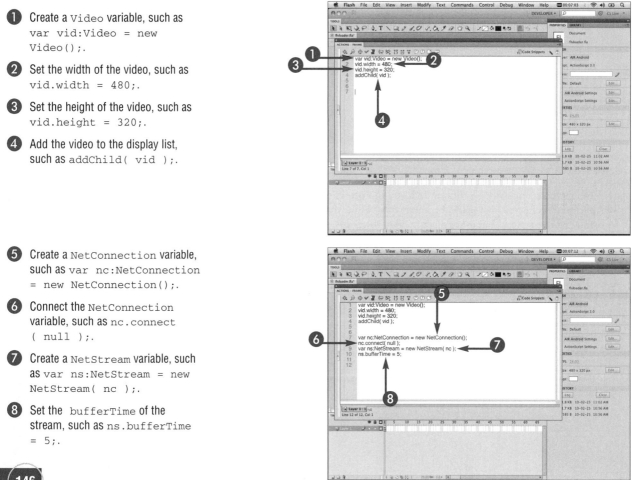

⑤ Create a NetConnection variable, such as `var nc:NetConnection = new NetConnection();`.

⑥ Connect the NetConnection variable, such as `nc.connect ( null );`.

⑦ Create a NetStream variable, such as `var ns:NetStream = new NetStream( nc );`.

⑧ Set the bufferTime of the stream, such as `ns.bufferTime = 5;`.

9. Set the `client` property, such as `ns.client = this;`.

10. Create an `onMetaData` function on the `client` object.

11. Listen for `NetStatusEvent.NET_STATUS` events on the stream.

12. Create an event handler function, such as `onStatus`.

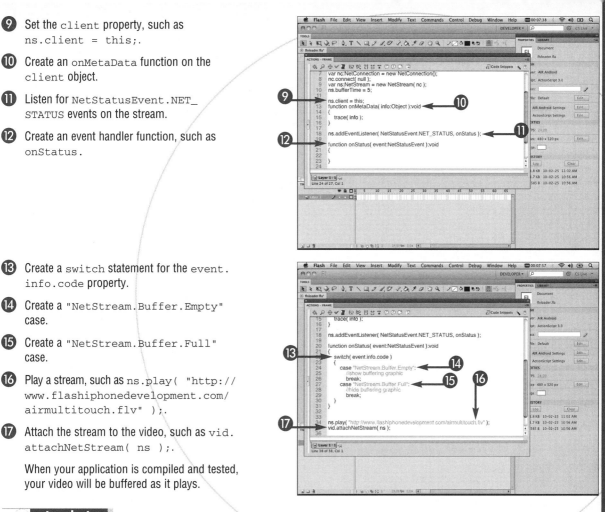

13. Create a `switch` statement for the `event.info.code` property.

14. Create a `"NetStream.Buffer.Empty"` case.

15. Create a `"NetStream.Buffer.Full"` case.

16. Play a stream, such as `ns.play( "http://www.flashiphonedevelopment.com/airmultitouch.flv" );`.

17. Attach the stream to the video, such as `vid.attachNetStream( ns );`.

When your application is compiled and tested, your video will be buffered as it plays.

Apply It

There are many other useful messages that get sent with a `NetStatusEvent.NET_STATUS` event when fired. `NetStream.Play.StreamNotFound` is fired when you try to play a video file that does not exist. `NetStream.Play.Start` and `NetStream.Play.Stop` are fired when the stream is being started and stopped. `NetStream.Pause.Notify` and `NetStream.Unpause.Notify` are fired when the stream has been paused and then resumed. Here is an example:

```
function onNetStatus( event:NetStatusEvent ):void {
switch( event.info.code ){
case "NetStream.Play.StreamNotFound":
break;
case "NetStream.Play.Start":
break;
case "NetStream.Play.Stop":
break;
case "NetStream.Pause.Notify":
break;
case "NetStream.Unpause.Notify":
break;
}
}
```

147

Control
a Video

After you have your video playing and buffering properly, it is time to add some controls. When creating the visual elements for your controls, make sure that they do not overlap the video in any way. Doing so will cause them to be redrawn unnecessarily and take valuable CPU processing away from the video. This section will focus on the code behind your controls; it will be up to you to implement the interface in order to affect the video.

After your video has started playing, you will want to give the user the option to pause the video or stop the video. Pausing the video can be done by calling the `NetStream.pause()` method. This stops the video at its current position, while the buffer continues to fill. Currently, there is no `stop` method in the `NetStream` class; however, you

can properly implement stop functionality by pausing and then seeking to the beginning of the video.

You can seek to a specific time in the video using the `NetStream.seek()` method. The `seek` method seeks the video to the closest key frame at the location specified. This means that you will not always go to the exact time in seconds that you specified, but to the closest key frame before or after.

To resume a video that is currently paused, call the `NetStream.resume()` method. If the video is already playing, calling this method will have no effect.

When the user has finished watching the video and has moved onto a different section in your application, you want to make sure that you close the video stream. This will stop all data that is currently playing in the stream and make the stream available for another use, such as playing a different video.

Control a Video

① Click Window.

② Click Common Libraries.

③ Click Buttons.

The Buttons Library panel appears.

④ Select buttons to use as video controls.

⑤ Drag them to the Stage.

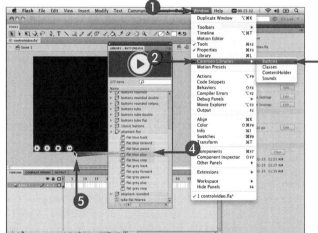

⑥ Select a button on the Stage.

⑦ Give it an instance name, such as `play_btn`.

⑧ Repeat steps **6** and **7** for each button.

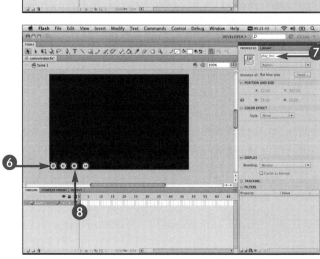

Note: *The code shown here continues the example from the section "Buffer a Video."*

9 In the Actions panel, add a click event listener and an event handler for the Play button.

10 Resume the stream, such as `ns.resume();`.

11 Add a click event listener and an event handler for the Pause button.

12 Pause the stream, such as `ns.pause();`.

13 Create a click event listener and an event handler for the Stop button.

14 Pause the stream, such as `ns.pause();`.

15 Seek to the beginning of the video, such as `ns.seek( 0 );`.

16 Create a click event listener and an event handler for the Forward button.

17 Seek the video 2 seconds from its current position, such as `ns.seek ( ns.time + 2.0 );`.

When your application is compiled and tested, your controls will be included with your video.

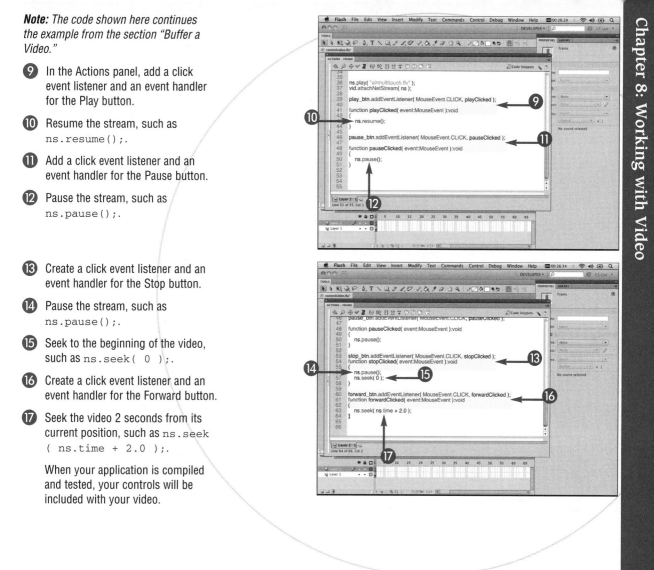

Apply It

The example in this section shows how you can pause and resume a `NetStream` instance by calling the `NetStream.pause()` and `NetStream.resume()` methods. There is also a nice convenience method implemented on the `NetStream` class called `togglePause()`. Calling this method will either pause or resume the stream, depending on what current state it is in. This makes your pause and resume logic a lot simpler, and you have to implement only one method and one button that changes its visual state when clicked:

```
function togglePause():void
{
stream.togglePause();
}
```

Set the Volume of a Video

Y ou set the volume of a video through the NetStream object. Similar to the SoundChannel class, the NetStream class has a soundTransform property, which can be used to affect the volume of your video.

The soundTransform property is set to an instance of the SoundTransform class. Setting the value of the volume property on an instance of the SoundTransform class will adjust the volume. This value is a number between 0 and 1. Setting the volume to 0 will mute the audio, whereas setting it to 1 will set the audio to full volume.

In order to set the volume of the NetStream, you must reset its soundTransform property every time that you want to adjust the volume. This means that accessing the volume property of a previously set soundTransform instance will

not adjust the volume of the sound that is currently playing. For example, the following code would not affect the volume of the sound track currently being played in a video:

```
stream.soundTransform.volume = 0.5;
```

This is true for all objects that have soundTransform properties, such as MovieClip and SoundChannel.

Keep in mind that some users will be using headphones when using your application. This makes it extremely important to set the initial volume of your video so that it mixes well with all the other sounds in your application. The more control that you can give the users with regards to the volume of the audio in your application, the better the users' experience will be. The last thing that you want is the users to rip their headphones off their heads because the sound is too loud or mute the sound altogether because it is poorly mixed.

Set the Volume of a Video

1. Create a Volume On button symbol.

2. Create a Volume Off button symbol.

Note: For more details on how to create button symbols, see Chapter 2, "Getting Started with Flash CS5."

3. Place both buttons on the Stage at the same location.

4. Give them instance names, such as on_btn and off_btn.

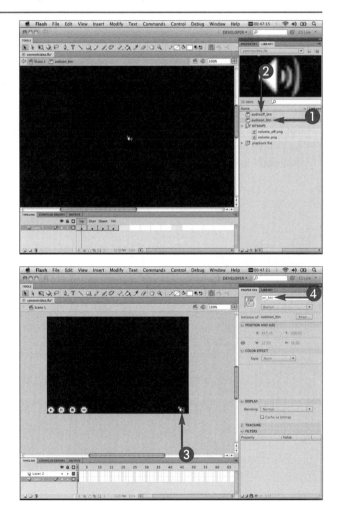

Note: *The code shown here continues the example from the section "Control a Video."*

⑤ Hide the On button.

⑥ Create a click event listener and an event handler for the On button.

⑦ Set the volume of the stream to 1, such as `ns.soundTransform = new SoundTransform( 1 );`.

⑧ Hide the On button.

⑨ Show the Off button.

⑩ Create a click event listener and an event handler for the Off button.

⑪ Set the volume of the stream to 0, such as `ns.soundTransform = new SoundTransform( 0 );`.

⑫ Show the On button.

⑬ Hide the Off button.

When your application is compiled and tested, buttons to turn the volume on and off will be included with your video.

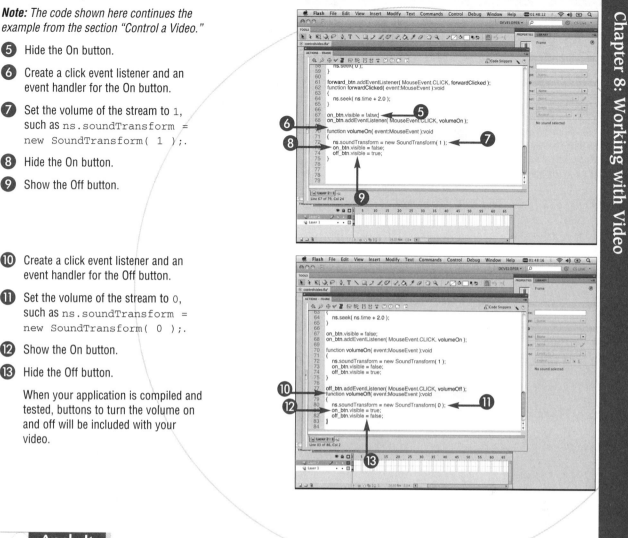

Apply It

Because users will often be using headphones when using your application, panning the audio can have a great impact on the user experience. A great example of this is the Mail application for Mac OS X. The default sound for when you successfully send an email is a swooshing sound that pans from left to right. It is not a feature that would cause you to use that email application over another, but you could argue that it definitely adds to the experience.

Setting the pan of your sounds can be done through the `SoundTransform.pan` method. This method functions in the same manner as the `volume` property. However, the `pan` property values range from -1 to 1. A value of -1 pans a sound fully to the left speaker, a value of 1 pans a sound fully to the right speaker, and a value of 0 sets the pan of the sounds to be in the center.

Here is an example of setting the audio of a video to be panned fully to the left speaker:

```
var transform:SoundTransform = new SoundTransform();
transform.pan = -1;
ns.soundTransform = transform;
```

Embed Fonts in Your Application

n order for your text to appear properly in your application, you will need to embed the fonts used in your application. Android devices come with a very limited set of fonts pre-installed on them, so it is recommended that you embed all your fonts. You need to specifically embed fonts only when they are used in dynamic text fields because fonts in static text fields are automatically included with your application.

The process for embedding fonts in Flash CS5 has greatly improved. Previously to Flash CS5, fonts were embedded on a dynamic or an input text field. If you accidentally embedded extra characters that you did not need, you would have to track down the text field in your file and adjust it. Flash CS5 now has a Font Embedding dialog

box that allows you to manage all your embedded fonts from a single location.

In this dialog box, you can select fonts to embed in your application, as well as its character set. It is important to embed only the characters that are required for your application because the more characters you embed, the bigger the file size of your application will be.

You can also export your fonts so that you can access them from ActionScript. This allows you to set the font of a `TextField` instance dynamically.

When choosing a font to use in your application, it is important to understand the font license agreement of that font. If you have downloaded a font to use from the Internet, make sure to check that you have the proper permissions before using it.

Embed Fonts in Your Application

Embed a Font in Your Application

1. Click the Text tool.

2. Click here and select Classic Text.

3. Click here and select Dynamic Text.

4. Drag a text field on the Stage.

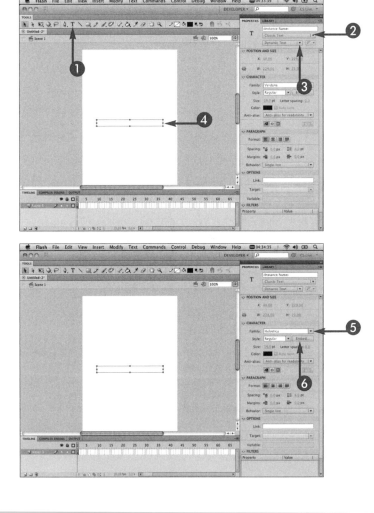

5. Click here and select a font, such as Helvetica.

6. Click Embed.

The Font Embedding dialog box appears.

7 Click Uppercase.

8 Click Lowercase.

9 Click Numerals.

10 Click Punctuation.

The font will now be embedded with your application when it is compiled.

Export for ActionScript

11 Click the ActionScript tab.

12 Click Export for ActionScript.

13 Give the font a class name, such as Helvetica.

14 Click OK.

The font can now be accessed and used with ActionScript.

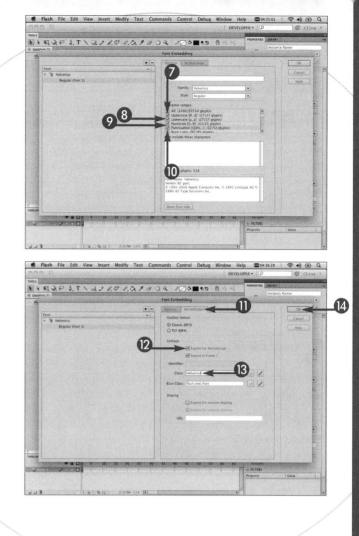

Extra

The new Font Embedding dialog box is a big improvement in managing the fonts and characters that are embedded in your application. There is, however, another way to a summary of every single character for every font that is embedded in your final application. In the Publish Settings dialog box on the Flash tab, there is Generate Size Report check box. Selecting this will generate a report of all the assets in your file and how much of the final file size of your application they account for. When your application is compiled, the report can be viewed in the Output panel. A text file is also created in the same directory as your SWF file, which allows you to compare reports as you develop.

In the Fonts section, you will be able to see each character that you have embedded for a specific font. This allows you to make sure that you are embedding only the characters that you need, which gives you a greater control over the final file size of your application.

The size report also shows you the file sizes of all your images, sounds, and embedded videos.

Create an Input TextField

Adobe has done a great job of creating the same experience for the users when they are inputting text in an AIR for Android application compared to that of a native Android application. Any input text field in your application will have all the same features by default, such as predictive text.

When selecting a font for your input `TextField`, make sure that your fonts are embedded into your application. This will ensure that your fonts are rendered properly when inputting text. For more details on embedding fonts, see the preceding section, "Embed Fonts in Your Application."

If you want the predictive text to appear, make sure that your text field is high enough for it to be visible.

When a user touches an input field in order to start typing, the keyboard will automatically appear. If your content is at the bottom of the screen, your content will automatically be pushed up in order to show it above the keyboard. When your user is finished inputting text, the keyboard will disappear, and your content will be readjusted to its original position. This is convenient because it makes sure that your content is always visible to your user, without your having to manage it.

Currently, you cannot control the type of keyboard that appears for a specific `TextField`. You may have noticed with some Android applications that the SDK has several different keyboard types, such as a number pad and a URL keyboard, just to name a few. Currently, AIR for Android applications by default use the default alphabet keyboard.

Create an Input TextField

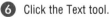

① Click the Text tool.

② Click here and select Classic Text.

③ Click here and select Static Text.

④ Create a label on the Stage.

⑤ Type text for your label, such as **username:**.

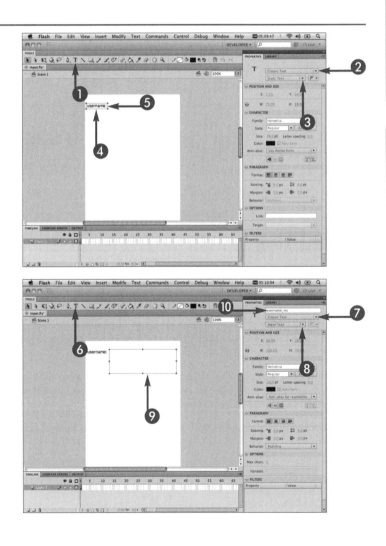

⑥ Click the Text tool.

⑦ Click here and select Classic Text.

⑧ Click here and select Input Text.

⑨ Create an input field on the Stage.

⑩ Give it an instance name, such as `username_txt`.

⑪ Click here and select a device font, such as Helvetica.

⑫ Click here and select Use Device Fonts.

⑬ Click the background button to create a border around your text field.

The text field is set to receive user input.

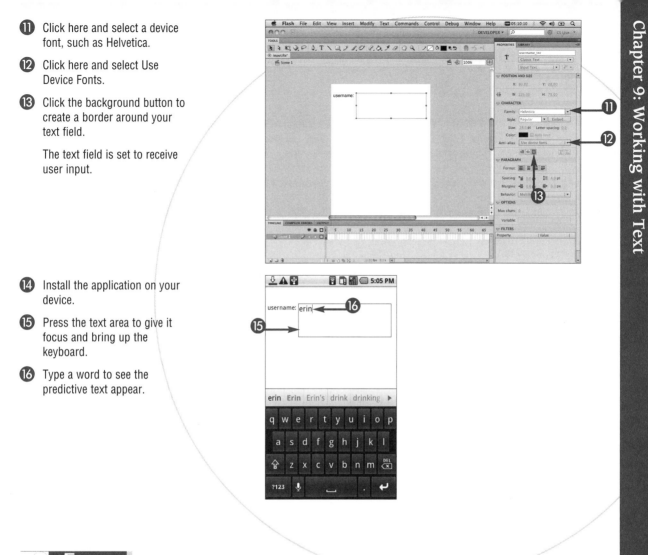

⑭ Install the application on your device.

⑮ Press the text area to give it focus and bring up the keyboard.

⑯ Type a word to see the predictive text appear.

Extra

The keyboard layout can vary between Android devices. Some devices have a hide keyboard button, whereas others do not. To ensure that the keyboard is hidden across devices, the text input field must lose focus. The easiest way for this to occur is when the user touches the screen anywhere outside the bounds of an input `TextField`. This is not very intuitive for users. However, you can take advantage of this by creating a visual element, such as a cancel button, that when pressed by the user will hide the keyboard. The interesting thing about this method is that you do not need to create any listeners for that button in ActionScript in order to close the keyboard. When the user touches the screen over the button, the keyboard will automatically hide. If the user touches another input text field, the keyboard will stay shown, allowing the user to enter text into that field.

Pressing the Back key on the device will also hide the keyboard. This functionality happens automatically in the AIR Runtime, and you do not have to listen for the key press.

Create a Password TextField

O ne of the most common items that a user will input into your application is a login credential. This usually includes a password field, in which the user's input is often masked for security reasons. This prevents somebody from getting a hold of your device and being able to see your password if it is stored somewhere on the device.

When the user types into a password field, the last character that was pressed will show unmasked for a certain period of time or until he or she presses another character. This allows the user to make sure that he or she hit the correct character on the on-screen keyboard. Password text fields do not use the auto correction feature of your device.

Setting the `displayAsPassword` property on the `TextField` class enables you to hide the input characters by using asterisks or circles instead of showing the characters. When a `TextField` is set to be a password-enabled `TextField`, the copy commands will be disabled. This is a security measure to stop people from retrieving passwords from a device that is not theirs.

When allowing your users to log in in your application, it is a good practice to allow them to have their credentials stored on the device. This would allow the application to automatically log the users in, saving them from having to type their username and password every time that they start the application. There are several ways to store this information on the device, which are explored in more detail in Chapter 10, "Saving State."

Create a Password TextField

Note: You can combine the steps in the preceding section, "Create an Input TextField," with this one to create a login form.

1. Click the Text tool.
2. Click here and select Classic Text.
3. Click here and select Static Text.
4. Create a label on the Stage.
5. Type text for your label, such as **password:**.

6. Click the Text tool.
7. Click here and select Classic Text.
8. Click here and select Input Text.
9. Create an input field on the Stage.
10. Give it an instance name, such as `password_txt`.

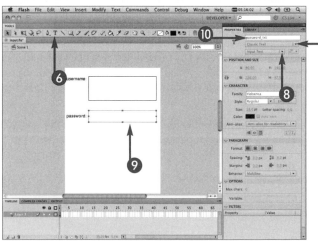

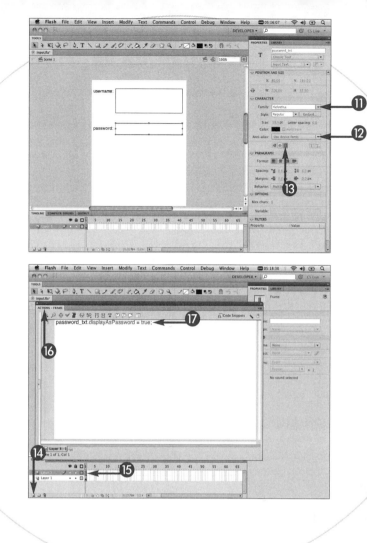

⑪ Click here and select a device font, such as Helvetica.

⑫ Click here and select Use Device Fonts.

⑬ Click the background button to create a border around your text field.

The text field is set to receive user input.

⑭ Click the New Layer button.

A new layer is added to the Timeline.

⑮ Select a frame to which to add ActionScript.

⑯ Open the Actions panel.

⑰ Set the text field to display as a password, such as `password_txt.displayAsPassword = true;`.

The password characters will now be hidden as they are typed.

Apply It

If you are creating a form that has several input fields, you may want to give the user the ability to go to the next field without pressing it to give it focus. This is especially true when the keyboard is visible and hiding the next input `TextField`. Most Android applications that give users this ability supply a Next button directly above the keyboard. Tapping the Next button will force the focus to the next `TextField` in the form. To change the focus from one `TextField` to another, set the `focus` property of the `stage`:

```
function onNextButtonClicked( event:TouchEvent ):void
{
stage.focus = nextTextField_txt;
}
```

Without a Next button, the user will have to tap outside of the text field area to hide the keyboard to select the next input text field. This can be very annoying if there are many fields and will cause the user to take longer to completely fill out your form.

Using TLF TextFields

Adobe has created a new Text Layout Framework (TLF), which is an extensible ActionScript library built on top of the new text-rendering engine in Flash Player 10. The text engine solves many of the problems that Flash has faced over the years when it comes to text.

The new framework supports bidirectional text, vertical text, and over 30 writing systems, including Arabic, Hebrew, Chinese, Japanese, Korean, Thai, Lao, and the major writing systems of India. TLF also gives you greater control over kerning, ligature, case, digit case, and digit width.

You are also able to create additional text containers or columns and have your text flow from one to the other automatically and flow around inline images. TLF also supports proper copying and pasting and undoing when

editing text. This is not the same as the method used by Android applications, as this is available on all text field types.

Previously, there was a major workflow issue with fonts between the Mac OS X and Windows development environments. Sometimes your text fields would shift position in your FLA file when opened on Mac OS X. This has caused major problems when working in large teams and with clients. The new text engine has solved these issues to allow for a more consistent workflow between platforms.

Because the Text Layout Framework is written in ActionScript, you could see some performance decreases when using some of its advanced features. When using the new text framework, your file links to the textLayout. swc file, which contains all the ActionScript code for the framework.

Using TLF TextFields

1 Click the Text tool.

2 Click here and select TLF Text.

3 Click here and select a type, such as Read Only.

4 Draw a text field on the Stage.

5 Type some text, such as **Hello World**.

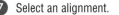

6 Click here and select Use Device Fonts.

7 Select an alignment.

The TLF text field is created.

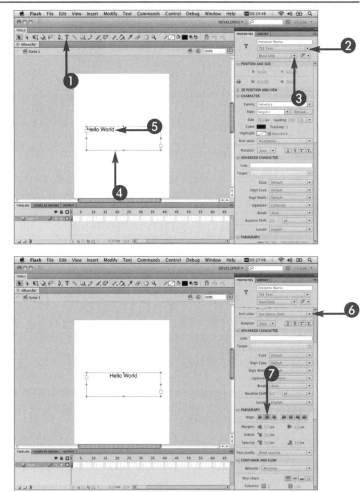

8 Click File.

9 Click ActionScript Settings.

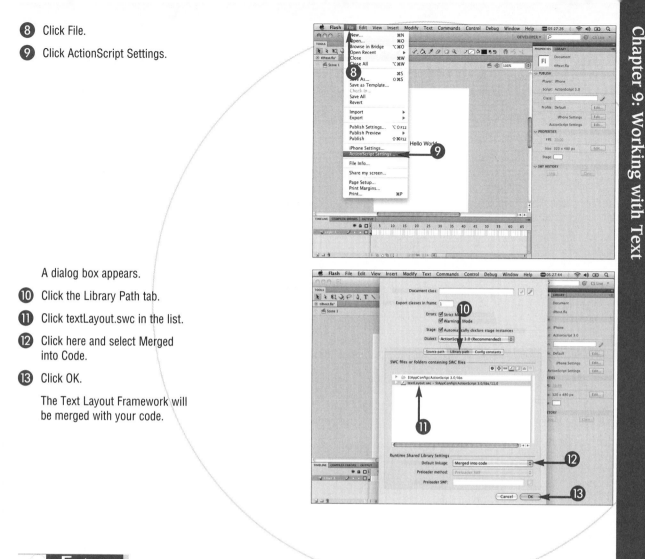

A dialog box appears.

10 Click the Library Path tab.

11 Click textLayout.swc in the list.

12 Click here and select Merged into Code.

13 Click OK.

The Text Layout Framework will be merged with your code.

Extra

The new Text Layout Framework has provided developers and designers with a rich set of text controls in order to create the next generation text-based applications. This could not have come at a better time because the mobile reader market is about to explode, if it has not already. Devices such as the Amazon Kindle, Sony Reader, and Barnes & Noble nook already have a foothold in the mobile reader marketplace. However, new tablet devices are destined to take the industry to the next level. There are a number of Android tablet computers set to release in 2010 that will run Adobe AIR applications and Flash Player 10.1.

Content makers have already begun developing digital versions of their content. The *New York Times* has released an Adobe AIR application that allows users to read the latest articles online, in a format that is similar to what they would expect from the printed version. This experience would not be possible without the new columns and text flow containers in the Text Layout Framework. With the new mobile devices running AIR, the *New York Times* will be able to capitalize on another customer touch point and revenue stream.

Create a Scrollable TextField

Mobile devices have very limited screen real estate, and there will probably be times when you have a large piece of text that will need to be scrolled. The Flash Player for the desktop automatically scrolls the text field when you scroll the mouse wheel, when the mouse is over the top of the text field. Because there is no mouse wheel support on mobile devices, you will need to implement other methods.

One method would be to add all the text to the text field and change its height based on the amount of text. If the text field was a display container, you could move the container on the y-axis as the user's finger moves up and down.

Another way would be to change the scrollV property of the text field based on the current direction that the user

is scrolling. The `TextField.getLineIndexAtPoint()` method allows you to find the current line of text underneath a given x and y location. Using this method to track which line of text the user's finger is currently over allows you to determine which direction he or she wants to scroll the text. Comparing the current line that the finger is under with the last line from a previous frame will give you the difference in lines of text. Adding the difference to the current scrollV value will move the text up or down the same amount of lines as the difference.

This method allows you to have large amounts of text in a small text field and does not require more display objects or complicated caching methods.

Create a Scrollable TextField

1 Create a multiline text field on the Stage.

Note: See the section "Create an Input TextField" for more information.

2 Give it an instance name, such as text_txt.

3 Open the Actions panel.

4 Create an int variable, such as var startLine:int;.

5 Create another int variable, such as var lastLine:int;.

6 Set the text field to a large string.

7 Add a mouse down listener to the text field, such as text_txt.addEventListener(MouseEvent.MOUSE_DOWN, onPress);.

8 Create an event handler method, such as onPress.

9 Set the start line, such as startLine = text_txt.getLineIndexAtPoint (e.localX, e.localY);.

10 Set the last line to the start line, such as lastLine = startLine;.

11 Listen for the mouse up event on the text field, such as text_txt.addEventListener (MouseEvent.MOUSE_UP, stopScrolling);.

⑫ Add an enter frame listener, such as `addEventListener( Event.ENTER_ FRAME, onFrame );`.

⑬ Create an event handler, such as `stopScrolling`.

⑭ Remove the enter frame event listener.

⑮ Create an event handler, such as `onFrame`.

⑯ Get the text line under the finger, such as `var currentline = text_txt. getLineIndexAtPoint( text_txt. mouseX, text_txt.mouseY );`.

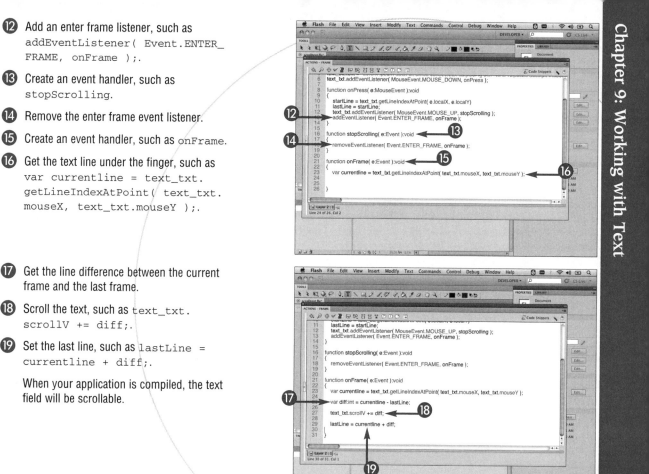

⑰ Get the line difference between the current frame and the last frame.

⑱ Scroll the text, such as `text_txt. scrollV += diff;`.

⑲ Set the last line, such as `lastLine = currentline + diff;`.

When your application is compiled, the text field will be scrollable.

Apply It

There are a few more cases in which you do not want to scroll the text. The `getLineIndexAtPoint()` method will return −1 if the point is not over the text field. If this is the case, you want to remove the event listener for the enter frame event. Also, you do not want to scroll the text if you are at the top or at the bottom of text. Adding the following code to the `onFrame` method after the `diff` variable will solve for these cases:

```
if( currentline == -1 ){
removeEventListener( Event.ENTER_FRAME, onFrame );
}
if( diff > 0 ){
if(text_txt.bottomScrollV==text_txt.maxScrollV+text_txt.numLines) return;
}
else if( diff < 0 ){
if( text_txt.scrollV == 0 ) return;
}
```

Create a Local SharedObject

Local shared objects, often referred to as *Flash cookies,* are data files that are created by Flash applications and stored locally on your machine. Flash Web applications and sites use local shared objects to store user information so that it can be retrieved upon the user's return. Unlike normal browser cookies, local shared object files are encoded in the ActionScript Message Format (AMF). This enables you to save complex objects such as `ByteArray` and does not limit you to simple text strings.

The ActionScript Message Format is a proprietary format created by Adobe that is used to serialize ActionScript objects so that they can be passed back and forth between other clients or servers. Flash applications use AMF when communicating with a Flash Remoting Server and Flash Media Server and to another Flash application through a `LocalConnection` instance.

Creating a local shared object in a Flash Android application creates a file in the /data/data/app.<appID>/<appID>/LocalStore/#SharedObjects directory. The name of the file is determined by the unique name that you entered in the `SharedObject.getLocal()` method. If the file already exists, the data from the file is returned to your `SharedObject` instance; if not, an empty file is created for you.

When you are creating a name for your local shared object, most characters are supported, with the exception of spaces and these specials: ~, %, &, \, ;, :, ", ', ,, <, >, ?, and #.

If, for whatever the reason, a local shared object cannot be created by the `getLocal()` method, an `Error` will be thrown. It is a good practice to surround the instantiation of your local shared object with a `try ... catch` statement in order to properly handle the error if it is thrown.

Create a Local SharedObject

① Select the frame on the Timeline to which to add ActionScript code.

② Open the Actions panel.

③ Create a `SharedObject` instance, such as `var so:SharedObject;`.

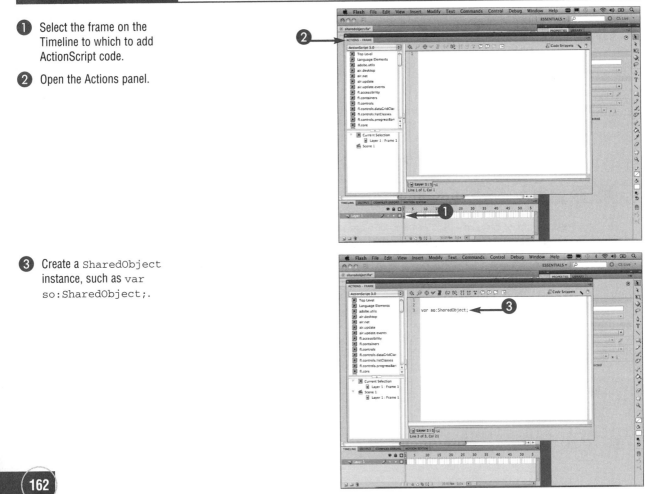

④ Get a reference to the local
`SharedObject`, such as =
`SharedObject.getLocal()`.

Note: If the `SharedObject` *does not exist,
it will be created.*

 ⑤ Type a name for your `SharedObject`,
such as `"scores"`.

The local `SharedObject` instance is
created.

Note: *The* `SharedObject` *file is not
created on the file system until data has
been written to it.*

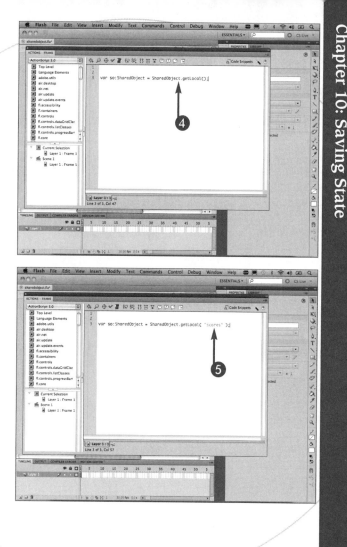

Extra

There are several different ways to explore the file system of your device in order to see if your `SharedObject` file was successfully written to the device. However, the /data folder on your device requires that you have root access in order to view the contents of the folder. By default, all Android devices do not allow you to gain access to this directory to view it, whether it is from a Terminal window or the Android Eclipse plug-in.

There are several ways you can gain access to the root user by unlocking your device. If you decide to do this, you must understand that this will void any warranties on your device and has the potential to lock you out of your device for good. Unlocking your device will also erase all of the data on it, so make sure to back everything up before attempting it.

One of the easier methods is to use Superboot, available at http://bit.ly/ceFYY5. Depending on your operating system, the instructions are slightly different; however, if you follow them, the process should take no more than about ten minutes.

Write to a SharedObject

After you have created your local shared object, you can write data to it. A SharedObject instance has a data property, which stores all the data in your local shared object. The data property is a simple Object and contains a collection of attributes and properties that you would like to save. These properties can be of any ActionScript type, such as ByteArray, XML, Array, Number, and Boolean.

Each piece of data that you want to save in a local shared object must be set as a property of the data property object. Directly assigning the data property to another object, such as myso.data = myobject;, will be ignored, and your data will not be saved.

After you have placed all the data that you want to save in your SharedObject instance data property, you can

call the flush() method to have it immediately saved to the file system of your device. If you choose not to use this method, the data will be written to the file system when the shared object session ends. This can occur if the SharedObject instance is garbage-collected because there are no longer any references to it or when your application closes. Be careful when relying on this method, as there are instances, such as your application crashing, in which your data may not be saved.

Writing data to the local file system of the device can be a performance-intensive task if done in short intervals. If you can avoid calling the flush() method every time that you store new data in the data property, you will see some performance gains.

Write to a SharedObject

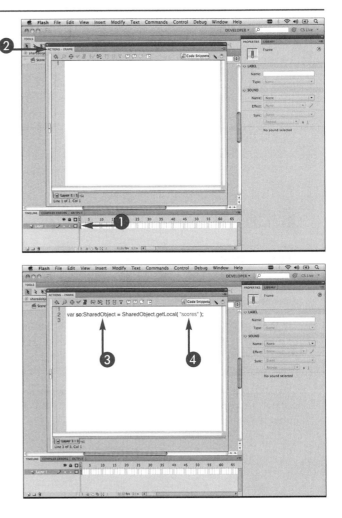

1. Select the frame on the Timeline to which to add ActionScript code.

2. Open the Actions panel.

3. Create a SharedObject instance, such as var so:SharedObject = SharedObject.getLocal();.

4. Type a name for your SharedObject, such as "scores".

5 Store a `String` variable in the `SharedObject`, such as `so.data.name = "julian";`.

6 Store an `int` variable in the `SharedObject`, such as `so.data.score = 1580;`.

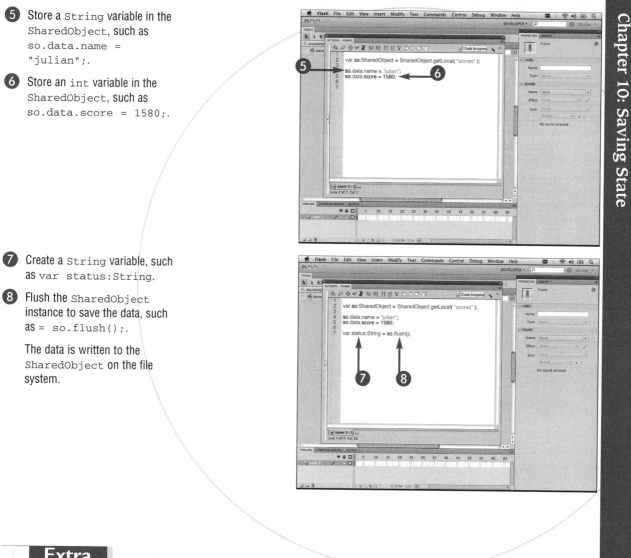

7 Create a `String` variable, such as `var status:String`.

8 Flush the `SharedObject` instance to save the data, such as `= so.flush();`.

The data is written to the `SharedObject` on the file system.

Extra

In addition to writing to a local shared object, you can delete any data that you have stored. If you want to delete a single property, you can use the `delete` keyword. Setting the property to null or undefined will not delete the value from the local shared object.

```
delete so.data.myattribute;
```

If you want to delete all the data from your local shared object at once, you can use the `clear()` method on the `SharedObject` class. This method purges all data and also deletes the shared object from the local file system of the device. The instance is still active; however, it no longer contains any data.

```
var so:SharedObject = SharedObject.getLocal( "scores" );
so.clear();
```

Load Data from a SharedObject

A local shared object stores its data as key value pairs in a file that is encoded with the ActionScript Message Format. When your SharedObject instance is instantiated by calling the SharedObject.getLocal() method, the file is decoded, and all the key value pairs are added to the data property object of your instance.

Reading the attributes from the data property is very similar to writing the data. For example, if you stored a username property in the local shared object, the syntax may look something like the following:

```
myso.data.username = "lori";
```

To retrieve the value of the username, simply place the property on the other side of the equals operator:

```
var username:String = myso.data.username as
  String;
```

Because the data property is a base ActionScript Object, it does not know the data types of all its properties and attributes. To get the best performance out of your ActionScript code, you will want to strongly type all your variables. This has a number of benefits besides the increase in performance. During development, if the compiler knows what data type your variable is, it allows you to use code hinting to see all the properties and methods associated with that class. It also can catch many compiler errors, especially if you are trying to pass the wrong type of object in as an argument to a function.

Using the as keyword enables you to cast an unknown variable to a specific data type. If the value that you are casting is not of that type, your variable will be set to null.

Load Data from a SharedObject

1. Select the frame on the Timeline to which to add ActionScript code.

2. Open the Actions panel.

3. Create a SharedObject instance, such as var so:SharedObject = SharedObject.getLocal();.

4. Enter a name for your SharedObject, such as "scores".

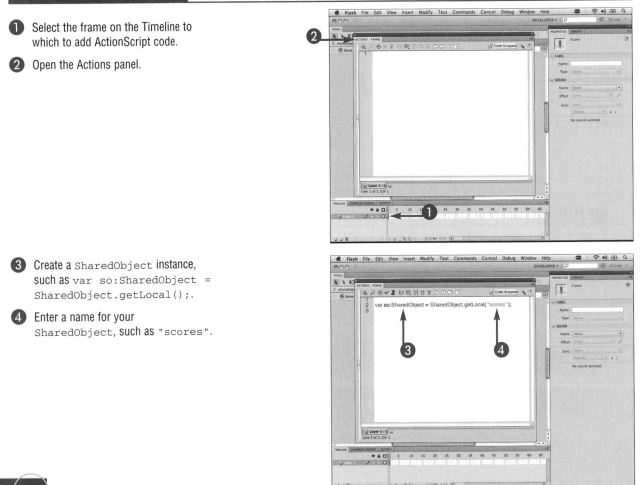

166

Note: *Save some data in your* `SharedObject`. *For more details, see the preceding section, "Write to a SharedObject."*

⑤ Retrieve a `String` variable, such as `var username:String = so.data.name as String;`.

⑥ Retrieve an `int` variable, such as `var score:int = so.data. score as int;`.

⑦ Trace your data, such as `trace ( username, score );`.

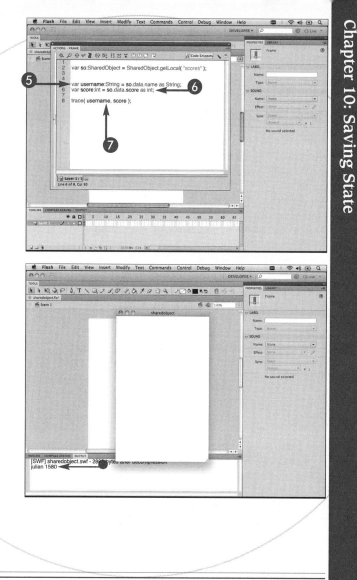

⑧ Press ⌘+Enter (Ctrl+Enter) to test your movie.

● The data that you retrieved is shown in the Output panel.

Apply It

If you are unsure of what properties and data you have stored in your local shared object, you can iterate over the `data` property. This enables you to inspect all the key value pairs that you have stored. Using the `for .. in` statement allows you to iterate over all the dynamic properties of an object. All fixed properties, such as variables and methods defined in the class definition, are omitted from enumeration. Properties are kept in no particular order and can appear to be random. The order in which your properties appear when iterating over its object will be different every time and should not be relied on. Here is an example:

```
for (var prop:String in so.data )
{
    trace(prop, "=", so.data[ prop ]);
}
```

Connect to a SQLite Database

With the release of Adobe AIR 1.0, we were introduced to a set of ActionScript APIs to communicate with SQLite databases. These allowed developers to store and retrieve information in their applications. The Android OS also has a SQLite framework, which enables you to communicate with SQLite databases through the same set of ActionScript APIs.

The SQLConnection class is used to manage the creation of and connection to a SQLite database file. When a SQLConnection instance attempts to connect to a database file, it will connect to it if it already exists or create it if it does not.

When you attempt to connect to a database file, you must specify the path in order to successfully connect to it or create it. You want to carefully pick a location in the

application sandbox of your application. Certain directories and folders are not guaranteed to be preserved during an application update. The ideal folder to use is the File.applicationStorageDirectory directory. This will ensure that your database files are maintained when the user updates your application. Placing your database in the application storage directory will ensure that no other application will have access to your SQLite database. This will prevent other applications from potentially modifying the database.

When selecting a file for your database file, the entire directory must exist. If one of the folders does not exist, the SQLConnection instance will throw an error.

To open the connection to your database file, use the openAsync() method on the SQLConnection class.

Connect to a SQLite Database

① Create a SQLConnection instance, such as var conn:SQLConnection = new SQLConnection();.

② Create a File instance, such as var db:File = File. applicationStorageDirectory. resolvePath();.

③ Type the path to your database file, such as "leaderboard.db".

④ Create a listener for when the database is opened, such as conn.addEvent Listener(SQLEvent.OPEN, onDatabaseOpen);.

⑤ Create a listener for any errors, such as conn.addEventListener (SQLErrorEvent.ERROR, errorHandler);.

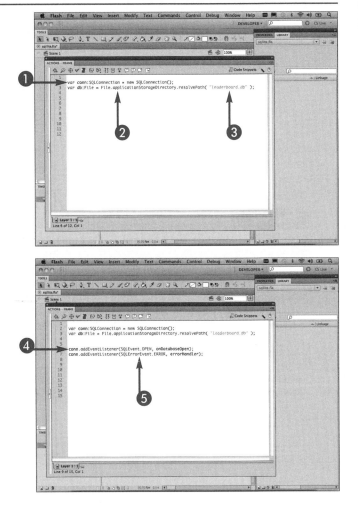

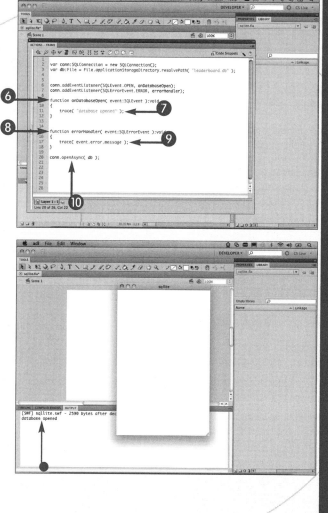

6 Create an event handler for the open event, such as `onDatabaseOpen`.

7 Add a `trace` statement to show a successful connection to the database, such as `trace( "database opened" );`.

8 Create an event handler for the error event, such as `errorHandler`.

9 Trace any errors that occur, such as `trace(event.error.message );`.

10 Open the database, such as `conn.openAsync( db );`.

11 Press ⌘+Enter (Ctrl+Enter) to test your movie.

● Your `trace` statements appear in the Output panel.

Extra

`SQLConnection` instances operate in two distinct modes, asynchronous and synchronous. The example in this section uses the `openAsync()` method, which uses the asynchronous mode. With the asynchronous method, any SQLite database operations occur in the background and separate from the main thread. Each `SQLConnection` instance runs in its own thread to maximize performance. This allows the user to continue to interact with the application while database operations are executing. When using the asynchronous method, you will need to register event listeners in order to determine when a database operation has successfully completed.

Using the `open()` method will create a connection using synchronous execution. This method does not require you to add any event listeners to determine when an operation has successfully completed. This makes the synchronous method more desirable for developers; however, it causes the commands to run in the main thread. This means that any database operation will cause the rest of the application to pause, including any animations and touch events, until the operation is complete. Because events are not fired with this method, you will need to surround your database operation methods with `try .. catch` blocks in order to capture any errors that occur.

Create a SQLite Table

After you have opened a connection to a SQLite database, you can create a table within it to store information. A database table consists of a predetermined number of columns and any number of rows. Each column is identified by its name, which is given upon creation. Along with a unique name, each column has a type of data associated with it.

The following are valid types for your table columns: TEXT, NUMERIC, INTEGER, REAL, Boolean, Date, XML, XMLList, Object, and NONE.

To create a table in your database, you can execute a CREATE TABLE SQL statement. You can also specify to create the table only if it does not already exist. Each table in your database has a unique name in order to distinguish which table you would like to select or insert data into.

The SQLStatement class gives you the ability to execute any SQL statement against a SQLConnection instance that has already been opened. Setting the sqlConnection property of the SQLStatement class allows you to link your SQL statement to an open SQL connection. The text property of the SQLStatement class specifies the actual SQL statement to execute, in this case the CREATE TABLE statement.

After your SQL statement is created and linked to an open connection, you can call the execute() method in order to execute the SQL statement on your database. If your SQLConnection instance was opened using the asynchronous method, you will need to register event listeners on your SQLStatement instance in order to determine when your statement has finished executing successfully. If you are using the synchronous method, be sure to surround your execute code with a try .. catch block to catch any errors.

Create a SQLite Table

Note: The code shown here continues the example from the preceding section, "Connect to a SQLite Database."

① Create a String instance variable, such as var sql:String = "";.

② Create a table if it does not exist, such as CREATE TABLE IF NOT EXISTS.

③ Give your table a name, such as scores.

④ Create an ID column, such as "(id INTEGER PRIMARY KEY AUTOINCREMENT, " +.

⑤ Create a name column, such as "name TEXT, " +.

⑥ Create a related column, such as one for scores, as in "score INTEGER)";.

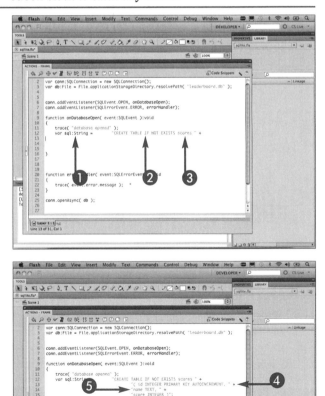

7 Create a `SQLStatement` variable, such as `var sqlStat:SQLStatement = new SQLStatement();`.

8 Set the connection for the SQL statement, such as `sqlStat.sqlConnection = conn;`.

9 Set the SQL string to the statement, such as `sqlStat.text = sql;`.

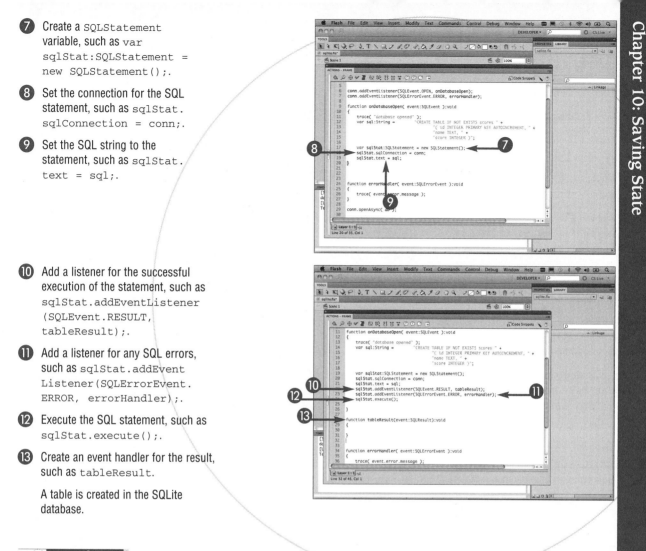

10 Add a listener for the successful execution of the statement, such as `sqlStat.addEventListener (SQLEvent.RESULT, tableResult);`.

11 Add a listener for any SQL errors, such as `sqlStat.addEvent Listener(SQLErrorEvent. ERROR, errorHandler);`.

12 Execute the SQL statement, such as `sqlStat.execute();`.

13 Create an event handler for the result, such as `tableResult`.

A table is created in the SQLite database.

Apply It

For each column created in your database table, you can specify a default value when doing an `INSERT` command. This can be done by using the `DEFAULT` constraint after the column data type, and the value can be `NULL`, a string constant, a number, or an expression enclosed in parentheses. This is especially useful when you want to add the time in which the row was inserted into the database into a date or time column. To help with this, there are three special keywords: `CURRENT_TIME`, `CURRENT_DATE`, and `CURRENT_TIMESTAMP`. The `CURRENT_TIME` keyword format is HH:MM:SS, the `CURRENT_DATE` format is YYYY-MM-DD, and the `CURRENT_TIMESTAMP` format is YYYY-MM-DD HH:MM:SS. Here is what the SQL statement would look like to add a time column with a default value to the example's scores table:

```
var sql:String = "CREATE TABLE IF NOT EXISTS scores (" +
" id INTEGER PRIMARY KEY AUTOINCREMENT, " +
" name TEXT, " +
" score INTEGER," +
" time DATE DEFAULT CURRENT_TIMESTAMP" +
")";
```

Insert Data into a SQLite Table

Inserting data into a SQLite database table is similar to creating the table. You use the same methods for creating and executing a SQLStatement instance as you did earlier. The only difference is the text property, which represents the SQL statement to execute. The INSERT SQL command is used to insert values into the table.

The INSERT statement uses the VALUES keyword to insert a single row into an existing table. If no column list is specified, the number of values specified must match the same number of columns in the table. If a column list is present, the number of values must match the number of columns specified. Any columns in the table that are not specified in the column list will be filled with their default value or with NULL if no default value is specified.

You should be aware that there are security concerns when inserting values when a user has the ability to input data. Concatenating an INSERT statement with user input could allow the user to enter another SQL statement, which could be run and affect your database — potentially erasing it all. This is called a *SQL injection attack* and can be prevented with the use of the parameters property on the SQLStatement class.

Parameters are used to allow for the typed substitution of unknown values at the time of the SQL construction. The use of parameters is the only way to guarantee that the proper data type will be stored in the database. If parameters are not used, the text representation of the class based on the associated column's type affinity will be used.

Insert Data into a SQLite Table

Note: *The code shown here continues the example from the preceding section, "Create a SQLite Table."*

1. Create a String variable, such as var sql:String = "";.

2. Insert data into your table, such as INSERT INTO scores.

3. List the columns to insert data into, such as (name,score).

4. List parameters for the values, such as values(:name, :score).

5. Create a SQLStatement variable, such as var sqlStat:SQLStatement = new SQLStatement();.

6. Set the connection for the SQL statement, such as sqlStat.sqlConnection = conn;.

7. Set the SQL string to the statement, such as sqlStat.text = sql;.

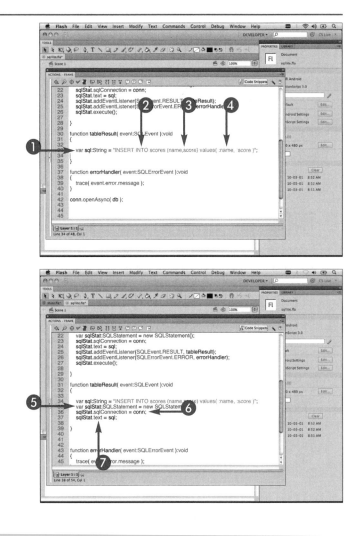

8 Set the parameter for the name value, such as `sqlStat.parameters[ ":name" ] = "julian";`.

9 Set the parameter for a related value, such as one for a score, as in `sqlStat.parameters[ ":score" ] = 150;`.

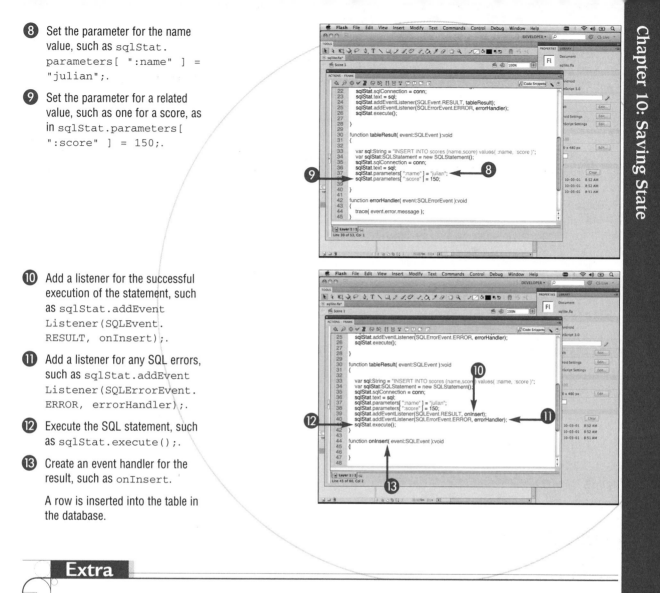

10 Add a listener for the successful execution of the statement, such as `sqlStat.addEventListener(SQLEvent.RESULT, onInsert);`.

11 Add a listener for any SQL errors, such as `sqlStat.addEventListener(SQLErrorEvent.ERROR, errorHandler);`.

12 Execute the SQL statement, such as `sqlStat.execute();`.

13 Create an event handler for the result, such as `onInsert`.

A row is inserted into the table in the database.

Extra

The example here explores one of the three different techniques to use the INSERT statement. The second INSERT statement method takes its data from a SELECT statement. If no column list is specified, the number of columns in the result of the SELECT statement must exactly match the number of columns in the table. If a column list is specified, the number of columns in the result must match the number named in the list. A new entry is created for every row returned by the SELECT statement. For more details on how to use the SELECT statement, see the following section, "Select Data from a SQLite Table."

In the example of the scores table, you could have created a table in your database called `topfive`, in which you insert the top five scores from the scores table. Your SQL statement would look like this:

```
var sql:String = "INSERT INTO topfive (name,score) SELECT name,score FROM scores ORDER BY score
    DESC LIMIT 5";
```

The third INSERT statement method uses the default values of the columns in the table. A new row is created in the database with each column filled with its default value.

Select Data from a SQLite Table

After your SQLite database table is populated with data, you can use the SELECT SQL statement to retrieve specific data from it. Retrieving data from a table is a two-step process. The first step is to execute a SQL SELECT statement with a SQLStatement instance.

SELECT statements can be very simple or very complex. In its simplest form, the SELECT statement enables you to select specified columns from a table in the database. You can also use the * in place of specific columns to select all the columns of the table. This method will return all the data for each row returned by the SQL statement.

You can use the WHERE clause to limit the number of rows that are returned. An equation is used after the WHERE keyword to filter which rows to return, such as SELECT * FROM scores WHERE name='miles'.

You can also use the LIMIT clause to place an upper bound on the number of results to return. A negative number will cause there to be no upper bound.

After the SELECT statement has successfully executed and returned results from the database, you can retrieve a SQLResults object by calling the getResults() method on the same SQLStatement instance that executed the SELECT. The data property of the SQLResults object is an Array containing all the results of the SQL statement that was executed. Each entry in the Array represents a row in the database table. The data property will be null if the SQL statement returns 0 rows or if it is not a SELECT statement.

Select Data from a SQLite Table

Note: The code shown here continues the example from the preceding section, "Insert Data into a SQLite Table."

① Create a String variable, such as `var sql:String = "";`.

② Select what columns to select from the table, such as `SELECT *`.

③ Type **FROM**.

④ Select what table to select from, such as `scores`.

⑤ Create a SQLStatement variable, such as `var sqlStat: SQLStatement = new SQLStatement();`.

⑥ Set the connection for the SQL statement, such as `sqlStat. sqlConnection = conn;`.

⑦ Set the SQL string to the statement, such as `sqlStat.text = sql;`.

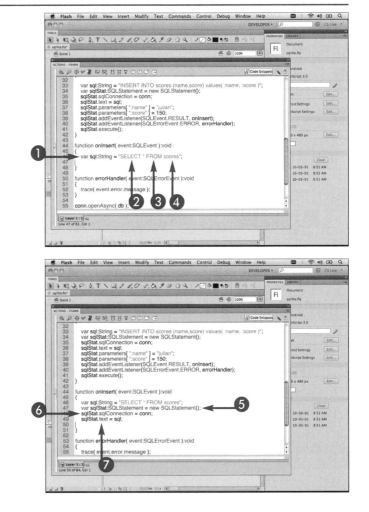

8 Add a listener for the successful execution of the statement, such as `sqlStat.addEventListener (SQLEvent.RESULT, onSelect);`.

9 Add a listener for any SQL errors, such as `sqlStat.addEvent Listener(SQLErrorEvent. ERROR, errorHandler);`.

10 Execute the SQL statement, such as `sqlStat.execute();`.

11 Create an event handler for the result, such as `onSelect`.

12 Create a `SQLResult` variable, such as `var result:SQLResult = SQLStatement( event. target ).getResult();`.

13 Loop through the rows.

14 Iterate over the properties of the row.

15 Output the property and its value, such as `trace( prop, result.data[ i ][prop] );`.

The queried data is returned from the database.

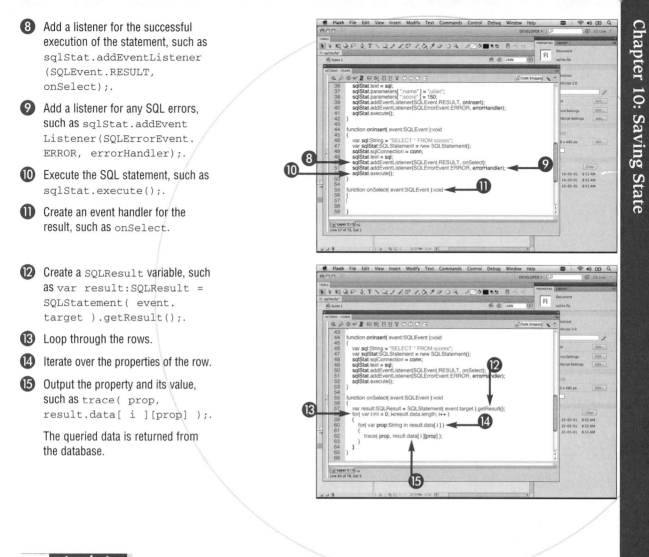

Apply It

When using the `SELECT` statement to return a set of rows from the database, you may want to have them ordered in a certain way. By default, they are returned in the same order that they were inserted into the database. If you take the leaderboard example, you will want to return the scores in order from highest to lowest. Ordering the results as they are returned is far more efficient than ordering them after they have been returned in ActionScript. You can use the `ORDER BY` clause to order the returned results in conjunction with your `SELECT` statement:

```
var sqlStat:SQLStatement = new SQLStatement();
sqlStat.sqlConnection = conn;
var sql:String = "SELECT * FROM scores ORDER BY score DESC";
sqlStat.text = sql;
sqlStat.addEventListener(SQLEvent.RESULT, onSelect);
sqlStat.addEventListener(SQLErrorEvent.ERROR, createError);
sqlStat.execute();
```

Update Data in a SQLite Table

After your database table becomes populated with data, you will probably find yourself wanting to update the data in the table. One option would be to delete all the rows that you would like to update and then reinsert them into the table with their new values. This would require more steps than necessary and would not be very efficient. There is a SQL command that allows you to do this all in one step. The UPDATE SQL statement enables you to update the value of a specific column in selected rows of a table.

The SET keyword is used to specify specific columns in your table and the new values you would like to update them to. Each assignment in an UPDATE statement specifies a column name to the left of the equals sign

and an arbitrary expression to the right of it. The expression can be a value from other columns or a completely new one. It is important to note that all expressions are evaluated before any assignments are made. To update multiple columns at the same time, separate each assignment with a comma.

A WHERE clause can also be used in your UPDATE statement to restrict which rows in the table are updated. Omitting the WHERE clause will cause all rows to be affected by the update. The ORDER BY clause in an UPDATE statement is used only to determine which rows fall within the limit. The order in which the rows are modified is arbitrary and is not determined by the ORDER BY clause.

Update Data in a SQLite Table

Note: *The code shown here continues the example from the preceding section, "Select Data from a SQLite Table."*

 Create a String variable, such as var sql:String = "";.

② Type **UPDATE**.

③ Set the database table name, such as scores.

④ Type **SET**.

⑤ Select a column to update, such as name=.

⑥ Set the new value of the column, such as 'Julian Dolce'.

⑦ Type **WHERE**.

⑧ Select a column to check against, such as name=.

⑨ Set the value to check against, such as 'julian'.

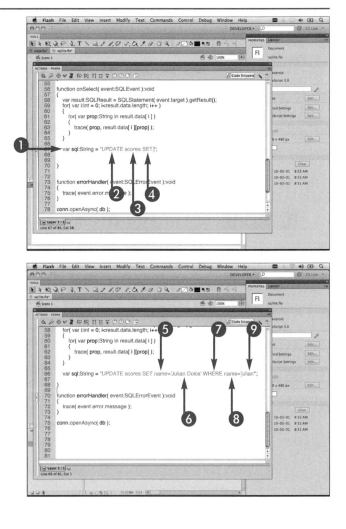

⑩ Create a `SQLStatement` variable, such as `var sqlStat: SQLStatement = new SQLStatement();`.

⑪ Set the connection for the SQL statement, such as `sqlStat. sqlConnection = conn;`.

⑫ Set the SQL string to the statement, such as `sqlStat.text = sql;`.

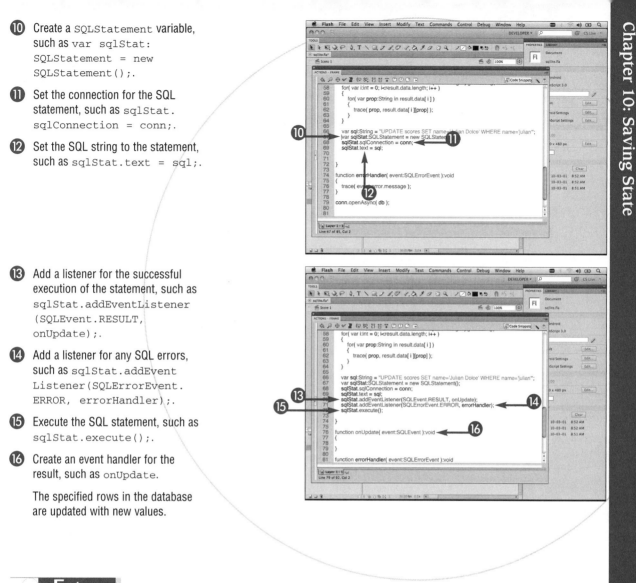

⑬ Add a listener for the successful execution of the statement, such as `sqlStat.addEventListener (SQLEvent.RESULT, onUpdate);`.

⑭ Add a listener for any SQL errors, such as `sqlStat.addEvent Listener(SQLErrorEvent. ERROR, errorHandler);`.

⑮ Execute the SQL statement, such as `sqlStat.execute();`.

⑯ Create an event handler for the result, such as `onUpdate`.

The specified rows in the database are updated with new values.

Extra

You can make specific columns in your database table contain unique values. In the example here, you could have specified the name column to be unique. This would mean that when a user tried to submit a second score with the same name, it would be ignored, as there is already a row with the same value. To work around this, you would check to see if the name already exists and then update the score value and if it did not exist, insert the data into the database.

You can also use the `INSERT OR REPLACE` statement, which will do this for you in one statement. The following SQL statement syntax checks the name value for any rows that already exist with the same value and either updates or inserts the new row:

```
var sql:String = "INSERT OR REPLACE INTO scores (name,score) values ('julian', 5000)";
```

Delete Data from a SQLite Table

You are able to delete rows from your database using the DELETE SQL statement. The DELETE statement starts with the DELETE FROM keywords and is followed by the name of the table from which it will remove records. Following the table name is the WHERE keyword, which can be used to supply an expression to evaluate against. Those rows that match the expression will be removed. The result of the expression must always return either true or false in order to properly determine whether it should remove the row or not.

If no WHERE keyword and expression are supplied, all rows will be removed from the table. When using this method to delete all the rows from a table, SQLite uses an optimization in order to remove all the rows, without having to visit each row of the table individually. This truncate optimization makes the delete run much faster.

When using string values in your expressions, you must use single quotes around the value that you want to evaluate against. For example, WHERE name=julian will throw an error because it tries to look for the column named julian. To fix this, here is the proper syntax: WHERE name='julian'. This applies only to strings, as integer values do not require quotes in order to properly evaluate.

You can also combine multiple expressions to narrow down the set of rows to delete from the table. To combine the expressions, you can use the AND keyword. For example, the following SQL statement would remove all rows in the table in which the name is equal to "julian" and the score is equal to 4000: DELETE FROM scores WHERE name='julian' AND score=4000.

Delete Data from a SQLite Table

Note: The code shown here continues the example from the preceding section, "Update Data in a SQLite Table."

1 Create a function that will delete names from the table, such as deleteName.

2 Pass in a name argument as a String, such as name:String.

3 Create a String variable, such as var sql:String = "";.

4 Type **DELETE FROM**.

5 Set the table name, such as scores.

6 Type **WHERE**.

7 Set the column to check against, such as name=.

8 Create a parameter index, such as :name.

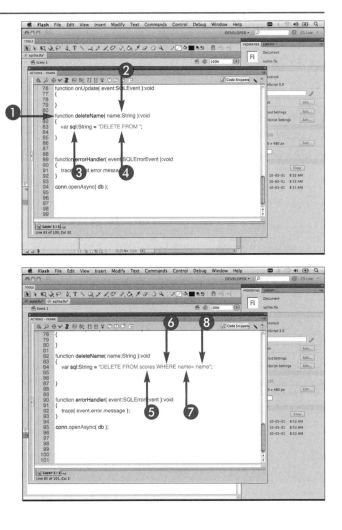

⑨ Create a `SQLStatement` variable, such as `var sqlStat: SQLStatement = new SQLStatement();`.

⑩ Set the connection for the SQL statement, such as `sqlStat. sqlConnection = conn;`.

⑪ Set the SQL string to the statement, such as `sqlStat.text = sql;`.

⑫ Set the parameter for the name that is passed in, such as `sqlStat. parameters[ ":name" ] = name;`.

⑬ Add a listener for the successful execution of the statement, such as `sqlStat.addEventListener (SQLEvent.RESULT, onDelete);`.

⑭ Add a listener for any SQL errors, such as `sqlStat.addEventListener (SQLErrorEvent.ERROR, errorHandler);`.

⑮ Execute the SQL statement, such as `sqlStat.execute();`.

⑯ Create an event handler for the result, such as `onDelete`.

The specified rows are deleted from the table in the database.

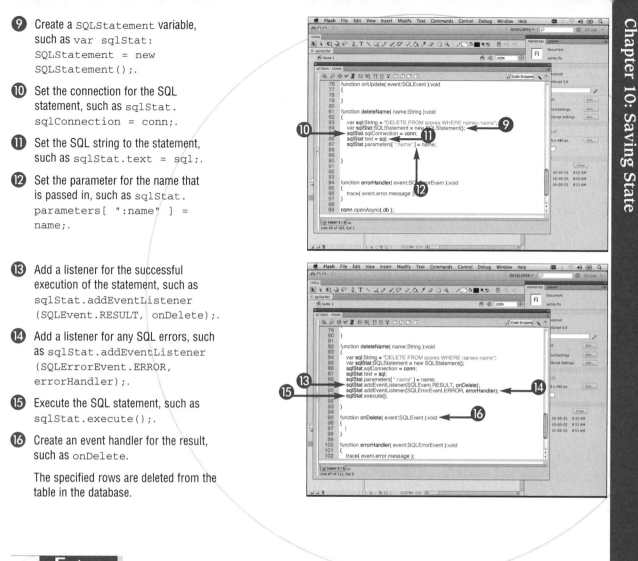

Extra

Indexes help us retrieve information quicker. For example, if you are looking for a specific topic in this book, it is quicker to look it up in the index, instead of reading the book from start to finish, in order to find it. The same applies for tables in your database. When selecting data using the SELECT statement, every row is visited, which could affect speed, depending on how many rows you have in the table. Creating an index for specific columns will reduce the number of rows that need to be visited when running your SELECT statement. In the leaderboard example, you may want to create an index on the name column if you are doing a lot of selects based on its value. The trade-off, however, is an index will cause INSERT statements to be slower because the index needs to be regenerated after every insert. You could use the DROP INDEX statement to delete the index before an INSERT and then re-create it afterwards. In most instances, this is necessary only when dealing with very large data sets. To create your index, execute the following SQL statement:

```
var sql:String = "CREATE INDEX name_idx ON scores (name)";
```

Handle
Application Exits

Unlike other device platforms, such as the iPhone, the Android platform allows multiple applications to be open at any given time. Because multiple applications can be open at any given time, chances are your application will not exit when the user navigates away from it or it is interrupted by your device. For more details on how to listen for when your application loses focus, see the section "Handle Application Deactivation" later in this chapter.

One of the most common ways that your application will quit is either by explicitly calling the NativeApplication. exit() method yourself or the user telling the application to force-stop in the Settings application on the device.

The NativeApplication class dispatches an event when your application is exiting. Listening for this event

enables you to perform any needed last-second cleanup of objects or save the state of your application. This event will not be fired when either of the methods mentioned earlier cause your application to exit. There is a good chance you will never receive this event; however, it does not hurt to include it in case it does get fired.

The most common case for when to tell your application to exit is when the user has pressed the Back key on the device, so there is no reason for your application to continue to run. Because you will not receive the Event.EXITING event when you call the NativeApplication.exit() event, be sure to do any cleanup before you call the method.

When your application exits, make sure to write any important data to the file system and stop all sounds and other media as quickly as possible. There is no guarantee that your application will finish performing all its tasks before your application finally exits.

Handle Application Exits

① Create a NativeApplication variable, such as var application: NativeApplication;.

② Set the variable to your application's NativeApplication, such as = NativeApplication. nativeApplication.

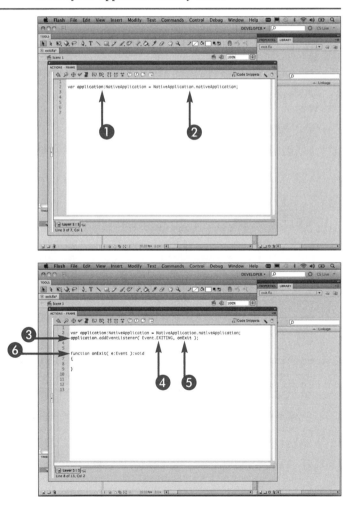

③ Add a listener to your application, such as application.addEvent Listener( );.

④ Listen for the Event.EXITING event.

⑤ Set an event handler to be fired, such as onExit.

⑥ Create an event handler function for the event, such as onExit.

⑦ Create a method to perform exit tasks, such as `performExitTasks`.

⑧ Stop all sounds, such as `SoundMixer.stopAll();`.

⑨ Call the `performExitTasks` method.

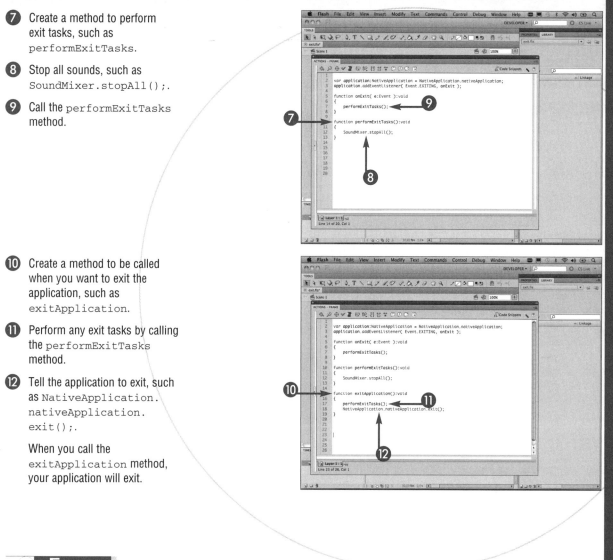

⑩ Create a method to be called when you want to exit the application, such as `exitApplication`.

⑪ Perform any exit tasks by calling the `performExitTasks` method.

⑫ Tell the application to exit, such as `NativeApplication.nativeApplication.exit();`.

When you call the `exitApplication` method, your application will exit.

Extra

When your application exits, you will want to save any necessary data as fast as possible. If the save process takes too long, there is a chance that the application will quit without completing the entire save. In order to prevent this, you will want to limit the data to be as small as possible.

After all your data is saved, you can try and do any cleanup of your application. This would be no different than the regular code cleanup you would do when disposing of objects that are no longer needed. Make sure that all your animations and Timelines have stopped. Stop all timers and enter frame loops. Remove any remaining listeners on any live objects. Also, close any network requests, sockets, and file streams that you may still have open.

All of these will make sure that your application is completely cleared from memory when your application quits. If your application causes memory leaks when it closes, the user may have to reboot his or her device in order to clear its memory.

Save Application States

I t has become common practice when developing mobile applications to launch your application in its last known state. For example, if you are developing a game and the user is playing the game when the application quits, you will want to launch the game to a state in which the user can simply pick up where he or she left off.

Another reason it is recommended you save the state of your application often is that your application can quit unexpectedly. As mentioned previously, listening for the application exiting event is a great place to save the state of your application. However, you should not rely on this too much, as that event may not get fired every time your application quits. This is especially true in the event that the user has force-stopped the application from the Settings application on the device.

It will be up to you to determine how often you save the state of your application. Different types of applications will call for different methods. For example, if you are developing a game, you may want to save more often than an application.

This chapter has discussed two different methods of how to save states of your application. A SharedObject is probably all that is needed when saving states as a SQLite database may be overkill. Saving the state information of your application to a file on the device is an additional option. For more details on working with files, see Chapter 11, "Working with Files." You will want to implement the method that will allow you to not only save the data efficiently, but also load it quickly when your application starts.

Save Application States

1. Create a function to save the section when it changes, such as `function saveCurrentSection():void{}`.

2. Set a `String` argument as the section to save, such as `section:String`.

3. Create a `SharedObject` variable, such as `var so:SharedObject = SharedObject.getLocal();`.

4. Set the name of your `SharedObject`, such as `"state"`.

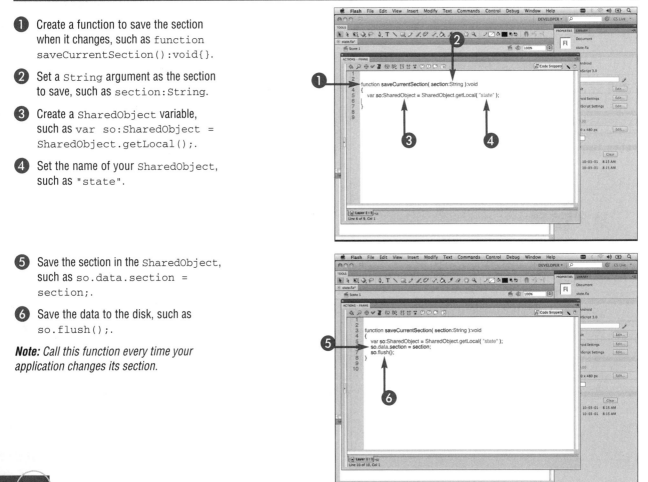

5. Save the section in the `SharedObject`, such as `so.data.section = section;`.

6. Save the data to the disk, such as `so.flush();`.

Note: Call this function every time your application changes its section.

7 Create a function to load the last saved section, such as `function getLastSection()`.

8 Give it a return type of `String`.

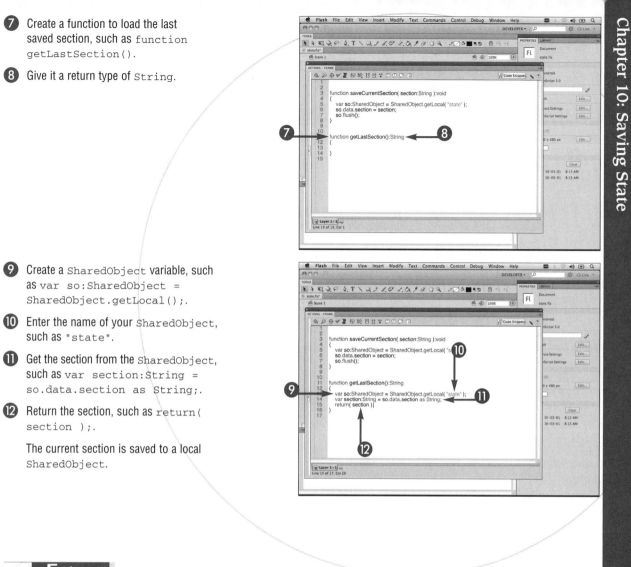

9 Create a `SharedObject` variable, such as `var so:SharedObject = SharedObject.getLocal();`.

10 Enter the name of your `SharedObject`, such as `"state"`.

11 Get the section from the `SharedObject`, such as `var section:String = so.data.section as String;`.

12 Return the section, such as `return( section );`.

The current section is saved to a local `SharedObject`.

Extra

Saving the state of your application does not have to be a complex process. You do not have to save every single interaction point between the user and your application. Simply saving which section of your application was last viewed is usually enough for most applications. But there are instances in which the data may become more complex, and it will be up to you to decide what data is most important to save for when the user returns. If you are creating a game, you should save the state after each level at the very least. This allows the user to continue the game, also saving his or her score. Depending on the type of game, however, you may be able to save more frequently, such as when the user takes a turn or makes a move in the game. This can easily be done with a casual game but is harder for an action or driving game. When deciding what data and how often to save it, ask yourself what makes sense for the user to continue when the game is loaded. You can also give him or her an option upon relaunching the game to continue the last game or start a new one.

Handle Back and Menu Button Presses

Android devices, such as the Nexus One, have a set of buttons just underneath the screen. The most common ones are Back, Menu, Home, and Search. Most applications use the Back and Menu buttons on the device as a way to interact with the applications.

The Android SDK has a specific style of menu that appears when you press the Menu button. If you plan on integrating a menu, it is a good idea to try to design your menu with the same look and feel as the Android SDK so that the user will be familiar with it. The Menu button allows you to hide some of the more popular tasks of your application, giving you more room to display important information. Accessing application settings, refreshing data, and composing new messages are all great examples of items to place in your menu.

The Back button is most often used for returning to the previous screen in your application. It is very similar to the Back button in a browser, but instead of going to your last Web page, you are going to the last screen or section in your application. It is also often used as a way to close pop-up windows that may appear in your application. This saves you from having to add a close or OK button to any pop-ups.

When the user presses either the Back or Menu button, a `KeyboardEvent` is fired, just as if it was a key press on a keyboard. The key code for the Back button is 94, and the key code for the Menu button is 95.

Handle Back and Menu Button Presses

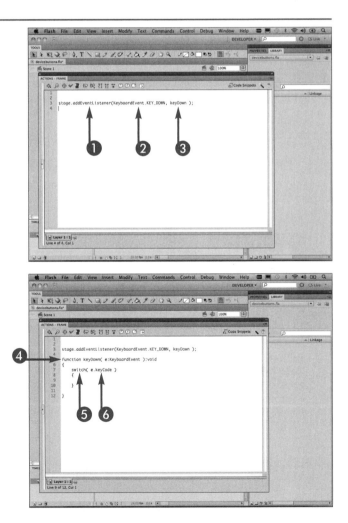

① Add an event listener to the Stage, such as `stage.addEvent Listener();`.

② Listen for the `KeyboardEvent. KEY_DOWN` event.

③ Add an event handler, such as `keyDown`.

④ Create a `KeyboardEvent` handler, such as `function keyDown ( e:KeyboardEvent ) :void{}`.

⑤ Create a `switch` statement.

⑥ Switch on the key code that was pressed, such as `e.keyCode`.

7 Add a `case` for the Back button, such as `case Keyboard.BACK:`.

8 Output that the Back button was pressed, such as `trace( "back button pressed" );`.

9 Add a `break;`.

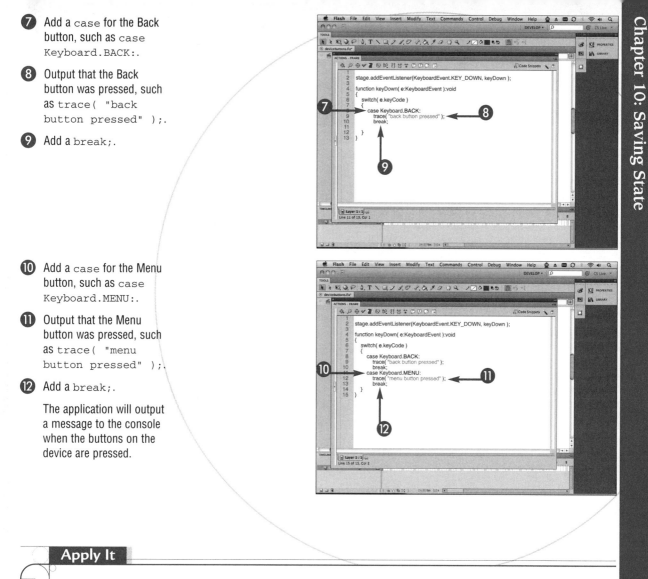

10 Add a `case` for the Menu button, such as `case Keyboard.MENU:`.

11 Output that the Menu button was pressed, such as `trace( "menu button pressed" );`.

12 Add a `break;`.

The application will output a message to the console when the buttons on the device are pressed.

Apply It

By default, the Back button brings you back to the home screen of the device and places your application in the background. To prevent this behavior, you can call the `Event.preventDefault()` method so that you can handle any Back button presses in your application. Here is what your key press event handler method would now look like:

```
function keyDown( e:KeyboardEvent ):void{
                switch( e.keyCode )
                {
                    case Keyboard.BACK:
                        trace( "back button pressed" );
                        e.preventDefault();
                        break;
                }
}
```

185

Handle Application Deactivation

Android devices can have multiple applications running at the same time. This is a huge benefit as it allows you to jump between applications without having to close one to open the other. When your application loses focus, it is put into background mode. To make sure that your application does not use up valuable CPU and battery, make sure to stop all intensive tasks when your application is put into background mode.

There are a number of different reasons that your application can put placed into background mode. The user can press the Home button or the Back button on the device in order to launch a new application. Your application may have launched a URL that caused another application to launch and receive focus. Or you may have received an interruption such as a phone call.

The `NativeApplication` class will fire an `Event.DEACTIVE` event when your application is placed in background mode. Each application will handle this event differently. This would be a great place to save the state of your application and save any important data. It is also a good idea to stop all the sounds that are currently playing, as they will continue to play when the application is in the background.

After your application has performed all its tasks for going into the background, you can listen for `Event.ACTIVATE` to be fired from the `NativeApplication` class, telling you that your application has regained focus. This allows you to unpause your application and continue where the user last left off.

Handle Application Deactivation

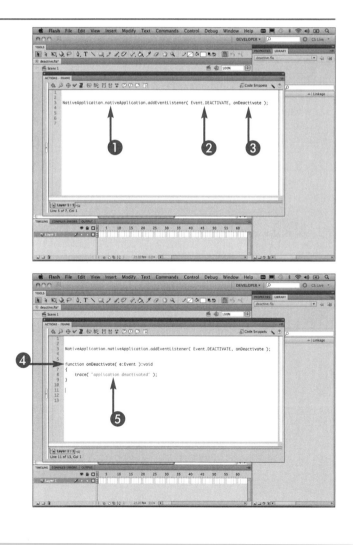

1 Add an event listener to the application, such as `NativeApplication.nativeApplication.addEventListener()`.

2 Listen for the `Event.DEACTIVATE` event.

3 Add an event handler, such as `onDeactivate`.

4 Create an event handler method, such as `onDeactivate`.

5 Output a message when the application is deactivated, such as `trace( "application deactivated" );`.

6 Add an event listener to the application, such as `NativeApplication. nativeApplication. addEventListener();`.

7 Listen for the `Event. ACTIVATE` event.

8 Add an event handler, such as `onActivate`.

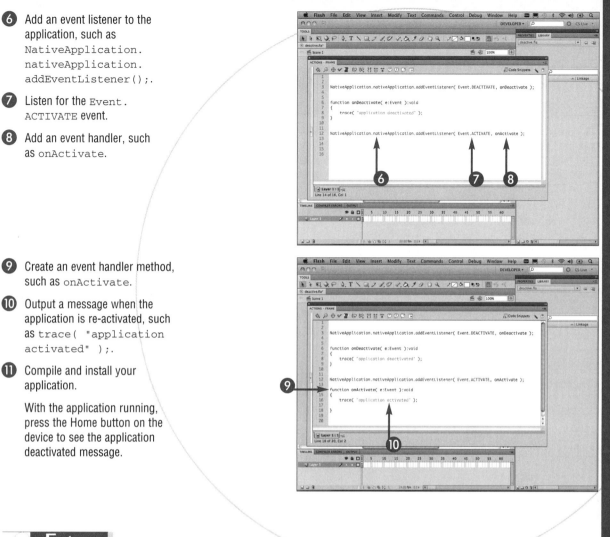

9 Create an event handler method, such as `onActivate`.

10 Output a message when the application is re-activated, such as `trace( "application activated" );`.

11 Compile and install your application.

With the application running, press the Home button on the device to see the application deactivated message.

Extra

There are many different things you can do when your application is deactivated in order to make sure that your application does not take up valuable CPU usage and memory. You can call the garbage collector to make sure that all the items that it has yet to collect are collected. This will free up any additional memory that your application no longer needs. You can start the garbage collector with the following syntax:

```
System.gc();
```

Another important task is to reduce the frame rate of your application. This will reduce the amount of code that is executed when your application is placed in the background. To dynamically change the frame rate of your application, use the following syntax:

```
stage.frameRate = 2;
```

If you set the frame rate to a low number when the application is placed in the background, make sure to reset it when the application becomes active again.

Reference Files and Directories

An Android application can read and write files to the device's local file system. Each application is placed in its own directory and, for security purposes, has access to read and write to those directories only. The path to your application on the device is similar to the following: /data/data/app.com.mobileflash development.filepaths/. This path is known as the application home and is referred to as <Application_Home>.

There are a few common directories that are created in the application home directory when it is installed on your device. You can use these directories to write preference files, save documents, and save the state of your application. The `File` class contains static properties that allow you to access these directories.

`File.applicationDirectory` is located at <Application_Home>/app/assets. This is the directory that contains the SWF file of your application. This is the same directory that all your files are bundled to when bundling them with the Flash IDE. This directory is a read-only directory.

`File.applicationStorageDirectory` is located at <Application_Home>/<app ID>/Local Store. Use this directory for saving any files that are specific only to your application. For example, you may save preference files or SQLite databases. Files in this directory will be kept when an application is updated.

`File.documentsDirectory`, `File.userDirectory`, and `File.desktopDirectory` all resolve to the root directory of your SD card, /sdcard. You can use this directory to place files so that other applications may have access to them. You might also consider a folder in this location for any temporary files that your application may save.

Reference Files and Directories

Create Text Fields

1. Click the Text tool.

2. Draw a text field on the Stage.

3. Click here and select Classic Text.

4. Click here and select Dynamic Text.

5. Give the text field an instance name, such as application_txt.

6. Click here and select Multiline.

7. Click here and select a font, such as Arial.

8. Click here and select Use Device Fonts.

9. Copy the text field on the Stage.

10. Paste a new text field on the Stage.

11. Give it an instance name, such as documents_txt.

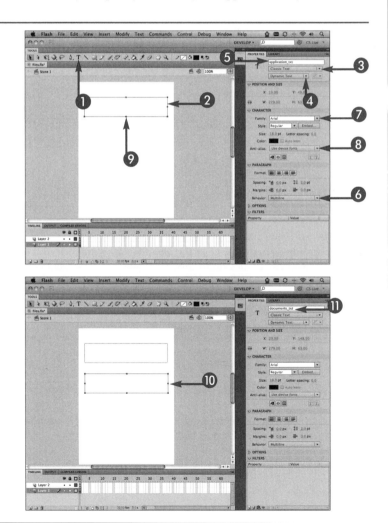

⑫ Paste another new text field on the Stage.

⑬ Give it an instance name, such as `user_txt`.

Set the Text Fields to Your Application's Directories

⑭ Open the Actions panel.

⑮ Import the `File` class.

⑯ Set the text to the application path, such as `application_txt.text = File.applicationDirectory.nativePath;`.

⑰ Set the text to the documents path, such as `documents_txt.text = File.documentsDirectory.nativePath;`.

⑱ Set the text to the application home path, such as `user_txt.text = File.userDirectory.nativePath;`.

The path to the application directories are placed in the text fields on the Stage.

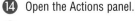

Extra

You should use caution when you are targeting any of the `File.documentsDirectory`, `File.userDirectory`, and `File.desktopDirectory` directories in order to store your files on the SD card. Because any application has access to these directories, any application can read, write, and delete files placed there. If you decide to put files here, make sure that you create a folder specifically for your application. You will also need to add `<uses-permission android:name="android.permission.WRITE_EXTERNAL_STORAGE" />` to your application descriptor file, in order to save files to the SD card.

Other applications have also used the /sdcard/data/<app_id> folder path when saving files to the SD card.

Storing files on the SD card can be very useful for sharing files between applications, but this is also a good location for storing any temporary cache files. For example, a Twitter application that loads profile images for a tweet may cache the file to the local file system, as opposed to loading it over the Internet every time. The application can check the local file system first to see if it exists, and if it does not, it will download it and save it to the disk.

Write Files

You can write files to the local file system of the device using the `File` class and the `FileStream` class. You can write any type of file to the file system as long as you know how to properly encode the file. Any text file format is the easiest type of file to write to the file system.

The first step to writing a file is to create a `File` instance, which is a representation of a path to a file or directory on the file system. This can be an existing file or directory or one that does not currently exist. The `File` class has a number of static properties that map to specific directories on the file system, as shown in the preceding section, "Reference Files and Directories." You can use the `resolvePath()` method to create a new

`File` object with a path relative to the current path of the `File` instance.

After you have created a reference to your file location, you can use the `FileStream` class to write to the file. The `FileStream` class is very similar to the `ByteArray` class and has all the same methods for reading and writing bytes to the object. In most cases, you will simply be dealing with text files and can use the `FileStream.writeUTFBytes()` method in order to write any `String` instance variables to the file.

After you have written all the data to the file, make sure to close the stream by calling the `FileStream.close()` method. Upon closing the stream, you will no longer be able to write data to the file.

Write Files

1. Create a `File` variable, such as `var file:File`.

2. Select a directory for your file, such as `File.applicationStorage Directory`.

3. Resolve the path, such as `resolvePath();`.

4. Create a name for your file, such as `preferences.txt`.

5. Create a `FileStream` variable, such as `var stream:FileStream = new FileStream();`.

6. Add a listener to the stream, such as `stream.addEventListener();`.

7. Listen for the `IOErrorEvent.IO_ERROR` event.

8. Specify an event handler function, such as `onIOError`.

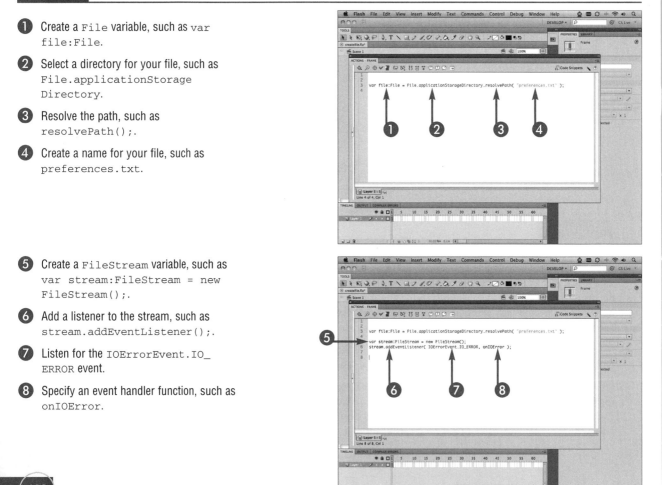

9. Create the event handler function, such as `onIOError`.

10. Output the event, such as `trace( event );`.

11. Open the stream, such as `stream.openAsync();`.

12. Select the file to open.

13. Open the file in the `FileMode.WRITE` mode.

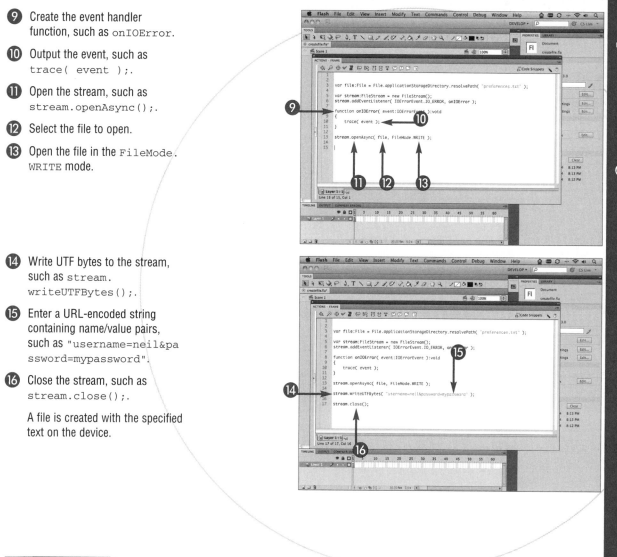

14. Write UTF bytes to the stream, such as `stream.writeUTFBytes();`.

15. Enter a URL-encoded string containing name/value pairs, such as `"username=neil&password=mypassword"`.

16. Close the stream, such as `stream.close();`.

A file is created with the specified text on the device.

Apply It

You can also write a `ByteArray` instance to the `FileStream` object. This makes it very easy to save non-text-based file formats such as images. Chapter 6, "Working with Images," discusses encoding PNG images from a `BitmapData` instance. The PNG image is encoded into a `ByteArray`, which can be saved to the file system:

```
var bd:BitmapData = new BitmapData( 200, 200, false, 0xFFFF0000 );
var png:ByteArray = PNGEncoder.encode( bd );
var stream:FileStream = new FileStream();
var file:File=File.applicationStorageDirectory.resolvePath("my.png");
stream.open(file, FileMode.WRITE );
stream.writeBytes( png );
stream.close();
```

Read Files

R eading files is very similar to writing files. You can read any file that you have access to on the file system. To select a file to read, you create a `File` object to the path of the file that you want on the file system.

When reading files, it is always a good idea to make sure that it exists before trying to read it. The `exists` property on the `File` class will return `false` if it does not exist and `true` if it does.

If your file exists, you can create a `FileStream` instance that points to your `File` and use the `FileMode.READ` property when calling the `openAsync()` method. Opening the file asynchronously causes the file to be opened and read into the buffer on a separate thread. This prevents any

performance degradation on the main thread, which may cause animations and sound to pause while reading the file.

In order to determine when the file has been completely read into the buffer, you can listen for the `Event.COMPLETE` event on the `FileStream` object. After the file has been completely read into the buffer of the `FileStream` instance, you can use any of the `read` methods on it to read the data. When you are reading any kind of text file, you can use the `readUTFBytes()` method. When reading UTF bytes, you need to specify how many bytes you would like to read at any given time. You can use the `bytesAvailable` property on the `FileStream` class to determine how many bytes there are from the current position of the buffer to the end of the buffer. If the current position of the buffer is 0, this will allow you to read the entire file.

Read Files

1 Create a `File` variable, such as `var file:File`.

2 Select a directory for your file, such as `File.applicationStorage Directory`.

3 Resolve the path, such as `resolvePath();`.

4 Create a name for your file, such as `preferences.txt`.

5 Create a `FileStream` variable, such as `var stream:FileStream = new FileStream();`.

6 Listen for the complete event on the stream, such as `stream. addEventListener( Event. COMPLETE, onComplete );`.

7 Open the file, such as `stream. openAsync();`.

8 Select the file to open.

9 Open the file in the `FileMode. READ` mode.

10 Create an event handler method, such as `onComplete`.

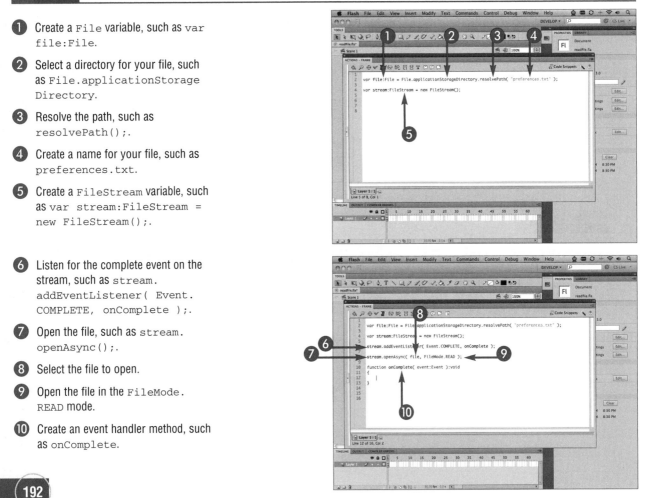

11. Create a `String` variable, such as `var str:String`.

12. Read UTF bytes of the stream, such as `stream.readUTFBytes();`.

13. Read all the bytes available in the stream, such as `stream.bytesAvailable`.

14. Create a `URLVariable` variable, such as `var variables: URLVariables = new URLVariables();`.

15. Decode the text read from the file, such as `variables.decode( str );`.

16. Output your variables, such as `trace( variables. username, variables. password );`.

17. Close the stream, such as `stream.close();`.

The text is read from the file.

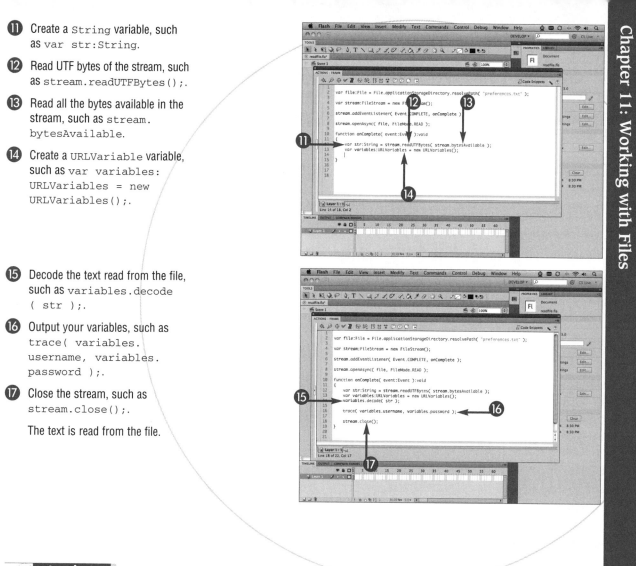

Apply It

You can also read an entire file to a `ByteArray` instance. This is very useful when dealing with binary file formats, such as images, databases, and binary property list files. You will need to understand the format of the file in order to properly parse a binary file. After you have your file in a `ByteArray` instance, you can also send it over a `Socket` connection. Connecting to a socket server on your computer or over the network enables you to send your files to your computer to back them up and save them:

```
var ba:ByteArray = new ByteArray();
stream.readBytes( ba );
//sending the files over a connected Socket class
ba.position = 0;
socket.writeBytes( ba );
socket.flush();
```

Update Files

When you open a file in either the `FileMode.READ` or `FileMode.WRITE` mode, you can perform only the specified task. For example, when reading a file, you can only read the file and cannot use any of the write methods to write data to the file. The same is true for when you are writing a file.

The `FileMode.UPDATE` mode allows you to open a file that you can read and write at the same time. This comes in handy when dealing with preferences files. For example, when your application starts up, it will read a preferences file from the file system in order to initialize your application. This could be something simple such as automatically logging in the user or determining which section of your application to start in. After the file has been read, there is a high probability that you will want

to overwrite the data in the file to reflect the user's interactions with your application.

Without the ability to open the file in the update mode, you would have to open the file twice — once to read it and once to write it. Opening the file in the update mode enables you to keep the stream to the file open for as long as you need it. This can have a dramatic effect on performance as you do not have to open the file and re-create a new `FileStream` and `File` instance.

It is important to keep track of the position of the buffer as you read and write to it. When you initially read the entire file, the position of the buffer is located at the end. If you want to overwrite the entire file, you will need to set the position of the buffer to the beginning of the file. Otherwise, you will simply write your data at the end of the file.

Update Files

① Create a `File` variable, such as `var file:File;`.

② Select a directory for your file, such as `File.applicationStorage Directory.resolvePath()`.

③ Create a name for your file, such as `preferences.txt`.

④ Create a `FileStream` variable, such as `var stream:FileStream = new FileStream();`.

⑤ Listen for the complete event on the stream, such as `stream. addEventListener( Event. COMPLETE, onComplete );`.

⑥ Open the file, such as `stream. openAsync();`.

⑦ Select the file to open.

⑧ Open the file in the `FileMode. UPDATE` mode.

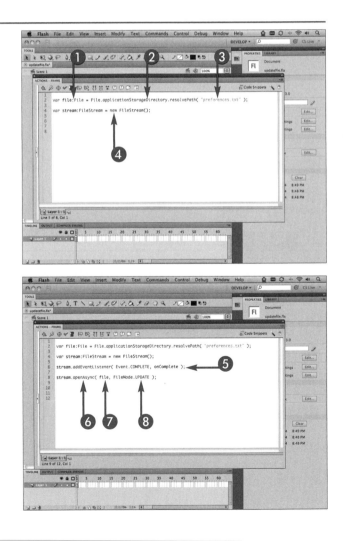

9. Create an event handler method, such as onComplete.

10. Create a String variable, such as var str:String.

11. Read the entire file, such as stream.readUTFBytes(stream.bytesAvailable);.

Note: The position of the buffer in the stream is now located at the end of the file.

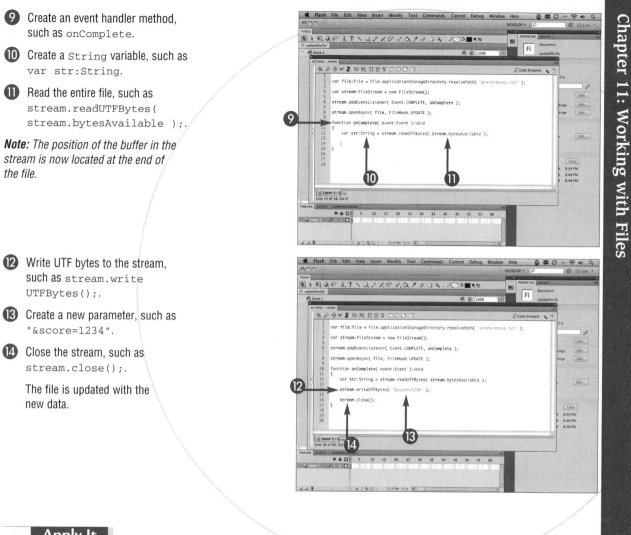

12. Write UTF bytes to the stream, such as stream.write UTFBytes();.

13. Create a new parameter, such as "&score=1234".

14. Close the stream, such as stream.close();.

The file is updated with the new data.

Apply It

The truncate() method on the FileStream class enables you to trim the file from its current location specified by the position property. This allows you to keep your files below a given file size easily. For example, you may have set up a logging system in your application to log events or errors to a file on the file system of the device. Over time, this file could grow to be unnecessarily large. You can use the File.size property in order to determine the size of the file in bytes. The following is an example of truncating a file to keep it under a given size:

```
var file:File=File.applicationStorageDirectory.resolvePath("log.txt");
var stream:FileStream = new FileStream();
stream.open(file, FileMode.UPDATE);
if (file.size > 1000)
{
    stream.position = 1000;
    stream.truncate();
}
stream.close();
```

Append Files

I f you know that you always want to write to the end of the file, you can use the FileMode.APPEND mode when opening your file. When the file is opened in the append mode, data is always written to the end of the file when any write method is called on the FileStream instance. This makes it easier to write to the end of the file, as you never have to worry about what position the buffer is currently at before writing the data.

If the file does not exist prior to opening it, the file will still be created just as it would when opening the file in the write mode. Also, when the file is opened in append mode, you are able only to write to the file and cannot read it. If you need the ability to read and write the file, open the file with the FileMode.UPDATE mode. For more

details on how to update files, see the preceding section, "Update Files."

Popular uses for opening files in the append mode is when you are writing to a log file. A log file can come in a variety of forms, such as a history of the user's actions when interacting with your application or a list of errors if any are to occur in your application. These can be valuable, especially when you allow other people to test your application during development. If the user experiences a crash or finds a portion of the application that is broken, you can have him or her send you the log files saved by the application. This will give you more details and help you track down the problem faster and more effectively.

Append Files

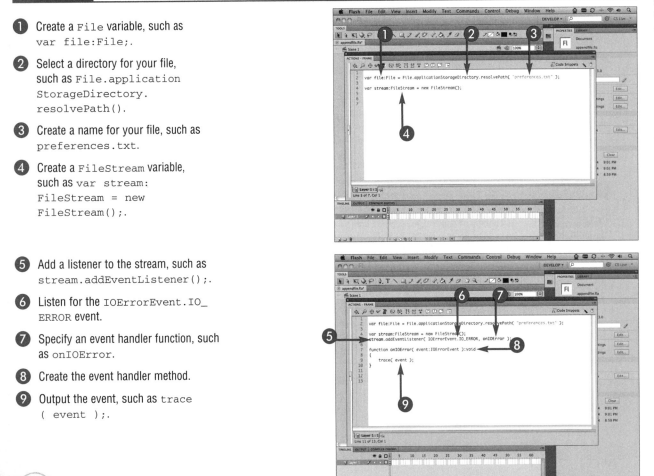

① Create a File variable, such as
var file:File;.

② Select a directory for your file, such as File.application
StorageDirectory.
resolvePath().

③ Create a name for your file, such as preferences.txt.

④ Create a FileStream variable, such as var stream:
FileStream = new
FileStream();.

⑤ Add a listener to the stream, such as stream.addEventListener();.

⑥ Listen for the IOErrorEvent.IO_ ERROR event.

⑦ Specify an event handler function, such as onIOError.

⑧ Create the event handler method.

⑨ Output the event, such as trace (event);.

10 Open the file, such as
`stream.openAsync();`.

11 Select the file to open.

12 Open the file in the
`FileMode.APPEND` mode.

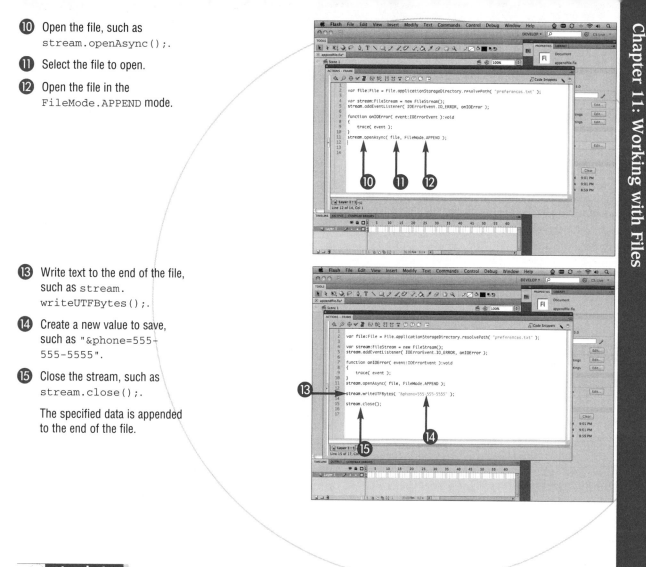

13 Write text to the end of the file,
such as `stream.
writeUTFBytes();`.

14 Create a new value to save,
such as `"&phone=555-
555-5555"`.

15 Close the stream, such as
`stream.close();`.

The specified data is appended
to the end of the file.

Apply It

The new network API classes in AIR 2.0 make it easy to create an application for the desktop that can communicate with your Android application. The new `ServerSocket` class enables you to accept incoming `Socket` connections from the device. After the data is received from a connected socket, you can save the file to the local file system. Here is a very basic example of an AIR application that creates a socket server:

```
var server:ServerSocket = new ServerSocket();
server.addEventListener(ServerSocketConnectEvent.CONNECT, onConnect );
server.bind( 5555, "localhost" );
server.listen();
private function onConnect( event:ServerSocketConnectEvent ):void{
var socket:Socket = event.socket;
//listen for any data arriving on this socket.
}
```

Handle Files Synchronously

There are two ways to open files, asynchronously and synchronously. Throughout this chapter, the examples have shown opening files asynchronously because this method is more popular for mobile development. When you open files asynchronously, all file operations occur on a separate thread from the main one. This will allow your interface and application to remain responsive when performing file commands.

However, there are times when you want to pause the main thread from continuing while you are writing to your file. One example may be when your application is exiting. If you try to write code asynchronously when you receive an exiting event from your application, your data may not be written before the application closes. In this example, there is no guarantee that your data will be written synchronously either because the Android OS may halt your code and exit in the case of a crash. However, you have a better chance of it occurring if your data is written synchronously.

To open files synchronously, simply call the open() method on the FileStream class instead of the openAsync() method. When you open your file with the open() method, you can either read the file or write to the file immediately afterwards. There is no need to register for complete events when using this method. Your application will pause until all the data in the file is read into the buffer before continuing to execute the next line of code in your application.

If you are reading or writing very small pieces of data, this method may work well enough for you, as you may not see a significant delay in responsiveness in your application. It also makes your development easier as you do not have to worry about adding and removing event listeners for when the data is available.

Handle Files Synchronously

1. Create a File variable, such as var file:File.

2. Select a directory for your file, such as File.applicationStorage Directory.

3. Resolve the path, such as resolvePath();.

4. Create a name for your file, such as preferences.txt.

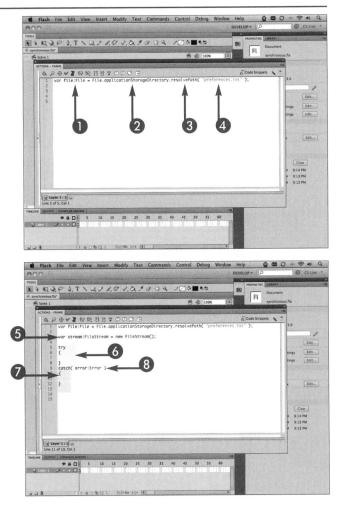

5. Create a FileStream variable, such as var stream:FileStream = new FileStream();.

6. Create a try block.

7. Create a catch block.

8. Catch for any errors, such as error:Error.

9 Open the stream, such as `stream.open();`.

10 Select the file to open.

11 Open the file in the `FileMode.READ` mode.

12 Create a `String` variable, such as `var str:String`.

13 Read the entire file, such as `stream.readUTFBytes( stream.bytesAvailable );`.

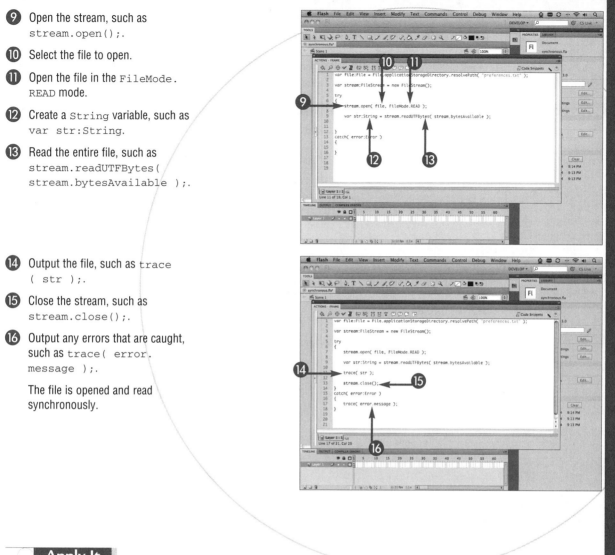

14 Output the file, such as `trace ( str );`.

15 Close the stream, such as `stream.close();`.

16 Output any errors that are caught, such as `trace( error.message );`.

The file is opened and read synchronously.

<hr />

Apply It

When creating a `File` object for a specific file location, you must make sure that the entire path to the file is valid. For example, the following `File` variable would throw an error because the full path to the file does not exist:

```
var file:File = File.applicationStorageDirectory.resolvePath("AppData/data.xml");
```

The reason this would fail is because the AppData directory does not exist in the user directory of the application.

To make sure that your file is successfully created in this location, you would need to check to see if the directory existed and if it did not, create it. You can use the following syntax to create a directory:

```
var file:File=File.applicationStorageDirectory.resolvePath("AppData");
file.createDirectory();
```

Copy Files

As mentioned earlier in this chapter, you cannot write files to the same directory as your application. The reason for this is that each application needs to be digitally signed when it is compiled. Adding or removing files from this directory may cause the application to be no longer valid and could cause it to no longer launch.

There may be times that you want to bundle files with your application and have them be updated throughout the life of the application. A good example of this would be when you are using a SQLite database. You may want to bundle a database with your application that contains information for your application. If you kept the database in the application directory, you would never be able to update or add new data to it.

To work around this issue, you can copy your file from the application directory to a directory to which you have write access. It is important that you copy and not move the file as this may cause the application to be invalid.

There are two methods that you can use to copy a file to a new location: The copyTo() and copyToAsync() methods of the File class give you the ability to copy your files synchronously or asynchronously, respectively. Both of these methods also allow you to specify whether to overwrite the file if it already exists.

When your application launches, it can check to see if the file already exists in a write access directory, and if it does not, it can copy the file from your application directory.

Copy Files

Note: Do not forget to bundle the source file with your application. For more details, see the section "Bundle Images with Your Application" in Chapter 6.

Note: Bundling a text file uses the same process as bundling an image.

 Create a File variable, such as var sourcefile:File.

② Select a directory for your file, such as File.applicationDirectory. resolvePath();.

③ Create a name for your file, such as preferences.txt.

④ Create a File variable, such as var destfile:File.

⑤ Select a directory for your file, such as File.applicationStorage Directory.resolvePath();.

⑥ Create a name for your file, such as preferences.txt.

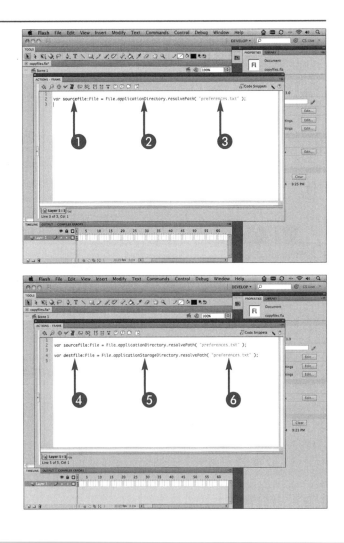

7 Register a listener for the complete event, such as `sourcefile.addEventListener( Event.COMPLETE, copyComplete );`.

8 Create an event handler method, such as `copyComplete`.

9 Output that the file has been successfully copied, such as `trace( "copy complete" );`.

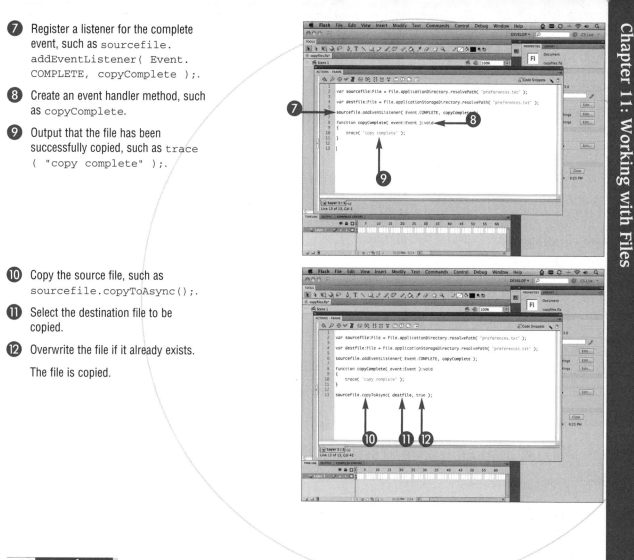

10 Copy the source file, such as `sourcefile.copyToAsync();`.

11 Select the destination file to be copied.

12 Overwrite the file if it already exists.

The file is copied.

Apply It

It is possible that you will be copying files that are big in size. Because copying files from your application bundle will most likely occur during the startup procedure of your application, you will most likely favor the `copyToAysnc()` method. This will allow your application to start up as quickly as possible. However, if your application requires those files to be in the new location before your application can be interacted with, you will want to provide the user visual feedback that a copy is occurring. You can register a listener for the complete event on the `File` instance in order to know when the copy has completed successfully:

```
sourcefile.copyToAsync( destinationFile, true );
sourcefile.addEventListener( Event.COMPLETE, copyComplete );
function copyComplete( event:Event ):void
{
trace( "copy complete" );
}
```

Load
SWF files

Earlier chapters in the book demonstrate how to load different types of media, such as images (Chapter 6), videos (Chapter 8), and sounds (Chapter 7). With AIR for Android, you can also load SWF files at runtime. This is an extremely important feature because it allows you to create external files, which can either be loaded from the local file system of the device or from a Web server on the Internet. This is one of the big features missing from the Flash CS5 iPhone Packager, which may potentially alter your development process in order to develop for the iPhone platform.

With AIR for Android, you are able to load any external ActionScript 3 SWF, and it will execute as you would expect if you were developing an AIR application for the desktop or a Flash application for the Web.

If you decide to load the SWF from the device, you need to make sure that it is bundled with your application when it is compiled. After the application is compiled, you can use the `Loader` class in order to load the SWF at runtime. The `Loader` class is a subclass of the `DisplayObject` class, which means that it can be added to the display list just like any other visual asset, such as a `MovieClip`. You can add an instance of the `Loader` class at any time after it has been instantiated. You do not have to wait until your SWF file has been completely loaded in order to add it to the display list.

The `load()` method on the `Loader` class accepts an instance of the `URLRequest` class, which represents the location of the file that you are loading.

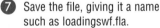

Load SWF files

Create a File to Load

1. Create a new FLA file.

2. Save the file, giving it a name such as circle.fla.

3. Click the Oval tool.

4. Draw a circle on the Stage.

5. Publish the file.

   The file is published as circle.swf.

Bundle a File

6. Create a new FLA file.

7. Save the file, giving it a name such as loadingswf.fla.

8. Click File.

9. Click AIR Android Settings.

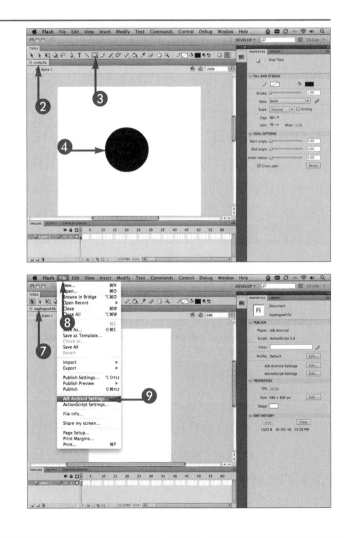

The Application & Installer Settings dialog box appears.

10 Click the + button.

The Open dialog box appears.

11 Click the file to bundle, such as circle.swf.

12 Click Open.

The file will now be bundled with your application.

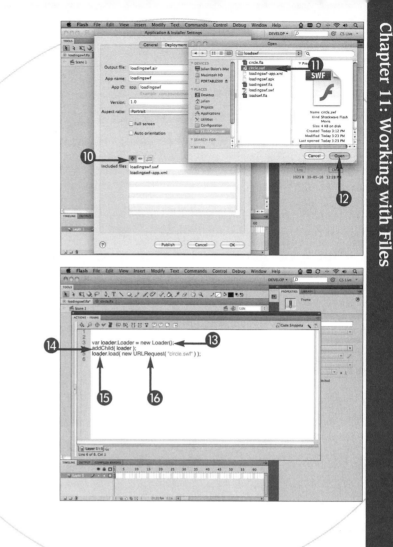

Load the SWF

13 Create a Loader variable, such as `var loader:Loader = new Loader();`.

14 Add it to the display list, such as `addChild( loader );`.

15 Call the `load()` method, such as `loader.load();`.

16 Create a URLRequest variable, such as `new URLRequest( "circle.swf" )`.

17 Compile and install your application.

The external SWF will be loaded.

Extra

If you happen to be loading a file from the Internet or a large file from the file system, you want to make sure that you are providing the user with some sort of visual feedback that your application is loading something. Mobile devices can often have slow download speeds, and not having a progress indicator can lead to confusion that your application has frozen or broken.

You can add a listener to the `Loader.contentLoaderInfo` property in order to receive progress updates, as shown in the following:

```
var loader:Loader = new Loader();
loader.contentLoaderInfo.addEventListener( ProgressEvent.PROGRESS, onProgress );
loader.load( new URLRequest( "circle.swf" ) );
function onProgress( e:ProgressEvent ):void{
trace( e.bytesLoaded/e.bytesTotal );
}
```

Retrieve Your Current Location

Android devices, such as the Google Nexus One phone, have the capability to determine your location through wireless networks as well as the onboard GPS chip. Using wireless networks is less accurate but is functional without a view of the sky. When selected, the device will use WiFi and/or mobile networks, such as cell towers, in order to determine your location. Using the GPS chip is more accurate but also uses more battery. Using GPS satellites to determine your location requires that you are in an open area. You can select which to use in the Location & Security section of the Settings application.

The Geolocation class enables you to retrieve information about your current location from your device. The geographical location is identified by longitude and latitude positions, which are returned in the WGS 84 standard format.

The Geolocation class dispatches an update event when a change in geographical location is detected. Each update dispatches a new GeolocationEvent, which returns properties of your current location, such as the longitude, latitude, altitude, speed, and timestamp of the latest change in location.

You can set the time interval for updates in milliseconds by calling the Geolocation.setRequestedUpdate Interval() method. The update interval is used only as a hint to conserve the battery power, and the actual time between updates may be greater or lesser than this value. Omitting this call will result in the device using a default interval for its updates.

You can check if the Geolocation.isSupported property is true to see if the device has the capability to retrieve the current location.

Retrieve Your Current Location

① Create a Geolocation instance, such as var geo:Geolocation;.

② Check if Geolocation is supported, such as if(Geolocation. isSupported).

③ Instantiate a new Geolocation variable, such as geo = new Geolocation();.

④ Set the update interval, such as geo.setRequestedUpdate Interval(100);.

⑤ Register an event listener for the update event, such as geo.add EventListener(Geo locationEvent.UPDATE, geolocationUpdate Handler);.

6 Create an `else` statement.

7 Output that `Geolocation` is not supported, such as `trace( "No geolocation support." );`.

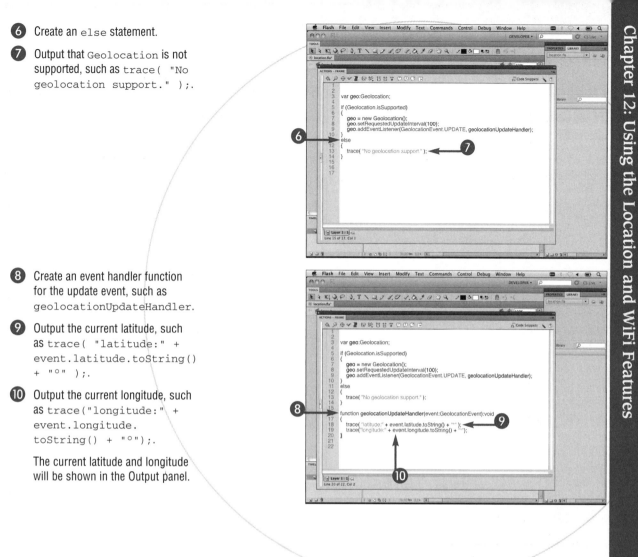

8 Create an event handler function for the update event, such as `geolocationUpdateHandler`.

9 Output the current latitude, such as `trace( "latitude:" + event.latitude.toString() + "°" );`.

10 Output the current longitude, such as `trace("longitude:" + event.longitude.toString() + "°");`.

The current latitude and longitude will be shown in the Output panel.

Extra

When you are developing an application that interacts with the GPS of the device, you will have to install your application on your device in order to use the `Geolocation` class. The process of installing an application on a device is pretty straightforward. However, you may want to test locally on your computer to make sure that everything is working correctly and there are no errors in your code before installing on your device. If you find yourself wanting to do this, you can set dummy longitude and latitude values in your code.

There is an application in the Android Market called *GPS Status*. This application displays the current longitude and latitude of your device. It also gives you the option to share your location in a variety of different ways. You can even email it to yourself so that you can copy and paste the location coordinates into your code.

This information comes in really handy as it enables you to insert dummy data into your application, allowing you to test it on your computer before installing it on your device.

Map Your Location with Yahoo!

Google provides an add-on to the Android SDK that enables you to embed maps inside your application. This library gives you the ability to include and interact with maps in your application. This is very similar to having the Maps application embedded in your application. Currently, this native Android framework is not included in the AIR for Android SDK, but there are many mapping APIs available for Flash.

Yahoo! has a map API for Flash that can be used in your AIR for Android applications. You will need to download the YahooMap.swc from the Yahoo! developer site at http://developer.yahoo.com/flash/maps/, as well as register your application in order to get an application ID. Yahoo! has many great samples that you can use to help get you started.

You can add the YahooMap.swc file in the Advanced ActionScript 3.0 Settings dialog box on the Library Path tab. It is important after you have included the file with your project that you set it to be merged into the rest of your code when your project is compiled. Skipping this step will result in your application not running.

The Yahoo! map component has all the map features you would expect, such as zoom, pan, and the ability to switch between map, satellite, and hybrid-style maps. After the map has been initialized, you can center it at a specified latitude and longitude position.

Make sure to read the license that comes with the API to make sure that you have the proper permission to include it in your application.

Map Your Location with Yahoo!

Add the Map API to Your Application

Note: First, you must download and import the YahooMap.swc file from http://developer.yahoo.com/flash/maps/.

1️⃣ Click File → ActionScript Settings.

2️⃣ Click the Library Path tab.

3️⃣ Click the Browse to SWC File button.

4️⃣ Click the SWC file that you imported.

5️⃣ Click here and select Merged into Code.

6️⃣ Click OK.

Display the Map at Your Current Location

7️⃣ Import the necessary classes.

8️⃣ Create a `Geolocation` instance.

9️⃣ Create a new `YahooMap` instance.

🔟 Register an initialize event listener, such as `map. addEventListener( YahooMapEvent. MAP_INITIALIZE, mapInitialized );`.

⑪ Initialize the map, such as `map.init();`.

⑫ Enter your Yahoo! App ID.

⑬ Enter the width and height of the map.

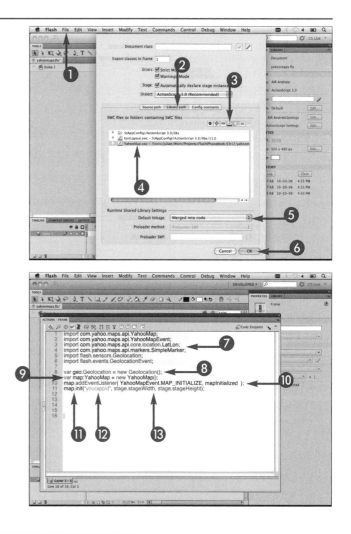

⑭ Create an event handler, such as
`mapInitialize`.

⑮ Set the initial map zoom level, such as `map.zoomLevel = 4;`.

⑯ Register for `Geolocation` updates, such as `geo.addEventListener ( GeolocationEvent.UPDATE, onGeoUpdate );`.

⑰ Create an event handler, such as `onGeoUpdate`.

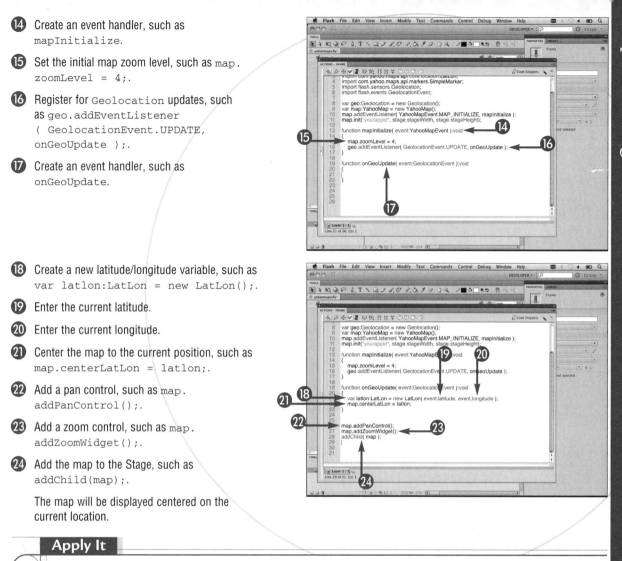

⑱ Create a new latitude/longitude variable, such as `var latlon:LatLon = new LatLon();`.

⑲ Enter the current latitude.

⑳ Enter the current longitude.

㉑ Center the map to the current position, such as `map.centerLatLon = latlon;`.

㉒ Add a pan control, such as `map.addPanControl();`.

㉓ Add a zoom control, such as `map.addZoomWidget();`.

㉔ Add the map to the Stage, such as `addChild(map);`.

The map will be displayed centered on the current location.

Apply It

There will be times when you want to find the latitude and longitude of a specific address. Calling the `geocode()` method on an `Address` instance will return a `LatLon` instance for that address. There is the possibility that more than one result will be returned to you. The following example automatically grabs the first one that is returned, as this should be the most accurate:

```
var address:Address = new Address("345 Park Ave, San Jose, CA 95110");
address.addEventListener(GeocoderEvent.GEOCODER_SUCCESS, geocodeAddress);
address.geocode();
function geocodeAddress (event:GeocoderEvent):void
{
var address:Address = event.target as Address;
var result:GeocoderResult = address.geocoderResultSet.firstResult;
map.zoomLevel = result.zoomLevel;
map.centerLatLon = result.latlon;
}
```

continued ➡

The Yahoo! maps API also enables you to add a marker to the map at a given latitude and longitude location. Using the `Geolocation` class, you can retrieve the current geographical location of the device and place a marker at this location on the map.

Registering an event for the `Geolocation` class update event will allow you to update the position of your marker as your geographical location changes. The `MarkerManager` class in the Yahoo! API has a `resetPosition()` method, which enables you to update the position of a marker. This method is very useful as it saves you from having to remove the original marker and adding a new one at the new location.

The `SimpleMarker` class in the Yahoo! API is a very simple marker that you can add to the Stage. It is not the

nicest-looking marker, though, so you will likely want to add your own custom graphic. To create your own custom marker, create a `MovieClip` symbol in the Library and center your graphic in it. Then export it for ActionScript and set the base class to `com.yahoo.maps.api.markers.Marker`. Your custom marker graphic will then be a subclass of the `Marker` class and have all the capabilities that other map markers do.

As well as update the position of your marker when your geographical location changes, you will want to center the map to the same location. Keeping your marker centered will ensure that your marker is never off the screen unless you manually pan the map. To pan the map, place a finger on the map and drag it in the direction that you want to move.

Map Your Location with Yahoo! *(continued)*

Add a Marker to Your Map

① Import a marker image to the Library.

Note: See Chapter 6, "Working with Images," for more information.

② Create a `MovieClip` symbol, such as `marker_mc`.

Note: See Chapter 2, "Getting Started with Flash CS5," for more information.

③ Center the image to the registration point of the movie clip.

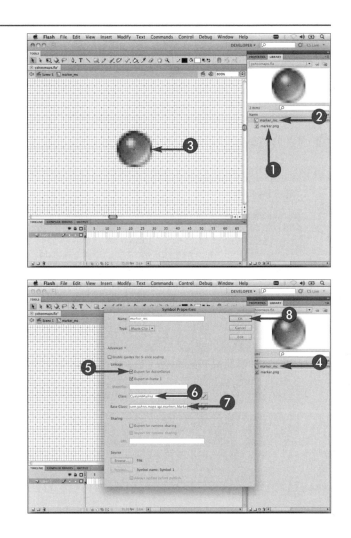

④ Right-click the `MovieClip` symbol and click Properties.

The Symbol Properties dialog box appears.

⑤ Click Export for ActionScript.

⑥ Give your symbol a class name, such as `CustomMarker`.

⑦ Give your symbol the base class of `com.yahoo.maps.api.markers.Marker`.

⑧ Click OK.

9 In the Actions panel, create an instance of your marker, such as `var marker:Custom Marker = new CustomMarker();`.

10 Set the `latlon` property of the marker, such as `marker. latlon = latlon;`.

11 Add the marker to the map, such as `map.markerManager. addMarker(marker);`.

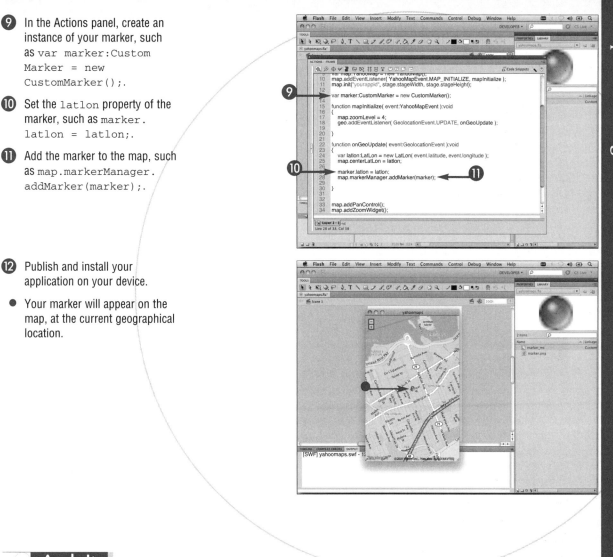

12 Publish and install your application on your device.

● Your marker will appear on the map, at the current geographical location.

Apply It

The Yahoo! maps API also has the capability to perform a local search for specific items. For example, you could search for all Starbucks locations nearby. By creating an instance of the `LocalSearch` class, you can use the `searchLocal()` method to perform your search. An array of `LocalSearchItem` instances will be returned, which you can use in order to place a marker on the map.

```
var localSearch:LocalSearch = new LocalSearch();
localSearch.addEventListener( LocalSearchEvent.SEARCH_SUCCESS, searchSuccess );
localSearch.searchLocal( "Starbucks", map.zoomLevel, map.centerLatLon, 5 );
function searchSuccess( event:LocalSearchEvent ):void{
var localResults:LocalSearchResults = event.data as LocalSearchResults;
var results:Array = localResults.results;
}
```

Map Your Location with Google

I n addition to the Yahoo! Maps API for Flash, Google has an API for their maps that are compatible with Flash and AIR for both the desktop and Android. One of the big benefits of using the Google Maps API is that it will be consistent with the Maps application on your Android device. It can be implemented so that it looks and feels just like it is the built-in maps framework.

Google provides an .swc file that you can embed in your Flash applications in order to access the Google Maps API. After you have downloaded it from the Google Maps Code repository, adding it to your .fla file can be done through the ActionScript Settings dialog box. After you access the ActionScript Settings dialog box, you use the

Library Path tab to bring up a list of .swc files and folders containing .swc files that will be compiled with your application. You then select the Google maps .swc file and make sure that it will be merged into the code.

Before you can start using the Google Maps API, you will need to obtain an API key from Google. When signing up for your key, Google will ask you to enter in a URL to a Web site where the application will be hosted. Because you are developing a mobile application and not a Web application, you can enter in your personal or company Web site URL. It is important to remember the URL because you will need to pass it to the Maps API when developing your application.

Map Your Location with Google

Obtain the Google Maps API

1 In a Web browser, go to the Google Maps Flash SDK URL, http://code.google.com/apis/maps/documentation/flash/.

2 Click SDK.

The SDK starts to download.

3 After the SDK is downloaded, unzip the sdk.zip file.

4 Click Sign Up for a Google Maps API Key.

The Google Maps SDK sign-up page appears.

5 Click here to check the terms of service check box.

6 Enter a URL to associate with your key.

7 Click Generate API Key.

Your API key is generated.

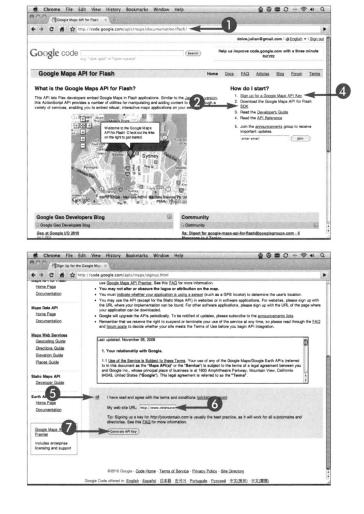

Add the Google Maps API to Your Application

⑧ In Flash, click File → ActionScript Settings.

The Advanced ActionScript 3.0 Settings dialog box appears.

⑨ Click the Library Path tab.

⑩ Click the Browse to SWC File button.

The Browse to SWC File dialog box appears.

⑪ Click the Maps .swc that you downloaded in step **2**.

⑫ Click Open.

The .swc file is now added to the list of libraries to include with your application.

⑬ Click the .swc file in the list.

⑭ Click here and select Merged into Code.

⑮ Click OK.

You are returned to your .fla file.

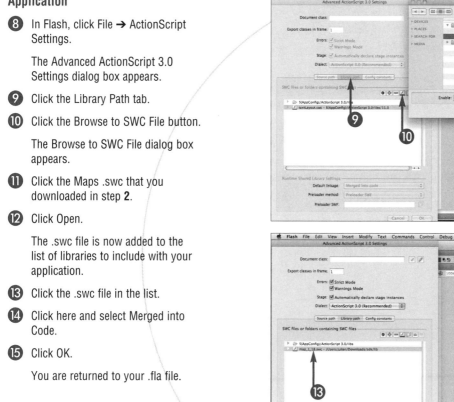

Extra

Merging an .swc file with your code takes all the compiled ActionScript code and assets inside it and merges them with your application. This treats the assets as if they were in your Library and you had the original class files. This is extremely convenient, as you do not have to worry about loading the .swc file externally or have to deal with any potential security restrictions that may be caused by this. The downside of this is that it will increase the file size of your main application, causing it to take longer to load initially.

A way to get around this on the Web is to set up the .swc file to be a runtime shared library. This will cause it to be loaded by your application externally. However, this method is not recommended for mobile applications. To load the library, create a new .fla file that simply merges the .swc file that you want to load into the code and load the compiled .swf. This can help in making sure that your user is presented with content as quickly as possible when your application is started and that additional files and assets are loaded as needed.

continued ➡

After you have downloaded the Google Maps .swc file, included it with your .fla, and obtained an API key from Google, you are ready to start development. The Flash Google Maps API has everything you would expect from a Google Map.

The main class that you will interact with is the Map class. The Map class is a display object that handles displaying the actual map tiles and any interaction with controls, overlays, and markers. It also has two properties, key and url, which allow you to provide your API key and the URL that you used when obtaining your key to the Maps API.

Before you can interact with the map, you must wait until it has fully initialized. This can be done by listening for the MapEvent.MAP_READY event on your Map instance. After the MAP_READY event has been received, you can

begin to interact with the map. For instance, you can center the map on your current location by listening to the Geolocation class for location updates.

As shown earlier in this chapter, the Geolocation class provides you with the current latitude and longitude of the device. By passing these values into the Map. setCenter() method, you can center the map on the screen at these coordinates.

The Marker class can also be used in order to place markers on the map. There are some simple built-in markers that you can add, as well as style, but you can also use a custom marker to place your own image on the map. When creating your marker, simply pass the latitude and longitude where you want to place your marker and add it to the map.

Map Your Location with Google (continued)

Use the Google Maps API in Your Application

16 Import the necessary files in the com. google.maps package, such as import com.google.maps.*;.

17 Import the Marker class, such as import com.google.maps.overlays.Marker;.

18 Create a Map instance, such as var map:Map = new Map();.

19 Add your API key, such as map.key = "MYAPIKEY";.

20 Add your URL, such as map.url = "http://www.deleteaso.com";.

21 Set the size of the map, such as map. setSize(new Point(480, 800));.

22 Add an event listener for the MAP_READY event, such as map.addEventListener (MapEvent.MAP_READY, onMapReady);.

23 Add the map to the display list, such as this.addChild(map);.

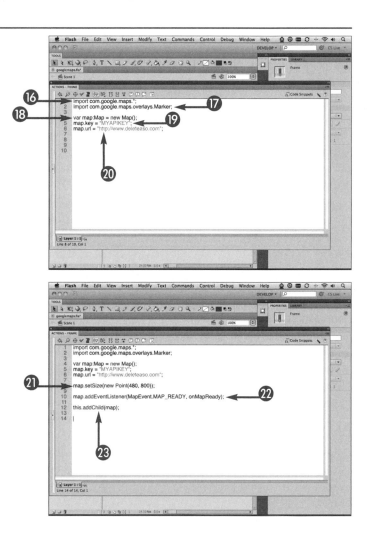

24 Create a `Geolocation` instance, such as `var geo:Geolocation = new Geolocation();`.

25 Create a handler for the MAP_READY event, such as `onMapReady`.

26 Listen for location updates, such as `geo.addEventListener( GeolocationEvent.UPDATE, onGeoUpdate );`.

27 Create a handler for the location update event, such as `onGeoUpdate`.

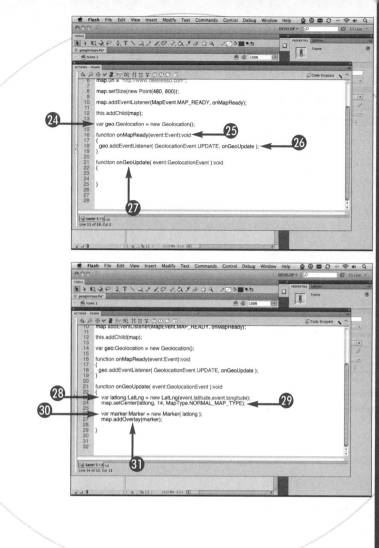

28 Create a `LatLng` variable, such as `var latlong:LatLng = new LatLng(event.latitude, event.longitude);`.

29 Center the map with the current location, such as `map.setCenter (latlong, 14, MapType. NORMAL_MAP_TYPE);`

30 Create a `Marker` instance, such as `var marker:Marker = new Marker( latlong );`.

31 Add the marker to the map, such as `map.addOverlay(marker);`.

32 Compile and install your application.

The map will be centered at your current location, marked by a marker.

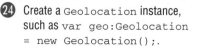

Apply It

You can also add the standard controls to your map, which allow your users to interact with it, just as they are probably used to in a Web browser. There are three common controls, the zoom control, the position control, and the map type control. Each of these controls can be added to the map after it has been initialized. You could change the `onMapReady` method from the example in this section to look like this, in order to add the controls:

```
function onMapReady(event:MapEvent):void {
  geo.addEventListener( GeolocationEvent.UPDATE, onGeoUpdate );
  map.addControl(new ZoomControl());
  map.addControl(new PositionControl());
  map.addControl(new MapTypeControl());
}
```

Determine Your Speed

The Geolocation class does a great job of enabling you to retrieve your current geographic location from the device. When the device detects a change in location, a GeolocationEvent is dispatched, and an instance containing information about the update is passed to the event handler function. As well as determine the latitude and longitude of your current location from the GeolocationEvent instance, you can determine the speed at which you are traveling.

The GeolocationEvent.speed property returns a number that represents your speed in meters per second. There are some simple equations that convert this into something more meaningful for your application. The example in the steps shows the equation for converting the number to kilometers per hour. Use the following equation if you want to convert it to miles per hour:

```
var mph:Number = Math.
  round((mps*360000)/160934.4));
```

The accuracy of the speed property will vary, depending on the accuracy of the GPS data that you receive. It will also vary between different devices. It has been my experience that it has been fairly accurate.

The speed property should be used more as a novelty instead of relying on it for very accurate data. For example, using it to see what your top speed is during a run or a bike ride is far more effective than using it as a replacement for the speedometer in your car.

You can also determine the time of when each update occurs. The timestamp property on the GeolocationEvent class returns the number of milliseconds since the runtime was initialized.

Determine Your Speed

1. Click the Text tool.

2. Draw a text field on the Stage.

3. Click here and select Classic Text.

4. Click here and select Dynamic Text.

5. Give the text field an instance name, such as speed_txt.

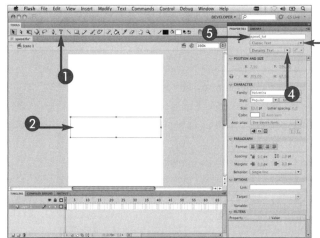

6. In the Actions panel, check to see if Geolocation is supported, such as if(Geolocation.isSupported){}.

7. Create an else statement if it is not supported, such as else{}.

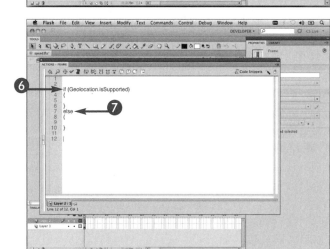

8 Create a `Geolocation` variable, such as `var geo:Geolocation = new Geolocation();`.

9 Add an event listener, such as `geo.addEventListener(GeolocationEvent.UPDATE, geolocationUpdateHandler);`.

10 Output a message if `Geolocation` is not supported, such as `trace( "No geolocation support" );`.

11 Create an event handler function.

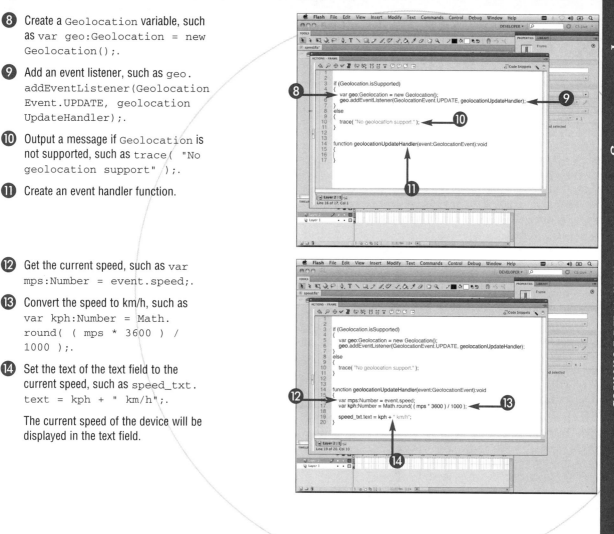

12 Get the current speed, such as `var mps:Number = event.speed;`.

13 Convert the speed to km/h, such as `var kph:Number = Math.round( ( mps * 3600 ) / 1000 );`.

14 Set the text of the text field to the current speed, such as `speed_txt.text = kph + " km/h";`.

The current speed of the device will be displayed in the text field.

Apply It

The `GeolocationEvent` class also contains a property that represents your altitude in meters. Combining both `altitude` and `speed` properties, you could measure how fast you ascend or descend in altitude. For example, you could measure your top speed skiing down a hill while measuring the change in altitude from the top to the bottom of the run:

```
var geo:Geolocation = new Geolocation();
geo.addEventListener(GeolocationEvent.UPDATE, geolocationUpdateHandler);
function geolocationUpdateHandler(event:GeolocationEvent):void
{
    trace( "altitude", event. altitude );
}
```

Check for an Internet Connection

C hances are your application will at some point require a connection to the Internet. It may be to simply send analytic tracking for user interactions or to submit a score to an online leaderboard. It could also be as complicated as a multiplayer game over a socket connection or streaming video from a media server, such as Flash Media Server. It is a good practice to check for the presence of an Internet connection before attempting to send data.

If an Internet connection is not found, you can hide the portions of your application that require it — for example, not displaying a Submit button in order to submit a score. You can also save the score locally for the user, and the next time that he or she launches the application with an Internet connection, you can submit the scores.

The `URLMonitor` and `SocketMonitor` classes enable you to monitor the availability of a specific host or service. The `URLMonitor` class is used to monitor the availability of a specified `URLRequest` instance. Calling the `start()` method of the `URLMonitor` class will attempt to hit the specified URL. After the monitor has determined whether the URL is available or not, a `StatusEvent.STATUS` event will be fired. The value of the `code` property for the event instance will be set to `"Service.available"` if the URL is available and `"Service.unavailable"` if it is unavailable. However, it is best practice to check the value of the `available` property of your `URLMonitor` instance.

Setting the `pollInterval` property of a `URLMonitor` instance will cause it to check the availability of the URL at the specified interval in milliseconds. Calling the `stop()` method will stop the monitoring of the service.

Check for an Internet Connection

1. Click File → ActionScript Settings.

   The ActionScript Settings dialog box appears.

2. Click the Library Path tab.

3. Click the Browse to SWC File button.

4. Click the aircore.swc file in the Adobe Flash CS5/AIK2.0/frameworks/libs/air folder.

5. Click here and select Merged into Code.

6. Click OK.

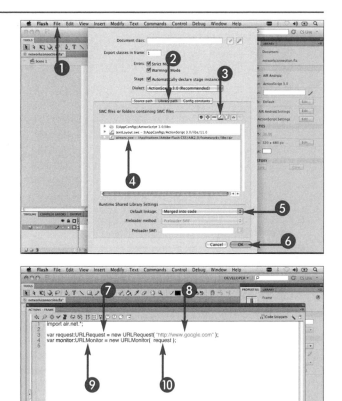

7. In the Actions panel, create a new `URLRequest` variable, such as `var request:URLRequest = new URLRequest();`.

8. Enter a valid URL to monitor, such as `http://www.google.com`.

9. Create a new `URLMonitor` variable, such as `var monitor:URL Monitor = new URLMonitor();`.

10. Enter the `request` variable in the constructor.

⑪ Add a listener to the monitor, such as `monitor.addEventListener();`.

⑫ Listen for the `StatusEvent.STATUS` event.

⑬ Enter an event handler method, such as `onStatus`.

⑭ Start the monitor, such as `monitor.start();`.

⑮ Create an event handler function.

⑯ Stop the monitor, such as `monitor.stop();`.

⑰ Output the monitor's availability, such as `trace( monitor.available);`.

The availability of the service will be shown in Output panel.

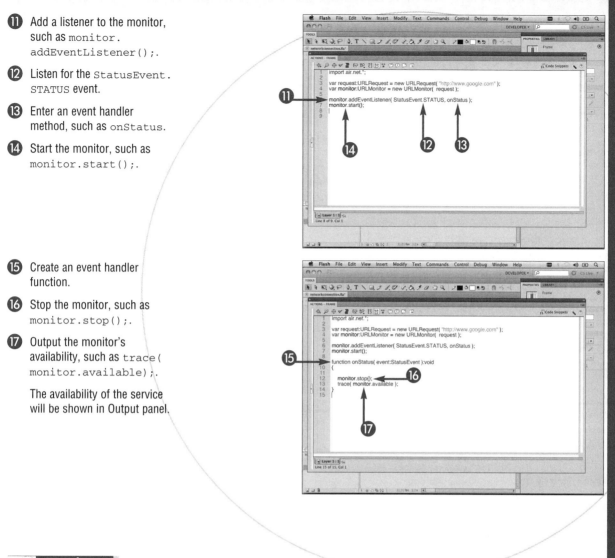

Apply It

The `SocketMonitor` class works the same way the `URLMonitor` class works, except instead of monitoring a URL or HTTP service, it monitors a host and port. Both classes are subclasses of the `ServiceMonitor` class and share many of the same properties and methods. When creating a `SocketServer` instance, you specify the host and the port in its constructor:

```
var monitor:SocketMonitor = new SocketMonitor("192.168.1.102", 4444);
monitor.addEventListener( StatusEvent.STATUS, onStatus );
monitor.start();
function onStatus( event:StatusEvent ):void
{
trace( monitor.available );
}
```

Set the System Idle Mode

The greatest thing about smartphones and devices is having your applications and information with you at all times. Mobile devices are becoming more and more like minicomputers, and we depend on them just as much — if not more. The biggest obstacle for any portable device, laptops included, is battery life. The more your application does, the more it will drain the battery.

In order to help prolong the battery life on the device, you can set it to go into Sleep mode if it does not register a touch on the screen. When the device goes into Sleep mode, the screen turns off, and the device locks. Because of the different ways that these devices allow users to interact, this can be an issue. For example, a game that

uses only the accelerometer as its input will not register a screen touch, so the screen could turn off right in the middle of a game.

This scenario is not ideal, and you will need to tell the device to remain awake. When disabling the Sleep mode of the device, be sure to disable it only when necessary. For example, if you are building a game, only disable it during game play and when the game launches. This allows the device to go into Sleep mode when it is not critical that it stay awake. This will help conserve the battery power of your user's device.

The `NativeApplication.systemIdleMode` property allows you to tell the device to stay awake, as well as set it back to the normal mode of the device.

Set the System Idle Mode

Set Application Permissions

1 Open the application descriptor file.

2 Add the `WAKE_LOCK` permission, such as `<uses-permission android: name="android.permission. WAKE_LOCK"/>`.

3 Add the `DISABLE_KEYGUARD` permission, such as `<uses-permission android: name="android.permission. DISABLE_KEYGUARD"/>`.

The necessary application permissions are set.

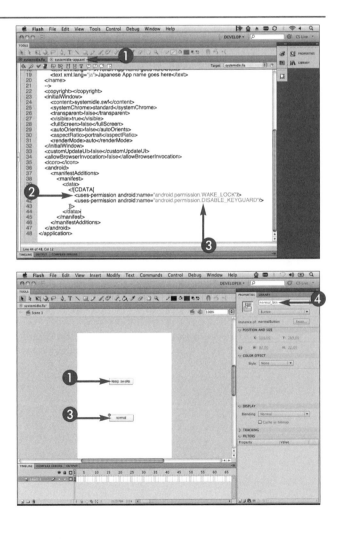

Create Buttons

1 Create a `Button` symbol and add it to the Stage.

Note: See Chapter 2 for more information.

2 Give it an instance name, such as `awake_btn`.

3 Create another `Button` symbol and add it to the Stage.

4 Give it an instance name, such as `normal_btn`.

Have the Buttons Set Awake and Normal Idle Modes

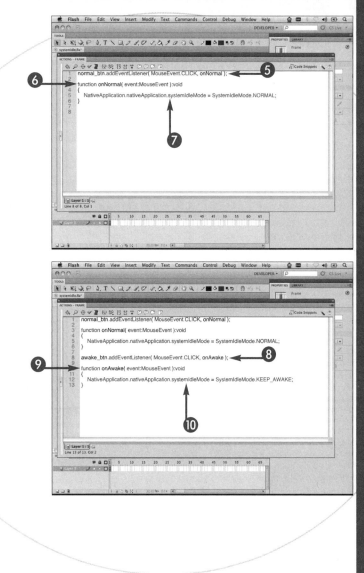

⑤ In the Actions panel, add a listener for the click event, such as `normal_btn.addEventListener( MouseEvent.CLICK, onNormal );`.

⑥ Create an event handler function, such as `onNormal`.

⑦ Set the system Idle mode to normal, such as `NativeApplication.nativeApplication.systemIdleMode = SystemIdleMode.NORMAL;`.

⑧ Add a listener for the click event, such as `awake_btn.addEventListener( MouseEvent.CLICK, onAwake);`.

⑨ Create an event handler function, such as `onAwake`.

⑩ Set the system Idle mode to awake, such as `NativeApplication.nativeApplication.systemIdleMode = SystemIdleMode.KEEP_AWAKE;`.

When the `awake_btn` button is clicked, the device will remain awake.

When the `normal_btn` button is clicked, the device will sleep after a certain period of inactivity.

Apply It

When your application exits, the system Idle mode is reset back to normal, allowing the device to enter Sleep mode when needed. However, you should not rely on this at all times; it is best practice to set the system Idle mode back to normal yourself when your application exits. This will make sure that the device will return to Sleep mode as expected. You can listen for the exiting event of the application to determine when the application is about to close:

```
var application:NativeApplication = NativeApplication.nativeApplication;
application.addEventListener( Event.EXITING, onExit );
function onExit( e:Event ):void
{
application.removeEventListener( Event.EXITING, onExit );
application.systemIdleMode = SystemIdleMode.NORMAL;
}
```

Display Web Pages

I f you have done any AIR desktop development, you may be familiar with the HTMLLoader class, which enables you to display HTML using the WebKit engine bundled with the AIR Runtime. Including the AIR Runtime version of the WebKit with the AIR Mobile profile will greatly increase the size and memory footprint of runtime. Because most mobile devices have a native implementation of WebKit, Adobe has chosen to leverage the native implementation instead of bundling its own. This keeps the runtime size down but limits the amount of communication between ActionScript and JavaScript, which is available in the HTMLLoader class.

To allow developers to display HTML content in their applications, Adobe has introduced the StageWebView class. The StageWebView class can display HTML content in two ways. The loadURL() method loads a remote URL

from the Internet. By default, loading a remote URL causes the native browser to be launched with that URL. The default behavior can be changed by listening for the LocationChangeEvent.LOCATION_CHANGING event and prevented by calling event.preventDefault().

The StageWebView.loadString() method enables you to display an HTML string as HTML content in your application. The HTML string can be a full formatted HTML Web page source or simply a block of text. Because the StageWebView class has the native scroll bars and zoom and pan features built into the control, it is a great solution for displaying large blocks of text to the user.

If your content relies on loading data from the Internet, be sure to set the <uses-permission android:name= "android.permission.INTERNET" /> permission in your application descriptor. For more details on application permissions, see Chapter 3.

Display Web Pages

Display a URL

① Create a StageWebView variable, such as var web:StageWebView = new StageWebView();.

② Set the position and dimensions of the Web view, such as web.viewPort = new Rectangle(0, 0, stage.stageWidth, stage. stageHeight);.

③ Set the Stage of the Web view, such as web.stage = this.stage;.

④ Listen for the LOCATION_CHANGING event, such as web.addEvent Listener(LocationChange Event.LOCATION_CHANGING, locationChanging);.

⑤ Create an event handler, such as locationChanging.

6 Prevent the default redirect behavior, such as `e.preventDefault();`.

7 Load the URL, such as `web.loadURL( e.url );`.

8 Load the initial URL, such as `web.loadURL( "http://www.google.com" );`.

The Web page is loaded in your application.

Display an HTML String

1 Create a `StageWebView` variable, such as `var web:StageWebView = new StageWebView();`.

2 Set the position and dimensions of the Web view, such as `web.viewPort = new Rectangle ( 0, 0, stage.stageWidth, stage.stageHeight );`.

3 Set the Stage of the Web view, such as `web.stage = this.stage;`.

4 Create an HTML formatted string.

5 Load the HTML string, such as `web.loadString( str );`.

The HTML string is loaded into the Web view.

Extra

The `StageWebView` class also provides you with other basic browser functionality if you want to provide users with a browser interface. The `stop()` method stops the current load request, the `reload()` method reloads the current page, and the `historyBack()` and `historyForward()` methods allow you to navigate the browsing history of your Web view. In addition to these methods, you can use the `title` property to retrieve the HTML title of the currently loaded page, as well as the `location` property for retrieving the currently loaded URL.

Because the `StageWebView` class is not added to the display list of your application, it cannot be removed from the Stage as if it were a display object. Your Web view instance can be removed from the Stage using the following syntax:

```
web.dispose();
```

Make Phone Calls

A ndroid devices have a custom URL scheme to enable developers to present users with a link to a telephone number. Creating a link to a telephone number is very similar to creating a link to a Web page. However, you substitute the `http://` protocol with `tel:`. The `tel` URL scheme takes any valid phone number as its parameter. When navigating to a valid `tel` URL, the Phone application will launch, and the number will be dialed without prompting the user.

It is a good practice to show an alert to the users, allowing them to confirm that they want to dial the specified number. The Mail application does this when a telephone number is detected in an email.

The Phone application supports most, but not all, of the special characters in the `tel` URL scheme. For example,

if a `tel` URL contains the * or # characters, the Phone application does not attempt to dial the corresponding phone number. This helps in preventing users from redirecting phone calls or changing the behavior of the Phone application. Also, if any space characters are detected in the URL string, the Phone application will not launch, as these spaces are not supported.

When dealing with an unknown source, such as allowing the user to enter a telephone number into an input text field, you should make sure that all special characters that are not valid characters in the URL are escaped properly. You can use the `encodeURI()` method to escape the URL string properly. When a string is encoded, all characters are encoded as UTF-8 escaped sequences unless they belong to a small subset of characters. To see the full list of characters, refer to the help files.

Make Phone Calls

① Create a `Button` symbol and place it on the Stage.

Note: See Chapter 2, "Getting Started with Flash CS5," for more information.

② Give it an instance name, such as `phone_btn`.

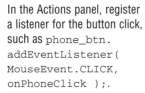

③ In the Actions panel, register a listener for the button click, such as `phone_btn.addEventListener( MouseEvent.CLICK, onPhoneClick );`.

④ Create an event handler function, such as `onPhoneClick`.

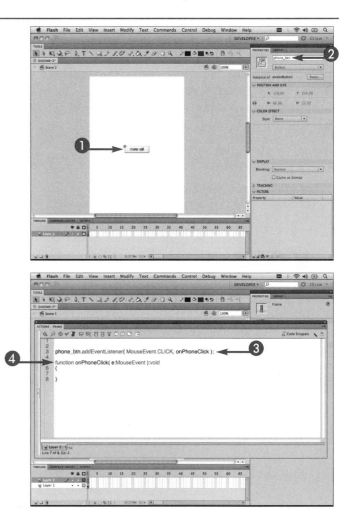

⑤ Create a `String` variable for the phone number, such as `var number:String = "+1-555-555-5555";`.

⑥ Create a `String` variable for the URL, such as `var url:String = "tel:";`.

⑦ Add the `number` variable to the `url` variable, such as `+ number`.

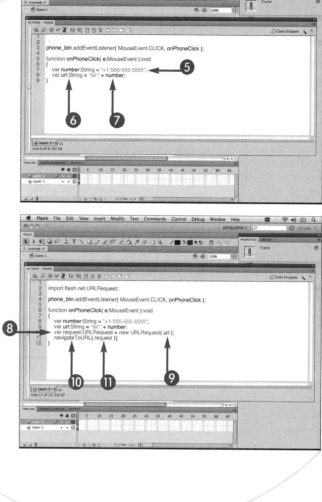

⑧ Create a `URLRequest` variable, such as `var request:URLRequest = new URLRequest();`.

⑨ Add the URL to the request.

⑩ Type **navigateToURL();**.

⑪ Add the `request` variable as an argument.

After you compile and install the application on a device, when the button is pressed, the Phone application will launch.

Apply It

You can also place the telephone number as a link in a text field that renders HTML text. To set the text field to render HTML text, you must select the Render As HTML button in the Properties panel of the text field. It is the middle button located directly underneath the Anti-Alias drop-down list. After the text field has been set to render HTML text, you can set the `htmlText` property of the text field to a `String` containing HTML text. Here is the syntax to create a telephone number link in a text field:

```
mytext_txt.htmlText = 'My telephone number is <u><a href="tel:+1-555-555-5555">
1-555-555-5555</a></u>';
```

Make sure that the font for the text field is big enough to allow the user to tap the link. If the font is too small, users will have a hard time registering a tap on the URL portion of the text.

Open the Mail Application

Opening the Mail application to send a message is the same process as if you were in a browser. The `mailto` URL scheme allows you to compose a new email message with certain fields prefilled. In its simplest form, a `mailto` URL contains only a recipient's email address, which follows the `mailto:` protocol. Any additional fields that you want to have prefilled are added as query string parameters after the recipient's email address.

You can use the `to` query string parameter in order to add additional email addresses to the To: field of the email. The `cc` query string parameter enables you to add email addresses to the carbon copy field. The `bcc` query string parameter enables you to add email addresses to the blind carbon copy field. If you want to add multiple

email addresses to any of these fields, you can separate additional email addresses by a comma.

You may have multiple email applications installed on your device, such as Gmail and Email. When a `mailto` link is clicked, a pop-up message will appear, asking which application to launch in order to compose the email.

Setting the `subject` query string parameter fills the Subject: field of the email. The `body` query string parameter allows you to prefill the body of the email with text. Because the `=`, `?`, and `&` characters are reserved in the `mailto` scheme, any parameters that contain these characters must be encoded. You will need to encode each parameter separately and not the entire URL as that will cause reserved characters, which are used to separate parameters, to be encoded as well.

Open the Mail Application

① Create a `Button` symbol and place it on the Stage.

Note: *See Chapter 2 for more information.*

② Give it an instance name, such as `email_btn`.

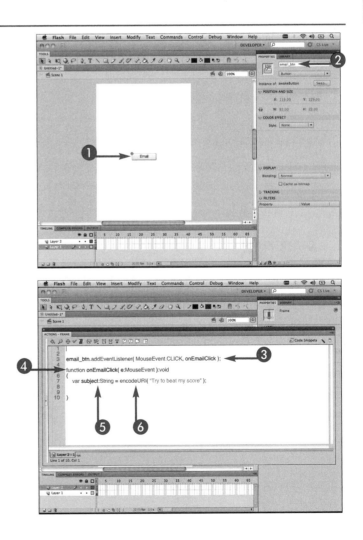

③ In the Actions panel, register a listener for the button click, such as `email_btn.addEventListener( MouseEvent.CLICK, onEmailClick );`.

④ Create an event handler function, such as `onEmailClick`.

⑤ Create a `String` variable for the subject of the email, such as `var subject:String = "Try to beat my score"`.

⑥ Encode the variable, such as `encodeURI();`.

7. Create a `String` variable for the email body, such as `var body:String = "I just scored 15429 in Sushi Toss! Can you beat my score?".`

8. Encode the variable, such as `encodeURI();.`

9. Create a `String` variable, such as `var url:String = "";.`

10. Add the `mailto:` protocol.

11. Add an email address, such as `name@email.com.`

12. Add a `?`.

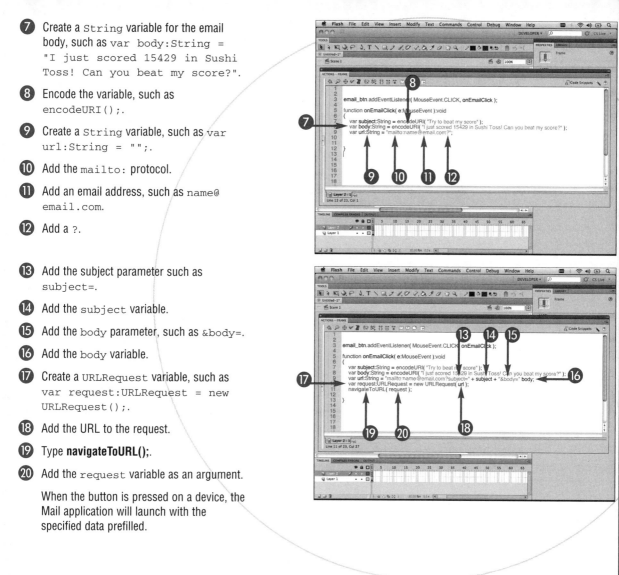

13. Add the subject parameter such as `subject=.`

14. Add the `subject` variable.

15. Add the `body` parameter, such as `&body=.`

16. Add the `body` variable.

17. Create a `URLRequest` variable, such as `var request:URLRequest = new URLRequest();.`

18. Add the URL to the request.

19. Type **navigateToURL();**.

20. Add the `request` variable as an argument.

When the button is pressed on a device, the Mail application will launch with the specified data prefilled.

Apply It

Currently, the `mailto` URL scheme does not support attachments. A common integration point of the Mail application in a mobile application is being able to send images with your email. However, this currently cannot be accomplished with AIR for Android. You can, although, include HTML in the body of your email. The following is an example of HTML in the body of your email:

```
var html:String = "<a href='http://www.deleteaso.com'>My Blog</a>";
var subject:String = "link to my blog";
var url:String = "mailto:name@email.com?subject=" + encodeURI(subject) + "&body=" +
  encodeURI(html);
navigateToURL( new URLRequest( url ) );
```

Open the Maps Application

Chapter 12, "Using the Location and WiFi Features," discusses how you can integrate maps inside your application. Another alternative to this is being able to launch the native Maps application to a specific geographical location. The downfall to this is having your application exit, in order to show the map. Depending on the type of application you are creating, this may be acceptable. Unlike the other URL schemes in this chapter, the map URL does not start with a custom scheme identifier, such as maps. Instead, a regular http URL is used, targeted at the Google Maps servers. If the Maps application is not found, a browser will be launched and will go to the Google Maps page.

Most of the Google Maps parameters are supported; however, using an unsupported parameter may cause the Maps application to fail to launch. The following are the

available Google Maps parameters: The q parameter is treated as if a query had been typed into the query box on the maps.google.com page. Note that q=* is not supported. The near parameter is the location part of the query. The ll parameter represents the latitude and longitude points in decimal format and separated by commas for the center of the map. The t parameter sets the type of map to display. Valid options for this parameter are m for maps, k for satellite, and h for hybrid. The z parameter sets the zoom level of the map ranging from 1–20. The sll parameter is the latitude and longitude points from which a business search should be performed. The spn parameter is the approximate latitude and longitude span.

Two parameters that cannot be included are view=text and dirflg=r.

Open the Maps Application

1 Create a Button symbol and place it on the Stage.

Note: *See Chapter 2 for more information.*

2 Give it an instance name, such as map_btn.

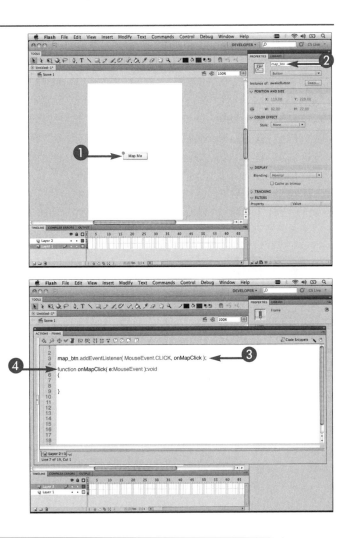

3 In the Actions panel, register a listener for the button click, such as map_btn. addEventListener(MouseEvent. CLICK, onMapClick);.

4 Create an event handler function, such as onMapClick.

5 Create a `String` variable, such as `var url:String = "";`.

6 Add the Google Maps URL, such as `http://maps.google.com/maps`.

7 Add the latitude and longitude parameter, such as `?ll=`.

8 Enter a latitude, such as `40.770401835894084`.

9 Add a comma.

10 Enter a longitude, such as `-73.97420883178711`.

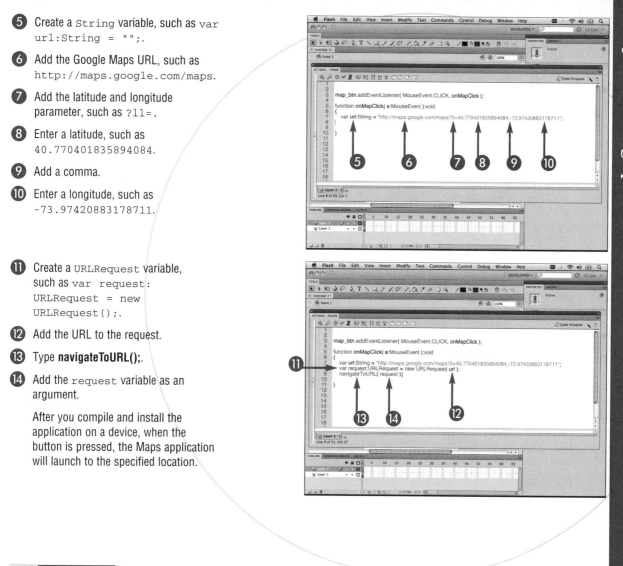

11 Create a `URLRequest` variable, such as `var request: URLRequest = new URLRequest();`.

12 Add the URL to the request.

13 Type **navigateToURL();**.

14 Add the `request` variable as an argument.

After you compile and install the application on a device, when the button is pressed, the Maps application will launch to the specified location.

Apply It

As well as show the current location on the map, you can generate driving directions between two addresses. By setting the `saddr` parameter as the source address and the `daddr` parameter as the destination address, you can have driving directions displayed on the map between the two addresses. Here is an example of getting the driving directions between the Google head office and the Adobe head office:

```
var saddr:String = encodeURI("1600 Amphitheatre Parkway, Mountain View, CA 94043");
var daddr:String = encodeURI("345 Park Ave, San Jose, CA 95110");
var url:String = "http://maps.google.com/maps?saddr="+saddr+"&daddr="+daddr;
navigateToURL( new URLRequest( url ) );
```

Open the Messaging Application

The sms URL scheme makes it easy to open the Messaging application from your applications. The Messaging application is where you can send text messages or SMS messages to other SMS-enabled devices. The sms URL scheme can be used to simply open the Messaging application, or you can open it to a new message with a phone number already prefilled.

The URL scheme starts with sms: and is followed by the phone number to compose the text message to. The phone number can contain digits 0 through 9 and the plus (+), hyphen (-), and period (.) characters. Any additional characters or text must not be included in the URL. If the sms URL does not have a phone number included with it, the Messaging application will open to its default screen.

There are currently some options for the sms URL scheme that are not supported on the Android. For example, you can specify only one phone number per URL. In the specification, it states that you can add multiple phone numbers by separating them with commas. In reality, however, if a comma is used to separate two phone numbers, the entire string will be treated as one phone number.

Similarly to the mailto URL scheme, the sms URL scheme has a body parameter. This parameter is used to prefill the message portion of the text message. Unfortunately, this parameter is not supported by the Messaging application, and if you use it, you may get unexpected results.

Open the Messaging Application

① Create a Button symbol and place it on the Stage.

Note: See Chapter 2 for more information.

② Give it an instance name, such as sms_btn.

③ In the Actions panel, register a listener for the button click, such as sms_btn.
addEventListener
(MouseEvent.CLICK,
onSMSClick);.

④ Create an event handler function, such as
onSMSClick.

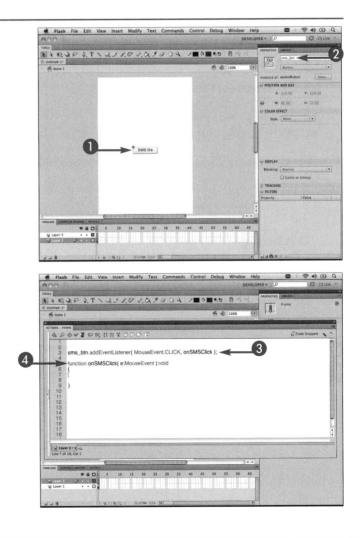

5 Create a `String` variable, such as `var url:String = "";`.

6 Add the `sms` URL protocol, such as `sms:`.

7 Add a phone number to text, such as `1-555-555-5555`.

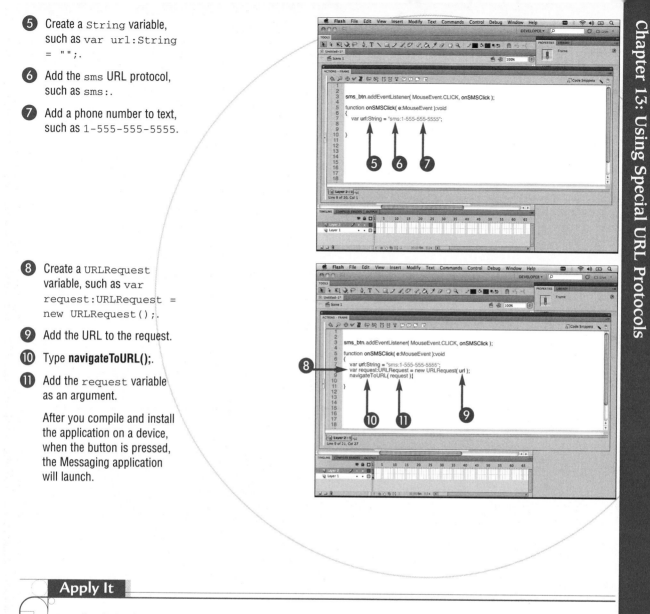

8 Create a `URLRequest` variable, such as `var request:URLRequest = new URLRequest();`.

9 Add the URL to the request.

10 Type **navigateToURL();**.

11 Add the `request` variable as an argument.

After you compile and install the application on a device, when the button is pressed, the Messaging application will launch.

Apply It

As well as being launched from your applications, the `sms` URL can be used as an HTML link on a Web page in the Browser application. You can also include an `sms` URL in HTML text that is rendered in a `TextField`. To apply HTML text to your `TextField`s, you must first select the Render As HTML button in the Properties panel of the `TextField`. After you select this, you can set the `htmlText` property of your `TextField` to the HTML text `String`:

```
var html:String = '<u><a href="sms:+1-555-555-5555">Send me a text message</a></u>';
mytext_txt.htmlText = html;
```

Play a YouTube Video

The YouTube URL protocol can be used to play videos in the YouTube application. If the YouTube application is not available or found, the Browser application will open to the YouTube Web site. Similar to linking to the Maps application, the YouTube URL protocol does not use a `youtube` scheme identifier. Instead, it uses a regular `http` protocol, which points to the YouTube servers.

Before you can link to a specific YouTube video, you must first get the unique identifier for that video. The unique identifier for a video can be found at the end of the URL in the Address bar when on the video page of the YouTube site. For example, if the URL to your video is http://www.youtube.com/watch?v=Nr32TcO7fmM, the unique video identifier will be `Nr32TcO7fmM`.

There are two different ways you can format the link to a YouTube video. The first is similar to the URL you would

see in the Address bar if you went to the video in a browser on your desktop — `http://www.youtube.com/watch?v=VIDEO_IDENTIFIER`, in which `VIDEO_IDENTIFIER` is the identifier of your video. When in a browser, this URL will bring you to the page for your video on YouTube.

The second URL format is slightly different from the first — `http://www.youtube.com/v/VIDEO_IDENTIFIER`, in which `VIDEO_IDENTIFIER` is the identifier of your video. If you went to this URL in a browser, it would display the video full screen outside the shell of the YouTube Web site.

When navigated to, both URL formats will exit your application and launch the YouTube application. If the video can be played on the device, it will automatically be launched and start to play.

Play a YouTube Video

① In a Web browser, navigate to the YouTube video page.

② Copy the video identifier.

③ Create a `Button` symbol and place it on the Stage.

Note: See Chapter 2 for more information.

④ Give it an instance name, such as `youtube_btn`.

230

5 In the Actions panel, register a listener for the button click, such as `youtube_btn.addEvent Listener( MouseEvent. CLICK, onYBClick );`.

6 Create an event handler function, such as `onYBClick`.

7 Create a `String` variable, such as `var url:String = "";`.

8 Add the YouTube URL, such as `http://www.youtube.com/v/`.

9 Add the video identifier, such as `Nr32TcO7fmM`.

10 Create a `URLRequest` variable, such as `var request:URL Request = new URLRequest();`.

11 Add the URL to the request.

12 Type **navigateToURL();**.

13 Add the `request` variable as an argument.

After you compile and install the application on a device, when the button is pressed, the YouTube application will launch, and the video will begin to play.

Extra

It is important to note that not all YouTube videos can be played on your device. If you link to a video that is not supported for playback on the device, you will receive an error message. Videos that were uploaded to YouTube before your device was released are the ones that may not be supported on the device. This is because they were not encoded in a format that your device understands. Since the release of the iPhone and Android devices, YouTube has started to encode its videos using the H.264 video codec, which is a supported video codec for the most smartphones. For any videos that were uploaded and not encoded with the H.264 video format, YouTube has been re-encoding them in order to support various devices. However, there is the possibility that your video did not get re-encoded yet, so you should make sure to test all your videos before submitting your application. If you have recently uploaded your video to YouTube, it will most likely support playback on the device.

Submit Updates to Twitter

Mobile devices have become the premier social devices on the market today. The ability to keep in touch with your friends and contacts wherever you are is a key element to the success of any new mobile device. Games and applications are taking advantage of this by integrating social media into them. Many games enable you to post your score to your Twitter feed. Integrating Twitter and other social media touch points gives developers free advertising within their users' social media networks.

Submitting text to users' Twitter feeds can be done using the Twitter API. The `twitter.com/statuses/update.xml` URL is used to POST the status string. You will need to have a method for the users to input their Twitter usernames and passwords. It is a good idea to store these locally so that the users do not have to input them every time. The username and password get added to the URL, creating the URL `http://username:password@twitter.com/statuses/update.xml`.

The status query string parameter is used to set the status update text. You can use a `URLVariables` instance to store this variable. Your `URLVariables` instance is then set to the `data` property of your `URLRequest` instance for the URL.

To send the Twitter status update, use a `URLLoader` instance. This allows you to listen for result events to be fired when the URL has been submitted. Registering a listener for the `IOErrorEvent.IO_ERROR` event enables you to notify the users that there was an error in submitting their Twitter status. This could be caused by an incorrect username or password, or there may be issues with the Twitter API. If an `Event.COMPLETE` event is fired, the submission was successful.

Submit Updates to Twitter

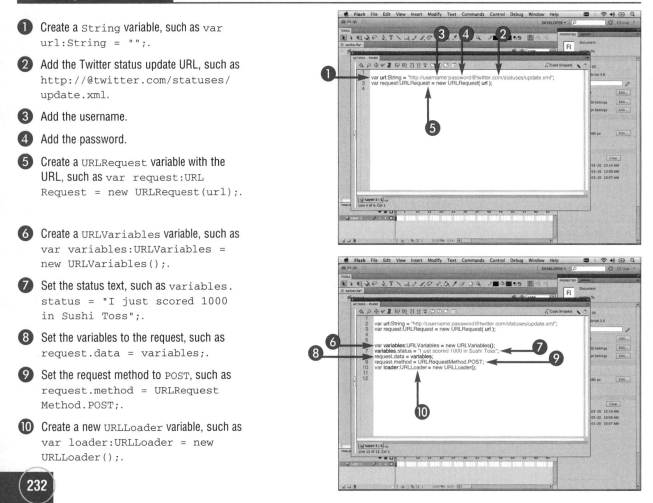

1. Create a `String` variable, such as `var url:String = "";`.

2. Add the Twitter status update URL, such as `http://@twitter.com/statuses/update.xml`.

3. Add the username.

4. Add the password.

5. Create a `URLRequest` variable with the URL, such as `var request:URLRequest = new URLRequest(url);`.

6. Create a `URLVariables` variable, such as `var variables:URLVariables = new URLVariables();`.

7. Set the status text, such as `variables.status = "I just scored 1000 in Sushi Toss";`.

8. Set the variables to the request, such as `request.data = variables;`.

9. Set the request method to POST, such as `request.method = URLRequestMethod.POST;`.

10. Create a new `URLLoader` variable, such as `var loader:URLLoader = new URLLoader();`.

⑪ Listen for any errors, such as
`loader.addEventListener`
`(IOErrorEvent.IO_ERROR,`
`ioError );`.

⑫ Create an event handler function,
such as `ioError`.

⑬ Output any errors, such as `trace`
`( e.toString() );`.

⑭ Listen for any complete events, such
as `loader.addEventListener`
`(Event.COMPLETE, onComplete );`.

⑮ Create an event handler function, such as
`onComplete`.

⑯ Output the result data, such as `trace(`
`loader.data as String );`.

⑰ Load the request, such as `loader.`
`load( request );`.

The status update will be posted to Twitter.

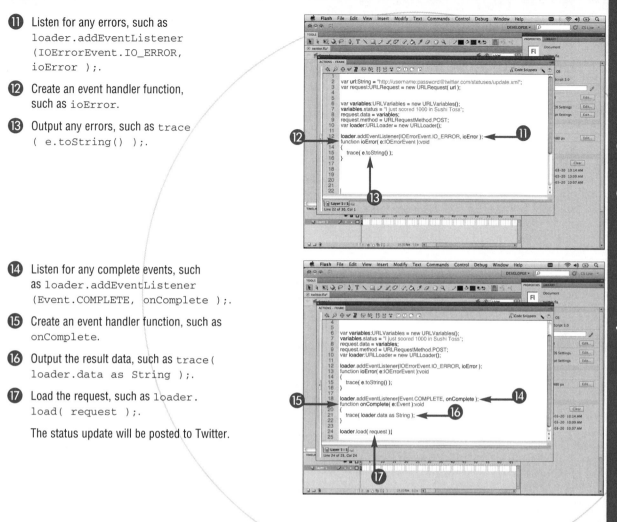

Apply It

Twitter has exposed an entire set of API methods for you to integrate with. If you want to integrate more of Twitter's features in your application, you can use one of the many open source ActionScript Twitter libraries. My favorite is `twitterscript`, available at http://code.google.com/p/twitterscript/, which was originally developed by Twitter and later open sourced in order for it to be maintained and kept current with API changes. The following is an example of how to use the `twitterscript` API to load the home Timeline of a user:

```
var twitter:Twitter = new Twitter();
twitter.setAuthenticationCredentials(username, password );
twitter.addEventListener(TwitterEvent.ON_HOME_TIMELINE_RESULT, onHomeResult );
twitter.loadHomeTimeline();
private function onHomeResult(event:TwitterEvent):void {
for( var i:int = 0; i<event.data.length; i++ ){
var status:TwitterStatus = event.data[ i ] as TwitterStatus;
trace( status.text );
}
}
```

Display Ads with Smaato

If you decide to create a free application, you can add advertising to your application in order to receive some earnings. Many of the free applications in the store use this method to allow users to download a free version of the application and turn off the ads if they purchase the full app. Smaato is one of the leading mobile advertising companies on the market today. Its API enables you to place ads inside your application as images or as text. To get started integrating ads in your application, go to the Smaato Web site at www.smaato. com and register for an account.

After you have registered for an account and set up your application, you will be given a PublisherID and an AdSpaceID. Keep these on hand because you will need them when constructing the ad request. You can also use

0 for both IDs if you want to test the API without registering your application.

When making an ad request, you can specify in which format the results will be returned. The easiest format to work with is XML. Having the result data in XML enables you to easily parse the image URL and the URL to navigate to when the user taps the image. After the URL of the image has been parsed, a second request will need to be made in order to load the image into the banner. This can be done using the Loader class. For more details on loading external images, see Chapter 6, "Working with Images."

When designing your application, you will want to account for a banner dimension size of 300 x 50.

Display Ads with Smaato

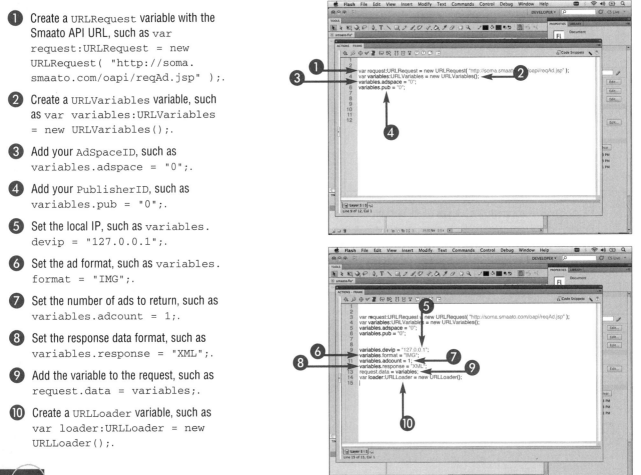

1. Create a URLRequest variable with the Smaato API URL, such as var request:URLRequest = new URLRequest("http://soma. smaato.com/oapi/reqAd.jsp");.

2. Create a URLVariables variable, such as var variables:URLVariables = new URLVariables();.

3. Add your AdSpaceID, such as variables.adspace = "0";.

4. Add your PublisherID, such as variables.pub = "0";.

5. Set the local IP, such as variables. devip = "127.0.0.1";.

6. Set the ad format, such as variables. format = "IMG";.

7. Set the number of ads to return, such as variables.adcount = 1;.

8. Set the response data format, such as variables.response = "XML";.

9. Add the variable to the request, such as request.data = variables;.

10. Create a URLLoader variable, such as var loader:URLLoader = new URLLoader();.

⑪ Listen for the complete event, such as
`loader.addEventListener( Event.COMPLETE, onComplete );`.

⑫ Load the request, such as `loader.load( request );`.

⑬ Create an event handler function.

⑭ Parse the data as XML, such as `var data:XML = new XML(loader.data as String);`.

⑮ Parse the status, such as `var status:String = data.*::status.toString();`.

⑯ Check the status, such as `if( status == "success" ){}`.

⑰ Parse the ad, such as `var ad:XMLList = data.*::ads.*::ad;`.

⑱ Parse the image URL, such as `var link:String = ad.*::link.toString();`.

⑲ Create a `Loader` variable, such as `var l:Loader = new Loader();`.

⑳ Load the image, such as `l.load( new URLRequest( link ) );`.

㉑ Add the image to the display list, such as `addChild( l );`.

The ad will be displayed in your application.

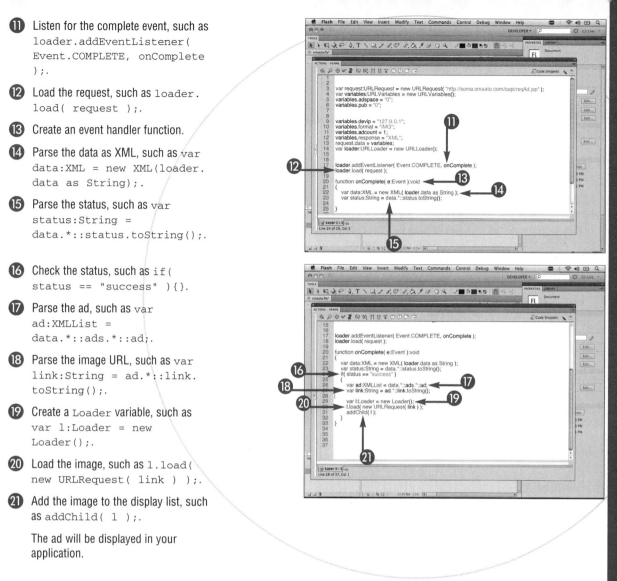

Apply It

After the image for the ad has been loaded, you can register it to listen for a `MouseEvent.CLICK` event in order to navigate to the URL of the ad. The following is a continuation of the example to add this functionality:

```
addChild( l );
var clickurl:String = ad.*::action.@target.toString();
l.addEventListener( MouseEvent.CLICK, onAdClick );
function onAdClick( e:MouseEvent ):void{
var request:URLRequest = new URLRequest( clickurl );
navigateToURL( request );
}
```

Track with Google Analytics

I ntegrating a form of analytics in your application is important in understanding how your users are using your application. Checking how many people have downloaded your application is only part of understanding how popular your application is. It allows you to see which portions of your application users are using more than others. It also enables you to determine if there are any features in your application that users are not using.

One of the more popular analytics suites is Google Analytics. Google Analytics provides a great feature set and is free to use. When you set up your application with Google Analytics, a unique ID will be generated for your application. You will want to copy your ID, as you will use it in your application. Google has also developed an open source ActionScript 3.0 API, which you can use to help with tracking interactions within your application.

The `GATracker` class contains all the methods to send tracking calls to Google Analytics. The constructor has two required parameters: The first parameter is the main Stage of your application. `GATracker` uses the Stage or any other `DisplayObject` in the display list for debugging purposes. The second parameter is a `String` variable, which is the Google Analytics unique ID for your application.

After you have instantiated your `GATracker`, you can send tracking calls to the Google Analytics servers. The most common item to track is page views. Whenever your application switches its view or the user navigates to a new section, you will want to call the `trackPageview();` method on the `GATracker` instance, with a `String` representing the section as its parameter.

Track with Google Analytics

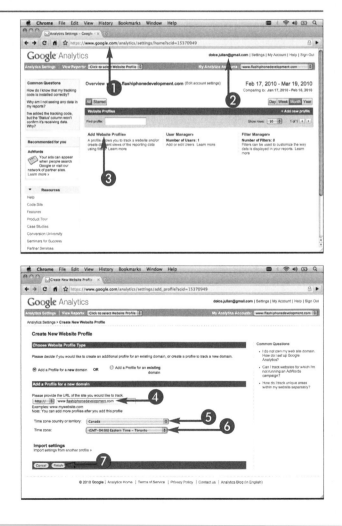

① In a Web browser, sign up for a Google Analytics account at www.google.com/analytics/.

② Log into your Google Analytics account.

The Google Analytics home page appears.

③ Click Add Website Profile.

The Create New Website Profile page appears.

④ Enter a URL to track against.

Note: *This will act as the domain for your application.*

⑤ Click here and select your country.

⑥ Click here and select your time zone.

⑦ Click Finish.

The Tracking Code page appears.

⑧ Select and copy the Web property ID.

Note: *You can download the Google API from the Google Code project at http://code.google.com/p/gaforflash/.*

⑨ In the Actions panel in Flash, import the necessary Google Analytics classes.

⑩ Create a GATracker variable, such as var tracker: AnalyticsTracker = new GATracker();.

⑪ Pass in the Stage as the first parameter.

⑫ Enter your Web property ID as the second parameter.

⑬ Track a page view, such as tracker.trackPage view("/home");.

The tracking request will be sent to Google.

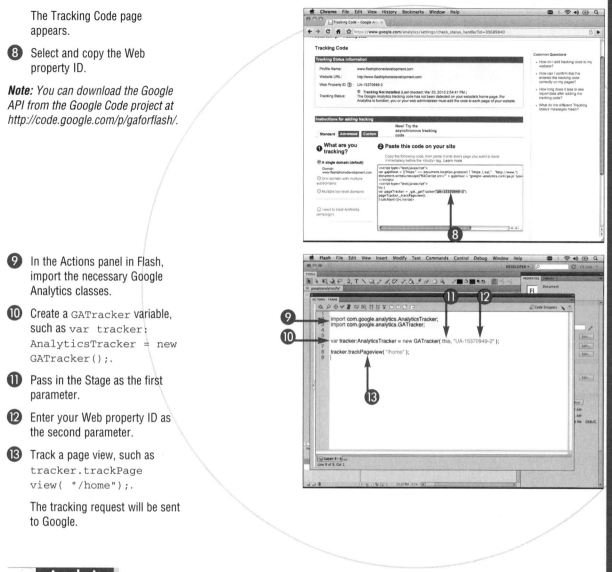

Apply It

As well as track page views, you can track events. Events can be anything that occurs in your application. Selecting a button, completing a level in a game, and successfully logging in are all examples of events that can be tracked. To track your event, call the trackEvent() method on the GATracker instance. The method takes four parameters: The first parameter is the category for the event. The second parameter is the action that created the event. The third parameter is an optional descriptor for the event. The last parameter is an optional value to be aggregated with the event. The following is an example of tracking a button click as an event:

```
var tracker:AnalyticsTracker = new GATracker( this, "GA-ID" );
btn.addEventListener( MouseEvent.CLICK, onButtonClick );
function onButtonClick( e:Event ):void{
tracker.trackEvent( "Button", "click", "Button", 123 );
}
```

Display Ads with AdMob

AdMob is one of the premier mobile advertising platforms on the market today. AdMob provides a variety of SDKs that you can use to distribute and monetize your applications. Currently, there is not a Flash for Android SDK; however, AdMob has just released a beta version of the Flash Lite SDK. The SDK is completely written in ActionScript 2.0 and will not work with the Android AIR Runtime, as all applications must be written in ActionScript 3.0.

Having the ActionScript 2.0 source code for the Flash Lite SDK, however, enables you to convert it to ActionScript 3.0. The ads that are served with the Flash Lite version are 192 pixels wide and 53 pixels high, which is not the optimal size for the Android. Having full control over the ad placement, you can be creative and place it in a location that will still look good.

After you sign up for an AdMob account, you can register a Flash Lite site. For each site that you create, a site ID will be generated for you. This ID is passed into the constructor of the AdMob class, which is included in the ad request.

The second parameter for the AdMob class constructor is the target holder for the ad that is returned. When the ad is loaded, it is placed at the top-left corner — or 0,0 — of the holder. Knowing the width of the ad and the width of the Stage, you can easily center the holder so that the ad is centered on the Stage after it has been loaded.

The third parameter is an optional Boolean, which specifies to set the ad request in test mode. This allows you to test the ads during development and turn on the live ads only when your application has been published to the Android Market. The default value for this parameter is false.

Display Ads with AdMob

1. Go to AdMob's Web site, www.admob.com, and create an account.

2. Obtain an AdMob site ID.

3. In the Actions panel in Flash, create a Sprite variable, such as var adHolder:Sprite = new Sprite();.

4. Set the x property of the Sprite, such as adHolder.x = .

5. Get the center of the Stage width, such as (stage.stageWidth/2).

6. Subtract half the width of the ad, such as -(192/2);.

7. Create an AdMob variable, such as var admob:AdMob = new AdMob();.

8. Enter your site ID.

9. Set the holder target for the ad.

10. Submit ad requests in test mode, such as true.

⑪ Add the ad container to the Stage, such as `addChild ( adHolder );`.

⑫ Load the ad, such as `admob. loadAd();`.

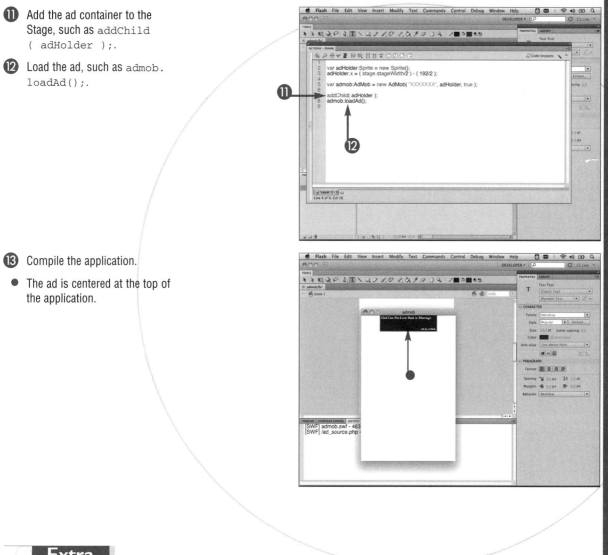

⑬ Compile the application.

● The ad is centered at the top of the application.

Extra

When you register your site with AdMob, you have the option to set the colors of your ad when it is displayed in your application. These can be changed anytime from the App Settings tab in the Settings for your site. The default ad style is a black background with white text. To change the colors, click the App Settings tab in the Settings section for your site. There are two options for the ad style: By default, Use Colors Set in Client Mode is selected. Selecting Use Colors Set Below will allow you to customize the colors. There is a text input box for the text color and background color in which you can enter the hex color values that you want. You can also select the color wheel icon beside each text box in order to show a list of predefined colors.

With your custom colors set for the ads that are returned, you will have more control over how they are integrated into the design of your application. One idea is to draw a colored bar across the entire width of the Stage the same color as the background of the ad.

Optimize Your Display List

One of the biggest bottlenecks when it comes to performance is the rendering of the display list. In comparison, your ActionScript code will outperform the rendering of your visual assets. So even if you have taken every step in order to make sure that your code is optimized to be as fast as possible, your visual assets may still be slowing your application down. There are several things to watch out for when creating your visual assets that will help you to make sure that your application will perform as fast as possible.

One tip is to make sure that you keep the display list as shallow as possible. Try not to have too many `DisplayObject`s with many nested clips. When a touch event occurs on the screen, the display list is traversed to find all the elements that are underneath the user's finger.

The deeper the display list, the longer the traversal will take. Keeping the list shallow will return those objects faster.

Another tip is to reduce the amount of items that overlap each other. The more items that are overlapping, the more compositing has to occur. In addition, try to reduce the amount of alpha (transparency) in your images. The more alpha there is in your image, the more the renderer has to composite what is underneath the alpha.

My third tip is to remove all your masks. Masking items will cause them to be redrawn to the screen every frame, even when a redraw is not necessary. This will cause an extreme decrease in performance as your application will render more than it needs to.

The example in the steps below shows how you could organize your visual assets in order to create a scrollable list.

Optimize Your Display List

Optimize a Scrollable List

1 Create a `MovieClip` symbol to represent a cell in the list.

Note: See Chapter 2, "Getting Started with Flash CS5," for more information.

2 Stack the cells on the Stage exceeding the height of the Stage.

Note: Make sure that the cells do not overlap and that they are on a whole pixel.

3 Click the Selection tool.

4 Select all the cells on the Stage.

Note: You can also press the ⌘+A (Ctrl+A) keyboard shortcut to select them all.

5 Convert the selected cells to a `MovieClip` symbol by pressing the F8 key.

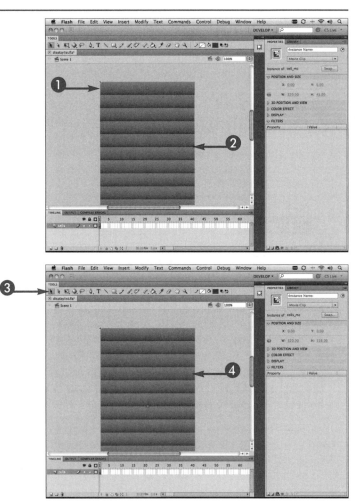

6 Create a new layer on the Timeline above the layer with the cells.

7 Click here to hide the layer with the cells on it.

8 Place a header graphic at the top of the Stage.

9 Place a footer graphic at the bottom of the Stage.

Note: *Covering objects are a way to reduce the number of masks needed.*

Test Your Movie

10 Press ⌘+ Enter (Ctrl+Enter).

● The extra cells are covered by the header and footer graphics.

Cells are not overlapped or masked, which improves performance.

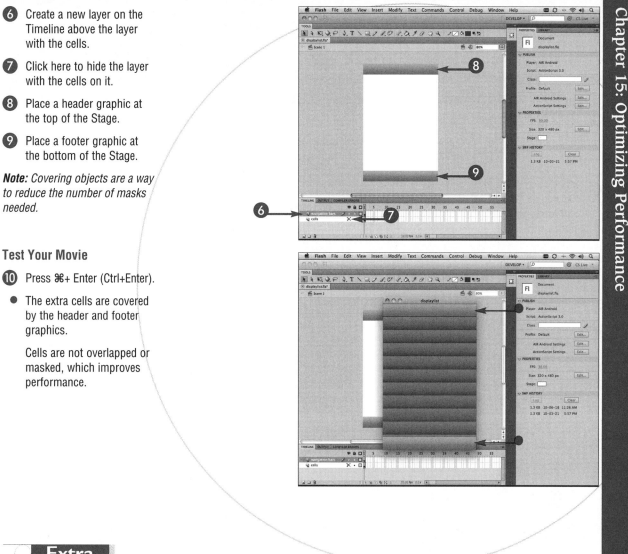

<div class="extra">

Extra

Using vectors can have a big impact on the performance of your application. A good practice to follow is to eliminate the use of vector objects unless absolutely necessary. This may not always be possible — for example, if you are creating a paint application. In these instances, you may be able to get a good enough performance if the application is not that intensive. However, if you are creating a game and you have some illustrated characters and objects in vector, you will want to export them to images. The amount of detail and complex vector points that an animated character can have is so great that the renderer will have a hard time keeping up with a decent frame rate.

From within the Flash IDE, you can easily export each frame as a PNG or other image format. Reimporting your vector assets as images will greatly improve your chances of achieving a decent frame rate. Exporting a lot of frames from a Timeline animation can be a very time-consuming process. You can automate this by creating a JSFL script file, which will move the play head to each frame and export it to an image.

</div>

Manage
Mouse Events

As mentioned in the preceding section, "Optimize Your Display List," keeping your display list shallow will have an impact on the performance of your application. One of the reasons is how mouse and touch events are handled within ActionScript 3.0.

There are three phases to a MouseEvent. The capturing phase is the first phase and occurs when an event is fired. The event starts with the topmost parent display object, or the Stage, and works its way down the display list hierarchy until it reaches the target in which the event originated. The second phase is the target phase, which occurs when the event reaches the display object from which the event originated. The third phase is the bubbling phase. During the bubbling phase of an event, the event follows the reverse path of the capturing event, all the way to the topmost parent display object.

With this knowledge, you can see how having deeply nested display lists can easily and quickly cause a decrease in performance, as the event will visit each item in the display list in both the capturing and bubbling phases.

There are a couple methods on the Event class that enable you to stop the event in its current phase. The stopPropagation() method prevents the processing of any event listeners in any nodes subsequent to the current node in the event flow. Calling this method will not have any effect on the current node, and it can be called during any phase of the event.

The stopImmediatePropagation() method prevents the processing of any event listeners in the current and subsequent nodes in the event flow. This method takes effect immediately and affects event listeners in the current node. However, you should note that this does not cancel the behavior of the associated event.

Manage Mouse Events

① Add a Button symbol to the Stage.

Note: *See Chapter 2 for more information.*

② Give it an instance name, such as btn.

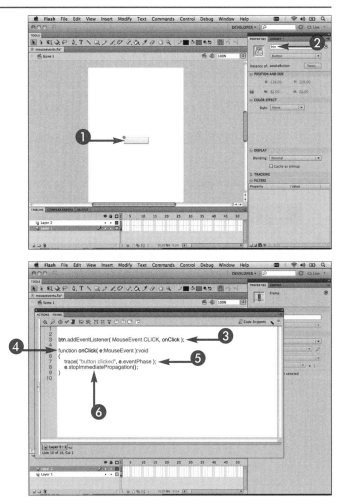

③ In the Actions panel, add a CLICK listener to the Button, such as btn.addEvent Listener(MouseEvent. CLICK, onClick);.

④ Create an event handler function.

⑤ Output the phase of the event, such as trace("button clicked", e.eventPhase);.

⑥ Stop the event from bubbling up, such as e.stopImmediate Propagation();.

7 Listen for the bubbled event on the Stage, such as `stage.addEvent Listener(MouseEvent. CLICK, onStageClick );`.

8 Create an event handler function.

9 Output the phase of the event, such as `trace("stage clicked", e.event Phase);`.

10 Press ⌘+ Enter (Ctrl+Enter) to test your movie.

● Check the Output panel to see the event phases.

The propagation of the event has been stopped and will not bubble.

Note: *You can remove the* `e.stop ImmediatePropagation();` *line of code in order to see the event bubble up to the Stage.*

Apply It

When the user drags his or her finger while it is pressed on the screen, a `MouseEvent.MOUSE_MOVE` event is fired. This event can be fired multiple times a frame as the finger moves quickly across the screen, which can decrease performance. The following is an example of how to use the `Event.ENTER_FRAME` event to track the position of a touch:

```
stage.addEventListener( Event.ENTER_FRAME, onFrame );
function onFrame( e:Event ):void{
var x:Number = stage.mouseX;
var y:Number = stage.mouseY;
trace( x, y );
}
```

Understanding cacheAsBitmap

The cacheAsBitmap property is a property that exists on all DisplayObject instances. If the cacheAsBitmap property is set to true, a bitmap representation of the display object will be cached internally. To get the highest performance increases in your application, use this method in conjunction with setting the rendering mode to GPU.

When your display object is cached using the cacheAsBitmap property, it is sent to the GPU. This enables you to perform simple translations along the x and y axis without having the display object reuploaded to the GPU. This works very well with display objects whose states remain fairly constant.

If there are any changes to the bounds of the display object — for example, if the object is scaled or rotated — the bitmap will be re-created and uploaded to the GPU.

For more information on scaling and rotating display objects, see the following section, "Understanding cachAsBitmapMatrix."

The cacheAsBitmap property is automatically set to true when a filter is applied to the display object. If you set cacheAsBitmap to false and then apply a filter, it will set the property to true. After all filters are removed from the display object or the filter array is empty, the property will be reset to its previous value.

When the cacheAsBitmap property is set to true, the rendering does not change. However, the display object snaps to the nearest pixel. To ensure that you do not see a visual shift in your display objects when setting the cacheAsBitmap property, make sure that all your elements are on whole pixels.

Understanding cacheAsBitmap

 ① Create a MovieClip symbol and place it on the Stage.

Note: See Chapter 2 for more information.

② Give it an instance name, such as sushi_mc.

Note: You can set the cacheAsBitmap property in the IDE as well as in code.

③ Click Cache As Bitmap.

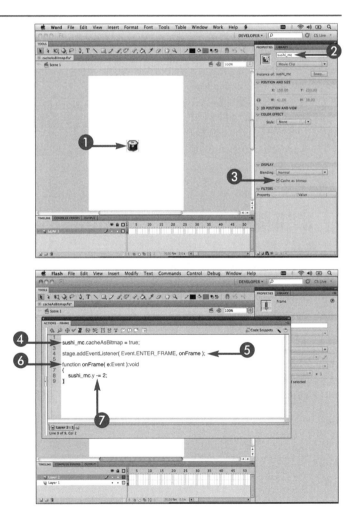

④ In the Actions panel, cache the symbol, such as sushi_mc.cacheAsBitmap = true;.

⑤ Register a listener for the enter frame event, such as stage.addEventListener(Event.ENTER_FRAME, onFrame);.

⑥ Create an event handler.

⑦ Move the symbol incrementally every frame, such as sushi_mc.y -= 2;.

8 Click File → Open.

The Open dialog box appears.

9 Click the application descriptor file.

10 Click Open.

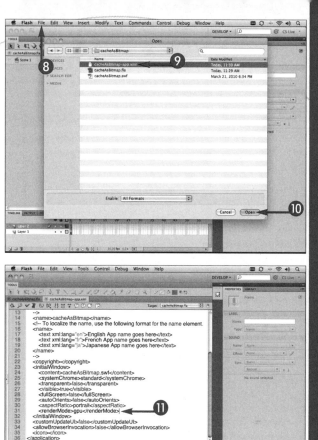

The application descriptor file is opened.

11 Set the `<renderMode>` node to `gpu`.

When you compile and install your application on your device, the `cacheAsBitmap` property will upload a representation of the display object to the GPU.

Apply It

The `opaqueBackground` property on a `DisplayObject` instance specifies whether it is opaque and the color value of the background. Setting this property to a number value creates an opaque background on the object to the color value that the value specifies. If it is set to null, the background of the display object will be transparent. When the `cacheAsBitmap` property is set to `true`, setting the display object to opaque can improve rendering performance. It is important to note that the opaque background region does not respond to mouse events.

```
myshape.opaqueBackground = 0x000000;
myshape.cacheAsBitmap = true;
```

Understanding cacheAsBitmapMatrix

The preceding section, "Understanding cacheAsBitmap," explores how to use the cacheAsBitmap property to upload display objects to the GPU. This works well if the bounds of the display object do not change, such as if it is not scaled or rotated. If your display objects are required to be scaled or rotated, however, you can use the cacheAsBitmapMatrix property to prevent the bitmap from being re-created and uploaded to the GPU.

Setting the cacheAsBitmapMatrix property to a valid Matrix instance will define how the display object is rendered when cacheAsBitmap is set to true. Your application will use this Matrix as a transformation matrix when rendering the bitmap version of the display object.

When the cacheAsBitmapMatrix property is set, the application will retain a cached version of the bitmap when a transformation of the display object occurs, such as rotation, scale, and translation. When the rendering mode of the application is set to GPU, the display object will be stored as texture in video memory. This allows all supported transformations to occur on the GPU, which can perform these transformations much faster than the CPU.

Simply setting the property to the identity matrix — for example, new Matrix(); — usually suffices, however, if you use any Matrix instance to upload a different bitmap to the GPU. It is best practice to set the Matrix to the size that it will appear in the application.

Transformations of the display object are not required to occur on the matrix. After the cacheAsBitmapMatrix property is set, you can use the rotation and scale properties of the display object in order to transform the object.

Understanding cacheAsBitmapMatrix

① Create a MovieClip symbol and place it on the Stage.

Note: *See Chapter 2 for more information.*

② Give it an instance name, such as sushi_mc.

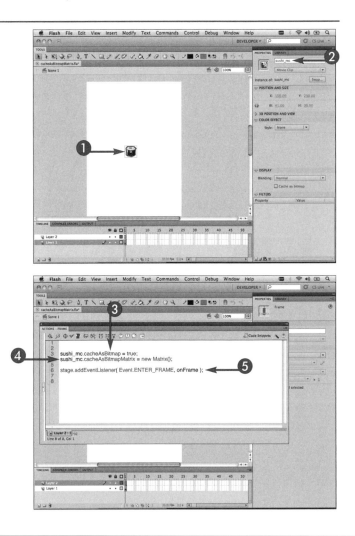

③ In the Actions panel, cache the symbol, such as sushi_mc.cacheAsBitmap = true;.

④ Cache the matrix, such as sushi_mc.cacheAsBitmapMatrix = new Matrix();.

⑤ Register a listener for the enter frame event, such as stage.addEventListener(Event.ENTER_FRAME, onFrame);.

6 Create an event handler.

7 Move the symbol incrementally every frame, such as `sushi_ mc.y -= 2;`.

8 Rotate the symbol incrementally every frame, such as `sushi_ mc.rotation += 10;`.

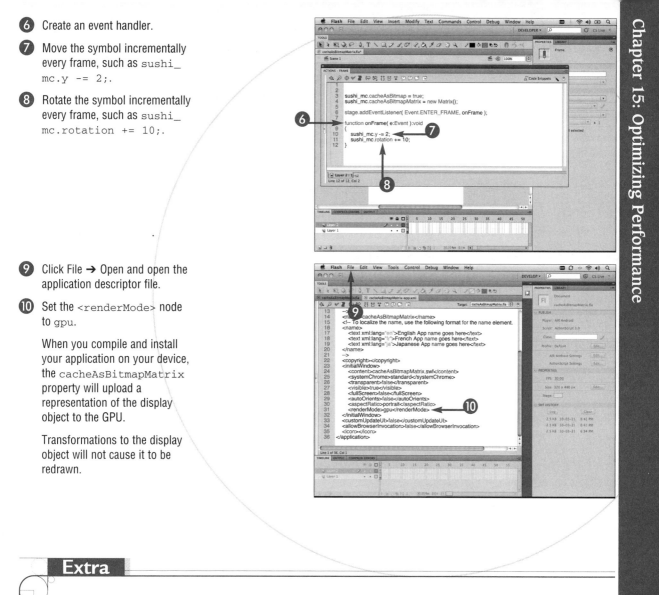

9 Click File → Open and open the application descriptor file.

10 Set the `<renderMode>` node to `gpu`.

When you compile and install your application on your device, the `cacheAsBitmapMatrix` property will upload a representation of the display object to the GPU.

Transformations to the display object will not cause it to be redrawn.

Extra

It is important to understand that the `cacheAsBitmapMatrix` property works only on 2D surfaces, as the texture that is uploaded is only a 2D surface. If you want to use a 3D surface, you simply set the z property to 0 or the value that you want. Setting the z property automatically sets your display object to be a 3D surface. The following syntax sets a `Sprite` instance to be a 3D surface:

```
mysprite.z = 0;
```

There is also an easy way to set the `cacheAsBitmapMatrix` to the same `Matrix` as it currently is on the Stage:

```
mysprite.cacheAsBitmapMatrix = sprite.transform.matrix.clone();
```

This is very useful when your display object has already been transformed before you set the matrix.

Show Your Trace Statements

I f you have been developing Flash applications for quite some time, you are probably very familiar with the trace() method. The trace() method enables you to output values to the Output panel within the Flash IDE.

The trace() statement can have multiple parameters passed into it. All arguments are outputted to the Output panel on a single line, with multiple arguments separated by a space.

The remote debugging capabilities of the Flash IDE allows you to receive your trace statements in the IDE when testing on the device. In order for this to work, your device must have WiFi turned on and be connected to the same network as the computer running the Flash IDE. You will also need to set the Android deployment type to Device Debugging. When your application is published in this

mode, you will be asked to enter the IP address of your computer when your application is launched.

If the Flash IDE is waiting for a remote player to connect, the application will attempt to connect to your computer over WiFi and start a remote debugging session. You can select Begin Remote Debug Session from the Debug menu in the Flash IDE to set up the IDE to receive the connection from your application. This should be done before you enter your IP address on the device.

The IP address of your computer can be found in the Network Preferences on Mac OS X or by running the ipconfig command from a command line in Windows.

In order to connect to the remote debugger on your computer, you will need to give your application Internet permissions. For more details on application permissions, see Chapter 3, "Developing Your First Application."

Show Your Trace Statements

1 Open the Actions panel.

2 Create a trace statement.

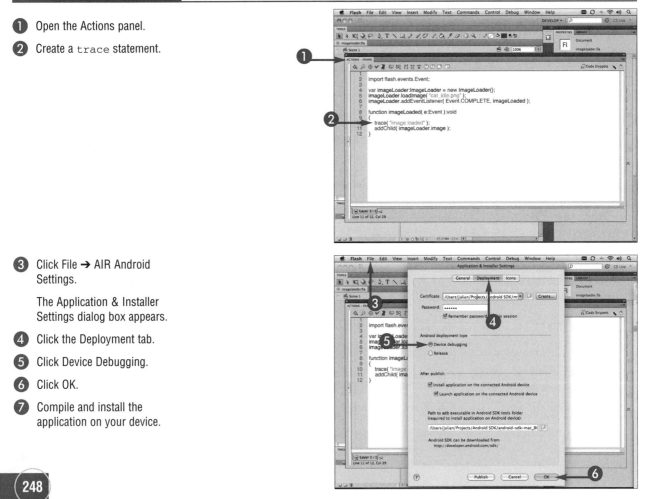

3 Click File → AIR Android Settings.

The Application & Installer Settings dialog box appears.

4 Click the Deployment tab.

5 Click Device Debugging.

6 Click OK.

7 Compile and install the application on your device.

8 Click Debug.

9 Click Begin Remote Debug Session.

10 Click ActionScript 3.0.

11 Launch the application on your device.

12 If prompted, enter the IP address of your computer.

● The workspace is changed to DEBUG.

● The `trace` statement is shown in the Output panel.

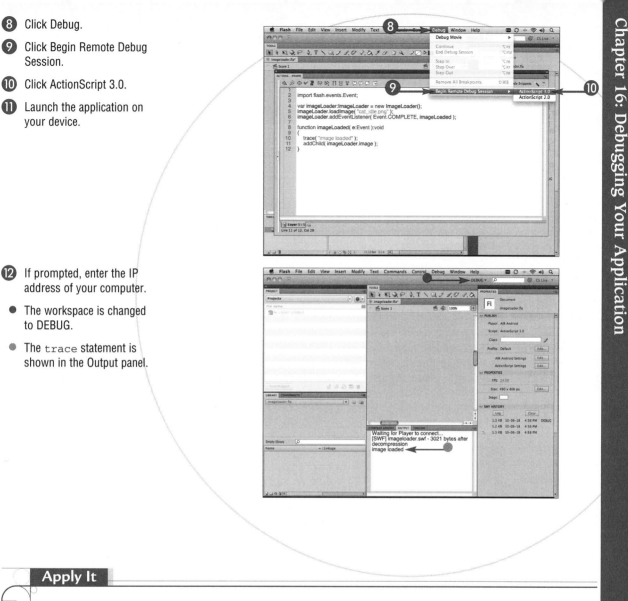

Apply It

The Output panel and the `trace()` method work well for outputting very simple expressions. They do not do well, however, when dealing with complex objects. There are several alternatives available to you. The POWERFLASHER SOSmax Socket Output Server is a great tool for more complex output from Flash. It runs as an XML-based socket server on your computer, which you can connect to from your device. Here is an example of how to connect to the application from your device:

```
var socket:XMLSocket = new XMLSocket();
socket.addEventListener( Event.CONNECT, onConnect );
socket.connect( "10.0.0.1", 4444 );
function onConnect( e:Event ):void{
socket.send( "connected to device" );
}
```

Create Breakpoints

W hen you are trying to debug a complex issue or problem with your code, the trace() method may not give you enough information. If there is a lot of code executing at a given time and it is outputting lots of trace statements to the Output panel, it may be difficult to decipher where the problem is. Having the ability to pause your application from continuing allows you at any given time to see the result of a line of code.

Setting a breakpoint lets you stop the application at a specific line of code. It is important to understand that there must be valid code on the same line as the breakpoint. For example, if you set a breakpoint on a line without code or a comment, the application will not stop at that breakpoint.

Breakpoints can be set in the Actions panel, the Script window, and the Debugger. All breakpoints set in the Actions panel are saved with the FLA and will be present the next time you open the file. Breakpoints set in the Script window and Debugger are not saved and are available only for the current development session.

When editing an external ActionScript file in the Script window, there are several shortcut commands that can be used to add and remove breakpoints. Pressing the ⌘+B (Ctrl+B) keyboard shortcut will toggle a breakpoint at the line of code on which the cursor has focus. There are also options from the Debug main menu item that allow you to remove all the breakpoints for a given file or from all ActionScript files.

Create Breakpoints

Set a Breakpoint in the Actions Panel

1 Open the Actions panel.

2 Click in the left column, next to the line of code at which you want to set a breakpoint.

A breakpoint is added.

Remove All Breakpoints

1 Right-click in the window.

2 Click Remove Breakpoints in This File.

All the breakpoints in the FLA are removed.

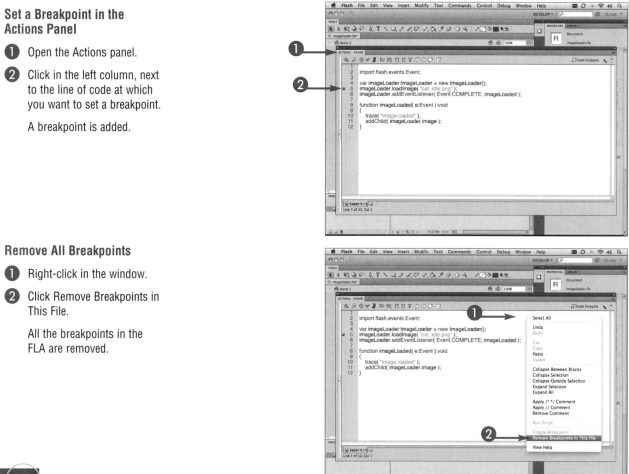

Set a Breakpoint in the Script Window

1 Click File → Open.

2 Navigate to and select an ActionScript 3.0 class file.

3 Click Open.

● The class file opens in the Script window.

4 Click in the left column.

A breakpoint is added.

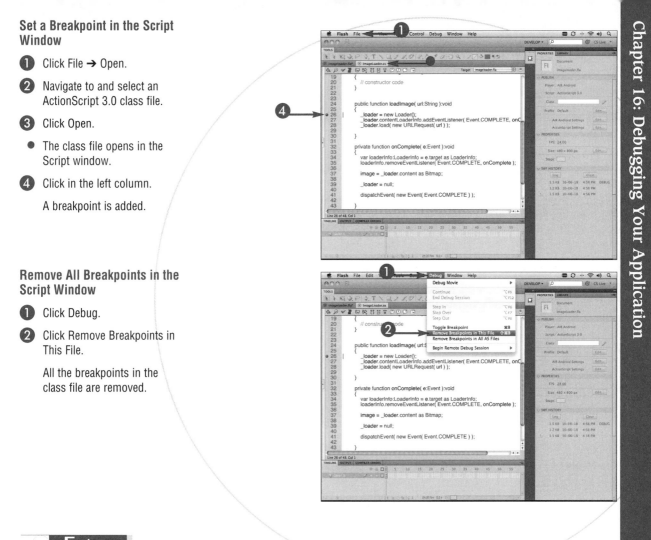

Remove All Breakpoints in the Script Window

1 Click Debug.

2 Click Remove Breakpoints in This File.

All the breakpoints in the class file are removed.

Extra

Breakpoints added in the Script window can also be saved in the AsBreakpoints.xml file, which is located in the configuration directory for Flash.

On a Windows XP machine, the AsBreakpoints.xml file can be found at the following location:

Windows Hard Drive\Documents and Settings\User\Local Settings\Application Data\Adobe\Flash CS5\language\Configuration\Debugger\

On a Windows 7 machine, the AsBreakpoints.xml file can be found at this location:

Windows Hard Drive\Users\<username>\AppData\Local\Adobe\Flash CS5\en_US\Configuration\Debugger

On a Mac OS X machine, the AsBreakpoints.xml file can be found here:

Macintosh HD/Users/User/Library/Application Support/Adobe Flash CS5/Configuration/Debugger/

AsBreakpoints.xml is a simple XML file that has a node for each file containing a breakpoint. For each breakpoint in the file, a child node is created with the line of which the breakpoint exists as an attribute.

Using the Flash CS5 Debugger

fter you have set some breakpoints in your code, you can use the Flash CS5 ActionScript 3.0 Debugger to have your application pause at each breakpoint. Debugging your application works the same for any Flash application, whether it is running on a device or running locally on your computer.

In some instances, you will need to specify to permit debugging in the Flash Publish Settings dialog box; however, specifically for Android development, you can omit this step. Debugging your application is different from testing your movie, or pressing ⌘+Enter (Ctrl+Enter). When you open the Debugger, selecting the appropriate debug scenario, your application will be compiled, and the Flash IDE will switch to the Debug workspace.

The Debug workspace displays panels that you can use to help debug your application effectively. You can also

select this workspace from the workspace drop-down list located at the top right of the application bar.

The Debugger will pause at any line of code that throws an Error. Most of the time Errors are thrown because the Debugger has encountered a null variable. Having the debugger stop on the specific line that caused the Error enables you to easily determine the null variable.

When using the Flash Debugger to debug a remote application, the Debugger will wait for two minutes for the remote application to connect. If a connection is not made within the two minutes, the Debugger times out, and you have to restart the remote debug session.

After a debug session has started, it can be stopped by clicking End Debug Session on the Debug main menu. You can also close the compiled file in order to end the session.

Using the Flash CS5 Debugger

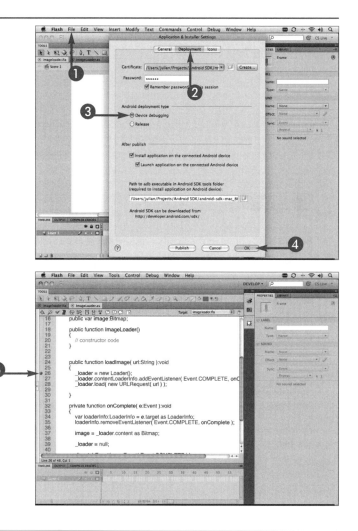

1 Click File → AIR Android Settings.

The Application & Installer Settings dialog box appears.

2 Click the Deployment tab.

3 Click Device Debugging.

4 Click OK.

5 Add a breakpoint to your application.

Note: For more details on adding breakpoints, see the preceding section, "Create Breakpoints."

6 Publish and install the application on your device.

7 Click Debug.

8 Click Begin Remote Debug Session.

9 Click ActionScript 3.0.

10 Launch the application on your device.

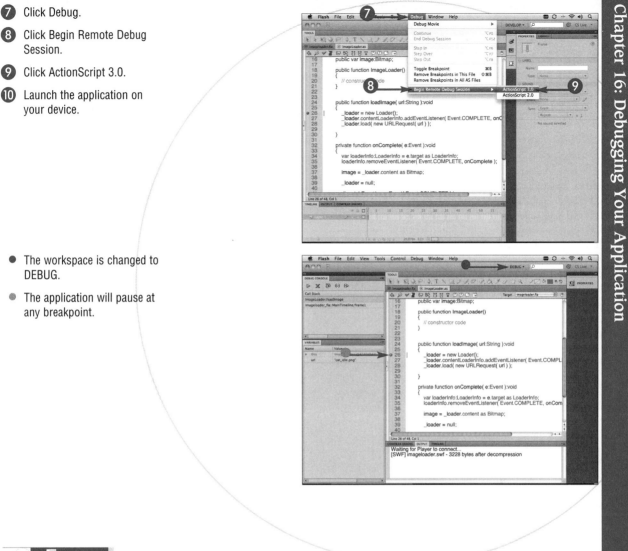

- The workspace is changed to DEBUG.

- The application will pause at any breakpoint.

Understanding the Debug Console

The Debug Console contains many useful features of the Flash CS5 Debugger. In most instances, this panel should automatically be shown when the Flash IDE workspace is changed to Debug. However, if for whatever reason it does not appear, you can show it by selecting it from the Debug Panels menu from the Window main menu.

There are two important parts of the Debug Console, the top menu bar and the Call Stack list. The top menu bar consists of a set of controls that allows you to control the Debugger. When the Debugger pauses at a breakpoint, you can click any of the buttons in the top bar to continue executing the application.

The Continue button continues running the application until it reaches the next breakpoint. The End Debug Session button closes the Debugger and the application, ending the current session. The Step Over button executes the line of code at which it has stopped and then pauses the application on the next line of code. The Step In button causes the Debugger to execute the current line of code and enter the Break mode. If the line of code calls another method, it will then step into that method. If you step into a different method, you can choose to step over or into each line, just as you would if the Debugger had stopped on a breakpoint. You can also click the Step Out button in order to return to the method that you stepped in from.

When the Debugger pauses your application from executing, the Call Stack shows a list of the remaining functions that are waiting to finish executing. Click an item in the list to jump to that method or script.

Understanding the Debug Console

① Add a breakpoint to your application.

② Set up a debugging session.

Note: For more details on adding breakpoints and debugging your application, see the sections earlier in this chapter.

③ Launch your application on your device.

④ Click the Step Over button.

● The debugger jumps to the next line of code to execute and pauses.

⑤ Click an item in the Call Stack list.

● The Debugger navigates to that
location in the code.

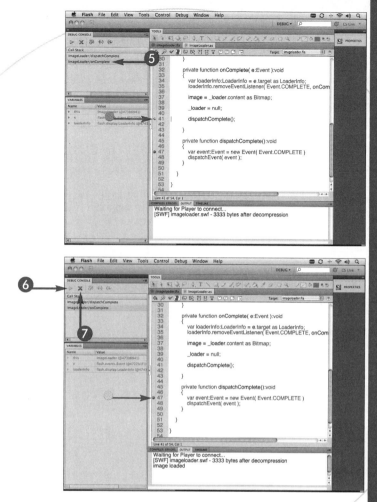

⑥ Click the Continue button.

● The Debugger continues executing
code until it reaches another
breakpoint or there is no more
code to execute.

⑦ Click the End Debug Session button
when you are finished debugging
your application.

The debugging session closes.

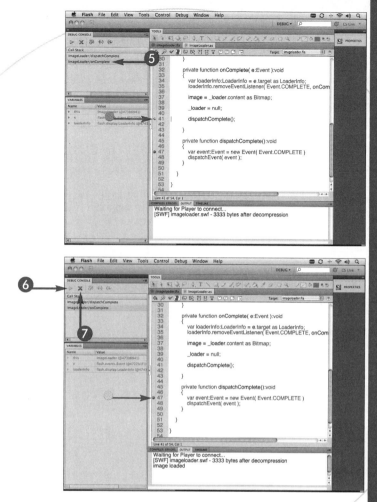

Extra

To make your debugging experience as efficient as possible, it is a really good idea to memorize the keyboard
shortcuts for the stepping methods in the Debug Console. Being able to quickly jump in, out, and over code will
increase the speed in which you can debug your application. You can find the keyboard shortcuts by selecting
Debug from the main menu. The shortcut key is located to the right of the item.

If you find that the default keyboard shortcut keys are not convenient, you can change them to something that
works better for you. To customize the keyboard shortcuts, click Flash → Keyboard Shortcuts on a Mac OS X
machine or Edit → Keyboard Shortcuts on a Windows machine.

Before you can customize the keyboard shortcuts, you must first create a duplicate of the default keyboard
shortcuts. To duplicate the set, click the Duplicate Set button, which is the first button to the right of the Current
Set drop-down list. Each set is stored in an .mfx file in the Flash Configuration folder. This makes it easy to share
shortcuts with other members of your team.

Understanding the Variables Panel

The Variables panel lists all the current objects and variables in the current scope. By default, the Variables panel should be shown when Flash switches to the Debug workspace. However, if for some reason it does not appear, you can show it using the Debug Panels menu on the Window main menu.

The Variables panel consists of two columns, Name and Value. The Name column shows the name of the variable in your code, and the Value column shows the value of that variable. This is extremely useful for tracking down any null variable Errors, as sometimes it can be hard to tell which object is null based on the Error message.

For any complex objects, such as classes, objects, arrays, and dictionaries, you can expand them to view their contents and properties. Being able to drill into objects

within Arrays and Dictionary objects is an extremely powerful tool in debugging your application. Without the Debugger, you would have to perform some heavily nested if statements in order to properly trace the objects and properties that you are interested in.

You can also change the value of a variable in the Variables panel. Double-clicking the Value column of the variable that you want to edit will change the row into an editable text input. After you edit the value, the new value will be used during the next code execution.

By default, there are certain types of variables that are hidden from the Variables panel. Clicking the panel preferences button will bring up a list of all the available types to be shown.

Understanding the Variables Panel

1 Add a breakpoint to your application.

2 Start debugging your application.

Note: For more details on adding breakpoints and debugging your application, see the sections earlier in this chapter.

3 Click the arrow to expand any complex objects in the Variables panel.

④ Click an item in the Call Stack list.

⑤ Click the arrow to expand any complex objects in the Variables panel.

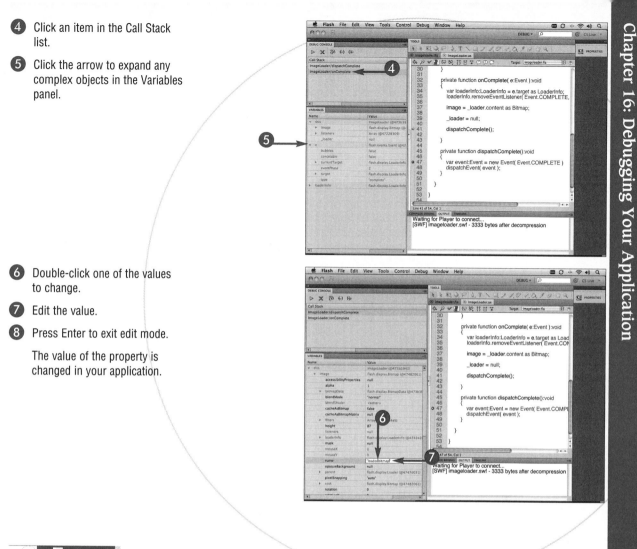

⑥ Double-click one of the values to change.

⑦ Edit the value.

⑧ Press Enter to exit edit mode.

The value of the property is changed in your application.

Extra

Changing variables on the fly can be used for more than just debugging. Being able to tweak parameters in a physics simulation or game can be useful, as it does not make you recompile the application in order to see the changes. It also enables you to test the effects on your application if variables are set to different values.

The Variables panel is updated when you click an item in the Call Stack list. This potentially allows you to track down bugs because you will be able to see the evolution of a variable as each item in the Call Stack is executed. It also allows you to see which variables are available within a given scope.

If you try to change a variable to a data type other than its current data type, the Variables panel will revert the value to its last valid value. For example, changing an int variable value to a String is not permitted through the Variables panel.

Unfortunately, you are not able to instantiate variables from the Variables panel. For example, an Array variable whose current value is null cannot be changed.

Debug with the Android Eclipse Plug-in

The earlier sections of this chapter show how to use the Flash CS5 IDE to debug your applications. This workflow is extremely useful if you are using the Flash CS5 IDE to develop your applications. However, this workflow may not be as efficient if you are using an Eclipse-based editor, such as Flash Builder or FDT.

Google provides a plug-in for Eclipse that gives you the ability to debug your applications. See Chapter 1, "Getting Started with Android Development," for more details on downloading and installing the Android Eclipse plug-in. The plug-in adds a new perspective to Eclipse called *DDMS* (Dalvik Debug Monitor Service). Switching to this perspective gives you options to debug your application.

The LogCat console can be used to show all the `trace` statements in your application. It shows debug statements from the entire device, including applications that you have not developed. You can create a filter that will show only `trace` statements from your application to make it easier to see only the `trace` statements that you are interested in.

If you are testing your application in the Android emulator, there are several options that allow you to send it information that is available only on a device. The Emulator Control panel enables you to simulate an incoming telephone call and an incoming SMS message. This allows you to see how your application performs if it is running when these events occur. You can also send your application GPS coordinates in order to simulate a change in location.

Simulating events in the emulator is useful if you do not have a device to test on and your application requires GPS.

Debug with the Android Eclipse Plug-in

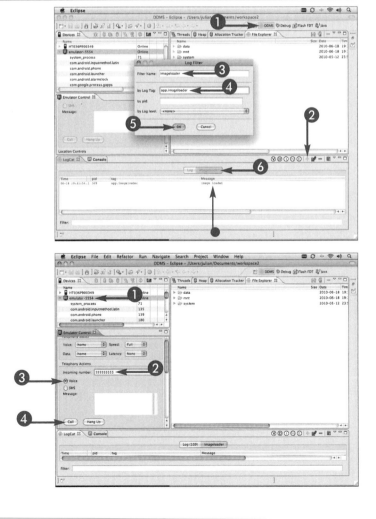

Create a LogCat Filter

1. In Eclipse, switch to the DDMS perspective.

2. Click the Add Filter button.

    The Log Filter dialog box appears.

3. Enter a filter name, such as `imageloader`.

4. Type your App ID, such as `app.imageloader`.

5. Click OK.

6. Click your filter tab.

    ● The LogCat output is filtered.

Simulate a Phone Call

1. Click your emulator in the Devices panel.

2. In the Emulator Control panel, type an incoming number.

3. Click Voice.

4. Click Call.

    The selected emulator instance receives the phone call.

Simulate an SMS Message

① Click your emulator in the Devices panel.

② In the Emulator Control panel, type an incoming number.

③ Click SMS.

④ Type a message.

⑤ Click Send.

The selected emulator instance receives the SMS message.

Simulate Receiving GPS Coordinates

① Click your emulator in the Devices panel.

② In the Location Controls section of the Emulator Control panel, click the Manual tab.

③ Click Decimal.

④ Type a longitude.

⑤ Type a latitude.

⑥ Click Send.

The GPS coordinates are sent to the emulator.

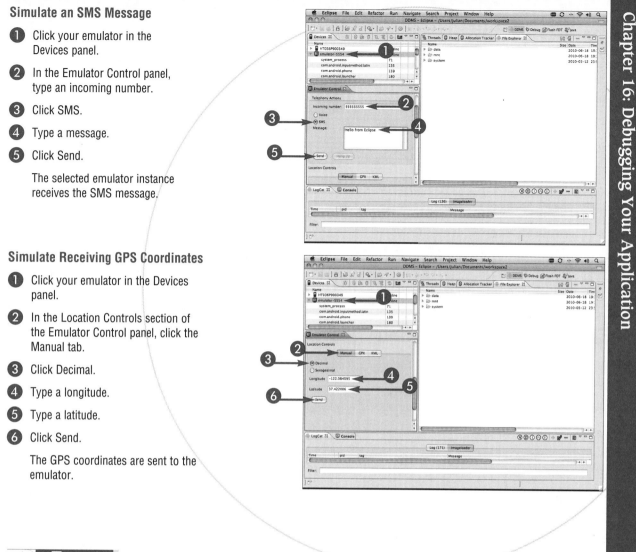

Extra

All the debugging that you can perform in the Android Eclipse plug-in can also be done from the command line. To view the LogCat console, open a Terminal or command prompt window and use the following command:

```
adb logcat
```

You can also interact with the emulator by connecting to its port and then running the commands to simulate a call or send GPS coordinates. The following commands will simulate an incoming phone call in the emulator:

```
telnet localhost 5554
gsm call 555555555
```

Take Screenshots of Your Application on Your Device

There will be many times when you will want to take screenshots of your application on your device. Most likely, you will want to have screenshots to use for marketing purposes; however, you also need to upload screenshots of your application to the Android Market when uploading your application.

Some mobile devices enable you to capture images of their screens by pressing a combination of keys on the devices. Android devices do not have this capability; however, screenshots can be taken with a tool in the Android SDK called *DDMS,* as well as the Eclipse Android plug-in.

When you take screenshots of your device, they will be at the same resolution as the screen resolution of the device.

For example, if you have a Nexus One phone, your screenshots will be taken at 480 x 800 pixels. In most cases, you would want your screenshots to be taken at 100% of the original size. However, the Android Market accepts screenshots in two different sizes only: 320 x 480 pixels and 480 x 854 pixels. If your screenshots are not at these sizes, you should resize them accordingly in an image-editing application such as Photoshop. Also, any landscape screenshots will be cropped.

The DDMS tool can take screenshots of any connected device or emulator. It can be found in the tools folder of the Android SDK and can be run from the command line.

Take Screenshots of Your Application on Your Device

① In a Terminal or command prompt window, type **ddms**.

② Press Enter.

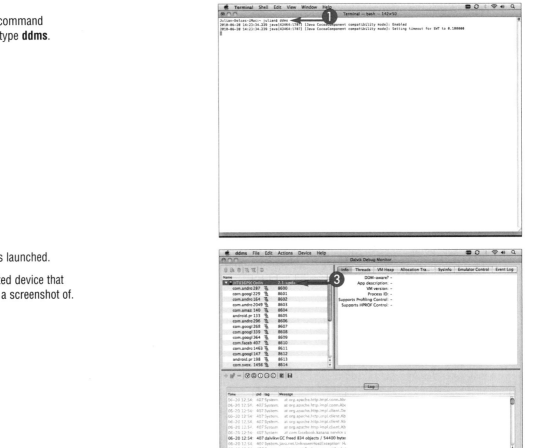

The DDMS tool is launched.

③ Click the connected device that you want to take a screenshot of.

④ Click Device.

⑤ Click Screen Capture.

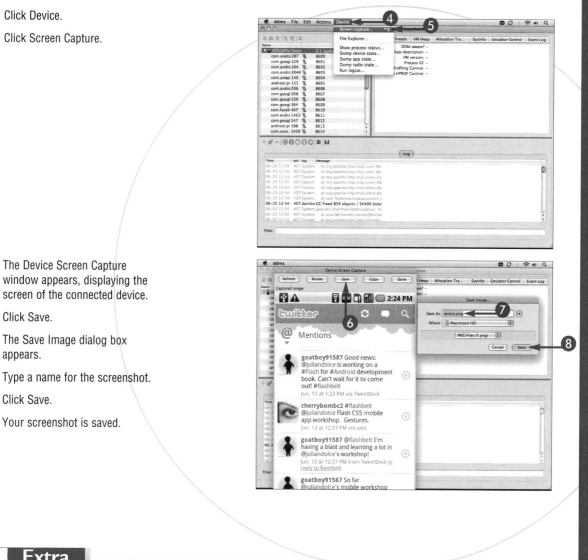

The Device Screen Capture window appears, displaying the screen of the connected device.

⑥ Click Save.

The Save Image dialog box appears.

⑦ Type a name for the screenshot.

⑧ Click Save.

Your screenshot is saved.

Extra

As well as upload screenshots of your application to the Android Market, you also upload a promotional graphic. This graphic should be 180 pixels wide and 120 pixels high. The image format can be either a 24-bit PNG or a JPEG, but it must not contain any alpha. This promotional graphic will appear in the Android Market on the device, if it is featured. A featured graphic can be shown on the home screen of the Market, as well as the home screen of a category. Application promotional graphics appear on a white-to-green gradient background. With this in mind, make sure that your graphic will look good against this background. Stay away from similar colors and choose complementary colors as much as you can. You want your graphic to stand out from the background in order to catch the user's eye. Because it can be difficult to browse and find applications on an Android device, it is extremely important that you create a pleasing promotional graphic. This may be your only opportunity to attract customers.

Create an
Application Icon

Every application binary that is uploaded to the Android Market must contain an application icon. This icon will be shown on the home screen of the Android device and will be used to launch your application on the device. It will also be used in the Android Market in the listing for your application.

Throughout the book, it has been mentioned that Android devices come with many different screen resolutions. In order for your icon to support the many different screen sizes, you should make three different icon sizes — one that is 36 x 36 pixels, one that is 48 x 48 pixels, and one that is 72 x 72 pixels. Each icon should be saved as a transparent 24-bit PNG.

When designing your application, consider the type of background it will be on. The launcher background is usually very dark, which may make black icons hard to

see. In addition, a colored glow is placed around the icon. For newer devices, such as the Nexus One, this color is orange. This may also factor into the look of your icon.

Google has provided developers and designers with a very comprehensive style guide for icons. Google has also released a Photoshop template file with all the different types of effects that you can incorporate into your icons. You can find the icon template file at Google's Android Developers site, on the Icon Design Guidelines page, at http://developer.android.com/guide/practices/ui_ guidelines/icon_design.html.

After your icons have been designed, you can add them to your application through the Flash IDE. All icons can be added from the Icons tab in the AIR Android Settings dialog box. Each icon size will automatically be packaged properly so that it can be used on the correct screen size.

Create an Application Icon

Create Application Icons

1 Open an image-editing application, such as Photoshop.

2 Create a 72 x 72 pixel icon.

3 Create a 48 x 48 pixel icon.

4 Create a 36 x 36 pixel icon.

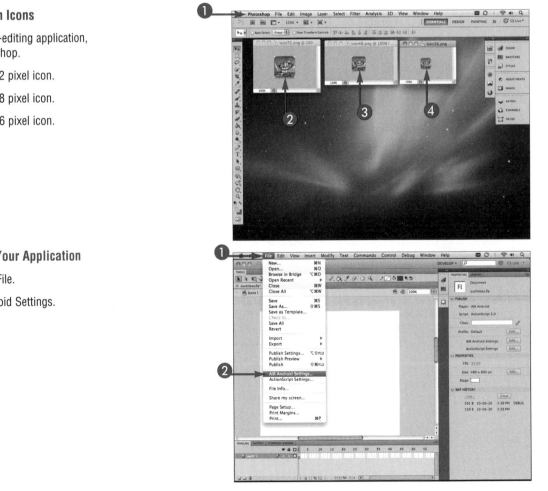

Add the Icons to Your Application

1 In Flash, click File.

2 Click AIR Android Settings.

The Application & Installer Settings dialog box appears.

③ Click the Icons tab.

④ Click Icon 36 x 36.

⑤ Click the folder icon.

The Open dialog box appears.

⑥ Click the 36 x 36 icon.

⑦ Click Open.

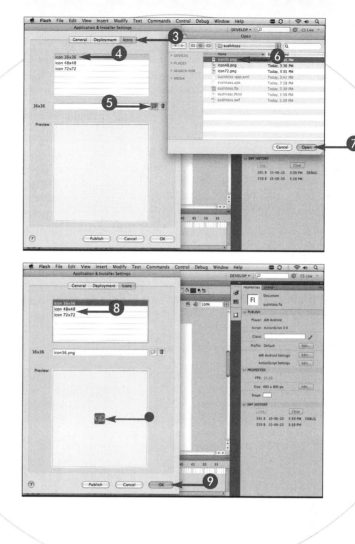

● The icon is shown in the Preview window.

⑧ Repeat steps 4 to 7 for the remaining two icons.

⑨ Click OK.

When your application is published, your icons will be bundled with it.

Extra

The Android icon style guide is extremely detailed and is far too big to explain it all here. It is recommended that you read it in full before designing your icon. It is a good practice to follow the guidelines so that your icon matches the rest of the look of the device. If you look at enough Android icons, you can begin to see the similarities between them. Your icon design should be modern instead of antique, minimal and not complicated, matte instead of glossy, and textured instead of flat vector. Your icons should never be cropped, should always be front facing, and should never have any perspective to them. Your icon should always be lit from the top. Also, in the icon template Photoshop file mentioned earlier, there is a list of good colors and materials to use in your icon design. Try to limit the number of different colors in your icon.

Also in the icon template file, there are a number of effects such as drop shadows and highlights that you can use to make your icon look consistent with others on Android devices.

Publish Your Application for the Android Market

This is the moment you have been waiting for. You have finished development of your application and tracked down and squashed all the bugs that your testers have found. You are now ready to publish your application for submission to the Android Market. To successfully upload your application to the Android Market, your application must be signed with a certificate that is valid beyond October 22, 2033. You may also want to create a specific certificate for this application if you have been using a generic one for development.

You will use the AIR Android Settings dialog box to make the necessary changes in order to publish for the Android Market. The General tab contains some basic information about your application. Make sure that the app name is the same name that you want to have shown in

the Market and on the device. Also, make sure that the version is correct. If this is the first time you are going to submit your application, you should set the version to 1.0 or something similar.

On the Deployment tab, you will make sure that your certificate is correct and valid for the correct length of time. Enter the password that you created when you created your certificate.

Up until now, you have most likely been publishing your application in Debug mode, in order to properly debug your application on your device. Now that your application is ready to be submitted to the Android Market, you will set the Android deployment type to Release.

After all the publish settings have been updated, you can publish your application. It is not a bad idea to test it on your device one last time before uploading it.

Publish Your Application for the Android Market

① Click File.

② Click AIR Android Settings.

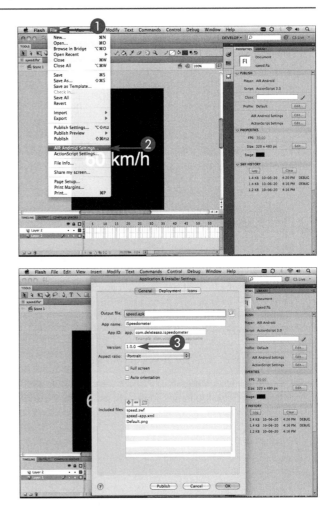

The Application & Installer Settings dialog box appears.

③ Type the version number, such as 1.0.0.

4 Click the Deployment tab.

5 Click Release.

6 Click Publish.

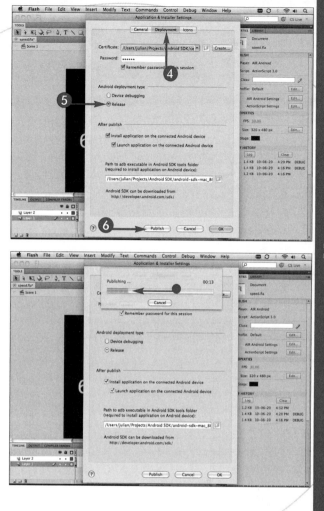

● The Publishing progress dialog box appears, showing you the status of your submission.

After the progress bar reaches the end, your application is published.

Extra

If you have been using the command line to compile your applications, you will have to change the development credentials in your script to match those of your distribution credentials, as mentioned earlier. You will also need to change the -target switch in order to have your application be compiled for Android Market distribution. The following is an example of publishing for the Android Market:

```
/Applications/Adobe\ Flash\ CS5/AIK2.5/bin/adt -package -target apk -storetype pkcs12 -keystore
  mycert.p12 -storepass password files.apk files-app.xml files.swf
```

Upload Your Application to the Android Market

After you have successfully published your application for the Android Market, you are ready to upload it through the Android Market Publish portal. Along with your application, you will be uploading all the necessary artwork, such as screenshots and application icons. If you plan on charging for your application, you will need to have signed up for a Google Checkout merchant account. In order to do so, you will need to have your banking and tax information ready. If you have not created an Android Market account yet, see Chapter 1, "Getting Started with Android Development," for more details.

After you have logged into your Android Market account, you can begin the upload process. There are five portions of the upload process, each equally important. If you have

all your material ready, it should not take you very long to fill out the form; however, take your time to make sure that it is filled out correctly.

The first section of the form is where you can upload all the assets for your application, such as the application itself, screenshots, and your promotional graphic. The promotional graphic is optional, as are the screenshots. If you choose to upload screenshots of your application, you must upload two.

For each asset, there is a Choose File button that enables you to browse for the file that you want to upload. You can then upload the asset to the Android Market. After each asset is uploaded, a representation of the asset will be displayed on the page.

Upload Your Application to the Android Market

1. In a Web browser, go to http://market.android.com/publish.

2. Type your account email address.

3. Type your account password.

4. Click Sign In.

Your Android Market profile page is shown.

5. Click Upload Application.

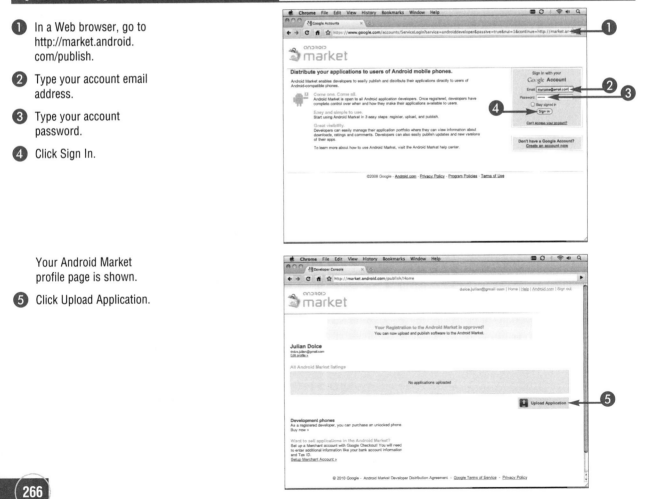

The Upload an Application form appears.

6 Click Choose File.

A file browser dialog box appears.

7 Click your .apk file.

8 Click Open.

● The filename is displayed on-screen.

9 Click Upload.

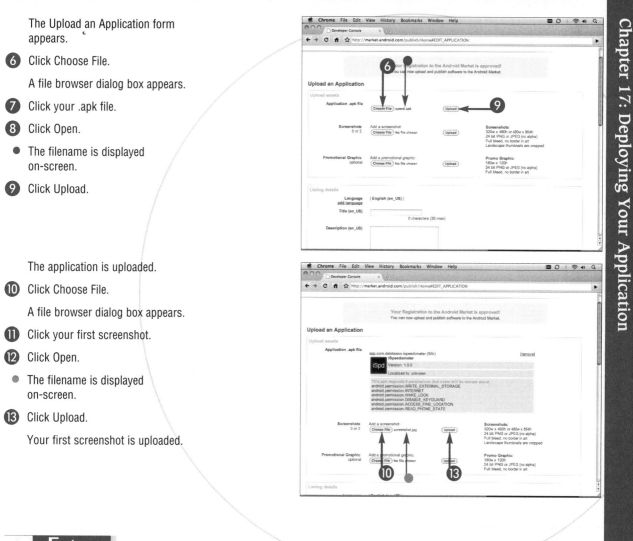

The application is uploaded.

10 Click Choose File.

A file browser dialog box appears.

11 Click your first screenshot.

12 Click Open.

● The filename is displayed on-screen.

13 Click Upload.

Your first screenshot is uploaded.

Extra

If you are creating an application and want to distribute your application outside of the Android Market, you can. This gives you the ability to host the Android application on your Web site. If you work for a company that already develops and sells applications, you could place your Android application for sale the same way. This would bypass Google's retaining 30% of the application sale price. This is very much different than what is allowed on other mobile platforms, such as the iTunes App Store.

However, with the increase in flexibility, not all devices are able to install applications from third-party, or unknown, sources. In order for a device to install non-Market applications, the Unknown Sources item in the Application Settings must be checked. To open the Application Settings, launch the Settings application and select Applications from the main list.

This is easy for some developers and most power users; however, the average consumer will most likely not trust an application that is not downloaded from the Android Market. So if your application is targeted at the general user, it is probably a better idea to upload it to the Android Market.

continued →

After you have uploaded all the assets for your application, you can move onto the second part of the form, Listing Details. In this section, you will add the name of your application, a description of your application, and promotional text.

Your application name can be a maximum of 30 characters and is displayed under the icon on the home screen. This should be the same as the name you set in the Flash AIR Android Settings dialog box. If your application name is one really long word, it may wrap onto two lines, which may make it hard to read.

The description text for your application can be a maximum of 325 characters. This text will appear on your application page in the Android Market, and it will be the key piece of text that determines whether a customer purchases and downloads your application.

Give customers a very high-level overview of your application and its key features.

The promotional text is optional and is required only if you have uploaded a promotional graphic earlier in the form. The promotional text appears next to the promotional graphic when it is featured in specific locations in the Android Market. You have only 80 characters to sell your application, so make each one count.

Selecting an application type is fairly straightforward, as there are only two options, Applications and Games. Depending on which type of application you have developed, the category you can select will differ.

The rest of the form consists of contact information and agreeing to the terms of use. Make sure to read the Android Content Guidelines before you submit your application to ensure that you have followed them all.

Upload Your Application to the Android Market *(continued)*

⑭ Click the Add Another link.

⑮ Click Choose File.

A file browser dialog box appears.

⑯ Click your second screenshot.

⑰ Click Open.

● The filename is displayed on-screen.

⑱ Click Upload.

Your second screenshot is uploaded.

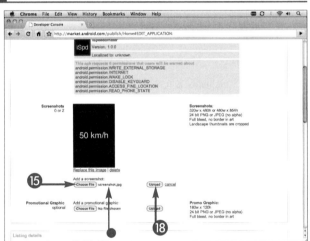

⑲ Type a title for your application.

⑳ Type description text for your application.

㉑ Click here and select an application type.

㉒ Click here and select a category.

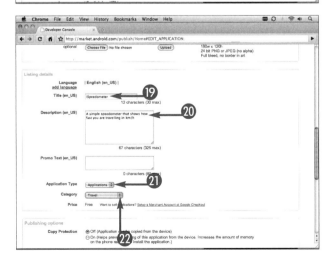

㉓ Select if you want to add copy protection to your application.

Note: *See the Extra section below for more details on copy protection.*

㉔ Type your Web site URL.

㉕ Type your email address.

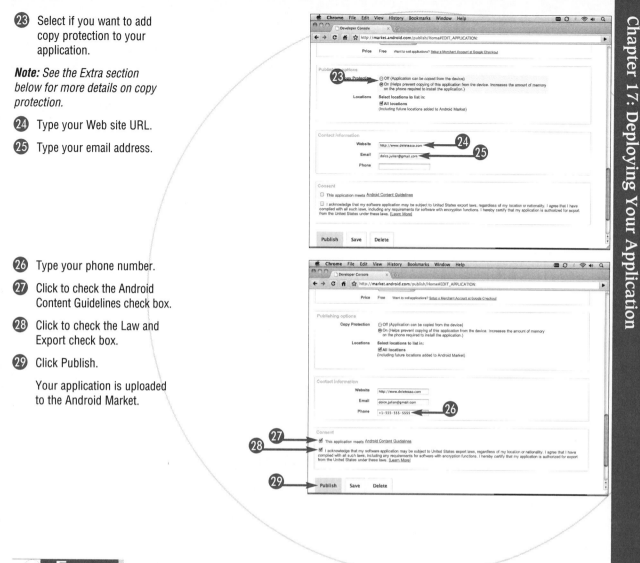

㉖ Type your phone number.

㉗ Click to check the Android Content Guidelines check box.

㉘ Click to check the Law and Export check box.

㉙ Click Publish.

Your application is uploaded to the Android Market.

In the Publishing Options section of the form, you have the ability to apply copy protection to your application. This will help prevent users from copying your application off of their device. Adding copy protection to your application will increase the amount of memory on the device required to install the application. However, if you are selling your application, chances are you will want to add this protection. This will prevent users from downloading the application to their computers and installing it on other devices.

Even if you have created a free application, keeping users from distributing the application is a good idea. Knowing that your application can be downloaded only from the Android Market allows you to keep control of it.

The trade-off in increased memory is, for most people, worth the extra protection.

ActionScript Class Reference

The following is a list of the ActionScript 3 classes available for AIR Android applications. Some of the classes that are available for the browser plug-in or the desktop AIR Runtime but are not available for Android have been omitted. For a complete ActionScript 3 class reference, visit the documentation on the Adobe Web site, http://help.adobe.com/en_US/FlashPlatform/reference/actionscript/3/.

The classes are listed alphabetically. Each class listing denotes the class name; its package; what class it extends, if any; its properties; its constants; and its methods.

Accelerometer

Package: flash.sensors

Extends EventDispatcher

Properties:

isSupported:Boolean

muted:Boolean

Methods:

Accelerometer()

setRequestedUpdateInterval()

ActionScriptVersion

Package: flash.display

Extends Object

Constants:

ACTIONSCRIPT2:uint

ACTIONSCRIPT3:uint

AccelerometerEvent

Package: flash.events

Extends Event

Properties:

accelerationX:Number

accelerationY:Number

accelerationZ:Number

timestamp:Number

Constant:

UPDATE:String

Methods:

AccelerometerEvent()

clone()

toString()

AntiAliasType

Package: flash.text

Extends Object

Constants:

ADVANCED:String

NORMAL:String

ApplicationDomain

Package: flash.system

Properties:

`currentDomain:ApplicationDomain`

`domainMemory:ByteArray`

`parentDomain:ApplicationDomain`

Constant:

`MIN_DOMAIN_MEMORY_LENGTH: uint`

Methods:

`ApplicationDomain()`

`getDefinition():Object`

`hasDefinition():Boolean`

ArgumentError

Package: Top Level

Extends Error

Method:

`ArgumentError()`

arguments

Package: Top Level

Properties:

`callee:Function`

`length:Number`

Array

Package: Top Level

Extends Object

Property:

`length:uint`

Constants:

`CASEINSENSITIVE:uint`

`DESCENDING:uint`

`NUMERIC:uint`

`RETURNINDEXEDARRAY:uint`

`UNIQUESORT:uint`

Methods:

`Array()`

`concat():Array`

`every():Boolean`

`filter():Array`

`forEach():void`

`indexOf():int`

`join():String`

`lastIndexOf():int`

`map():Array`

`pop():*`

`push():uint`

`reverse():Array`

`shift():*`

`slice():Array`

`some():Boolean`

`sort():Array`

`sortOn():Array`

`splice():Array`

`toLocaleString():String`

`toString():String`

`unshift():uint`

ActionScript Class Reference (continued)

AsyncErrorEvent

Package: flash.events

Extends ErrorEvent

Property:

error:Error

Constant:

ASYNC_ERROR:String

Methods:

AsyncErrorEvent()

clone():Event

toString():String

BevelFilter

Package: flash.filters

Extends BitmapFilter

Properties:

angle:Number

blurX:Number

blurY:Number

distance:Number

highlightAlpha:Number

highlightColor:uint

knockout:Boolean

quality:int

shadowAlpha:Number

shadowColor:uint

strength:Number

type:String

Methods:

BevelFilter()

clone():BitmapFilter

Bitmap

Package: flash.display

Extends DisplayObject

Properties:

bitmapData:BitmapData

pixelSnapping:String

smoothing:Boolean

Method:

Bitmap()

BitmapData

Package: flash.display

Extends Object

Implements IBitmapDrawable

Properties:

height:int

rect:Rectangle

transparent:Boolean

width:int

Methods:

applyFilter():void

BitmapData()

clone():BitmapData

colorTransform():void

compare():Object

copyChannel():void

copyPixels():void

dispose():void

draw():void

fillRect():void

floodFill():void

generateFilterRect():Rectangle

getColorBoundsRect():Rectangle

getPixel():uint

getPixel32():uint

getPixels():ByteArray

hitTest():Boolean

lock():void

merge():void

noise():void

paletteMap():void

perlinNoise():void

pixelDissolve():int

scroll():void

setPixel():void

setPixel32():void

setPixels():void

setVector():void

threshold():uint

unlock():void

BitmapDataChannel

Package: flash.display

Extends Object

Constants:

ALPHA:uint

BLUE:uint

GREEN:uint

RED:uint

BitmapFilterQuality

Package: flash.filters

Extends Object

Constants:

HIGH:int

LOW:int

MEDIUM:int

ActionScript Class Reference (continued)

BitmapFilterType

Package: flash.filters

Extends Object

Constants:

FULL:String

INNER:String

OUTER:String

BlurFilter

Package: flash.filters

Extends BitmapFilter

Properties:

blurX:Number

blurY:Number

quality:int

Methods:

BlurFilter()

clone():BitmapFilter

BlendMode

Package: flash.display

Extends Object

Constants:

ADD:String

ALPHA:String

DARKEN:String

DIFFERENCE:String

ERASE:String

HARDLIGHT:String

INVERT:String

LAYER:String

LIGHTEN:String

MULTIPLY:String

NORMAL:String

OVERLAY:String

SCREEN:String

SHADER:String

SUBTRACT:String

Boolean

Package: Top Level

Extends Object

Methods:

Boolean()

toString():String

valueOf():Boolean

BreakOpportunity

Package: flash.text.engine

Extends Object

Constants:

ALL:String

ANY:String

AUTO:String

NONE:String

Package: flash.utils

Extends Object

Implement IDataInput, IDataOutput

Properties:

```
bytesAvailable:uint
defaultObjectEncoding:uint
endian:String
length:uint
objectEncoding:uint
position:uint
```

Methods:

```
ByteArray()
compress():void
readBoolean():Boolean
readByte():int
readBytes():void
readDouble():Number
readFloat():Number
readInt():int
readMultiByte():String
```

```
readObject():*
readShort():int
readUnsignedByte():uint
readUnsignedInt():uint
readUnsignedShort():uint
readUTF():String
readUTFBytes():String
toString():String
uncompress():void
writeBoolean():void
writeByte():void
writeBytes():void
writeDouble():void
writeFloat():void
writeInt():void
writeMultiByte():void
writeObject():void
writeShort():void
writeUnsignedInt():void
writeUTF():void
writeUTFBytes():void
```

Camera

Package: flash.media

Extends EventDispatcher

Properties:

```
activityLevel:Number
bandwidth:int
currentFPS:Number
fps:Number
height:int
index:int
```

```
isSupported:Boolean
keyFrameInterval:int
loopback:Boolean
motionLevel:int
motionTimeout:int
muted:Boolean
name:String
names:Array
quality:int
width:int
```

(continued)

Camera *(continued)*

Methods:

getCamera()

setKeyFrameInterval()

setLoopback()

setMode()

setMotionLevel()

setQuality()

CameraRoll

Package: flash.media

Extends EventDispatcher

Properties:

supportsAddBitmapData:Boolean

supportsBrowseForImage:Boolean

Methods:

addBitmapData()

browseForImage()

CameraRoll()

Capabilities

Package: flash.system

Extends Object

Properties:

avHardwareDisable:Boolean

hasAccessibility:Boolean

hasAudio:Boolean

hasAudioEncoder:Boolean

hasEmbeddedVideo:Boolean

hasIME:Boolean

hasMP3:Boolean

hasPrinting:Boolean

hasScreenBroadcast:Boolean

hasScreenPlayback:Boolean

hasStreamingAudio:Boolean

hasStreamingVideo:Boolean

hasTLS:Boolean

hasVideoEncoder:Boolean

isDebugger:Boolean

language:String

localFileReadDisable:Boolean

manufacturer:String

os:String

pixelAspectRatio:Number

playerType:String

screenColor:String

screenDPI:Number

screenResolutionX:Number

screenResolutionY:Number

serverString:String

version:String

CapsStyle

Package: flash.display

Extends Object

Constants:

NONE:String

ROUND:String

SQUARE:String

Class

Package: Top Level

Extends Object

ColorCorrection

Package: flash.display

Extends Object

Constants:

DEFAULT:String

OFF:String

ON:String

ColorCorrectionSupport

Package: flash.display

Extends Object

Constants:

DEFAULT_OFF:String

DEFAULT_ON:String

UNSUPPORTED:String

ColorTransform

Package: flash.geom

Extends Object

Properties:

alphaMultiplier:Number

alphaOffset:Number

blueMultiplier:Number

blueOffset:Number

color:uint

greenMultiplier:Number

greenOffset:Number

redMultiplier:Number

redOffset:Number

Methods:

ColorTransform()

concat():void

toString():String

CompressionAlgorithm

Package: flash.utils

Extends Object

Constants:

DEFLATE:String

ZLIB:String

ActionScript Class Reference (continued)

DataEvent

Package: flash.events

Extends TextEvent

Property:

data:String

Constants:

DATA:String

UPLOAD_COMPLETE_DATA:String

Methods:

clone():Event

DataEvent()

toString():String

DefinitionError

Package: Top Level

Extends Error

Method:

DefinitionError()

Dictionary

Package: flash.utils

Extends Object

DisplayObject

Package: flash.system

Extends EventDispatcher

Implements IBitmapDrawable

Properties:

accessibilityProperties:
AccessibilityProperties

alpha:Number

blendMode:String

blendShader:void

cacheAsBitmap:Boolean

filters:Array

height:Number

loaderInfo:LoaderInfo

mask:DisplayObject

mouseX:Number

mouseY:Number

name:String

opaqueBackground:Object

parent:DisplayObjectContainer

root:DisplayObject

rotation:Number

rotationX:Number

rotationY:Number

rotationZ:Number

scale9Grid:Rectangle

scaleX:Number

scaleY:Number

scaleZ:Number

scrollRect:Rectangle

stage:Stage

transform:Transform

visible:Boolean

width:Number

x:Number

y:Number

z:Number

Methods:

getBounds():Rectangle

getRect():Rectangle

globalToLocal():Point

globalToLocal3D():Vector3D

hitTestObject():Boolean

hitTestPoint():Boolean

localToGlobal():Point

local3DToGlobal():Point

DisplayObjectContainer

Package: flash.display

Extends InteractiveObject

Properties:

mouseChildren:Boolean

numChildren:int

tabChildren:Boolean

textSnapshot:TextSnapshot

Methods:

addChild():DisplayObject

addChildAt():DisplayObject

areInaccessibleObjectsUnderPoint():Boolean

contains():Boolean

DisplayObjectContainer()

getChildAt():DisplayObject

getChildByName():DisplayObject

getChildIndex():int

getObjectsUnderPoint():Array

removeChild():DisplayObject

removeChildAt():DisplayObject

setChildIndex():void

swapChildren():void

swapChildrenAt():void

Endian

Package: flash.utils

Extends Object

Constants:

BIG_ENDIAN:String

LITTLE_ENDIAN:String

EOFError

Package: flash.errors

Extends Error

Method:

EOFError()

Error

Package: Top Level

Extends Object

Properties:

length:int = 1

message:String

name:String

Methods:

Error()

getStackTrace():String

toString():String

ErrorEvent

Package: flash.events

Extends TextEvent

Property:

errorID:int

Constant:

ERROR:String

Methods:

clone():Event

ErrorEvent()

toString():String

ActionScript Class Reference (continued)

EvalError

Package: Top Level

Extends Error

Method:

EvalError()

Event

Package: flash.events

Extends Object

Properties:

bubbles:Boolean

cancelable:Boolean

currentTarget:Object

eventPhase:uint

target:Object

type:String

Constants:

ACTIVATE:String

ADDED:String

ADDED_TO_STAGE:String

CANCEL:String

CHANGE:String

CLEAR:String

CLOSE:String

CLOSING:String

COMPLETE:String

CONNECT:String

COPY:String

CUT:String

DEACTIVATE:String

DISPLAYING:String

ENTER_FRAME:String

EXITING:String

FULLSCREEN:String

HTML_BOUNDS_CHANGE:String

HTML_DOM_INITIALIZE:String

HTML_RENDER:String

ID3:String

INIT:String

LOCATION_CHANGE:String

MOUSE_LEAVE:String

NETWORK_CHANGE:String

OPEN:String

PASTE:String

REMOVED:String

REMOVED_FROM_STAGE:String

RENDER:String

RESIZE:String

SCROLL:String

SELECT:String

SELECT_ALL:String

SOUND_COMPLETE:String

TAB_CHILDREN_CHANGE:String

TAB_ENABLED_CHANGE:String

TAB_INDEX_CHANGE:String

UNLOAD:String

USER_IDLE:String

USER_PRESENT:String

Methods:

clone():Event

Event()

formatToString():String

isDefaultPrevented():
Boolean

preventDefault():void

stopImmediatePropagation():
void

stopPropagation():void

toString():String

EventDispatcher

Package: flash.events

Extends Object

Implements IEventDispatcher

Methods:

addEventListener():void

dispatchEvent():Boolean

EventDispatcher():void

hasEventListener():Boolean

removeEventListener():void

willTrigger():Boolean

EventPhase

Package: flash.events

Extends Object

Constants:

AT_TARGET:uint

BUBBLING_PHASE:uint

CAPTURING_PHASE:uint

File

Package: flash.filesystem

Extends FileReference

Properties:

applicationDirectory:File

applicationStorageDirectory:
File

desktopDirectory:File

documentsDirectory:File

exists:Boolean

icon:Icon

isDirectory:Boolean

isHidden:Boolean

isPackage:Boolean

isSymbolicLink:Boolean

lineEnding:String

nativePath:String

parent:File

separator:String

systemCharset:String

url:String

userDirectory:File

Methods:

browseForDirectory():void

browseForOpen():void

browseForOpenMultiple():void

browseForSave():void

cancel():void

canonicalize():void

clone():File

copyTo():void

copyToAsync():void

createDirectory():void

createTempDirectory():File

createTempFile():File

deleteDirectory():void

deleteDirectoryAsync():void

deleteFile():void

deleteFileAsync():void

File()

getDirectoryListing():Array

getDirectoryListingAsync():
void

getRelativePath():String

getRootDirectories():Array

moveTo():void

moveToAsync():void

moveToTrash():void

moveToTrashAsync():void

resolvePath():File

FileFilter

Package: flash.net

Extends Object

Properties:

```
description:String
extension:String
macType:String
```

Method:

```
FileFilter():void
```

FileListEvent

Package: flash.events

Extends Event

Property:

```
files:Array
```

Constants:

```
DIRECTORY_LISTING:String
SELECT_MULTIPLE:String
```

Method:

```
FileListEvent()
```

FileMode

Package: flash.filesystem

Extends Object

Constants:

```
APPEND:String
READ:String
UPDATE:String
WRITE:String
```

FileReference

Package: flash.net

Extends EventDispatcher

Properties:

```
creationDate:Date
creator:String
extension:String
modificationDate:Date
name:String
size:Number
type:String
```

Methods:

```
browse():Boolean
cancel():void
download():void
FileReference()
upload():void
uploadUnencoded():void
```

FileReferenceList

Package: flash.net

Extends EventDispatcher

Property:

```
fileList:Array
```

Methods:

```
browse():Boolean
FileReferenceList()
```

FileStream

Package: flash.filesystem

Extends EventDispatcher

Implements IDataInput, IDataOutput

Properties:

bytesAvailable:uint

endian:String

objectEncoding:uint

position:Number

readAhead:Number

Methods:

close():void

FileStream()

open():void

openAsync():void

readBoolean():Boolean

readByte():int

readBytes():void

readDouble():Number

readFloat():Number

readInt():int

readMultiByte():String

readObject():*

readShort():int

readUnsignedByte():uint

readUnsignedInt():uint

readUnsignedShort():uint

readUTF():String

readUTFBytes():String

truncate():void

writeBoolean():void

writeByte():void

writeBytes():void

writeDouble():void

writeFloat():void

writeInt():void

writeMultiByte():void

writeObject():void

writeShort():void

writeUnsignedInt():void

writeUTF():void

writeUTFBytes():void

FocusDirection

Package: flash.display

Extends Object

Constants:

BOTTOM:String

NONE:String

TOP:String

FocusEvent

Package: flash.events

Extends Event

Properties:

direction:String

keyCode:uint

relatedObject:InteractiveObject

shiftKey:Boolean

Constants:

FOCUS_IN:String

FOCUS_OUT:String

KEY_FOCUS_CHANGE:String

MOUSE_FOCUS_CHANGE:String

Methods:

clone():Event

FocusEvent()

toString():String

ActionScript Class Reference (continued)

FrameLabel

Package: flash.display

Extends Object

Property:

```
frame:intname:String
```

FullScreenEvent

Package: flash.events

Extends ActivityEvent

Property:

```
fullScreen:Boolean
```

Constant:

```
FULL_SCREEN:String
```

Methods:

```
clone():Event
FullScreenEvent()
toString():String
```

Function

Package: Top Level

Extends Object

Methods:

```
apply():*
call():*
```

Geolocation

Package: flash.sensors

Extends EventDispatcher

Properties:

```
isSupported:Boolean
muted:Boolean
```

Methods:

```
Geolocation()
setRequestedUpdateInterval()
```

GeolocationEvent

Package: flash.events

Extends Event

Properties:

```
altitude:Number
heading:Number
horizontalAccuracy:Number
latitude:Number
longitude:Number
speed:Number
timestamp:Number
verticalAccuracy:Number
```

Constant:

```
UPDATE:String
```

Methods:

```
GeolocationEvent()
clone()
toString()
```

GestureEvent

Package: flash.events

Extends Event

Properties:

altKey:Boolean

commandKey:Boolean

controlKey:Boolean

ctrlKey:Boolean

localX:Number

localY:Number

phase:String

shiftKey:Boolean

stageX:Number

stageY:Number

Constant:

GESTURE_TWO_FINGER_TAP:String

Methods:

GestureEvent()

clone()

toString()

updateAfterEvent()

GesturePhase

Package: flash.events

Extends Object

Constants:

ALL:String

BEGIN:String

END:String

UPDATE:String

GradientGlowFilter

Package: flash.filters

Extends BitmapFilter

Properties:

alphas:Array

angle:Number

blurX:Number

blurY:Number

colors:Array

distance:Number

knockout:Boolean

quality:int

ratios:Array

strength:Number

type:String

Methods:

clone():BitmapFilter

GradientGlowFilter()

ActionScript Class Reference (continued)

GradientType

Package: flash.display

Extends Object

Constants:

```
LINEAR:String = "linear"
RADIAL:String = "radial"
```

Graphics

Package: flash.display

Extends Object

Methods:

```
beginBitmapFill():void
beginFill():void
beginGradientFill():void
clear():void
curveTo():void
drawCircle():void
drawEllipse():void
drawRect():void
drawRoundRect():void
endFill():void
lineGradientStyle():void
lineStyle():void
lineTo():void
moveTo():void
```

GraphicsBitmapFill

Package: flash.display

Extends Object

Implements IGraphicsData, IGraphicsFill

Properties:

```
bitmapData:BitmapData
matrix:Matrix
repeat:Boolean
smooth:Boolean
```

Method:

```
GraphicsBitmapFill()
```

GraphicsEndFill

Package: flash.display

Extends Object

Implements IGraphicsData, IGraphicsFill

Method:

```
GraphicsEndFill()
```

GraphicsGradientFill

Package: flash.display

Extends Object

Implements IGraphicsData, IGraphicsFill

Properties:

alphas:Array

colors:Array

focalPointRatio:Number

interpolationMethod:String

matrix:Matrix

ratios:Array

spreadMethod:String

type:String

GraphicsPath

Package: flash.display

Extends Object

Implements IGraphicsData, IGraphicsPath

Properties:

commands:Vector.<int>

data:Vector.<Number>

winding:String

Methods:

curveTo():void

lineTo():void

moveTo():void

wideLineTo():void

wideMoveTo():void

GraphicsPathCommand

Package: flash.display

Extends Object

Constants:

CURVE_TO:int

LINE_TO:int

MOVE_TO:int

NO_OP:int

WIDE_LINE_TO:int

WIDE_MOVE_TO:int

GraphicsPathWinding

Package: flash.display

Extends Object

Constants:

EVEN_ODD:String

NON_ZERO:String

GraphicsShaderFill

Package: flash.display

Extends Object

Implements IGraphicsData, IGraphicsFill

Properties:

matrix:Matrix

shader:Shader

ActionScript Class Reference (continued)

GraphicsSolidFill

Package: flash.display

Extends Object

Implements IGraphicsData, IGraphicsFill

Properties:

```
alpha:Number
color:uint
```

GraphicsTrianglePath

Package: flash.display

Extends Object

Implements IGraphicsData, IGraphicsPath

Properties:

```
culling:String
indices:Vector.<int>
uvtData:Vector.<Number>
vertices:Vector.<Number>
```

GraphicsStroke

Package: flash.display

Extends Object

Implements IGraphicsData, IGraphicsStroke

Properties:

```
caps:String
fill:IGraphicsFill
joints:String
miterLimit:Number
pixelHinting:Boolean
scaleMode:String
thickness:Number
```

GridFitType

Package: flash.text

Extends Object

Constants:

```
NONE:String
PIXEL:String
SUBPIXEL:String
```

IBitmapDrawable

Package: flash.display

ID3Info

Package: flash.media

Extends Object

Properties:

album:String

artist:String

comment:String

genre:String

songName:String

track:String

year:String

IDataInput

Package: flash.utils

Properties:

bytesAvailable:uint

endian:String

objectEncoding:uint

Methods:

readBoolean():Boolean

readByte():int

readBytes():void

readDouble():Number

readFloat():Number

readInt():int

readMultiByte():String

readObject():*

readShort():int

readUnsignedByte():uint

readUnsignedInt():uint

readUnsignedShort():uint

readUTF():String

readUTFBytes():String

IDataOutput

Package: flash.utils

Properties:

endian:String

objectEncoding:uint

Methods:

writeBoolean():void

writeByte():void

writeBytes():void

writeDouble():void

writeFloat():void

writeInt():void

writeMultiByte():void

writeObject():void

writeShort():void

writeUnsignedInt():void

writeUTF():void

writeUTFBytes():void

ActionScript Class Reference (continued)

IDynamicPropertyOutput

Package: flash.net

Method:

writeDynamicProperty():void

IDynamicPropertyWriter

Package: flash.net

Method:

writeDynamicProperties():void

IEventDispatcher

Package: flash.events

Methods:

addEventListener():void

dispatchEvent():Boolean

hasEventListener():Boolean

removeEventListener():void

willTrigger():Boolean

IExternalizable

Package: flash.utils

Methods:

readExternal():void

writeExternal():void

IGraphicsData

Package: flash.display

Extends Object

IGraphicsFill

Package: flash.display

Extends Object

IGraphicsPath

Package: flash.display

Extends Object

IGraphicsStroke

Package: flash.display

Extends Object

IllegalOperationError

Package: flash.errors

Extends Error

Method:

IllegalOperationError()

int

Package: Top Level

Extends Object

Constants:

MAX_VALUE:int

MIN_VALUE:int

Methods:

int()

toExponential():String

toFixed():String

toPrecision():String

toString():String

valueOf():int

InteractiveObject

Package: flash.display

Extends DisplayObject

Properties:

contextMenu:NativeMenu

doubleClickEnabled:Boolean

focusRect:Object

mouseEnabled:Boolean

tabEnabled:Boolean

tabIndex:int

Method:

InteractiveObject():void

InterpolationMethod

Package: flash.display

Extends Object

Constants:

LINEAR_RGB:String

RGB:String

InvalidSWFError

Package: flash.errors

Extends Error

Method:

InvalidSWFError()

IOError

Package: flash.errors

Extends Error

Method:

IOError()

IOErrorEvent

Package: flash.events

Extends ErrorEvent

Constant:

IO_ERROR:String

Methods:

clone():Event

IOErrorEvent()

toString():String

IURIDereferencer

Package: flash.security

Method:

dereference():IDataInput

JPEGLoaderContext

Package: flash.system

Extends LoaderContext

Property:

deblockingFilter:Number

JointStyle

Package: flash.display

Extends Object

Constants:

BEVEL:String

MITER:String

ROUND:String

Keyboard

Package: flash.ui

Extends Object

Properties:

capsLock:Boolean

CharCodeStrings:Array

numLock:Boolean

Constants:

A:uint

ALTERNATE:uint

B:uint

BACKQUOTE:uint

BACKSLASH:uint

BACKSPACE:uint

C:uint

CAPS_LOCK:uint

COMMA:uint

COMMAND:uint

CONTROL:uint

D:uint

DELETE:uint

DOWN:uint

E:uint

END:uint

ENTER:uint

EQUAL:uint

ESCAPE:uint

F:uint

F1:uint

F2:uint

F3:uint

F4:uint

F5:uint

F6:uint

F7:uint

F8:uint

F9:uint

F10:uint

F11:uint

F12:uint

F13:uint

F14:uint

F15:uint

G:uint

H:uint

HOME:uint

I:uint

INSERT:uint

J:uint

K:uint

KEYNAME_BEGIN:String

KEYNAME_BREAK:String

KEYNAME_CLEARDISPLAY:String

KEYNAME_CLEARLINE:String

KEYNAME_DELETE:String

KEYNAME_DELETECHAR:String

KEYNAME_DELETELINE:String

KEYNAME_DOWNARROW:String

KEYNAME_END:String

KEYNAME_EXECUTE:String

KEYNAME_F1:String

KEYNAME_F2:String

KEYNAME_F3:String

KEYNAME_F4:String

KEYNAME_F5:String

KEYNAME_F6:String

KEYNAME_F7:String

KEYNAME_F8:String

KEYNAME_F9:String

KEYNAME_F10:String

KEYNAME_F11:String

KEYNAME_F12:String

KEYNAME_F13:String

KEYNAME_F14:String

KEYNAME_F15:String

KEYNAME_F16:String

KEYNAME_F17:String

KEYNAME_F18:String

KEYNAME_F19:String

KEYNAME_F20:String

KEYNAME_F21:String

KEYNAME_F22:String

KEYNAME_F23:String

KEYNAME_F24:String

KEYNAME_F25:String

KEYNAME_F26:String

KEYNAME_F27:String

KEYNAME_F28:String

KEYNAME_F29:String

KEYNAME_F30:String

KEYNAME_F31:String

KEYNAME_F32:String

KEYNAME_F33:String

KEYNAME_F34:String

KEYNAME_F35:String

KEYNAME_FIND:String

KEYNAME_HELP:String

KEYNAME_HOME:String

KEYNAME_INSERT:String

KEYNAME_INSERTCHAR:String

KEYNAME_INSERTLINE:String

KEYNAME_LEFTARROW:String

KEYNAME_MENU:String

KEYNAME_MODESWITCH:String

KEYNAME_NEXT:String

KEYNAME_PAGEDOWN:String

KEYNAME_PAGEUP:String

KEYNAME_PAUSE:String

KEYNAME_PREV:String

KEYNAME_PRINT:String

KEYNAME_PRINTSCREEN:String

KEYNAME_REDO:String

KEYNAME_RESET:String

KEYNAME_RIGHTARROW:String

KEYNAME_SCROLLLOCK:String

KEYNAME_SELECT:String

KEYNAME_STOP:String

KEYNAME_SYSREQ:String

KEYNAME_SYSTEM:String

KEYNAME_UNDO:String

KEYNAME_UPARROW:String

KEYNAME_USER:String

L:uint

LEFT:uint

LEFTBRACKET:uint

M:uint

MINUS:uint

N:uint

NUMBER_0:uint

NUMBER_1:uint

NUMBER_2:uint

NUMBER_3:uint

NUMBER_4:uint

NUMBER_5:uint

NUMBER_6:uint

NUMBER_7:uint

NUMBER_8:uint

NUMBER_9:uint

NUMPAD:uint

NUMPAD_0:uint

NUMPAD_1:uint

NUMPAD_2:uint

NUMPAD_3:uint

NUMPAD_4:uint

NUMPAD_5:uint

NUMPAD_6:uint

NUMPAD_7:uint

(continued)

Keyboard *(continued)*

NUMPAD_8:uint	STRING_END:String	STRING_F30:String
NUMPAD_9:uint	STRING_EXECUTE:String	STRING_F31:String
NUMPAD_ADD:uint	STRING_F1:String	STRING_F32:String
NUMPAD_DECIMAL:uint	STRING_F2:String	STRING_F33:String
NUMPAD_DIVIDE:uint	STRING_F3:String	STRING_F34:String
NUMPAD_ENTER:uint	STRING_F4:String	STRING_F35:String
NUMPAD_MULTIPLY:uint	STRING_F5:String	STRING_FIND:String
NUMPAD_SUBTRACT:uint	STRING_F6:String	STRING_HELP:String
O:uint	STRING_F7:String	STRING_HOME:String
P:uint	STRING_F8:String	STRING_INSERT:String
PAGE_DOWN:uint	STRING_F9:String	STRING_INSERTCHAR:String
PAGE_UP:uint	STRING_F10:String	STRING_INSERTLINE:String
PERIOD:uint	STRING_F11:String	STRING_LEFTARROW:String
Q:uint	STRING_F12:String	STRING_MENU:String
QUOTE:uint	STRING_F13:String	STRING_MODESWITCH:String
R:uint	STRING_F14:String	STRING_NEXT:String
RIGHT:uint	STRING_F15:String	STRING_PAGEDOWN:String
RIGHTBRACKET:uint	STRING_F16:String	STRING_PAGEUP:String
S:uint	STRING_F17:String	STRING_PAUSE:String
SEMICOLON:uint	STRING_F18:String	STRING_PREV:String
SHIFT:uint	STRING_F19:String	STRING_PRINT:String
SLASH:uint	STRING_F20:String	STRING_PRINTSCREEN:String
SPACE:uint	STRING_F21:String	STRING_REDO:String
STRING_BEGIN:String	STRING_F22:String	STRING_RESET:String
STRING_BREAK:String	STRING_F23:String	STRING_RIGHTARROW:String
STRING_CLEARDISPLAY:String	STRING_F24:String	STRING_SCROLLLOCK:String
STRING_CLEARLINE:String	STRING_F25:String	STRING_SELECT:String
STRING_DELETE:String	STRING_F26:String	STRING_STOP:String
STRING_DELETECHAR:String	STRING_F27:String	STRING_SYSREQ:String
STRING_DELETELINE:String	STRING_F28:String	STRING_SYSTEM:String
STRING_DOWNARROW:String	STRING_F29:String	STRING_UNDO:String

Keyboard *(continued)*

STRING_UPARROW:String	W:uint
STRING_USER:String	X:uint
T:uint	Y:uint
TAB:uint	Z:uint
U:uint	**Method:**
UP:uint	isAccessible():Boolean
V:uint	

KeyboardEvent

Package: flash.events

Extends Event

Properties:

altKey:Boolean

charCode:uint

commandKey:Boolean

controlKey:Boolean

ctrlKey:Boolean

keyCode:uint

keyLocation:uint

shiftKey:Boolean

Constants:

KEY_DOWN:String

KEY_UP:String

Methods:

clone():Event

KeyboardEvent()

toString():String

updateAfterEvent():void

KeyLocation

Package: flash.ui

Extends Object

Constants:

LEFT:uint

NUM_PAD:uint

RIGHT:uint

STANDARD:uint

LineScaleMode

Package: flash.display

Extends Object

Constants:

HORIZONTAL:String

NONE:String

NORMAL:String

VERTICAL:String

ActionScript Class Reference (continued)

Loader

Package: flash.display

Extends DisplayObjectContainer

Properties:

content:DisplayObject

contentLoaderInfo:LoaderInfo

Methods:

close():void

load():void

loadBytes():void

Loader()

unload():void

LoaderContext

Package: flash.system

Extends Object

Properties:

applicationDomain:ApplicationDomain

checkPolicyFile:Boolean

securityDomain:SecurityDomain

Method:

LoaderContext()

LoaderInfo

Package: flash.display

Extends EventDispatcher

Properties:

actionScriptVersion:uint

applicationDomain:
ApplicationDomain

bytes:ByteArray

bytesLoaded:uint

bytesTotal:uint

childAllowsParent:Boolean

childSandboxBridge:Object

content:DisplayObject

contentType:String

frameRate:Number

height:int

loader:Loader

loaderURL:String

parameters:Object

parentAllowsChild:Boolean

parentSandboxBridge:Object

sameDomain:Boolean

sharedEvents:Event
Dispatcher

swfVersion:uint

url:String

width:int

Method:

getLoaderInfoByDefinition():
LoaderInfo

Matrix

Package: flash.geom

Extends Object

Properties:

a:Number

b:Number

c:Number

d:Number

tx:Number

ty:Number

Methods:

clone():Matrix

concat():void

createBox():void

createGradientBox():void

deltaTransformPoint():Point

identity():void

invert():void

Matrix()

rotate():void

scale():void

toString():String

transformPoint():Point

translate():void

Matrix3D

Package: flash.geom

Extends Object

Properties:

determinant:Number

position:Vector3D

rawData:Vector.<Number>

Methods:

append():void

appendRotation():void

appendScale():void

appendTranslation():void

clone():Matrix3D

decompose():Vector.<Vector3D>

deltaTransformVector():Vector3D

identity():void

interpolate():Matrix3D

interpolateTo():void

invert():Boolean

pointAt():void

prepend():void

prependRotation():void

prependScale():void

prependTranslation():void

recompose():Boolean

transformVector():Vector3D

transformVectors():void

transpose():void

MemoryError

Package: flash.errors

Extends Error

Method:

MemoryError():void

ActionScript Class Reference (continued)

Microphone

Package: flash.media

Extends EventDispatcher

Properties:

activityLevel:Number

code:String

enableVAD:Boolean

encodeQuality:int

framesPerPacket:int

gain:Number

index:int

isSupported:Boolean

muted:Boolean

name:String

names:Array

noiseSuppressionLevel:int

rate:int

silenceLevel:Number

silenceTimeout:int

soundTransform:SoundTransform

useEchoSuppression:Boolean

Methods:

getMicrophone()

setLoopBack()

setSilenceLevel

setUseEchoSuppression()

MouseEvent

Package: flash.events

Extends Event

Properties:

altKey:Boolean

buttonDown:Boolean

clickCount:int

commandKey:Boolean

controlKey:Boolean

ctrlKey:Boolean

delta:int

localX:Number

localY:Number

relatedObject:

InteractiveObject

shiftKey:Boolean

stageX:Number

stageY:Number

Constants:

CLICK:String

CONTEXT_MENU:String

DOUBLE_CLICK:String

MIDDLE_CLICK:String

MIDDLE_MOUSE_DOWN:String

MIDDLE_MOUSE_UP:String

MOUSE_DOWN:String

MOUSE_MOVE:String

MOUSE_OUT:String

MOUSE_OVER:String

MOUSE_UP:String

MOUSE_WHEEL:String

RIGHT_CLICK:String

RIGHT_MOUSE_DOWN:String

RIGHT_MOUSE_UP:String

ROLL_OUT:String

ROLL_OVER:String

Methods:

clone():Event

MouseEvent()

toString():String

updateAfterEvent():void

MovieClip

Package: flash.display

Extends Sprite

Properties:

currentFrame:int

currentFrameLabel:String

currentLabel:String

currentLabels:Array

currentScene:Scene

enabled:Boolean

framesLoaded:int

scenes:Array

totalFrames:int

trackAsMenu:Boolean

Methods:

gotoAndPlay():void

gotoAndStop():void

MovieClip()

nextFrame():void

nextScene():void

play():void

prevFrame():void

prevScene():void

stop():void

Multitouch

Package: flash.ui

Extends Object

Properties:

inputMode:String

maxTouchPoints:int

supportedGestures:Vector.<String>

supportsGestureEvents:Boolean

supportsTouchEvents:Boolean

MultitouchInputMode

Package: flash.ui

Extends Object

Constants:

GESTURE:String

NONE:String

TOUCH_POINT:String

Namespace

Package: Top Level

Extends Object

Properties:

prefix:String

uri:String

Methods:

Namespace():void

toString():String

valueOf():String

ActionScript Class Reference (continued)

NativeApplication

Package: flash.desktop

Extends EventDispatcher

Properties:

activeWindow:NativeWindow

applicationDescriptor:XML

applicationID:String

autoExit:Boolean

icon:InteractiveIcon

idleThreshold:int

menu:NativeMenu

nativeApplication:NativeApplication

openedWindows:Array

publisherID:String

runtimePatchLevel:uint

runtimeVersion:String

startAtLogin:Boolean

supportsDockIcon:Boolean

supportsMenu:Boolean

supportsStartAtLogin:Boolean

supportsSystemTrayIcon:Boolean

systemIdleMode:String

timeSinceLastUserInput:int

Methods:

activate():void

addEventListener():void

clear():Boolean

copy():Boolean

cut():Boolean

dispatchEvent():Boolean

exit():void

getDefaultApplication():String

isSetAsDefaultApplication():Boolean

paste():Boolean

removeAsDefaultApplication():void

removeEventListener():void

selectAll():Boolean

setAsDefaultApplication():void

NetConnection

Package: flash.net

Extends EventDispatcher

Properties:

client:Object

connected:Boolean

connectedProxyType:String

defaultObjectEncoding:uint

farID:String

farNonce:String

maxPeerConnections:uint

nearID:String

nearNonce:String

objectEncoding:uint

protocol:String

proxyType:String

unconnectedPeerStreams:
Array

uri:String

usingTLS:Boolean

Methods:

addHeader():void

call():void

close():void

connect():void

NetConnection()

NetStatusEvent

Package: flash.events

Extends Event

Property:

info:Object

Constant:

NET_STATUS:String

Methods:

clone():Event

NetStatusEvent()

toString():String

NetStream

Package: flash.net

Extends EventDispatcher

Properties:

bufferLength:Number

bufferTime:Number

bytesLoaded:uint

bytesTotal:uint

checkPolicyFile:Boolean

client:Object

currentFPS:Number

farID:String

farNonce:String

info:NetStreamInfo

liveDelay:Number

nearNonce:String

objectEncoding:uint

peerStreams:Array

soundTransform:
SoundTransform

time:Number

Constants:

CONNECT_TO_FMS:String

DIRECT_CONNECTIONS:String

Methods:

attachAudio():void

attachCamera():void

close():void

NetStream()

onPeerConnect():Boolean

pause():void

play():void

play2():void

preloadEmbeddedData():void

publish():void

receiveAudio():void

receiveVideo():void

receiveVideoFPS():void

resetDRMVouchers():void

resume():void

seek():void

send():void

setDRMAuthentication
Credentials():void

togglePause():void

NetStreamInfo

Package: flash.net

Extends Object

Properties:

audioBufferByteLength:Number

audioBufferLength:Number

audioByteCount:Number

audioBytesPerSecond:Number

audioLossRate:Number

byteCount:Number

currentBytesPerSecond:Number

dataBufferByteLength:Number

dataBufferLength:Number

dataByteCount:Number

dataBytesPerSecond:Number

droppedFrames:Number

maxBytesPerSecond:Number

playbackBytesPerSecond:Number

SRTT:Number

videoBufferByteLength:Number

videoBufferLength:Number

videoByteCount:Number

videoBytesPerSecond:Number

Constant:

EMBEDDED_CFF:String

Method:

toString():String

NetStreamPlayOptions

Package: flash.net

Extends EventDispatcher

Properties:

len:Number

oldStreamName:String

start:Number

streamName:String

transition:String

NetStreamPlayTransitions

Package: flash.net

Extends Object

Constants:

APPEND:*

RESET:*

STOP:*

SWAP:*

SWITCH:*

Number

Package: Top Level

Extends Object

Constants:

MAX_VALUE:Number

MIN_VALUE:Number

NaN:Number

NEGATIVE_INFINITY:Number

POSITIVE_INFINITY:Number

Methods:

Number()

toExponential():String

toFixed():String

toPrecision():String

toString():String

valueOf():Number

Object

Package: Top Level

Properties:

constructor:Object

prototype:Object

Methods:

hasOwnProperty():Boolean

isPrototypeOf():Boolean

Object()

propertyIsEnumerable():Boolean

setPropertyIsEnumerable():void

toString():String

valueOf():Object

ObjectEncoding

Package: flash.net

Extends Object

Property:

dynamicPropertyWriter:
IDynamicPropertyWriter

Constants:

AMF0:uint

AMF3:uint

DEFAULT:uint

Orientation3D

Package: flash.geom

Extends Object

Constants:

AXIS_ANGLE:String

EULER_ANGLES:String

QUATERNION:String

ActionScript Class Reference (continued)

OutputProgressEvent

Package: flash.events

Extends Event

Properties:

bytesPending:Number

bytesTotal:Number

Constant:

OUTPUT_PROGRESS:String

Methods:

clone():Event

OutputProgressEvent():void

toString():String

PerspectiveProjection

Package: flash.geom

Extends Object

Properties:

fieldOfView:Number

focalLength:Number

projectionCenter:Point

Method:

toMatrix3D():Matrix3D

PixelSnapping

Package: flash.display

Extends Object

Constants:

ALWAYS:String

AUTO:String

NEVER:String

Point

Package: flash.geom

Extends Object

Properties:

length:Number

x:Number

y:Number

Methods:

add():Point

clone():Point

distance():Number

equals():Boolean

interpolate():Point

normalize():void

offset():void

Point()

polar():Point

subtract():Point

toString():String

PressAndTapGestureEvent

Package: flash.events

Extends Event

Properties:

tapLocalX:Number

tapLocalY:Number

tapStageX:Number

tapStageY:Number

Constant:

GESTURE_PRESS_AND_TAP:String

Methods:

PressAndTapGestureEvent()

clone()

toString()

Proxy

Package: flash.utils

Extends Object

Methods:

callProperty():*

deleteProperty():Boolean

getDescendants():*

getProperty():*

hasProperty():Boolean

isAttribute():Boolean

nextName():String

nextNameIndex():int

nextValue():*

setProperty():void

ProgressEvent

Package: flash.events

Extends Event

Properties:

bytesLoaded:Number

bytesTotal:Number

Constants:

PROGRESS:String

SOCKET_DATA:String

Methods:

clone():Event

ProgressEvent()

toString():String

QName

Package: Top Level

Extends Object

Properties:

localName:String

uri:String

Methods:

QName()

toString():String

valueOf():QName

RangeError

Package: Top Level

Extends Error

Method:

RangeError()

ActionScript Class Reference (continued)

Rectangle

Package: flash.geom

Extends Object

Properties:

bottom:Number

bottomRight:Point

height:Number

left:Number

right:Number

size:Point

top:Number

topLeft:Point

width:Number

x:Number

y:Number

Methods:

clone():Rectangle

contains():Boolean

containsPoint():Boolean

containsRect():Boolean

equals():Boolean

inflate():void

inflatePoint():void

intersection():Rectangle

intersects():Boolean

isEmpty():Boolean

offset():void

offsetPoint():void

Rectangle()

setEmpty():void

toString():String

union():Rectangle

ReferenceError

Package: Top Level

Extends Error

Method:

ReferenceError()

RegExp

Package: Top Level

Extends Object

Properties:

dotall:Boolean

extended:Boolean

global:Boolean

ignoreCase:Boolean

lastIndex:Number

multiline:Boolean

source:String

Methods:

exec():Object

RegExp()

test():Boolean

Screen

Package: flash.display

Extends EventDispatcher

Properties:

bounds:Rectangle

colorDepth:int

mainScreen:Screen

screens:Array

visibleBounds:Rectangle

Method:

getScreensForRectangle():Array

ScreenMouseEvent

Package: flash.events

Extends MouseEvent

Properties:

screenX:Number

screenY:Number

Methods:

clone():Event

ScreenMouseEvent()

toString():String

ServiceMonitor

Package: air.net

Extends EventDispatcher

Properties:

available:Boolean

lastUpdated:Date

pollInterval:Number

running:Boolean

Methods:

augmentPrototype():void

checkStatus():void

ServiceMonitor()

start():void

stop():void

toString():String

Shape

Package: flash.display

Extends DisplayObject

Property:

graphics:Graphics

Method:

Shape()

SharedObject

Package: flash.net

Extends EventDispatcher

Properties:

client:Object

data:Object

defaultObjectEncoding:uint

fps:Number

objectEncoding:uint

size:uint

Methods:

clear():void

close():void

connect():void

flush():String

getLocal():SharedObject

getRemote():SharedObject

send():void

setDirty():void

setProperty():void

SharedObjectFlushStatus

Package: flash.net

Extends Object

Constants:

FLUSHED:String

PENDING:String

SimpleButton

Package: flash.display

Extends InteractiveObject

Properties:

downState:DisplayObject

enabled:Boolean

hitTestState:DisplayObject

overState:DisplayObject

soundTransform:
SoundTransform

trackAsMenu:Boolean

upState:DisplayObject

useHandCursor:Boolean

Method:

SimpleButton()

Socket

Package: flash.net

Extends EventDispatcher

Implements IDataInput, IDataOutput

Properties:

bytesAvailable:uint

connected:Boolean

endian:String

objectEncoding:uint

Methods:

close():void

connect():void

flush():void

readBoolean():Boolean

readByte():int

readBytes():void

readDouble():Number

readFloat():Number

readInt():int

readMultiByte():String

readObject():*

readShort():int

readUnsignedByte():uint

readUnsignedInt():uint

readUnsignedShort():uint

readUTF():String

readUTFBytes():String

Socket()

writeBoolean():void

writeByte():void

writeBytes():void

writeDouble():void

writeFloat():void

writeInt():void

writeMultiByte():void

writeObject():void

writeShort():void

writeUnsignedInt():void

writeUTF():void

writeUTFBytes():void

SocketMonitor

Package: air.net

Extends ServiceMonitor

Properties:

host:String

port:int

Methods:

checkStatus():void

SocketMonitor()

toString():String

Sound

Package: flash.media

Extends EventDispatcher

Properties:

bytesLoaded:uint

bytesTotal:int

id3:ID3Info

isBuffering:Boolean

length:Number

url:String

Methods:

close():void

extract():Number

load():void

play():SoundChannel

Sound()

SoundChannel

Package: flash.media

Extends EventDispatcher

Properties:

leftPeak:Number

position:Number

rightPeak:Number

soundTransform:SoundTransform

Method:

stop():void

SoundCodec

Package: flash.media

Extends Object

Constants:

NELLYMOSER:String

SPEEX:String

SoundLoaderContext

Package: flash.media

Extends Object

Properties:

bufferTime:Number

checkPolicyFile:Boolean

Method:

SoundLoaderContext()

SoundMixer

Package: flash.media

Extends Object

Properties:

bufferTime:int

soundTransform:SoundTransform

Methods:

areSoundsInaccessible():Boolean

computeSpectrum():void

stopAll():void

SoundTransform

Package: flash.media

Extends Object

Properties:

leftToLeft:Number

leftToRight:Number

pan:Number

rightToLeft:Number

rightToRight:Number

volume:Number

Method:

SoundTransform()

SpreadMethod

Package: flash.display

Extends Object

Constants:

PAD:String

REFLECT:String

REPEAT:String

SQLCollationType

Package: flash.data

Extends Object

Constants:

BINARY:String

NO_CASE:String

Sprite

Package: flash.display

Extends DisplayObjectContainer

Properties:

buttonMode:Boolean

dropTarget:DisplayObject

graphics:Graphics

hitArea:Sprite

soundTransform:SoundTransform

useHandCursor:Boolean

Methods:

Sprite()

startDrag():void

stopDrag():void

SQLColumnNameStyle

Package: flash.data

Extends Object

Constants:

DEFAULT:String

LONG:String

SHORT:String

SQLColumnSchema

Package: flash.data

Extends Object

Properties:

allowNull:Boolean

autoIncrement:Boolean

dataType:Boolean

defaultCollationType:String

name:String

primaryKey:Boolean

Method:

SQLColumnSchema()

ActionScript Class Reference (continued)

SQLConnection

Package: flash.data

Extends EventDispatcher

Properties:

autoCompact:Boolean

cacheSize:uint

columnNameStyle:String

connected:Boolean

inTransaction:Boolean

lastInsertRowID:Number

pageSize:uint

totalChanges:Number

Methods:

SQLConnection()

addEventListener()

analyze()

attach()

begin()

cancel()

close()

commit()

compact()

deanalyze()

detach()

getSchemaResult()

loadSchema()

open()

openAsync()

reencrypt()

releaseSavepoint()

removeEventListener()

rollback()

rollbackToSavepoint()

setSavepoint()

SQLError

Package: flash.errors

Extends Error

Properties:

detailArguments:Array

detailID:int

details:String

operation:String

Methods:

SQLError()

toString()

SQLErrorEvent

Package: flash.events

Extends Event

Property:

error:SQLError

Methods:

clone()

SQLErrorEvent()

toString()

SQLIndexSchema

Package: flash.data

Extends SQLSchema

Property:

table:String

Method:

SQLIndexSchema()

SQLMode

Package: flash.data

Extends Object

Constants:

CREATE:String

READ:String

UPDATE:String

SQLResult

Package: flash.data

Extends Object

Properties:

complete:Boolean

data:Array

lastInsertRowID:Number

rowsAffected:Number

Method:

SQLResults()

SQLSchema

Package: flash.data

Extends Object

Properties:

database:String

name:String

sql:String

Method:

SQLSchema()

SQLSchemaResult

Package: flash.data

Extends Object

Properties:

indicies:Array

tables:Array

triggers:Array

views:Array

Method:

SQLSchemaResult()

ActionScript Class Reference (continued)

SQLStatement

Package: flash.data

Extends EventDispatcher

Properties:

executing:Boolean

itemClass:Class

parameters:Object

sqlConnection:SQLConnection

text:String

Methods:

SQLStatement()

cancel()

clearParameters()

execute()

getResult()

next()

SQLTableSchema

Package: flash.data

Extends SQLSchema

Property:

columns:Array

Method:

SQLTableSchema():void

SQLUpdateEvent

Package: flash.events

Extends Event

Properties:

rowID:Number

table:String

Constants:

DELETE:String

INSERT:String

UPDATE:String

Methods:

clone()

SQLUpdateEvent():void

SQLViewSchema

Package: flash.data

Extends SQLTableSchema

Method:

SQLViewSchema():void

StackOverflowError

Package: flash.errors

Extends Error

Method:

StackOverflowError():void

Stage

Package: flash.display

Extends DisplayObjectContainer

Properties:

align:String

cacheAsBitmap:Boolean

displayState:String

focus:InteractiveObject

frameRate:Number

fullScreenHeight:uint

fullScreenSourceRect:Rectangle

fullScreenWidth:uint

height:Number

mouseChildren:Boolean

nativeWindow:NativeWindow

numChildren:int

orientation:String

quality:String

scaleMode:String

showDefaultContextMenu:Boolean

stageFocusRect:Boolean

stageHeight:int

stageWidth:int

supportsOrientationChange:Boolean

tabChildren:Boolean

tabEnabled:Boolean

textSnapshot:TextSnapshot

width:Number

Methods:

addChild():DisplayObject

addChildAt():DisplayObject

addEventListener():void

assignFocus():void

dispatchEvent():Boolean

hasEventListener():Boolean

invalidate():void

isFocusInaccessible():Boolean

removeChildAt():DisplayObject

setAspectRatio()

setChildIndex():void

setOrientation()

swapChildrenAt():void

willTrigger():Boolean

StageAlign

Package: flash.display

Extends Object

Constants:

BOTTOM:String

BOTTOM_LEFT:String

BOTTOM_RIGHT:String

LEFT:String

RIGHT:String

TOP:String

TOP_LEFT:String

TOP_RIGHT:String

ActionScript Class Reference (continued)

StageAspectRatio

Package: flash.display

Extends Object

Constants:

LANDSCAPE:String

PORTRAIT:String

StageDisplayState

Package: flash.display

Extends Object

Constants:

FULL_SCREEN:String

FULL_SCREEN_INTERACTIVE:String

NORMAL:String

StageOrientation

Package: flash.display

Extends Object

Constants:

DEFAULT:String

ROTATED_LEFT:String

ROTATED_RIGHT:String

UNKNOWN:String

UPSIDE_DOWN:String

StageOrientationEvent

Package: flash.events

Extends Event

Properties:

afterOrientation:String

beforeOrientation:String

Constants:

ORIENTATION_CHANGE:String

ORIENTATION_CHANGING:String

Methods:

clone()

StageOrientationEvent()

toString()

StageQuality

Package: flash.display

Extends Object

Constants:

BEST:String

HIGH:String

LOW:String

MEDIUM:String

StageScaleMode

Package: flash.display

Extends Object

Constants:

EXACT_FIT:String

NO_BORDER:String

NO_SCALE:String

SHOW_ALL:String

StageWebView

Package: flash.media

Extends EventDispatcher

Properties:

isFocusSupported:Boolean

isHistoryBackEnabled:
Boolean

isHistoryForwardEnabled:
Boolean

isSupported:Boolean

location:String

stage:Stage

title:String

viewport:Rectangle

Methods:

assignFocus()

dispose()

historyBack()

historyForward()

loadString()

loadURL()

reload()

StageWebView()

stop()

StaticText

Package: flash.text

Extends DisplayObject

Property:

text:String

StatusEvent

Package: flash.events

Extends Event

Properties:

code:String

level:String

Constant:

STATUS:String

Methods:

clone():Event

StatusEvent()

StyleSheet

Package: flash.text

Extends EventDispatcher

Property:

styleNames:Array

Methods:

clear():void

getStyle():Object

parseCSS():void

setStyle():void

StyleSheet()

transform():TextFormat

toString():String

ActionScript Class Reference (continued)

SWFVersion

Package: flash.display

Extends Object

Constants:

FLASH1:uint

FLASH2:uint

FLASH3:uint

FLASH4:uint

FLASH5:uint

FLASH6:uint

FLASH7:uint

FLASH8:uint

FLASH9:uint

SyncEvent

Package: flash.events

Extends Event

Property:

changeList:Array

Constant:

SYNC:String

Methods:

clone():Event

SyncEvent()

toString():String

SyntaxError

Package: Top Level

Extends Error

Method:

SyntaxError()

System

Package: flash.system

Extends Object

Properties:

ime:IME

totalMemory:uint

useCodePage:Boolean

Methods:

exit():void

gc():void

pause():void

resume():void

setClipboard():void

TabAlignment

Package: flash.text.engine

Extends Object

Constants:

CENTER:String

DECIMAL:String

END:String

START:String

TextBaseline

Package: flash.text.engine

Extends Object

Constants:

ASCENT:String

DESCENT:String

IDEOGRAPHIC_BOTTOM:String

IDEOGRAPHIC_CENTER:String

IDEOGRAPHIC_TOP:String

ROMAN:String

USE_DOMINANT_BASELINE:String

TextBlock

Package: flash.text.engine

Extends Object

Properties:

applyNonLinearFontScaling:Boolean

baselineFontDescription:FontDescription

baselineFontSize:Number

baselineZero:String

bidiLevel:int

content:ContentElement

firstInvalidLine:TextLine

firstLine:TextLine

lastLine:TextLine

lineRotation:String

tabStops:Vector.<TabStop>

textJustifier:TextJustifier

textLineCreationResult:String

userData:*

Methods:

createTextLine():Text

Linedump():String

findNextAtomBoundary():int

findNextWordBoundary():int

findPreviousAtomBoundary():int

findPreviousWordBoundary():int

getTextLineAtCharIndex():TextLine

releaseLines():void

TextColorType

Package: flash.text

Extends Object

Constants:

DARK_COLOR:String

LIGHT_COLOR:String

ActionScript Class Reference (continued)

TextDisplayMode

Package: flash.text

Extends Object

Constants:

CRT:String

DEFAULT:String

LCD:String

TextElement

Package: flash.text.engine

Extends ContentElement

Property:

text:String

Method:

replaceText():void

TextEvent

Package: flash.events

Extends Event

Property:

text:String

Constants:

LINK:String

TEXT_INPUT:String

Methods:

clone():Event

TextEvent()

toString():String

TextExtent

Package: flash.text

Extends Object

Properties:

ascent:Number

descent:Number

height:Number

textFieldHeight:Number

textFieldWidth:Number

width:Number

TextField

Package: flash.text

Extends InteractiveObject

Properties:

alwaysShowSelection:Boolean

antiAliasType:String

autoSize:String

background:Boolean

backgroundColor:uint

border:Boolean

borderColor:uint

bottomScrollV:int

caretIndex:int

condenseWhite:Boolean

contextMenu:NativeMenu

defaultTextFormat:TextFormat

displayAsPassword:Boolean

embedFonts:Boolean

gridFitType:String

htmlText:String

length:int

TextField (continued)

maxChars:int

maxScrollH:int

maxScrollV:int

mouseWheelEnabled:Boolean

multiline:Boolean

numLines:int

restrict:String

scrollH:int

scrollV:int

selectable:Boolean

selectionBeginIndex:int

selectionEndIndex:int

sharpness:Number

styleSheet:StyleSheet

text:String

textColor:uint

textHeight:Number

textWidth:Number

thickness:Number

type:String

useRichTextClipboard:
Boolean

wordWrap:Boolean

Methods:

appendText():void

getCharBoundaries():
Rectangle

getCharIndexAtPoint():int

getFirstCharInParagraph():
int

getImageReference():Display

Object

getLineIndexAtPoint():int

getLineIndexOfChar():int

getLineLength():int

getLineMetrics():
TextLineMetrics

getLineOffset():int

getLineText():String

getParagraphLength():int

getTextFormat():TextFormat

replaceSelectedText():void

replaceText():void

setSelection():void

setTextFormat():void

TextField()

TextFieldAutoSize

Package: flash.text

Extends Object

Constants:

CENTER:String

LEFT:String

NONE:String

RIGHT:String

TextFieldType

Package: flash.text

Extends Object

Constants:

DYNAMIC:String

INPUT:String

TextFormat

Package: flash.text

Extends Object

Properties:

align:String

blockIndent:Object

bold:Object

bullet:Object

color:Object

font:String

indent:Object

italic:Object

kerning:Object

leading:Object

leftMargin:Object

letterSpacing:Object

rightMargin:Object

size:Object

tabStops:Array

target:String

underline:Object

url:String

Method:

TextFormat()

ActionScript Class Reference (continued)

TextFormatAlign

Package: flash.text

Extends Object

Constants:

CENTER:String

JUSTIFY:String

LEFT:String

RIGHT:String

TextJustifier

Package: flash.text.engine

Extends Object

Properties:

lineJustification:String

locale:String

Methods:

clone():TextJustifier

getJustifierForLocale():TextJustifier

TextLine

Package: flash.text.engine

Extends DisplayObjectContainer

Properties:

ascent:Number

atomCount:int

descent:Number

hasGraphicElement:Boolean

mirrorRegions:Vector.
<TextLineMirrorRegion>

nextLine:TextLine

previousLine:TextLine

rawTextLength:int

specifiedWidth:Number

textBlock:TextBlock

textBlockBeginIndex:int

textHeight:Number

textWidth:Number

unjustifiedTextWidth:Number

userData:*

validity:String

Constant:

MAX_LINE_WIDTH:int

Methods:

dump():String

flushAtomData():void

getAtomBidiLevel():int

getAtomBounds():Rectangle

getAtomCenter():Number

getAtomGraphic():
DisplayObject

getAtomIndexAtCharIndex():
int

getAtomIndexAtPoint():int

getAtomTextBlockBeginIndex():
int

getAtomTextBlockEndIndex():
int

getAtomTextRotation():String

getAtomWordBoundaryOnLeft():
Boolean

getBaselinePosition():Number

getMirrorRegion():
TextLineMirrorRegion

TextLineCreationResult

Package: flash.text.engine

Extends Object

Constants:

COMPLETE:String

EMERGENCY:String

INSUFFICIENT_WIDTH:String

SUCCESS:String

TextLineValidity

Package: flash.text.engine

Extends Object

Constants:

INVALID:String

POSSIBLY_INVALID:String

STATIC:String

VALID:String

TextLineMetrics

Package: flash.text

Extends Object

Properties:

ascent:Number

descent:Number

height:Number

leading:Number

width:Number

x:Number

Method:

TextLineMetrics()

TextRenderer

Package: flash.text

Extends Object

Properties:

displayMode:String

maxLevel:int

Method:

setAdvancedAntiAliasingTable():void

TextRotation

Package: flash.text.engine

Extends Object

Constants:

AUTO:String

ROTATE_0:String

ROTATE_90:String

ROTATE_180:String

ROTATE_270:String

TextLineMirrorRegion

Package: flash.text.engine

Extends Object

Properties:

bounds:Rectangle

element:ContentElement

mirror:EventDispatcher

nextRegion:TextLineMirrorRegion

previousRegion:TextLineMirrorRegion

textLine:TextLine

ActionScript Class Reference (continued)

TextSnapshot

Package: flash.text

Extends Object

Property:

charCount:int

Methods:

findText():int

getSelected():Boolean

getSelectedText():String

getText():String

getTextRunInfo():Array

hitTestTextNearPos():Number

setSelectColor():void

setSelected():void

Timer

Package: flash.utils

Extends EventDispatcher

Properties:

currentCount:int

delay:Number

repeatCount:int

running:Boolean

Methods:

reset():void

start():void

stop():void

Timer()

TimerEvent

Package: flash.events

Extends Event

Constants:

TIMER:String

TIMER_COMPLETE:String

Methods:

clone():Event

TimerEvent()

toString():String

updateAfterEvent():void

Transform

Package: flash.geom

Extends Object

Properties:

colorTransform:ColorTransform

concatenatedColorTransform:ColorTransform

concatenatedMatrix:Matrix

matrix:Matrix

pixelBounds:Rectangle

TriangleCulling

Package: flash.display

Extends Object

Constants:

NEGATIVE:String

NONE:String

POSITIVE:String

TypeError

Package: Top Level

Extends Error

Method:

TypeError()

TypographicCase

Package: flash.text.engine

Extends Object

Constants:

CAPS:String

CAPS_AND_SMALL_CAPS:String

DEFAULT:String

LOWERCASE:String

SMALL_CAPS:String

TITLE:String

UPPERCASE:String

uint

Package: Top Level

Extends Object

Constants:

MAX_VALUE:uint

MIN_VALUE:uint

Methods:

toExponential():String

toFixed():String

toPrecision():String

toString():String

uint()

valueOf():uint

URIError

Package: Top Level

Extends Error

Method:

URIError()

URLLoader

Package: flash.net

**Extends
EventDispatcher**

Properties:

bytesLoaded:uint

bytesTotal:uint

data:data

Format:String

Methods:

close():void

load():void

URLLoader()

ActionScript Class Reference (continued)

URLLoaderDataFormat

Package: flash.net

Extends Object

Constants:

BINARY:String

TEXT:String

VARIABLES:String

URLMonitor

Package: air.net

Extends ServiceMonitor

Properties:

acceptableStatuses:Array

urlRequest:URLRequest

Methods:

checkStatus():void

toString():String

URLMonitor()

URLRequest

Package: flash.net

Extends Object

Properties:

authenticate:Boolean

cacheResponse:Boolean

contentType:String

data:Object

digest:String

followRedirects:Boolean

manageCookies:Boolean

method:String

requestHeaders:Array

url:String

useCache:Boolean

userAgent:String

Method:

URLRequest()

URLRequestDefaults

Package: flash.net

Extends Object

Properties:

authenticate:Boolean

cacheResponse:Boolean

followRedirects:Boolean

manageCookies:Boolean

useCache:Boolean

userAgent:String

Method:

setLoginCredentials
ForHost():*

URLRequestHeader

Package: flash.net

Extends Object

Properties:

name:String

value:String

Method:

URLRequestHeader()

URLRequestMethod

Package: flash.net

Extends Object

Constants:

DELETE:String

GET:String

HEAD:String

OPTIONS:String

POST:String

PUT:String

URLStream

Package: flash.net

Extends EventDispatcher

Implements IDataInput

Properties:

bytesAvailable:uint

connected:Boolean

endian:String

objectEncoding:uint

Methods:

close():void

load():void

readBoolean():Boolean

readByte():int

readBytes():void

readDouble():Number

readFloat():Number

readInt():int

readMultiByte():String

readObject():*

readShort():int

readUnsignedByte():uint

readUnsignedInt():uint

readUnsignedShort():uint

readUTF():String

readUTFBytes():String

URLVariables

Package: flash.net

Extends Object

Methods:

decode():void

toString():String

URLVariables():void

Utils3D

Package: flash.geom

Extends Object

Methods:

pointTowards():Matrix3D

projectVector():Vector3D

projectVectors():void

Vector

Package: Top Level

Extends Object

Properties:

fixed:Boolean

length:uint

Methods:

concat():Vector.<T>

every():Boolean

filter():Vector.<T>

forEach():void

indexOf():int

join():String

lastIndexOf():int

map():Vector.<T>

pop():T

push():uint

reverse():Vector.<T>

shift():T

slice():Vector.<T>

some():Boolean

sort():Vector.<T>

splice():Vector.<T>

toLocaleString():String

toString():String

unshift():uint

ActionScript Class
Reference (continued)

Vector3D

Package: flash.geom

Extends Object

Properties:

length:Number

lengthSquared:Number

w:Number

x:Number

y:Number

z:Number

Constants:

X_AXIS:Vector3D

Y_AXIS:Vector3D

Z_AXIS:Vector3D

Methods:

add():Vector3D

angleBetween():Number

clone():Vector3D

crossProduct():Vector3D

decrementBy():void

distance():Number

dotProduct():Number

equals():Boolean

incrementBy():void

nearEquals():Boolean

negate():void

normalize():Number

project():void

scaleBy():void

subtract():Vector3D

toString():String

VerifyError

Package: Top Level

Extends Error

Method:

VerifyError():void

Video

Package: flash.media

Extends EventDispatcher

Properties:

deblocking:int

smoothing:Boolean

videoHeight:int

videoWidth:int

Methods:

attachCamera():void

attachNetStream():void

clear():void

Video():void

Package: Top Level

Extends Object

Properties:

ignoreComments:Boolean

ignoreProcessingInstruction s:Boolean

ignoreWhitespace:Boolean

prettyIndent:int

prettyPrinting:Boolean

Methods:

addNamespace():XML

appendChild():XML

attribute():XMLList

attributes():XMLList

child():XMLList

childIndex():int

children():XMLList

comments():XMLList

contains():Boolean

copy():XML

defaultSettings():Object

descendants():XMLList

elements():XMLList

hasComplexContent():Boolean

hasOwnProperty():Boolean

hasSimpleContent():Boolean

inScopeNamespaces():Array

insertChildAfter():*

insertChildBefore():*

length():int

localName():Object

name():Object

namespace():*

namespaceDeclarations(): Array

nodeKind():String

normalize():XML

parent():*

prependChild():XML

processingInstructions(): XMLList

propertyIsEnumerable(): Boolean

removeNamespace():XML

replace():XML

setChildren():XML

setLocalName():void

setName():void

setNamespace():void

setSettings():void

settings():Object

text():XMLList

toString():String

toXMLString():String

valueOf():XML

XML()

XMLDocument

Package: flash.xml

Extends Object

Properties:

docTypeDecl:Object

idMap:Object

ignoreWhite:Boolean

xmlDecl:Object

Methods:

createElement():XMLNode

createTextNode():XMLNode

parseXML():void

toString():String

XMLDocument()

XMLNode

Package: flash.xml

Extends Object

Properties:

attributes:Object

childNodes:Array

firstChild:XMLNode

lastChild:XMLNode

localName:String

namespaceURI:String

nextSibling:XMLNode

nodeName:String

nodeType:uint

nodeValue:String

parentNode:XMLNode

prefix:String

previousSibling:XMLNode

Methods:

appendChild():void

cloneNode():XMLNode

getNamespaceForPrefix():String

getPrefixForNamespace():String

hasChildNodes():Boolean

insertBefore():void

removeNode():void

toString():String

XMLNode()

XMLNodeType

Package: flash.xml

Extends Object

Constants:

ELEMENT_NODE:uint

TEXT_NODE:uint

XMLSignatureValidator

Package: flash.security

Extends EventDispatcher

Properties:

digestStatus:String

identityStatus:String

referencesStatus:String

referencesValidationSetting:String

revocationCheckSetting:String

signerCN:String

signerDN:String

signerExtendedKeyUsages:Array

signerTrustSettings:Array

uriDereferencer:URIDereferencer

useSystemTrustStore:Boolean

validityStatus:String

Methods:

addCertificate():*

verify():void

XMLSignatureValidator()

XMLSocket

Package: flash.net

Extends EventDispatcher

Property:

connected:Boolean

Methods:

close():void

connect():void

send():void

XMLSocket()

INDEX

Bitmap class, 272
BitmapData class
  properties and methods, 273
  using, 110
BitmapData instance
  maximum width and height, 100
  saving to camera roll, 6, 112
BitmapDataChannel class, 273
BitmapFilterQuality class, 273
BitmapFilterType class, 274
bitmaps, filling shapes with, 41. *See also* cacheAsBitmapMatrix
  property
BlendMode class, 274
BlurFilter class, 274
Boolean class, 274
BreakOpportunity class, 274
breakpoints
  adding and removing, 250–251
  creating, 250–251
button size, considering, 77
button states, creating, 76–77
buttons, creating for system Idle mode, 218–219. *See also* Back
  button presses; menu button presses
ByteArray class, 275
ByteArray instance
  reading files to, 193
  using with sounds, 132–133
  writing to FileStream object, 191

C

cacheAsBitmap property, using, 244–245. *See also* bitmaps
cacheAsBitmapMatrix property, using, 246–247
calls, making, 222–223
Camera class, using, 116, 275–276
camera roll
  saving BitmapData instance to, 112
  saving images to, 112–113
CameraRoll class, 276
  described, 6
  selecting images from, 114–115
Capabilities class, 276
CapStyle class, 277
certificates, types of, 50
class names, convention for, 105
Class package, 277
clear() method, using with local SharedObjects, 165
code completion, using, 23
code hinting, providing, 23
codecs. *See* audio codecs; videos
Color Effects settings, applying to objects, 32
color schemes, trying, 81
ColorCorrection class, 277
ColorCorrectionSupport class, 277
ColorTransform class, 277

command line, compiling from, 54–55
command-line commands, using ANT with, 57
Compiler Errors panel, checking, 53
compiling from Flash Professional CS5, 52–53
CompressionAlgorithm class, 277
computeSpectrum method, using with sounds, 132–133
copyTo() method, using with files, 200
copyToAsync() method, using with files, 200–201
CPU usage, conserving, 187
Crop tool, using with videos, 139
cue points, adding to videos, 139
current location. *See* location

D

data property, using, 166–167
databases. *See* SQLite databases
DataEvent class, 278
DatagramSocket class in AIR 2.0, described, 8
DDMS (Dalvik Debug Monitor Service), 14–15, 258
Debug Console, using, 254–255
debugging with Eclipse plug-in, 258–259. *See also* Flash CS5
  Debugger
DefinitionError class, 278
delete keyword, using with properties, 165
designing applications, 65–66
development tools, using, 4–5
devices, installing applications on, 56–57
Dictionary class, 278
digital certificates, creating, 51
directories, referencing, 27, 188–189
dispatchEvent() method, using, 39
display list
  adding objects to, 34–35
  optimizing, 240–241
DisplayObject class, 278
DisplayObjectContainer class
  extending, 108
  properties and methods, 279
Document Settings dialog box, using, 44–45
draw() method, using, 110
drawing API, using, 40–41
driving directions, generating, 227

E

Eclipse plug-in, debugging with, 258–259
Eclipse-based IDEs, 4. *See also* Android Eclipse plug-in
email application, opening, 224–225
emulator, starting, 20–21
endFill() method, using, 40
Endian class, 279
EOFError class, 279
Error class, 279

INDEX

INDEX

O

`Object` classes, 303

objects

adding to display list, 34–35

adding to Stage with code, 34–35

applying Color Effects settings to, 32

applying filters to, 32

listing in current scope, 256

panning, 87

removing from Stage with code, 36–37

rotating, 84–85

setting size and position of, 32

`opaqueBackground` property, setting, 245

`openAsync()` method

using with files, 192

using with `SQLConnection` instance, 168–169

orientation

determining, 94–95

displaying in text field, 71

rotating content to, 70

`Orientation3D` class, 303

`OutputProgressEvent` class, 304

P

P12 certificate, creating, 50–51

packages, naming, 25, 105

page views, tracking with Google Analytics, 236–237

pan events, responding to, 86–87

password `TextField`, creating, 156–157

permissions

setting for applications, 60–61

setting for camera, 116

setting for microphone, 134

setting for system Idle mode, 218

`PerspectiveProjection` class, 304

Phone application, using, 222

phone calls, making, 222–223

`PixelSnapping` class, 304

`play()` method

using with sound files, 126–129

using with videos, 144

PNG file format, alpha channel in, 101

`PNGEncoder.encode` method, using, 111

`Point` class, 304

Portrait mode, using, 66–67, 71

`PressAndTapGestureEvent` class, 305

`ProgressEvent` class, 305

`ProgressEvent.PROGRESS` event, listening for, 109

`ProgressEvents`, using with sound files, 124

projects, creating, 44–45

properties

deleting, 165

editing in Flash, 32–33

setting in ActionScript, 33

`Proxy` class, 305

Publish settings, using, 46–47

Q – R

`QName` class, 305

`RangeError` class, 305

`Rectangle` class, 306

`ReferenceError` class, 306

`RegExp` class, 306

registration point

defined, 28

setting for zoom gestures, 83

`removeChild()` methods, using, 36–37

`removeEventListener()` method, using, 38

root user, gaining access to, 163

rotate events, responding to, 84–85

rotating content, 95–96

runtime

loading images at, 108–109

loading sounds at, 124–125

S

`Screen` class, 307

screen resolutions, considering, 66–67

screen size, considering in design, 66

`ScreenMouseEvent` class, 307

screenshots of applications, taking, 260–261

Script window, managing breakpoints in, 251

scrollable list, optimizing, 240–241

scrollable `TextField`, creating, 158, 160–161

`ServerSocket` class, described, 8, 197

`ServiceMonitor` class, 307

`Shape` class, 307

`Shape` objects, drawing, 40

shapes, filling with bitmaps, 41

`SharedObjectFlushStatus` class, 308

`SharedObjects`. *See also* local `SharedObjects`

described, 7

loading data from, 166–167

properties and methods, 308

verifying writing of, 163

writing, 164–165

`SimpleButton` class, 308

INDEX

Read Less–Learn More®

Visual®

There's a Visual book for every learning level...

Simplified®

The place to start if you're new to computers. Full color.

- Computers
- Creating Web Pages
- Digital Photography
- Internet
- Mac OS
- Office
- Windows

Teach Yourself VISUALLY™

Get beginning to intermediate-level training in a variety of topics. Full color.

- Access
- Bridge
- Chess
- Computers
- Crocheting
- Digital Photography
- Dog training
- Dreamweaver
- Excel
- Flash
- Golf
- Guitar
- Handspinning
- HTML
- iLife
- iPhoto
- Jewelry Making & Beading
- Knitting
- Mac OS
- Office
- Photoshop
- Photoshop Elements
- Piano
- Poker
- PowerPoint
- Quilting
- Scrapbooking
- Sewing
- Windows
- Wireless Networking
- Word

Top 100 Simplified® Tips & Tricks

Tips and techniques to take your skills beyond the basics. Full color.

- Digital Photography
- eBay
- Excel
- Google
- Internet
- Mac OS
- Office
- Photoshop
- Photoshop Elements
- PowerPoint
- Windows

...all designed for visual learners—just like you!

R.C.L.

FEV. 2011

G